Clipperton

Clipperton

A History of the Island the World Forgot

Jimmy M. Skaggs

Walker and Company
New York

First published in the United States of America in 1989
by Walker Publishing Company, Inc.

Published simultaneously in Canada by Thomas Allen & Son
Canada, Limited, Markham, Ontario

Library of Congress Cataloging-in-Publication Data

Skaggs, Jimmy M.
Clipperton: a history of the island the world forgot/Jimmy M. Skaggs.
p.   cm.
Bibliography: p.
Includes index.
ISBN 0-8027-1090-5
1. Clipperton Island—History.   I. Title.
DU950.C5S59   1989
996—dc20   89-8908
CIP

Printed in the United States of America

10 8 6 4 2 1 3 5 7 9

*for
Janeen,
Jessica,
and
Joy*

Contents

Preface

Curious how coincidence influences events. In late 1980 or early 1981, while researching another subject in a microfilm copy of the August 13, 1917, New York *Times,* I happened across a four-paragraph report of a contemporary melodrama. Although entirely irrelevant to my study, the article's provocative title— "Marooned 2 Years on Isle: Naval Commander Reports on Rescue of Mexican Women and Children"[1]—naturally caught my eye, and I read it.

A dozen hapless people, forgotten by Mexican authorities for several years, had been taken off an obscure Pacific atoll—of which I had never heard—by an unnamed American warship after all the island's men had been lost at sea in a small boat while seeking help. Finished reading, I resumed my work without giving the incident further thought.

No more than a couple of weeks passed when, lo and behold, while watching a "Jacques Cousteau Special" on the Public Broadcasting System, I encountered a similar tale, although Cousteau's yarn was far more salacious—replete with episodes of starvation, madness, rape, and murder. At the first opportunity I reread the article in the *Times;* it *was* the same story, but the newspaper account contained no mention of a mad light keeper who, according to survivors interviewed by Cousteau, had installed himself as "King of Clipperton island" and sorely abused the women and children.

Intrigued with what I thought to be an unusually harrowing episode of human drama, out of nothing more than personal interest I pursued the story part-time, as best as I could considering other, more pressing obligations. I did not know whether my effort would result in anything but the satisfaction of personal curiosity—if that, for it quickly became apparent that researching the place would not be a simple task.

In time, my digging uncovered C. Edward Morris's 1934 four-page article in the *New Outlook* about "The Island the World Forgot," which lamented the fact that in his official report to the United States Navy, Commander Harlan P. Perrill, captain of USS *Yorktown,* which had rescued the islanders, failed to include the "lurid details . . . of a macabre chapter in the history of the island . . . freely told in towns up and down the Mexican coast. . . ."[2]

I obtained a copy of Perrill's report, as well as that of the USS *Cleveland,* which, according to Morris, had been to the atoll in 1914. This started my correspondence with D. C. Allard, head of the Operational Branch Archives at the Naval Historical Center, Washington D.C. Navy Yard. No mere words of gratitude will ever absolve me of my considerable debt to this gentleman, whom I have never met. Not only did he see to it that I received the material I requested, but over the next several years he repeatedly assisted me, either by supplying copies of navy records in his possession that I required, or by introducing me to those who harbored the elusive materials.

Thus I became indebted for their assistance to Y. M. Anderson (acting head, Fleet Support Branch, Office of the Chief of Naval Operations, Washington, D.C.); B. F. Cavalcante (assistant head, Operational Archives Branch); Edwin R. Coffee (assistant chief, Modern Military Branch, National Archives and Records Service, Military Archives Division, National Archives); Wilbert B. Mahoney (Modern Military Headquarters Branch, Military Archives Division, National Archives); Lieutenant L. L. Moynihan (head, Fleet Support Branch, Office of the Chief of Naval Operations); and Richard A. von Dienhoff (Navy and Old Army Branch, Military Archives Division, National Archives).

By the time I had obtained the first of many U.S. Navy records detailing that proud service's experiences with the island, I encountered the writings of botanist Marie-Hélène Sachet, whose scholarly works included not only a cursory history of the place but, far more valuable to me, both a calendar of visits to the atoll through 1958, as best she had been able to compile it, and an excellent bibliography that naturally bulked with scientific literature. Her scholarship saved me untold labor. By mining her sources, as well as the bibliographies of those works she cited, over the next several years I pieced together the complete, untold story of Clipperton island—a far richer tale than I, Cousteau, or perhaps even Sachet herself had ever suspected.

Independently I had already discovered Captain Perrill's response to Morris's article in *New Outlook* and, far more important, his unexpunged letters to his wife, which had been published in 1937 but mostly overlooked by researchers ever since. These missives provided the missing details Morris had wished for regarding that "macabre chapter" in the atoll's story—and they explained why the navy officer and his entire crew had kept the whole thing secret for so many years.

Newspaper accounts of shipwrecks mentioned by Sachet led me to details of American corporate occupation of Clipperton island. Thus I became intrigued with what I judged to be incompetence on the part of the U.S. government in representing its citizens' legitimate business interests. In ferreting out this tale of "Foggy Bottom" ineptitude I was assisted by Conrad P. Eaton, librarian of the U.S. Department of State, Washington, D.C., and by J. Dane Hartgrove of the Diplomatic Branch, Civil Archives Division of the National Archives. Also most helpful was Antoinette Adam, research assistant at the Historical Society of Pennsylvania in Philadelphia, who provided copies of rare gazetteer entries crucial to the topic.

Seeking to round out the story of the island's ownership and Victor Emmanuel III's arbitration award, I pursued the life and times of George Emra Nunn, whose tardy study of Ferdinand Magellan had persuasively demonstrated Spanish discovery. For those details I was greatly assisted by the late dean of Latin American historians, Dr. John Francis Bannon, S.J., professor emeritus of history at St. Louis University, whose reminiscences of his graduate school days at the University of California, Berkeley, provided much insight into Nunn's research and publication delays—an interesting if tangential tale of American historiography and scholarly snobbery that ultimately found no place in the manuscript. I am nevertheless beholden to Douglas R. McManis of the American Geographical Society, New York, for copies of the Society's correspondence with Nunn and for permission to reproduce Nunn's map of Magellan's voyage, which originally appeared in *The Geographical Review,* as well as to university archivist J. R. K. Kantor, Bancroft Library, University of California, Berkeley, whose efforts on my behalf supplied other relevant aspects of Nunn's work there as a graduate student.

While researching the offbeat, top-secret story of U.S. naval occupation during World War II, I stumbled upon Franklin Delano Roosevelt's extraordinary involvement with this island—a largely unknown and heretofore untold chapter of the president's biography. For that information I wish to thank William R. Emerson, director of the Franklin D. Roosevelt Library, Hyde Park, N.Y., and his staff, especially Raymond Teichman, supervisory archivist, who located and made available a vast amount of unpublished material concerning the White House, the State Department, and the navy vis-à-vis the atoll.

My work has indebted me to numerous people, many of them strangers who have nevertheless unhesitatingly answered my requests for information about this most curious of topics. I appreciate the generosity of the following: entomologists Charles F. Harbison and David K. Faulkner of the Natural History Museum, San Diego, for allowing me unparalleled access to Harbison's unpublished research materials; Dr. Richard C. Murphy, vice president for science and Research, The Cousteau Society, Los Angeles, for permission to quote material from "The Cousteau Odyssey" and for the use of Society photographs; Clayton R. Barrow, Jr., editor-in-chief of the *Proceedings* of the United States Naval Institute, Annapolis, Maryland, for permission to quote and reproduce photographic materials from his publication; librarian Glen C. Creason and history department manager Mary S. Pratt of the Los Angeles Public Library, who located information regarding the *Thistle,* its shipwreck, and the rescue of its crew; and librarian Eleanore E. Wilkins of the U.S. Geological Survey, Menlo Park, California, who located obscure imprints relative to the island's geology.

At Wichita State University, my debt is enormous. Student assistants Lauri Dickerson, now an architect, and Jan Turkle, now a physician, did much of the early spadework in Ablah Library, where a good-humored staff indulged my investigation. Thoburn ("Buck") Taggart, interlibrary-loan librarian, patiently made the collective holdings of the nation's libraries readily available to me; government documents librarian Arlene Moore and her entire staff, especially Pauline F. Jopling, saved me much time by swiftly locating obscure public imprints; and Dr. Stephen K. Stoan, then Ablah's head of reference and now assistant director for public services, University of Texas at Arlington Library, and his entire staff at WSU deftly fielded my offbeat requests for assistance.

Dr. Ginette Adamson, associate professor and chair of the Department of Modern and Classical Languages and Literature, unselfishly used a portion of her valuable sabbatical in France to find otherwise unattainable French sources for me. And Dr. John Dreifort, associate professor and chairman of the Department of History, dug through notes of a long-past visit to the Roosevelt Library to locate references to the atoll he had observed while researching an aspect of Franco-American relations. Dr. David N. Fransworth, associate vice president for academic affairs and professor of political science, saved me much research regarding Victor Emmanuel III's decision.

Colleagues in the Department of Modern and Classical Languages at WSU rendered Spanish and French documents into English far faster and much more accurately than my stumbling attempts would have allowed. For their assistance I am most grateful to Dr. Wilson R. Baldridge, Professor Antoinette M. Tejeda, and Lecturer Brigitte Yanney.

Dr. William E. Full, associate professor of geology, and Dr. James H. Thomas, associate professor and chairman of the Department of American Studies, helped with photographic reproductions. Expert cartographer Heidi Mazzullo prepared the Clipperton island locator map.

Dr. Lloyd M. Benningfield, professor of electrical engineering and former dean of the WSU Graduate School, provided a stipend for the summer of 1986 that allowed me to complete my research and commence writing.

Several associates read early drafts of the manuscript, in part to help me avoid technical flaws but also to suggest approaches. At WSU, Dr. William R. Carper, professor of chemistry, not only translated technical material into language comprehendible to a layman but offered meaningful criticism regarding the manuscript's structure. Dr. John C. Gries, associate professor and chairman of the Department of Geology, spotted numerous errors and, I think, has saved me considerable embarrassment—all the while trying to figure out a practical way to visit the place. And

Dr. Phillip Drennon Thomas, professor of history and dean of the Fairmount College of Liberal Arts and Sciences, read and criticized the entire piece twice, which is surely service above and beyond.

Old friends elsewhere also assisted. Dr. Seymour V. ("Ike") Connor, professor emeritus of history, Texas Tech University, and my mentor, friend, and sometime coauthor, skillfully picked apart my first draft. His criticism, along with that of Fred Woodward, director of the University Press of Kansas, convinced me that a decidedly different tack was required. LaVone and Jane Pirner of Wichita, eclectic and discerning readers, offered insightful advice, and former WSU colleague Miss Margaret Ann Gray provided me with much more meaningful feedback than she ever suspected.

While I happily acknowledge the aid of many people during the preparation of this book, I alone am responsible for its shortcomings.

Notes

1. Page 18 of edition cited.

2. Morris, p. 32.

1

A Natural History

Clipperton island is one of the most obscure, isolated, and un-pleasant places on earth. Strange things happen thereabouts.

A narrow, low-lying coral ring situated 670 miles southwest of Acapulco, it sits alone in the mostly empty eastern North Pacific ocean. Geographically misplaced, its closest atoll neighbor is Pukapuka in the eastern Tuamotu archipelago, 2,600 miles to the southwest.

French-owned tropical Clipperton island was named for an English pirate, but its history is mostly Mexican and American. It is a curiosity of United States foreign policy, the only spot in the superpower's sphere that was excluded from the Monroe Doctrine.

This unique place is an odd setting for stories of imperialism and international intrigue. Leading luminaries include Ferdinand Magellan, Emperor Charles V, Hernán Cortés, Napoleon III, Porfirio Díaz (and several Mexican revolutionaries), Italian King Victor Emmanuel III (perhaps acting for dictator Benito Mussolini), Admiral Richard Byrd (who was unquestionably under secret orders from President Franklin Delano Roosevelt), and modern explorer Jacques Yves Cousteau. Supporting characters and tangential tales include pirates and buried treasure, castaways and truly heroic deeds, adventurers and mostly misadventures, scientists and sometimes surprising discoveries, sailors of numerous nations and curious clandestine missions, and even a fiendish villain—and rape and murder.

The stage measures less than four square miles, much of that area a stagnant lagoon that reeks of ammonia during the dry season. No tropical paradise, the atoll offers ships neither safe harbor nor shallow bottom offshore. Mariners can find anchorage at 20 to 45 fathoms close by, 100 yards or less off the wave-tossed southwestern shore, or further out at 250 yards or more off the northeastern coast; however, southwestern anchorage often proves to be dangerously close to shore, and as for the northeast, U.S. Navy *Sailing Directions* for the area warn that "Heavy squalls are frequent from the N to ENE direction and at such times it is advisable to be prepared to heave up and head for open water."[1]

Difficult to visit even in fair weather, the low-lying coral ring is so storm-lashed in the wet season as to be invisible to anyone sailing through nearby shipping lanes. "Soundings give but little warning when approaching from any direction," the navy cautions. "A high, breaking surf pounds the coral reef which encircles the atoll and at times completely sweeps across it and into the lagoon." Only the 69-foot-tall "Rock" can be seen in good weather for any distance, at ten miles or so; it looks somewhat like "a sail but on closer approach it appears to resemble an immense castle."[2]

Clipperton island is a nesting site for millions of birds, and their pungent odors sometimes waft on tropical breezes to passing ships, doubtlessly discouraging many who might otherwise be willing to brave violent breakers to surf ashore. Several of those who have landed in recent times insist that they felt quite uneasy, some even suggesting that this strange, somewhat surreal little place has an aura of the supernatural about it, replete with spirits and ghosts.

Usually uninhabited by humans, the island was settled late in the nineteenth century by American miners who processed its bird droppings as fertilizer. Over the ensuing three decades, hundreds of persons consequently lived and labored in its tropical heat, and over time many of them became desperate to leave. At least one sincerely believed that the island was driving him mad. Other residents behaved quite oddly. One was removed by authorities because, allegedly, he was insane. Another, undoubtedly island-crazed, drove himself and three companions at gunpoint into a shark-infested sea to their deaths.

Then, during World War I, through no fault of their own, islanders were cut off from the mainland in an incident the New York *Times* labeled "macabre."[3] With the inhabitants marooned, a madman ruled as despot, terrorizing a handful of women and children with whom he happened to be stranded—raping whomever he wanted, murdering any who resisted. It was genuine melodrama, with the U.S. Navy cast in the role of the cavalry to the rescue.

Later, President Roosevelt became intrigued with the place, which he considered critical to postwar America, and he ordered his navy to seize it, lest it fall into the clutches of Winston Churchill and become part of the British Empire. Military operations on and about the atoll, a closely guarded secret of World War II, quickly devolved to debacle, so much so that Roosevelt's preoccupation with it and its peculiar problems may have contributed to his poor performance at Yalta.

Clipperton island began millions of years ago as a volcanic seamount thousands of miles west of its present location. A relatively insignificant vent in the earth's crust caused by the constant deformation of tectonic plate movement, it has ever since moved steadily eastward, toward the Americas, on a conveyer-belt-like seabed that geologists say slowly spreads out from a midoceanic ridge. Over time Clipperton mountain uplifted to peak at perhaps 2,000 feet above sea level, or about three miles above the surrounding sea floor, before suddenly exploding in a fiery burst of pyrotechnics easily equal to that of Krakatoa in 1883, obliterating virtually everything above the waterline and leaving in its place a gaping, smoking crater some two miles in diameter.

Even as seawater flooded into a 300-foot-deep, bowl-shaped caldera, molten rock oozed up from the vent located along the southeastern coral rim. Individual volcanic spines pushed skyward, adhering laterally to one another as they rose nearly seven stories above the rim, forming a cavernous, two-acre glob of trachyte—now known as "the Rock."

Coral that for eons had clung to the mountain's upper flanks quickly colonized the shallower reaches of the drowned crater—the only newly habitable water within 1.4 million square miles. Over time the coral erected numerous reefs, slowing building an atoll in otherwise deep water, where none should be.

Throughout most of its existence, this atoll consisted primarily of two long narrow facing coral crescents built along opposing (western and eastern) crater rims. Between them, inside the two-mile-wide crater-lagoon, seven smaller, mostly submerged reefs took root upon igneous rock. The largest of these, the Grand Reef (some 300 acres in area, situated beside the Rock), eventually encircled the volcanic vent entirely. Others—mostly long thin slivers of coral that parallel the crescents like ghostly shadows in the water—over time grew to enclose most of the lagoon, 100 yards or more inshore.

So did the crescents. Even as the exploded mountaintop continued to rise from the seabed, eventually stranding about eight feet of coral crown above sea level, the outer reefs—steadily growing atop the crater rim—slowly came together. About the middle of the nineteenth century, both ends had met, creating a continuous, seven-mile-diameter ring that completely cut off the lagoon from the sea.

By then life had taken up residence on and about the atoll. Deluged by as much as 200 inches of rainfall annually (most of it falling in the June-to-November stormy wet season), the land-locked lagoon became a brackish freshwater lake, an inhospitable environment for marine creatures. Interior reefs quickly died. So did most fishes. By the middle of the twentieth century, only odd varieties of gobies, damselfish, shrimp, and surgeonfish survived; by 1980, merely pondweed and a few microscopic plants and animals were known to persist.

By contrast, tropical waters outside the coral ring are alive with creatures. As deep as man has explored the surrounding sea, 130 feet or so, he has marveled at abundance amid dead rock: coral, algae, plankton, small fishes, large fishes. Sharks thrive: blue, hammerhead, mako, nurse, thresher, tiger, and great white. Man-eaters are especially active offshore as well as in the atoll's shallows, much as they are near Australia's Great Barrier Reef. Frenzied feeding is commonplace about Clipperton and, perhaps, much underwater courtship as well.

Venomous yellow-bellied sea snakes also gather offshore, in swarms of a thousand or more individuals. They thrive in "ocean slicks"—zones where surface currents converge into "drift lines" that contain floating objects such as debris, fish, and carrion. Clipperton lies precisely along one of the Pacific's two great drift lines, but fortunately for island inhabitants, these deadly aquatic reptiles are not especially aggressive, save when mating, nor do they venture ashore; however, moray eels that likewise inhabit these waters regularly slither up from the deep and hunt in reef shallows, taking fish and unwary land crabs that forage for food in tidal pools along the shoreline. Like sharks, morays have attacked unsuspecting people who linger too long in the island's surf.

Conditions are not much safer ashore. The coral crown, which encircles the lagoon at a maximum of nine feet above sea level, offers little protection from a surrounding ocean that produces storms of truly awesome proportions. As the island is merely 700 miles north of the equator, tropical tempests are commonplace throughout much of the year. Waterspouts regularly sprout offshore.

Even though eastern Pacific hurricanes are neither as numerous nor as destructive as those of the Atlantic and Caribbean, or as dangerous as typhoons of the western Pacific and the China sea, or even as frequent as cyclones in the Indian ocean, they are commonplace. Many of them are conceived as tropical depressions quite near Clipperton island. From November to May, weather systems typically grow into moderate thunderstorms, but from May through October, when the cumulative impact of the tropical sun's rays is greatest on the surrounding sea, they fully mature.

On average, six tropical disturbances arise annually in adjacent waters, half of them becoming great storms. These usually slide harmlessly along the West coast of North America, hundreds of miles out to sea. Occasionally, a Pacific hurricane will skid northeastward and slam into the Mexican coast somewhere between the Gulf of Tehuantepec and the upper reaches of Baja California. One tempest in twenty will contain enough kick to cross the continent intact as a weather system and be reborn in the Gulf of Mexico; this apparently happened in 1850, killing hundreds of people in Mexico and the United States before the freak Pacific storm spent itself on the Louisiana coast.

Fortunately for mankind, the majority of eastern Pacific storms never threaten the mainland. Rather, they rake isolated islands, such as Hawaii, the Revilla Gigedo group off Baja California, and Clipperton.

Poor refuge from a turbulent sea though Clipperton may be, it has harbored an amazing spectrum of life. Relentless breakers pushed by opposing equatorial currents constantly pound its reef, sometimes from all directions at once. Over time the surf has laid down a continuous off-white carpet of beach sand around the lagoon shore, from time to time washing up onto it assorted life-forms, many of which—including man—have somehow survived.

This desolate, mostly featureless landscape is a difficult place on which to scratch out a living. The most prominent feature, the Rock, is located on the lagoon's side of the southeastern rim: it is a light-colored, 300-foot-long, 20-foot-wide formation that juts skyward almost 70 feet above the flat coral ring. No monolith, the Rock is an aggregation of many long, thin strands of fused trachyte that, up close, resemble organ pipes or standpipes.

The Rock's north and east faces are veritable vertical walls. Its south and west sides are broken and stair-stepped, creating a tumble-down or "immense castle" appearance from afar. The formation has been so worn by water and wind that some observers have likened it to an isolated block of weathered sandstone. In places, where bird droppings have liberally coated its surface, the Rock has a glazed white patina. Elsewhere, bird-splattered trachyte has been leached into a crumbly white material the consistency of chalk.

Dozens of separate vertical volcanic extrusions stretch skyward, sometimes touching and sometimes not, creating passages of varying sizes within the Rock. A few are roofless, but most have fused together overhead, creating caves inhabited by the island's creatures. Cavern floors are covered with beach sand, feathers, and bird droppings, and many of these malodorous caves wind entirely through the volcanic formation from top to bottom. Some are large enough for man to explore or even inhabit; however, most are merely tiny crevices between rock faces suitable only for nesting birds and surefooted lizards.

The Rock is connected to the coral rim by a finger of beach called "the Isthmus," which, before 1861, bordered a narrow, shallow southern entrance to the lagoon. Many men have dug deeply into these sands for pirates' treasure that was said to be buried near the Rock. Nearby, along the lagoon shore, are "Rock bay" and "Thumb point," which are formed by projections of beach adjacent to the Rock. Close by, another spit of sand called "the Hook" steadily grows toward the Rock as the sea relentlessly deposits new beach material.

Clockwise about the lagoon, along the western shore, is "Pincer bay," which consists of two fingers of sand jutting north and south and situated some 900 feet apart. Between them are three to fifteen islets, the precise number depending upon the water level in the lagoon; the largest, a remnant of reef, comprises 300 square feet.

One hundred feet off the lagoon's northwestern shore are five "Egg islands," the only portion of the interior reefs to be permanently above water. The largest comprises 800 square feet, the smallest less than 20. Midway along the northern shoreline is "Green point," a discolored stretch of sand that borders the other one-time entrance to the lagoon. From there to the Rock, neither the beach nor the featureless coral crown is remarkable.

At their widest point, along the northwestern shore, the limestone coral rim and interior beach sands together stretch 1,500 feet across, from ocean to lagoon; and at the narrowest, near Green point, they measure merely 130 feet. Rim to rim, along its longest axis, southeast to northwest, the atoll measures 2.6 miles, and by its shortest, southwest to northeast, 1.5 miles. Eighty-five percent of the island's area is lagoon, which ranges in depth from a few inches to at least 50 fathoms.

This unremarkable island takes on a rather sinister cast when its map is rotated 135 degrees, so that the southeastern coastline points north. Suddenly the atoll bears an uncanny resemblance to a human skull. The deep circular hole in the Grand Reef becomes a hollow left eye socket, staring back blankly. Submerged lagoon reefs that parallel the whole western interior shoreline metamorphose into a smirking, leering mouth, and the separate, smaller reef that lies off Pincer bay is transformed into an ugly gash that runs the entire length of the skull's left cheekbone, a scar worthy of a pirate. Even the Egg islands take on new qualities, becoming either the stubble of scraggly whiskers, or a patch of unsightly pimples, or both.

Clipperton's usual residents take no notice of such anthropomorphism. Their struggles to survive are drama enough.

Despite a punishing climate, this bleak little island harbors a remarkable variety of plants and animals, some of them unique. All resident life migrated here, mostly from the Americas, including thirty-eight varieties of fungi that either flew to the atoll as wind-borne spores or hitchhiked as parasites on transient birds. Primitive island life-forms include mildews and molds that thrive in damp conditions; these attach themselves to every surface, including grains of sand, and extract nutrients directly from the superabundance of bird droppings that litter the landscape, breaking down organic matter in the process. One third of the fungi are of the penicillium group, and none of the remainder species pose any particular health problems for other, regular residents. Three varieties of lichen, symbiotic unions of algae and fungi, cling to coral debris, and the acids they produce as a byproduct of life slowly crumble rocks the size of soccer balls into pea gravel, which in turn eventually becomes beach sand.

Botanists have classified thirty-five species of island algae, ranging from green pond scum, which covers every stagnant pool of water, no matter how small, to red-brown seaweed, which grows in protected coves on the lagoon's leeward side. Algae blackens coral all along the perimeter of the reef, and in places, as on Green point, it even discolors the island's off-white beach sands.

Three varieties of mosses, several sedges, and even a particularly hardy variety of bur grass exist. Thickets take root just above the waterline, sometimes surviving considerable distances from the lagoon, but always in clumps and clusters, and only where their tender shoots somehow escape the ravages of omnipresent land crabs.

Durable morning glories, whose vines periodically choke the island and then mysteriously vanish for years, as though drought-killed, quite possibly predate man on the atoll, but botanists believe that most other plants (bird-of-paradise, borage, coconut palm, jute, mustard, nightshade, ragweed, and waltheria among them) were imported, sometimes purposely, for none of them could have survived until human beings upset the island's natural balance.

Assorted animals also subsist in and about the lagoon's warm, primordial goo. All along the sandy interior shoreline, in marshy areas ranging from mud bogs to small ponds, amoeba and paramecia flourish. Sow bugs feed off microscopic life-forms and

inhabit protected coves where pond weeds grow. They are common as high as the splash zone. So too are three species of marine
worms and two varieties of aquatic snails, all of which feed
assorted predators, particularly birds. Periwinkles, edible first
cousins to delectable escargots, inhabit shallow ponds by the
untold thousands. Earthworms abound. Damselflies dart in and
out of the cover of sedge stands, searching for food and seeking
protection from lightning-fast lizards with long sticky tongues.

At the turn of the twentieth century, naturalists estimated that
five million crabs lived on the island, literally a case of infestation.
Rock crabs (*Geograpsus lividus, Pachygrapsus minutes,* and *Crangon
hawaiiens clippertoni*) live in modest numbers along both the seaside
reef and freshwater lagoon, moving freely from one environment
to the other. Land crabs (*Gecarcinus planatus, Gecarcoidea lalandei,*
and *Thalamita roosevelti*)—especially the numerically dominant
red-orange *G. planatus,* about which much will be said later—
share a similar life-style and overrun the island in incredible
numbers. Principally nocturnal, these fist-size crustaceans hole up
under rocks and ledges or loose sand during the day and scurry
about foraging, mostly at night. They cohabit with and frequently
feast off of sand fleas, six varieties of ants, four species of dung-
eating beetles, and an undetermined variety of cockroaches, silver-
fish, springtails, and guano-eating earwigs.

Humid-zone bugs thrive. Lantern flies (very large tropical insects with bulbous heads and colorful markings) are common, as
are shield bugs and damselflies. Water striders hop about the
lagoon during calms; they row with middle legs, steer with rear
ones, and seize hapless victims with front claspers. Gnats thus die
by the hundreds daily.

Woolly centipedes, some of which glow in the twilight, prefer
the cool, moist shade about the Rock, as do long-legged house
spiders. Pink-winged hawkmoths flutter around morning glory
flowers, and large, bright green caterpillars live among their vines.
Snout and owlet moths are numerous but hardly noticeable,
except to night feeders such as the predatory spiders that stalk
them. A dozen species of flies buzz about—from common green
house pests to exotic flesh flies that deposit eggs in open wounds
that they gouge out of assorted hosts with needle-sharp suckers,

their maggots eventually leaving behind either dead victims or dripping, cankerous sores.

Clipperton is a reptilian paradise. The island's skink (*Emoia cyanura arundeli*) is duplicated nowhere else on earth. These gold-striped lizards have no relative at all in the Americas, their closest kin being inhabitants of Pukapuka, 2,600 miles away. How this animal's ancestors crossed the equator against prevailing currents and winds defies plausible explanation.

When *E. cyanura arundeli* was first collected in 1897, it possessed a dark blue tail, a color characteristic that by 1958 had completely faded away. Until quite recently, these reptiles scurried only through the Rock's catacombs, snaring flies and other bugs with quick, sticky tongues, but once vegetation increased, mostly because of man, they abandoned the Rock for easier pickings elsewhere.

The solitary peak thus became the exclusive domain of the island's other lizard, an equally unique species of gecko (*Gehyra multilata*). These small, dull-brown creatures scamper up and down virtually perpendicular volcanic spines, often entering grottoes upside down along the ceilings. Folklore insists that the toes of geckoes are tipped with suction cups; actually, the soles of their feet are composed of thousands of microscopic backward-projecting hooks that fasten onto the tiniest surface irregularity. As do skinks, geckoes feed mostly at night on insects, but they keep a wary, independently rotating eye peeled for land crabs.

Dominating the atoll and its environs are incredibly vast numbers of birds, their great cacophonous screechings sometimes drowning out even the constant roar of the sea. The sum total of winged creatures that have visited Clipperton island over the eons is staggering, easily aggregating in the billions. Human visitors have been struck dumb by their numbers, both nesting and circling overhead. During any nesting season, a million or more birds thrive on these rich marine feeding grounds, representing a score of species that live mostly in harmony. In fair weather, no quadrant of the island's sky is without them.

Most species are transients. A half dozen varieties of ducks regularly winter there: pintails, blue-winged teals, canvasbacks, shovellers, baldpates, and coots. Coots especially thrive, cropping copious quantities of succulent November sedges for nesting material. Occasionally, and unaccountably, even barn swallows sometimes take up residence on the atoll.

Marine species are far more common. Wading birds—black-bellied plovers, tattlers, Hudsonian curlews, sandpipers, ibis—graze everywhere along the lagoon shore. Even so, they never seem to diminish the swarms of sow bugs upon which they constantly feed. A plover will even spear an unwary crab through its mouthpart, slam it against the hard coral to shatter its shell, and feast.

Overhead, countless petrels and shearwaters, both North Pacific cousins of the albatross, glide away much of their lives at sea, tirelessly soaring and occasionally swooping down to skim the crests of waves, their unblinking eyes searching for fish or carrion. These birds come ashore only to nest, and then rarely at Clipperton island. Follow-the-leader formations of brown pelicans also dive close to the atoll's shimmering sea, or, when resting, sit lazily on gentle sea swells well offshore. They too abhor this land, calling here only out of necessity and nesting elsewhere.

Of all the seabirds that regularly reside here, three dominate—frigates, gulls, and gannets. Vast numbers of purplish "Magnificent" frigate birds (*Fregata magnificens*) nest high on the beach, along the crest of the weathered coral crown where large rocks continuously break loose from the dead reef. Also known as "man-o'-war" birds and even incorrectly as "sea eagles," their wing span (approximately 7.5 feet) is the greatest in proportion to body weight (three to four pounds) of any avian species, which enables them to soar effortlessly on air currents while searching for squid, fish, young sea turtles, and carrion. Mostly, though, frigates are aerial bullies and thieves, mercilessly mugging gannets, gulls, and even other frigates until victims give up their catches, which a piratical man-o'-war will seize and devour in midair. If nesting, it will regurgitate its meal to feed its chicks.

Frigates are unfussy nesters. Like most of the island's birds, they begin breeding in November, once the worst of the stormy wet season has passed. Hens typically lay clutches of two eggs each, directly on the sand among the coral debris, seldom adding unnecessary adornments such as sedge stems to soften their chicks' entry into the world. Seemingly indifferent parents, frigates appear oblivious to the squawking plight of fledglings that wander down from the nesting area onto the lagoon beach, which is predominantly occupied by nesting gannets, more commonly known in these waters as "boobies." There, transgressing and flightless young "sea eagles" display amazingly little courage and are easily driven off the beach and back up onto the coral crown by territorially minded but equally young boobies—the very birds frigates will terrorize as adults.

Quarrelsome by nature, frigates have but one natural enemy on the island, the ubiquitous land crabs (especially *G. planatus*), which, if given the opportunity, will steal an unguarded egg or snatch an unwary chick. Nesting birds are ever-vigilant and brook no harassment from these squat crustaceans, who instinctively seem to understand as much. Except for terns that nest in out-of-the way places—high up on the Rock and on remote lagoon islands—frigates among the atoll's birds are the least annoyed by crabs, which scramble out of the way of the man-o'-wars' slashing, scimitar-hooked beaks—lest they lose a claw, an eye, or their very lives.

Terns, small forked-tailed gulls sometimes called "sea pigeons," prefer the safest reaches of the atoll. Their eggs are delicious, and birds have been conditioned by plundering seamen the world over as well as by omnipresent crabs on Clipperton island to nest mostly in remote places. Terns occupy every possible crevice of the Rock, their primary nesting site, and such high ground as they find on the low-lying lagoon islands, especially the Eggs. Because, in fair weather, these islets are no more than two feet above the usual water level of the lagoon, untold thousands of eggs and chicks are lost annually to choppy water and storm surges. Those birds unable to find nesting space elsewhere share the beach with gannets and crabs.

Inhospitable habitat though the atoll may be, it harbors four varieties of gulls. Noddy terns (*Anous stolidus*), so called because of a characteristically sleepy countenance (broken when they flutter suddenly airborne, screeching, as though startled awake), and white-capped noddies (*Micranous diamesus*) are the most common species. Difficult to tell apart, the latter, in addition to being white-capped, are somewhat smaller and grayer in plumage. Fairy terns (*Gygis candida*) nest here, but not in numbers as vast as

noddies. Least numerous are sooty terns (*Sterna fuliginosa*), also
called "wide-awakes" because of their shrill shrieks.

Of all the birds that call Clipperton island home, sooty terns
are by far the most endearing. They mate for life and are loyal
partners and helpmates, and stern but devoted parents. Alone
among the sea pigeons—indeed, among all the atoll's birds—
sooty terns do not foul the land, for they defecate at sea. Not even
when startled into flight will a sooty tern void its bowels. All
other avian species regularly shower the place. As a result, guano
has accumulated to a depth of several feet in some spots.

Foremost among the island's other fowl residents are blue
boobies (*Sula brewsteri*) and brown boobies (*S. piscatrix websteri*),
their large, webbed feet respectively color-coded. Called gannets
in the South Pacific, these pathetic little creatures are rivaled only
by "gooney birds" (black-footed albatrosses) for sheer naivete.
When nesting, boobies will allow man to approach quite close,
often squawking merely mild protests, or pecking out defensively
only when handled. Their eggs and flesh smack of rancid fish,
otherwise they might well be extinct. Homely birds, they have a
rather comic expression, and all of these characteristics led sixteenth-century Spaniards who sailed these waters to call them
bobos, or clowns.

Little about these clowns is appealing. They regularly foul their
own nests, squirting feces over mates, eggs, chicks, and neighbors
whenever they take flight. Typically, a booby eats sixty small fish
a day and excretes about 11 pounds of phosphate-rich guano
annually. The ground everywhere around their nests is littered
with their droppings. Over the eons, an abundance of rainfall has
percolated all the bird waste through the atoll's porous coral
bedrock, in places leaching it into large beds of almost pure
calcium phosphate, a rich natural fertilizer.

While some Clipperton island boobies nest at the Rock, having
taken up residence on cavern floors among quarrelsome terns that
they displace with superior size, most boobies set up housekeep-
ing unpretentiously in the sands that border the lagoon. Typically,
a pair of birds will claim about three square feet of beach, scoop
out a small hollow for a nest, and mate.

Virtually at that instant a land crab will appear and, just out of
pecking range, commence a relentless vigil. Covering everything

but its stem-mounted eyes with sand to shield itself from the broiling sun, it simply waits patiently. When within days the first egg is laid, the crustacean will skitter closer, dropping defensively to the ground and retracting its claws if threatened by the nesting bird. A crab will squat motionless until the slow-witted booby's attention lapses, then sneak closer still. Such a siege may last for a week, the harassed mother pushed to exhaustion while her indifferent mate snoozes nearby or fishes for them both. Ultimately, if the crustacean has not otherwise been successful, she will roll one of her two precious eggs toward her antagonist.

Tribute paid, that nest generally thereafter is left alone. How mindless, prehistoric creatures such as Clipperton island land crabs could possibly communicate among themselves about which nest has been taxed and which has not is unknown.

Fratricide, widespread elsewhere among wide-ranging tropical gannets (the stronger chick commonly pecks siblings to death as one or both parents look on disinterestedly), is rare on this atoll, probably because of crab predation. Since boobies typically lay only two eggs, infanticide is also rare, but that too has been observed occasionally.

Meanwhile, if, while rolling its loot away from the bird's nest, a marauding crab cracks a captured egg on the sharp coral debris, it will eat its prize then and there, shell and all, lest it be forced to share with others of its kind that are certain to flock to any feast, no matter how small. Should the booty survive, the crab becomes surrogate parent, protecting the egg from all rivals while awaiting the natural incubation of tropical sun and sand to hatch it. As soon as the chick pecks its way out of its shell, the crab will seize and devour it.

Once upon a time, green sea turtles regularly lumbered ashore to bury clutches of eggs in warm lagoon sands, but the animals' numbers have been so depleted worldwide by hunters that none has been observed at Clipperton island for more than a century. Likewise, fur and elephant seals once braved the surrounding shark-infested waters to clamber up on the coral rim to bask and breed. They remained seaside, near the constant breakers, where bulls called cows into harems. The tropical climate and relative isolation made the place an ideal rookery, until hunters happened onto the scene. None of these mammals has been observed on the atoll since the early nineteenth century.[4]

Then came man, then pigs.

Notes

1. Page 5.

2. *Ibid.*

3. "Macabre isle of passion," p. 1.

4. The foregoing description of Clipperton island is drawn from a variety of sources, all of which are cited in full in the Bibliography. Specifically, see works by Allison (1958, 1959); Anderson and Davis; W. J. Baldwin, *et al.*; Banks; Bartsch and Rehder; Beck; Chace; Chubb; A. H. Clark; H. L. Clark; Coquillett; J. Y. Cousteau (1980, 1981); J. M. Cousteau; Currie; Dawson; DeLaubenfels; Denniston; Edwords; Fraser; Garman; Gifford; Guppy; Hamilton; Harbison; Hartman; Heidemann; Heller; Heller and Snodgrass (1901, 1903); Hertlein; Hertlein and Emerson; Hurd; Hutchinson; Hyman; Ives; Jacobs; Johnson; Killip; J. H. Kimball; Lacrois; Limbaugh; Lipps (1968, 1969); McNeill; Menard; Menard and Fisher; Murphy (1980); Nelson, *et al.*; Obermuller; Owen; Pease; Rathbun (1902, 1918); Richardson; Sachet (1959, 1960, 1962); Schmitt (1939, 1940); Shoemaker; Slevin; Snodgrass and Heller (1902, 1904); Stager; W. R. Taylor; Teall; Truchan and Larson; Van Denburg and Slevins; Visher (1922, 1925); Wardley; Wetmore; G. W. Wharton; W. J. Wharton; and Yaldwyn and Wodzicki.

2

Island of Many Names
1521–1857

No one knows for certain who discovered Clipperton island, but circumstantial evidence strongly suggests that it was sighted by Ferdinand Magellan on January 24, 1521, during his historic circumnavigation of the globe. That fact is believed to have been suppressed for a time because of its implications for the Spanish Empire; as a result, the atoll was lost to history.

Little matter. Hundreds of years were to pass before Magellan's probable discovery of this unusual place would matter to anyone. By then, it would be seen by numerous other sailors, many of them renaming it in the process; however, there is no evidence whatsoever that anyone went ashore before 1825. After all, far greater opportunities for adventure—and wealth—existed elsewhere in the vast Pacific ocean.

Most accounts of Magellan's celebrated voyage around the world (1519–22)[1] place him nowhere near this obscure, smelly atoll, probably because generations of historians have unthinkingly overlooked the obvious. Magellan's flotilla could not possibly have tacked across the entire Pacific ocean along the course that expedition survivors later claimed, because all such possible routes lay across the very heart of the island-spattered South Pacific and consequently contain countless inviting landfalls—far too many places to be reconciled with merely the two desolate little islands actually sighted by the sixteenth-century explorers. Not until the early twentieth century did anyone grasp the significance of this contradiction and, as a consequence, conclude that Magellan had discovered Clipperton island.[2]

Most readers are generally familiar with Magellan's epic voyage, which, among other things, proved that the world was round. Setting sail from San Lucar, Spain, in 1519, this Portuguese soldier-of-fortune in Spanish employ led a five-ship flotilla on an expedition of discovery bound ultimately for the spice islands southeast of India.

Mindful of the Papal Line of Demarcation (1493) and the Treaty of Tordesillas (1494), which split the New World between the two pious Catholic kingdoms of Spain and Portugal forever, Spanish king Charles V forbade Magellan to trespass upon Portuguese waters. Thus unable to round the southern tip of Africa and sail along a known waterway to Indonesia, the adventurer instead groped his way through a labyrinth of islands off the tip of South America (now known as the Strait of Magellan) and into the expanse of water he called *el mar pacifico*. Thence, according to survivors, they generally sailed diagonally across the entire Pacific ocean to Guam in the Marianas, sighting merely two uninhabited and unremarkable desert islands along the way, which they individually named *San Pablo* and *Tiburones* ("Sharks") islands and, collectively, the "Unfortunate isles."

By then Magellan had lost two vessels to hardship and mutiny. Sailors aboard his three remaining ships were reduced to eating leather sail shrouds and, when they could catch them, shipboard rats. The men suffered terribly from malnutrition, which in turn induced scurvy; their gums hemorrhaged, and their teeth fell out. Several died. Because neither Unfortunate isle offered safe harbor or fresh food, they sailed on across unknown waters and empty sea, finally encountering the Mariana islands, where the explorers refreshed themselves, cavorting among friendly Polynesian people the Spaniards superciliously called *ladrones,* or "thieves," because of their light-fingeredness.

In time the explorers resumed their voyage of discovery, encountering islands (the present Philippines) they happily named for Lazarus, who had likewise experienced a miraculous deliverance from death. Ironically, Magellan was soon killed by natives. Survivors abandoned one leaky vessel, filled the other two to the gunnels with spices, and set sail separately for home. In 1522, *Victoria* limped into port at San Lucar with eighteen weary seamen aboard. Its cargo sold at auction for several times the entire cost of the expedition, lost ships included.

The explorers spoke of the extraordinary sights they had seen and of where they had been. Generations of scholars unthinkingly accepted these accounts at face value until, pondering Magellan's precise route across the Pacific, twentieth-century historian George E. Nunn concluded that survivors had not told the truth. Had Magellan tacked across the then uncharted ocean the way they and the Spanish government claimed, he would have traversed much of the South Pacific. Instead of the two desert islands that he and his scurvy-ridden crew actually saw, they would have encountered thousands of landfalls, among them hundreds of exotic places—some of them veritable tropical paradises replete with amorous, bare-breasted women eager (as subsequent exploration would amply demonstrate) to nurse randy, sixteenth-century sailors back to health, and beyond.

Nunn's evidence that Magellan actually went elsewhere includes the fact that Hernando de Bustamante, one of the eighteen survivors, eventually said that Magellan's route to the Marianas was considerably different than the one made public. The old man confessed on his deathbed that the ship's log had been fabricated in the Philippines.

Why such deception? Nunn contends that "there was always a motive for early Spanish writers on this subject to deceive their public."[3] The great distance across the Pacific indicated that all of the spice islands might well be within Portugal's half of the world, as defined by the Treaty of Tordesillas. For Spain to admit this would have been to abandon the Far East, which it was not about to do.

Nunn speculates that this blatant fraud was overlooked for hundreds of years because, except for García Jofre de Loaisa's expedition of 1526—which, once through the Strait of Magellan and into the Pacific, is known to have sailed generally northward, parallel to but well out of sight of the western coast of the Americas, to the established latitude of the Marianas (about 10° N), before turning due west—all subsequent Spanish trade with the Orient was through Mexico aboard Manila galleons. Thus, for centuries no mariner attempted to replicate Magellan's publicly reported route; had that happened, European exploration and exploitation of the island-rich South Pacific would have been pushed forward by two hundred years.

Seeking to determine where Magellan actually went, Nunn rejected a variety of possible routes across the ocean as containing far too many landfalls before his sleuthing led him to trace a course similar to that unquestionably sailed by Loaisa, who had been sent by King Charles V in 1526 for more spices. Alongside Loaisa as the expedition's chief pilot was Sebastián Cano, a survivor of Magellan's voyage who had captained *Victoria* on the last leg of its historic voyage; he undoubtedly knew these waters better than anyone else. Using that fact as a clue, Nunn drew a line eastward of but parallel to Cano's known trek across the Pacific. Nearby lay two uninhabited desert islands that closely fit descriptions of the Unfortunate isles. "San Pablo and Tiburones," Nunn therefore concluded, "may be identified with Clipperton and Clarion islands, in latitudes 10°17′ N. and 18°[21′] N., respectively, or approximately the reverse of the latitudes given in several of the accounts."[4]

Meanwhile, increasingly anxious about the fate of *Trinidad,* Magellan's other spice-laden vessel, in 1527 King Charles had written Hernán Cortés, conqueror of the Aztecs, and instructed him to investigate the whereabouts of the ship, which, Cano had said, planned to sail eastward from the spice islands across the Pacific to New Spain. He also ordered Cortés to provide assistance to Loaisa's expedition, which, the king predicted, would soon reach Mexico on its triumphant return voyage from his oriental islands—following *Trinidad*'s reported course.

Charles's letter reached Mexico virtually simultaneously with a handful of survivors from Loaisa's expedition who, separated by a storm near the tip of South America, had sailed by dead reckoning northward to Mexico's Gulf of Tehuantepec, thinking it to be Panama. They were rescued by friendly Indians and conveyed to Cortés, who was already quite interested in the western sea.

In fact, he had recently written the king about profitable possibilities: "I exult in the tidings brought me of the Great [Pacific] Ocean, for in it, as cosmographers and those learned men who know about the Indies inform us, are scattered the rich isles teeming with gold and spices and precious stones."[5]

Cortés informed his monarch that he had sent forty Spaniards to the town of Zacatula, north of present Acapulco, with instructions to build two medium-size caravels and two brigantines with which to explore the south seas. Volunteers for the expedition abounded. Indians who lived along New Spain's west coast repeatedly spoke of "an island inhabited only by women," Cortés wrote, "and . . . at given times men from the mainland visit them. If they conceive, they keep the female children but the males they throw away. This island is 10 days' journey from the province [of Ceguatan], and many of them [Ceguatan's inhabitants] went there and saw it." He added that the Indians "also told me that . . . [the island] is very rich in pearls and gold. I shall try to learn the truth about this island and shall make a full account to your Majesty."[6]

Coupling the king's orders with his own desire to find fabled "Feminia," Cortés placed a kinsman, Alvaro de Saavedra Cerén, in command of a three-ship flotilla that sailed from the west coast village of Zihautano on October 31, 1527, heading west by southwest. For two weeks Saavedra's flotilla hurried before trade winds that drove them southwestward more than 200 leagues, where they encountered a current that deflected them due westward. On Friday, November 15, when an estimated 700 miles from the mainland, Saavedra recorded in his log: "There appear many birds, land birds, and signs of land."[7]

Considering the persistent myth of a pleasure island inhabited by Amazons somewhere in the vicinity, it is truly remarkable that Saavedra did not investigate. Instead, he continued unwaveringly on course toward the distant spice islands, losing two ships before the expedition reached the Moluccas. There he happened upon survivors of Loaisa's expedition, whom he took aboard. Eventually he loaded his lone caravel with supplies and cloves and set course across the vast, empty ocean toward Mexico, but he quickly encountered what sailors on *Trinidad* had already discovered: both prevailing breezes and ocean currents were contrary to a direct eastward crossing of the Pacific. Twice the Spaniards were driven back to the spice islands by adverse winds, Saavedra dying in the last failed attempt.

In time Saavedra's outgoing route became a veritable shipping lane between Mexico and the Orient, but a half century would pass before a return route to the Americas would be discovered— the course of the Japanese Current that sweeps clockwise around the vast North Pacific basin. Even though hurried along by favorable westerly winds, return voyages nevertheless required nine months. Sailing through bitterly cold northern latitudes, seamen increasingly fell victim to scurvy and beriberi, a diet-induced thiamine deficiency that leads to neurological and gastrointestinal disorders, then to paralysis and death. By the time they reached Acapulco, few had strength enough to man pumps, much less trim sails; only by chance of light breezes were some crews of lumbering, top-heavy galleons able to slide into port, drop anchor, and, exhausted, await help from shore.

Despite such hardships, regular trade between Acapulco and Manila commenced in 1580, and for the next three centuries, Clipperton island's tale entwines with that of Spanish exploitation of the Philippines. Two vessels annually departed Acapulco for Manila, by regulation sailing on the tide no later than March 31 to avoid *vendevals*, gusty southwestern winds that sweep the Philippine sea from June through September.

Reported Antonio de Morga, counsel for the Holy Inquisition who traveled to the Philippines aboard a Manila galleon in 1603:

> *Inasmuch as the vessels on leaving Acapulco are wont sometimes to encounter calms, they set sail south from sixteen and one-half degrees, in which the port [of Acapulco] is situated, until they strike the brisas, which is situated generally at ten or eleven degrees. By this route they sail continually before the wind, and without changing sails, with fresh and fair brisas, and in other weather, for one thousand and eight hundred leagues [5,400 miles], without sighting any mainland or island [sic].*[8]

So long as ships avoided the late summer monsoon season, the outward passage was so placid that Spanish sailors called the ocean *mar de damas*, or "Ladies' sea." Eighteenth-century French Jesuit Père Taillandier, who traveled aboard a Manila ship to reach China reported: "One does not have to fear contrary winds, and since the winds that blow are always fresh, they temper the heat."[9]

Historian William Schurz, an authority on the Manila trade,

contends that misfortune rarely befell galleons on outward voyages. Caravels sometimes sailed too late and were consequently battered to bits on rocks somewhere in the Philippines by *vendevals,* and sometimes they were captured by pirates who trolled the Ladies' sea for silver-laden prizes. Even so, only about seventy of the four hundred or so ships that plied Acapulco-Manila shipping lanes over the ensuing two centuries were ever lost. A dozen outgoing vessels disappeared, including one rich galleon known to have been taken in 1705 by English buccaneer John Clipperton; however, most disasters occurred on the longer, far more dangerous Manila-Acapulco run that traversed the violent high latitudes of the North Pacific. There, another sixty vessels vanished.[10]

It seems remarkable that Manila galleon passenger Antonio de Morga failed to see Clipperton island, for situated at latitude 10°18' N, longitude 109°13' W, it lay precisely along the established transoceanic trade route.[11] In fact, lumbering Spanish caravels sometimes carried as many as eight hundred passengers across the picturesque sea, but none of them ever reported seeing land in the atoll's vicinity, or even what might have appeared to be a white sail on the horizon, or swarms of birds as thick as bees.

Nevertheless, contemporary Spanish mariners almost certainly knew about the place, even if none of them mentioned it. Mexican chronicler Antonio Garcia Cubas once explained this dearth of detail:

> *The South Seas was explored in all directions, and many of those navigators, particularly those coming from Mexican ports, stopped [sic] at [Clipperton] island, despite its being lost in the immense waters of the Ocean. One [should] not be surprised . . . by the impossibility of obtaining indications of such an island in the personal relations of the first Spanish explorers, if one pays attention to its little importance, since it consisted of a single rock, surrounded by breakers and coral reefs which developed through the years into an atoll with guano deposits.*[12]

Eighteenth-century maps (compiled mostly by landlubbers who relied primarily on hearsay for their maritime information) regularly depict one or more offshore islands at or about Clipperton's actual location. Several show an *Isla de los Medaños,* meaning

"Sandbank" or "Mudflat" island. Others locate an *Isla de Mudleda,* the meaning of which is obscure, *mudleda* perhaps being colloquial for *muda,* or "roost for birds of prey," such as frigates. A few charts place nearby an *Isla de Nublada*—"Cloudy," "Gloomy," or perhaps even "Apprehensive" island, the correct nuance being unknown. And some even position thereabouts either an *Isla de Pasión* or a *Roca de Pasión,* the origin of the name being obscure but likely relating somehow to popular legends of lusty women on pleasure islands.[13]

Doubtlessly confusing to early sailors and cartographers alike was the existence of *Roca Partida* ("Departure Rock"), a barren projection towering 110 feet above sea level (48 feet higher than Clipperton Rock) and situated at latitude 18°59′ N, longitude 112°04′ W, some 67 miles west of *Isla de Socorro* in the Revilla Gigedo islands, off Baja California, or approximately 800 miles north of Clipperton. *Roca Partida* was regularly seen by those aboard returning Manila galleons, and modern maritime descriptions report that the *Roca* itself "consists of two white pinnacle rocks connected by a low ridge. When viewed from a distance the island resembles a vessel under jury masts,"[14] a characterization remarkably similar to that of Clipperton Rock. Many early cartographers incorrectly placed *Roca Partida* too far south, actually in the vicinity of Clipperton island, doubtlessly leading some mariners mistakenly to believe that the two Pacific islands with prominent peaks were one and the same.

Little matter. Most Spaniards who slipped out of Acapulco's harbor on the tide bound for the Orient were far more interested in reaching veritable tropical paradises than in exploring uninhabited, obviously unimportant bird-splattered rocks, however they might be identified on contemporary maps. The Marianas and the Philippines beckoned; women there traded their favors for fishhooks. As Antonio de Morga observed: "The natives of those islands, who go about naked . . . go out to sea to meet the ships as soon as they discover them. . . ."[15]

With neither safe harbor nor alluring human habitation, the odd little atoll was merely ignored by Spaniards who sailed by it regularly.

★   ★   ★

Not so with the English pirate John Clipperton, or so legend insists. Some accounts of his exploits assert that the eighteenth-century brigand actually used this atoll as his south seas base of operation,[16] but it is quite doubtful that he ever set foot there. He reportedly first saw the place in mid-February 1705, when, like Magellan two centuries earlier, he was halfway around the world, but unlike the Portuguese explorer in Spanish employ, this English pirate would survive his epic voyage—it being merely one of three circumnavigations of the globe to his credit.

Nothing whatsoever is known of John Clipperton before 1703, when he sailed as midshipman aboard the privateer *St. George* with Captain William Dampier to raid Spanish shipping lanes in the Pacific. Likely Clipperton was just another shadowy figure among a brotherhood of criminals, a professional thief. European governments then regularly hired outlaws to make war upon rivals, rewarding buccaneers such as Clipperton and Dampier with plunder.

A recent celebrity in England, where his best-selling memoirs told of bloodcurdling adventure in far-off exotic lands, Captain Dampier was a drunkard recently adjudged by the British Admiralty as "not a fit person" to command "any of his majesty's ships."[17] Hired anyway by joint-stock investors who owned *St. George* and therefore claimed a share of the spoils, the old pirate proved to be a poor choice. He drank incessantly, and when his leadership was questioned, he booted a troublesome junior officer off the ship, picking Clipperton to take his place.

Off the coast of Chile, Dampier tried three times to capture the same French vessel—twice being beaten off by fewer guns and once being outsailed to the safety of the port at Lima. In Panama, during a hurricane, he led a hundred men to attack what he knew to be a poor village; their gunpowder failed to ignite, and they were beaten off by a handful of Spaniards and natives. Back aboard ship after the storm, Dampier ordered all sails unfurled rather than pit his well-armed vessel against a suddenly appearing Spanish man-o'-war, but his hardbitten crew of cutthroats refused to run. They fought the Spaniards to a draw, finally forcing the warship to retreat.

Virtually a sieve from big shot and small, *St. George* limped to the coast, Dampier looking for an island-obscured cove to beach her for repairs. There, in the Gulf of Nicoya in what is present-day Costa Rica, the Englishmen happened upon a forty-ton bark, which they captured without much ado. Dampier christened it *Dragon* and, at least according to one of his biographers, appointed John Clipperton to its command: "Now that he had a ship of his own, [Clipperton] decided that the moment had come to break with Dampier. It was all done very politely. He [Clipperton] complained that the *St. George* was unseaworthy. Dampier replied that if he didn't like her he could go off on his own account. . . . "[18] Pirate William Funnell, who was there, said later that Dampier and Clipperton had a "falling out," and as a result, "Mr. Clipperton, with twenty-one of our men, seized the bark. . . ."[19]

It is certain that Clipperton and his companions purloined part of *St. George*'s supplies and, late in 1704, independently sallied forth to troll the Ladies' sea for Manila galleons; however, no account of that voyage exists. Clipperton reportedly captured numerous Spanish vessels off Acapulco, all told taking more than four thousand gold doubloons. He is also said to have "discovered" the atoll.

James Burney, who penned the first comprehensive history of voyages and discoveries in the south seas, asserted that

> *from New Spain [in 1705] he [Clipperton] discovered the Island or Rock which was named after him, and which was noticed in the charts so early as to have place in that designed by Herman Moll [about 1730] for shewing the boundary-line of the [British] South Seas Company's privileges. It [Clipperton island] is laid down in latitude 10°20' N, and about a half a degree in longitude east of the meridian of Cape San Lucas [located at the southern tip of Baja California, or about 110° W]. It is said to have been seen by one of the fur traders on the northwest coast of America, and its situation to have been found very nearly as was before assigned [presumably by Clipperton].*[20]

Moll's map in fact locates Clipperton's island within one-half degree of its actual site and thereby constitutes persuasive circumstantial evidence that the pirate truly saw the atoll that ever since has borne his name. Nevertheless, no early account suggests that he ventured ashore, much less that he used it as a base for his nefarious activities. All such stories appear to have been the creations of twentieth-century imaginations.

About 1707 Clipperton returned to England, disappearing from public view until 1719, when he commanded the last privateering venture in British history, a circumnavigation of the globe. It ended in failure. Penniless, in 1722 he retired to Galway, Ireland, dying there within the week.

Six years after Clipperton reportedly discovered the place, passengers of two French merchantmen unquestionably sighted it. Bound for the Orient aboard *La Princesse* and *La Découverte,* companion trading vessels out of Havre that most recently had called at the port of Valparaíso, Frenchmen happened upon the island on April 3, 1711. Michel du Bocage, captain of *La Découverte,* fixed its location at 10°28′ N, 115°23′ W of Paris and recorded in his log: "A large tooth-shaped rock projects off the south point of the low-lying isle, which is battered by breakers. From the northeast the island seems paved with gravel and from a distance appears to have low brush. In the middle of the island is a great lake that appears marginally connected to the sea."[21]

Added a Monsieur de Prudhomme, passenger aboard *La Découverte:* "Since it was not on our map, and because we saw it on Easter, we named it *L'île de Passion.* It was mostly lagoon, and we saw no sign the island was inhabited. There were no trees, but low hedges seemed to cover parts of the land. Breakers continuously crashed ashore, and a dangerous current pulsed in and out of the lagoon at an opening near the rock."[22] An employee of the hydrographic service at the French Marine Ministry, Prudhomme also sketched the atoll from afar—the first known chart of the place—and independently placed its location at 10°19′ N, 110°47′ W of Paris.

Even though the French merchant vessels carried 1.2 million francs in precious metal for trade in the Orient, and even though their crews were doubtlessly eager to dally in Polynesia, the ships repeatedly circled the atoll for two days, albeit at a prudent distance—far away from the violent breakers—searching in vain for safe entrance to the huge lagoon. They abandoned the effort on April 6 and resumed course for the spice islands and, ultimately, China.

The island may also have been sighted five years later by Le

Gentil de la Barbinais, a mysterious Frenchman who claimed to have circumnavigated the globe between 1714 and 1718. Purportedly the agent for a private French trading company, the gentleman wrote in his memoirs that, given the then uneasy state of relations between Spain and France, his mission was quite sensitive and a closely guarded secret. He wrote that merchants for whom he worked "provided our ship, [identified only as] le V . . . , with an English commission, in the name of an Englishman who sailed with us with the title of Captain, but without exercising the functions; and that we might better pass for English, we engaged a number of English sailors as our crew."[23]

The gentleman stated that *le V . . .* followed Magellan's well-established route into the Pacific but, once into the vast ocean, deviated in order to call at the Peruvian port of Goacho (Huanchaco?) and at the Galapagos islands. Moreover, after having noted the publicly reported route and resulting "discovery" of *L'île de Passion* by the Frenchman Bocage, the gentleman stated that his vessel followed a similar heading to Guam in the Marianas, but it is unclear whether or not he also claims to have seen Bocage's *L'île de Passion* as, supposedly, *le V . . .* sailed by on the trade winds.

Little matter. Most maritime authorities consider Le Gentil de la Barbinais's *Nouveau voyage autour du monde,* published in two volumes in Paris in 1725, to have been a hoax concocted by an anonymous landlubber, perhaps a journalist, because at a time when the world was imperfectly explored, *Nouveau* contained utterly no new information. Every place mentioned in it, such as *L'île de Passion,* had been previously discovered or recently publicized, as by Bocage.

More than half a century passed before the island was again mentioned in print. Using a map that identified it as "Clipperton Rock," Charles Duncan, master of the English merchant vessel *Princess Royal,* is said to have sailed by in 1787. His chart, apparently adapted from Herman Moll's map of 1730, placed it at 4° N, and, according to nineteenth-century historian James Burney, Duncan carefully verified its existence in his log, improving upon its location by fixing its position at 6° N and 35° W of Valparaíso.[24] Inexplicably, soon thereafter "Duncan's Island" appeared on many English maps.

The next mariner to visit was the first person now believed to have set foot ashore. Born in 1795 in Rye, New York, Benjamin Morrell ran away to sea at age sixteen, sailing "before the mast" as a common seaman. During the War of 1812, he was twice captured by the British: the first time he escaped; the second, he was thrown into the dank hole of a prison ship anchored off Halifax, where he languished for the balance of the war. Afterward he became the protégé of Josiah Macy, master of *Edward,* a merchantman out of New York. Captain Macy taught the unlettered Morrell navigation and steadily promoted him until, in 1822 at age twenty-seven, he became skipper of his first ship, *Wasp.*

Thus Morrell commenced an extraordinarily adventurous life at sea about which he eventually penned *A Narrative of Four Voyages to the South Seas,* published in New York in 1832 by J. & J. Harper. According to it, Morrell was the first American to penetrate the Antarctic Circle, for he claimed to have reached 70° S—a feat surpassed only by the exploits of legendary Pacific explorer Captain James Cook. Morrell's commercial jaunts also took him to many exotic South Pacific islands, in some instances his crew being the first white men ever seen by natives.

For three years (1824–27) they explored Polynesia leisurely—fornicating, trading, and hunting seals as they went. This last endeavor eventually took them to Clipperton island.

After having scouted the channel islands off Los Angeles, Morrell wrote:

> *We now took the wind from the north, with fair weather, and steered to the south-east for Clipperton's Rock. In lat. 27°0' north, we took wind from north-east, which continued until the 17th of August.*
>
> *Aug. 17th. [1825]—We arrived at Clipperton's Rock, and at 4 P.M., came to anchor on the south-south-west side of the island, in 8 fathoms of water, sandy bottom, about one-fourth of a mile off-shore.*
>
> *This island is situated in lat. 10°15' north, long. 109° west and exhibits unequivocal proof of volcanic origin. It is low all around near the water, but a high rock rises in the centre [sic], which may be seen at the distance of 6 leagues [18 statute miles]. It produces a little shrubbery and some coarse grass, among which I think fresh water might be found by digging. The whole island is literally*

covered with sea-birds, such as gulls, whale-birds, gannets, and the booby [sic]. There are also a few small land-birds, which were probably blown from the American coast during the hurricane months. Fur-seal and sea-elephant resort here in small numbers in the proper seasons, and green turtles come hither to deposit their eggs. Among the few vegetable productions of this island we found a plant resembling sarsaparilla, which badly poisoned several of the crew who handled it.

After taking what few fur-seal could be found about the island, we got under way, and sailed for the Galapagos islands. . . .[25]

Not only was Morrell's location of the place an improvement, but from his account it is reasonable to infer that a party from his ship actually went ashore. If so, they were the first persons known to have done so, a fact generally ignored when the island later became the focus of an international dispute over ownership.

While many adventurers and scientists called at Clipperton soon after Morrell's visit, the most famous scientist of the nineteenth century passed it by. The voyage of HMS *Beagle* (1831–36), which carried young Charles Darwin to fame, following its visit to the remote and biologically curious Galapagos islands, tacked northwestward across the vast North Pacific—thus entirely missing the only atoll in the entire northeastern Pacific ocean, with its own unique flora and fauna.

Eventually, though, Clipperton island would come to be very closely associated with the Galapagos in the minds of many scientists, including Darwin. In his treatise on *Coral Reefs* (1842–46), Darwin wrote:

The western shores of America appear to be entirely without coral-reefs; south of the equator the survey of the Beagle, *and north of it the published charts show that this is the case. Even in the bay Panama, where coral flourish, there are no true coral-reefs, as I have been informed. . . . There are no coral-reefs in the* Galapagos *Archipelago, as I know from personal inspection; and I believe there are none on the* Cocos, Revilla-gigedo, *an other neighboring islands.* Clipperton Rock, 10° N., 109° W., *has lately been surveyed by Captain Belcher; in form it is like the crater of a volcano. From a drawing appended to the MS. plan in the Admiralty, it evidently is not an atoll. The eastern part of the Pacific presents an enormous area without any islands, except Easter, and Sala, and Gomez Islands, which do not appear to be surrounded by reefs.*[26]

Belcher's survey cited by Darwin had taken place from shipboard in 1839, not long after the voyage of *Beagle*. HMS *Sulpher*, similarly launched "for the express purpose of Maritime Discovery,"[27] was commissioned in 1835 and sailed under Captain (later Admiral) Frederick William Beechey, who had accompanied explorer Sir William Edward Parry on his celebrated adventure into the Arctic in 1819; tagging along as companion vessel was HMS *Starling*. Together the ships' companies were to fix accurately the location of numerous sites variously placed on contemporary maps and to find such new lands as might be encountered; however, Beechey was taken ill in Valparaíso and was succeeded in command by Edward Belcher, who would be knighted for his exploits on this voyage around the world.

Sulpher and *Starling* called at the Hawaiian islands, Nunivak island off Alaska, the Kamchatka peninsula in tsarist Russia, Vancouver island, which was then property of the Hudson Bay Company, and San Francisco bay, at that time Mexican territory. The Englishmen explored the Sacramento river upstream some 156 miles in longboats. They put in at Monterey, Acapulco, and the Gulf of Papagayo, where they trekked overland and mapped the Lake of Managua. Later they charted the Central American coast to Panama.

In May 1839, while visiting Cocos island, Belcher decided to sail to Clipperton. He explained in his report:

> *The existence of Clipperton Rock, or its attendant dangers, not being a clear point amongst navigators, determined me on steering for it, either to verify, rectify, or obliterate it from its assumed position. That I did so, will probably be deemed fortunate, for the extent of its dangers was certainly unknown to us. Yet today only, 8th May, 1839, have we made it one month from Cocos, or about 1,360 miles direct.*
>
> *At dawn, the rock was discovered by the* Starling *and ourselves,*

at nearly the same instant, then distant about fifteen miles, and presenting, owing to the sun's rays playing on its nearest face, the appearance of a brig close hauled. Unfortunately, the light baffling airs of the last month, accompanied by rain, which have worn our gear as well as patience nearly threadbare, prevented our doing anything effective towards its survey until after noon, when the weather cleared, and sun and wind favoured our operations. The name, Clipperton Rock, certainly misled us, and had we made the point at night, with a fair wind, would, almost inevitably, have severely damaged or destroyed both vessels. I certainly should have steered to pass it to the northward; merely assuming it to be a solitary rock.

Nothing in this name could lead a seaman to imagine a high rock, placed on the southern edge of a coral lagoon island, three miles long N. and S., by the same east and west [sic].

This rock can be seen fifteen miles. In thick weather the low coral belt, which appears like sand, will not be distinguished until close to it. The breakers on the eastern side do not afford sufficient warning for a vessel to trim or change course. On the northern part of the belt, the land is a little raised, and appears to be clothed with something like grass.

There are two entrances, which at high water may be safe; but at the moment we passed, the surf was too heavy, and the reflux show the rocks bare. The high rock is situated in latitude 10°17' N., longitude 109°19' W., the dangers from it northerly extending 2 miles easterly, and the same northwesterly. On the beach several large trees were observed, and an object which was thought to be part of a vessel near the westerly opening.

In the centre of the lagoon, as viewed from the mast-head, there is one large hole of blue water, and a second belt is connected with rock, attaching it to the eastern side of the island. This literally constitutes two islands, formed by its two openings; both are on the weather side of the island.

No living trees were seen, but the whole island was covered with gannets, boobies [sic], frigate pelican, and several kinds of tern, which had also been noticed in great numbers during the last week, at least five hundred miles to the eastward. From this an easterly current may be inferred, as these birds generally keep to its stream or tail course. (It does not follow, therefore, as a matter of course, as *noticed by some writers, that the appearance of birds denotes land to windward; they are more likely guided by tide.)*

No bottom was obtained by the Sulpher *with 150 fathoms of line, but the* Starling *had soundings with less than 100 on the northern side.*

Sharks, porpoises, and turtle were observed together. The former annoyed us much by biting at our patent logs, for which one was taken, and made example of. They were very large and literally swarmed. In all probability they were attracted by a shoal of file [fish] (balistidae), and other small fish, which had been feeding off our copper [bottom] since quitting the island of Cocos.[28]

Belcher does not make clear how long *Sulpher* and *Starling* lay off Clipperton island before setting sail for the Orient and, eventually, action in China during the Opium War, but they lingered long enough for him to take the most accurate fix of the atoll to date—his narrative also providing the most detailed description of the place yet published. Issued in two volumes by Dawsons of Pall Mall in London in 1843, Belcher's memoirs were seen by relatively few contemporary mariners, but his map, printed separately by the British Admiralty in 1849, was the first widely disseminated chart of the island, the manuscript version of which Charles Darwin consulted in the course of his research on coral reefs.[29]

A contemporary of Darwin and Belcher, Frederick Debell Bennett purposely looked for land in the general vicinity of Clipperton (although he did not call the island by that name), twice coming dangerously close without seeing anything. A fellow of the Royal College of Surgeons, London, in 1833 he sailed aboard *Tuscan,* a 300-ton whaler captained by T. R. Stavers, bound for the Pacific. Bennett later reported that his voyage "was undertaken chiefly on my part with a view to investigate the anatomy and habits of Southern Whales, and the mode of conducting the Sperm Whale Fishery, (a subject then untouched by the literature of any country), and to make as many observations on the state of the Polynesian, or any other lands we might visit, and to collect as many facts and examples in natural history as opportunity offers."[30]

They chased sperm whales across Polynesia, visiting tropical paradises between hunts. In the company of lusty fishermen, Bennett visited numerous as-yet-unspoiled havens sprinkled liberally throughout the South Pacific, including Tahiti. They also landed at Pitcairn island, where he met descendants of Fletcher Christian and other *Bounty* mutineers. Eventually they turned north and sailed to Hawaii, whose inhabitants were just beginning to resist Occidental influence. Bennett sympathized, believing that native culture was being devastated by Christian missionaries.

After harpooning and sea-butchering several sperm whales off Oahu island, *Tuscan* tacked eastward across the Pacific, sighting the California coast near the southern tip of the Baja peninsula. There, off Cape St. Lucas, they steered southeastward. In his memoirs, Bennett wrote:

> In lats. 10° and 9°, the nearest land being Cliporton's [sic] Rock, the sea had occasionally a green appearance; and many boobies came about the ship. Two of these birds were captured in the rigging. The one had a light-brown plumage; the beak blue, the legs yellow, or lemon-colour; its stomach contained eight flying fish. The other example had the plumage of its back slate-colour; the abdomen white, and the beak and legs blue.[31]

They continued to search for land, including

> [Charles] Duncan's Island, of doubtful existence, but laid in some of our charts, in lat. 6° N., long., 106° W. From the number of frigate-birds, (upwards of forty were around the ship at one time), boobies and other amphibious birds which we noticed on the same spot, we had reason to suspect the vicinity of land. On the 24th of December our course was supposed to have passed over the spot assigned to Duncan's Island, without any land being seen. It subsequently appeared, however, that our longitude (which was by chronometer) was at that time less easterly than we supposed, by 30 miles.[32]

Tuscan returned to England in 1837, and Bennett was made a fellow of the Royal Geographical Society. In 1840 the London publishing house of Richard Bentley published in two volumes his *Narrative of a Whaling Voyage Round the Globe*. Curiously, the accompanying "Chart shewing the tracks of the south seaman *Tuscan* in a voyage round the world from the year 1833 to 1836" dutifully locates the phantom "Duncan island," but not "Cliporton's Rock."

Increasingly, mariners confirmed that the atoll truly existed. The November 1851 issue of *Nautical Magazine* announced that "Captain Turnbill of the British barque *Elora,* at San Francisco, Aug. 4, reports that the island of Clipperton, in lat. of 16°16′ N., long. 109°20′ W., marked as a mere rock on all the charts of the Pacific; he saw a lagoon coral reef attached to it stretching 6 miles to the westward [sic]."[33]

Captain T. Harvey of HMS *Havana,* which had "sailed from Plymouth on the 13th of October, 1855, bent on contributing all she could for the benefit of science and her country,"[34] also plied these waters. He reported:

> On the 21st of August [1857, we] made Clipperton Island, bearing W.b.N.1/2N. Hauled up to pass South of it, and stood along the island, trying for soundings, but no bottom at 150 and 180 fathoms two miles distant. It was covered with myriads of birds, abundance of large drift wood and pieces of wreck. We also had plenty of porpoises about the ship. On the North side the sea was much less, and landing was apparently easy in whale boats. Our standard chronometer (Webb, 5021) gave the longitude within two miles of Sir Edward Belcher's. It is correctly stated as being visible within four or five leagues off, but it is a formidable danger and a wide berth should always be given it at night.[35]

Thus, by the middle of the nineteenth century the obscure, dangerous little atoll was steadily losing its anonymity.

Indeed, once John Clipperton stumbled upon it—if in fact he did—it passed from oblivion to limbo. Following Herman Moll's example, European mapmakers increasingly located a "Clipperton Island," or a "Clipperton Rock," and occasionally, even a "Clipperton Atoll" somewhere off Acapulco—sometimes near an *Isla de los Medaños* and sometimes near an *Isla de Pasión,* with which Spaniards aboard Manila galleons were obviously familiar, and other times near *L'île de Passion,* as the French had commenced to call the place.

Eventually, mariners came to realize that there was merely one island, and the old pirate's surname stuck to the place like guano to porous coral debris.

Notes

1. For examples, see works by Benson; Boorstin; Finger; Guillemard; Hildebrand; Parr (1953, 1964); Roditi; Wroth; and Zweig.

The most fanciful secondary account of the expedition ever penned (and passed off as serious history) is Charles McKew Parr's *So noble a captain: the life and times of Ferdinand Magellan* (1953), which was reissued in 1964 as *Ferdinand Magellan, circumnavigator;* both versions assert that Magellan actually landed on San Pablo, evidence for which is wholly lacking in both original and contemporary secondary sources. Parr writes (both titles, pp. 226–28): "During the four days they were on St. Paul [Clipperton], the navigators tried to ascertain its longitude, or east-west position on the globe. . . . [Magellan] probably calculated St. Paul's latitude, or north-south position, correctly; apparently it was about 15° south of the equator, but since its longitude was not ascertained we cannot identify it today."

2. Nunn, pp. 615–33.

3. *Ibid.*, p. 631.

4. *Ibid.*, p. 633. Although generally overlooked by historians, Nunn's investigation has been well received by scholars especially interested in Magellan. For example, see Nowell (ed.), *passim.*

5. [Cortés], p. 145.

6. *Ibid.*, p. 165. A variant of the Feminia legend is retold eloquently by Gary Jennings in his masterful novel *Aztec* (1980), p. 593: "I [the castaway narrator] wondered if I might eventually be cast up on The Islands of Women, of which I had heard storytellers tell, though none ever claimed to have been there in person. According to the legends, those were islands inhabited entirely by females, who spent all their time diving for oysters and extracting the pearl hearts from those oysters which had grown hearts. Only once a year did the women ever see men, when a number of men would canoe out from the mainland to trade cloth and other such supplies for collected pearls—and, while there, to couple with the women. Of the babies born of the brief mating, the island women kept only the female infants and drowned the males. Or so said the stories. I meditated on what would happen if I should land on The

Island[s] of Women uninvited and unexpected. Would I be immediately slain or subjected to sort of mass rape in reverse?"

7. Mexico, *Isla de la Pasión*, p. 77.

8. Morga, II, 201.

9. Quoted by Schurz, p. 633.

10. Schurz, *passim*.

11. See Toniolo; and "Clipperton island and the routes of Spanish ships."
Seeking to learn precisely who had discovered Clipperton island, in 1919 renowned Italian geographer A. R. Toniolo carefully examined the known routes of the Manila galleons and concluded that the little atoll was unquestionably on their prevailing tack, as well as that of vessels engaged in the contemporary trade between Mexico and Peru. Unaware of Magellan's probable route across the Pacific, Toniolo concluded (p. 105), "Because of Clipperton island's location, likely it was first seen by Manila galleons sailors."

12. Mexico, *Isla de la Pasión*, pp. 32–33.

13. Several early maps that locate assorted islands by various names are reproduced in Mexico, *Isla de la Pasión*, and France, *Memoire*.

14. U.S. Navy, *Sailing directions*, p. 5.

15. Morga, II, 201.

16. Numerous secondary accounts place pirates on Clipperton island, but no primary source confirms the legends. See, "England's Claim to Clipperton," p. 12; "Found them safe," p. 8; Edwords, p. 4; and Harbison, "Clipperton island: A Short History of Visits of Scientists to this Atoll" (MS, 1958), p. 1, in Harbison Papers.

17. Quoted in "William Dampier," p. 455.

18. Lloyd, p. 115.

19. Funnell, pp. 68–69.

20. Burney, IV, 447. See also Gerhard, who writes (p. 204, n. 12): "It was probably on this voyage that Clipperton discovered the island which bears his name, a small atoll 670 miles southwest of Cape Corrientes, very close to the westbound track of the Manila galleon."

21. Quoted in France, *Mémoire*, p. 129. According to Dahlgren, p. 480, *Princesse*'s master was Captain Benoît de Bénac.

22. Quoted in Sachet, *Geography,* p. 5.

23. [Barbinais], p. 16.

24. Burney, IV, 512.

25. Morrell, pp. 219–220.

26. Darwin (1925), p. 111. Isla del Coco, a possession of Costa Rica, is usually called "Cocos island" by English writers.

27. Belcher, I, v.

28. *Ibid.,* pp. 255–57. Belcher's mention of "part of a vessel near the westerly opening," that is, along the northeastern coastline, is Clipperton island's earliest reported shipwreck. Neither the identity of the vessel nor the circumstances of its destruction are known. Perhaps some unfortunate mariner tried to sail into the lagoon and failed.

29. A copy of Belcher's map is reproduced herein.

30. Bennett, I, v.

31. *Ibid.,* p. 291.

32. *Ibid.,* pp. 292–93.

33. "Nautical notices," p. 612.

34. Harvey, p. 302.

35. *Ibid.*

3

The Great Guano Rush
1856–1893

Although mariners were becoming increasingly aware (and wary) of the obscure little atoll, it undoubtedly would have remained unknown to the world at large until well into the twentieth century had not a great guano rush caused entrepreneurs of several nations to assess its mining potential. During the nineteenth century, a boom in commercial fertilizers reverberated throughout Western agriculture, and much money was to be made in the trade, even in such an unlikely spot as Clipperton island. Competing French and American firms consequently laid claims to its nitrates and phosphates, thereby raising the questions of ownership and sovereignty.

For eons, replenishment of soil fertility—be it purposely by farmers, or serendipitously by nature—relied upon farm manures or upon decayed vegetable matter (humus); however, because a burgeoning worldwide population required ever-greater agricultural productivity, scientists increasingly turned their attention to the dilemma articulated at the beginning of the nineteenth century by economist Thomas Robert Malthus—the Law of Diminishing Returns, which, as it applies to agriculture, means that intensively used land inevitably wears out.

Agronomists dug into the relationship between soil additives and crop yield and quickly observed that nitrogen and such minerals as calcium, potassium, and magnesium overcame infertility and significantly increased output. Progressive farmers applied this research, and their crops grew bigger and better. News spread, giving rise to an international fertilizer industry.

English entrepreneurs treated phosphatized rock deposits with sulfuric acid and created "Superphosphate," history's first commercial fertilizer; and German competitors soon produced agricultural-grade phosphoric acid from steel slag. Both commodities sold well, despite vigorous competition from an organic alternative—guano, the dried excrement of sea birds and bats.

Early in the century, guano deposits rich in sodium nitrate were discovered on the desert Chincha islands off Peru. Situated in the middle of the cold, dry Humboldt Current, these arid islands—roost to millions of seafowl that gorged themselves daily on fish from a brimming sea—were veritable guano factories. Copious droppings dried quickly in the desiccating climate, the residue containing unusually high concentrations of nitrogen and phosphorus, which were ideally suited to agricultural uses.

Eventually a Peruvian-British company commenced mining the guano beds, offering the product on the European market as a cheap alternative to Superphosphate. Guano quickly developed devoted users throughout Europe and the United States, a rising demand resulting in a global search to locate more reserves. Numerous other islands containing significant deposits were soon discovered, the majority within ten degrees of the equator—Anguar (sometimes called Ngeaur) island in the Caroline group of the western Pacific; Makatea near Tahiti; Nauru, northeast of the Solomon islands in the southeast Pacific; and Ocean island in the Gilbert group of Polynesian atolls. As a result, Western governments became very interested in bird droppings.

For example, on April 8, 1858, Emperor Napoleon III awarded "the deposits of guano . . . which are located on Clipperton island in the northern Pacific ocean, and on the Hounden or Dog islands in the northeast of the Pomotou, and Bird island in the southeast of the same group" to the trading house of Lockhart and Company of Le Havre. Two months later, the French Navy ordered Lieutenant Victor le Coat de Kervéguen to Le Havre to board *L'Amiral,* a merchant vessel operated by Lockhart and Company that was bound for the islands to inspect the concession. Inasmuch as France had yet to assert ownership over any of these places, the government sent Kervéguen as official representative to "take possession . . . of each of these islands in the name of the Emperor."[1]

The Second Empire had frequently followed an aggressive, imperialistic foreign policy designed to recapture national glory lost at Waterloo—what one writer has called "a rose-coloured view of the grandiose schemes of the past."² French troops joined forces with the British in the expedition against China (1857–60) that resulted in France acquiring China's southeastern Cochin province, including the rich Mekong delta. With Great Britain and Spain in 1861, France intervened militarily in insolvent Mexico, but its partners soon withdrew from this ill-conceived expedition to protect foreign creditors; French troops remained, and at the encouragement of native royalists Napoleon III manufactured a throne for Mexico and persuaded Archduke Ferdinand Maximilian of Austria-Hungary to occupy it. About then France also undertook construction of the Suez Canal, a project completed in 1869, about the time the Second Empire, Britain, and Italy jointly took charge of Tunisian finances to protect European creditors. Juxtaposed with these momentous events, Louis Napoleon's annexation of Clipperton island in 1858 was a caricature of economic imperialism—a French farce.

Within days of receiving orders, Lieutenant Kervéguen boarded *L'Amiral,* a merchant ship captained by J. Detaille, and they soon sailed for the Pacific. On "November 16, 1858, at 5:00 P.M., after 125 days of navigation, the island was seen at a distance of 15 to 18 miles," Detaille later reported to Lockhart and Company. The next day, "at 7:00 A.M., I started exploring the exterior of the island with the ship to discover a place of disembarkment and a place to drop the anchor. I went along at one-half mile away, which was all prudence allowed." After three days of tacking about the atoll, still unable to locate anchorage, he decided to send the second mate ashore in a dinghy "on the north side in a place which looked less dangerous to me . . . [with] four [of our] bravest crewmen."³

Their little vessel was quickly caught up in the breakers, which almost swamped it before drenched sailors rowed back into calmer waters. Finally, one of the men jumped into the shark-infested sea and swam ashore through rolling breakers and turbulent surf, hauling along behind him a length of rope that was attached to the dinghy's bow. A second seaman followed. Carrying three empty sacks, he pulled himself to land using the hand line. Very likely the second party ever to set foot on the undisturbed atoll—after the American Benjamin Morrell in 1825—the Frenchmen found themselves enveloped by the chaos of alarmed birds that shrieked abuse at the newcomers, flying off in all directions and leaving their "small eggs on the ground in the midst of big red crabs."[4]

Sailors encountered numerous "rotten dead trees, [undoubtedly] thrown there by the sea and the currents," but if they saw signs of shipwrecks, such as those suggested in 1843 by Edward Belcher, they failed to report them to Captain Detaille. They did observe that the ground was "stony white coral, devoid of vegetation . . . and littered with bird dropping." They took several samples from various sites along the northwestern shore, and when their collecting was done, "tied themselves to the rope and were pulled [back through the breakers] by the men who stayed in the boat, [with] sharks all around. Thanks be that both were rescued," Detaille eventually advised his employer, "but their samples were soaked with sea water."[5]

Considering the danger, Detaille hesitated to send men back for better samples. Instead, the following day he repeatedly sailed around the atoll's perimeter, searching for an easier landing place but finding none. He later reported to Lockhart and Company executives: "I was almost always on the mast, and I could see the shore almost as well as if I had been there." Even so, he hastened to add, "I was sorry not to make it to the shore, but we agreed it was too risky; the position of the ship was too dangerous for me to leave it."[6]

Lieutenant Kervéguen, whose specific mission it was to go ashore to proclaim French ownership, likewise remained aboard ship. Unable to fulfill the usual requirements of international law and diplomacy, he did what he considered to be the next best thing: on November 17, as the vessel made one final circuit about the atoll, he read Louis Napoleon's proclamation of annexation from the rolling deck of *L'Amiral,* the French Tricolor flapping overhead from the mainmast.

No one aboard ship thought the place was worth much. Detaille wrote in his report: "Upon analysis of what the second mate brought back, considering what I could deduce about the weather and wind during the four days we sailed near the island—the two which preceded the landing and the one which followed—I have concluded that the quality of the guano is very inferior. . . ."[7]

Detaille noted that torrential rains undoubtedly "wash out the guano and leach out all the organic parts which make it rich; the sun and the heat succeeding the storms finish evaporating the little ammonia left." What remained was pitifully poor. "If one filled a barrel with this guano, one would hardly get 100 kilos of material, half of which would be stone, and half the remainder would be water," Detaille calculated. "As to quantity, there must be little [guano, for] the [coral] belt is merely three to four metres high, and the sea breaks with [such] violence that . . . much guano is undoubtedly swept into the lagoon, which is saline, while more is washed into the sea . . . by constant rainfall."[8]

Even were its guano both superior and plentiful, the Frenchman theorized that exploitation of Clipperton island would not be feasible: "One could try to build a breakwater and a pier to load boats, but . . . the expenditure would be considerable, the dangers overwhelming, and I doubt that those works would resist a whole year, no matter how strong we could make them." Moreover, the island's climate was abominable. The health of the workers would surely suffer ill effects from "the humid heat and the steamy atmosphere."[9]

Kervéguen completely concurred:

> I admit my idea of guano is quite different [than what we found]; while I admit that I do not know very much about it, that this sand and madreporous debris piled up by man may have a great influence on impoverished ground; however, until I get a more competent declaration, I do not believe Clipperton island guano, always mixed with sand and madreporous debris, is in favorable condition for exploitation—particularly considering the very great distance that separates the island from France.[10]

Upon reaching Honolulu two weeks later, Captain Detaille dispatched his report to Lockhart and Company of Le Havre, along with two small samples. "To compose those two jars," he remarked, "I had to sort out a quantity ten times more considerable, the nine parts taken out were made of stones of which I send you a specimen."[11]

For his part, Kervéguen presented to the Foreign Office of the royal government of the Sandwich islands the following note, a copy of which was placed as an advertisement in the December 18, 1858, issue of Hawaii's leading newspaper, the *Polynesian:*

In the name of the Emperor, and in conformity with his orders, transmitted to us by the Minister of the Navy, we, the undersigned, Victor Le Coat de Kerveguen, Lieutenant, Commissioner of The Government of the Emperor of the French, do, hereby proclaim and declare, that, from this day forth, the full sovereignty of Clipperton Island, situated by 10°19' Latitude North, and 111°33' Longitude West of the Meridian of Paris, belongs to His Majesty the Emperor Napoleon III, and his heirs and successors in perpetuity.[12]

Reporting on this event, the newspaper added: "The Island, we are told, is low & small, but covered with guano."[13]

Interestingly, four days earlier—well before news of Kervéguen's ceremony off Clipperton island could possibly have reached Paris—the French government formally notified Great Britain that the atoll had been annexed "in the name of the Government of the Emperor,"[14] apparently because Napoleon III believed that the English, the leaders in the international fertilizer business, were France's chief rival for the property. He doubtlessly wished to stake early claim, lest Queen Victoria beat him to the birdshit.

Her Majesty's government apparently accepted the Second Empire's assertion of ownership without question, notwithstanding the atoll's English-sounding name, for it never subsequently challenged French authority. Ironically, a century later the British government would covet this dreary little place and take steps to control it.

Curiously and perhaps significantly, the Second Empire made no attempt whatsoever to notify the United States government of its claim, likely because Napoleon III was well aware that his action constituted a clear violation of the Monroe Doctrine—already a cornerstone of American foreign policy. Three decades earlier, and in the face of just such resurgent European imperialism, President James Monroe had proclaimed that the Americas were closed to "future colonization by any European powers . . . [and that the United States] should consider any attempt on their part to extend their system to any portion of this hemisphere as dangerous to our peace and safety."[15]

However unenforceable the Monroe Doctrine may have been in 1823 when originally pronounced, thirty-five years later—as France formally laid claim to Clipperton island—the United States was in a position to enforce the Doctrine, and did so regularly. Indeed, merely eight years after France quietly annexed the obscure atoll, the Johnson administration would invoke precisely that policy to force the French emperor to abandon his puppet regime in Mexico, Maximilian's empire.

Moreover, two years before Lieutenant Kervéguen asserted an imperfect claim to Clipperton island, the U.S. government, like that of France, had become very interested in bird droppings. On August 18, 1856, President Franklin Pierce signed into law the Guano Islands Act, which authorized any American citizen who "discovers a deposit of guano on any island, rock, or key, not within the lawful jurisdiction of any other government, and not occupied by the citizens of any other government, and who takes possession thereof, and occupies same, such island, rock, or key may, at the discretion of the President, be considered as appertaining to the United States."[16]

Even though many American politicians and most businessmen publicly praise the so-called virtues of free enterprise, celebrating it as *the* vital ingredient of the national experience, reality is far different. Over the course of history, the U.S. government has aided and abetted private enterprise far more than it has restrained it; a paternalistic public sector has protected businesses from foreign competition and provided generous bounties, subsidies, and other incentives to encourage domestic growth and development in the belief that what is good for the entrepreneur is also good for the nation, and vice versa—a pragmatic economic philosophy some historians have called "neo-mercantilism."

The Guano Islands Act is a clear expression of that philosophy, modified by the country's democratic experience. Whereas laws of the Second Empire as well as conventional diplomatic practices required Louis Napoleon to send a personal representative to annex the atoll, the Guano Islands Act authorized any U.S. citizen to act on behalf of himself and his government. Within thirteen years of the law's passage, Americans had claimed seventy-two tropical "guano islands." Many (but not all) of these places were in the Central Pacific, thousands of miles from American territorial waters; sovereignty over some of them was retained by the United States as late as 1980."[17]

Thus, while the U.S. government had solid diplomatic grounds as well as ample economic motivation to contest Louis Napoleon's claim to Clipperton island, it was unaware that the Second Empire had expanded off Central America's Pacific coast. Curiously, when the State department did eventually learn of that claim, four decades later, diplomats casually conceded title to the French without regard either to Monroe Doctrine implications or to its occupation under U.S. law.

Three years after French explorers Detaille and Kervéguen pronounced Clipperton island's guano to be inferior, John Griswold, an American prospector once described as "a young gentleman of scientific tastes, and a close and accurate observer,"[18] purposely landed on the atoll to assess its potential under the Guano Islands Act.

Obviously unaware of the specious French claim, Griswold wrote in his journal:

> On the 6th of August, 1861, we lay on our oars, just outside the breakers on the N.E. side. At half past six we were ashore, shooting in on a high roller, which left us high and dry on the beach, with a hole stove in our bow. The beach was covered with drift wood, and while the crew were collecting it, I started to examine the island.[19]

He drank from the land locked lagoon, pronouncing its waters to be potable if brackish, before walking to the Rock, which he inspected with interest. He explored its caves—"dreary-looking places, dark and wet"—and afterward scaled the peak to survey the scene—a bleak, lifeless expanse wholly without vegetation. After climbing down he judged the place to be nothing "but a coral platform, coral clinker and coral sand. We found nothing to detain us and left the island on the afternoon of the day on which we landed."[20]

Griswold, who soon abandoned his search for commercial guano deposits throughout the Pacific to fight in the Civil War, gave a sample of Clipperton pond weed to naturalist W. Harper

Pease, who copied appropriate passages from the explorer's journal, which he published four years later in the *Proceedings* of the California Academy of Natural Sciences. Pease also forwarded the specimen to the Academy's headquarters in San Francisco, but it was lost in 1906 along with other treasures when the city was razed by earthquake and fire. The son of the Connecticut shipbuilder whose yard fabricated the ironclad USS *Monitor,* Griswold never returned to his quest for wealth; slightly more than a year after visiting the atoll, he died in battle at Antietam.

Two decades passed before another prospector is known to have examined the place. On May 21, 1881, or so he would later claim, Captain Frederick W. Permien of the brig *Elise,* out of San Francisco, first sighted the island. He later swore in a court deposition that he had sailed within a quarter mile of it, observing "millions of birds [that] hovered over it. . . . I saw it was an island of some extent; and [supposed it to be] rich in guano."[21]

Despite a soft market for fertilizer caused by global oversupply, in 1892 Permien persuaded three San Francisco venture capitalists (A. A. Cornell, Peter J. Laflin, and John A. Magee, Jr.) to finance an expedition to the island to assess its worth. In case they found anything of value, they organized the Stoningham Phosphate Company, aggregating interest in the enterprise. Cornell and Magee bankrolled the expedition, and Laflin provided the schooner *Caleb Curtis,* which set sail on June 15 with Laflin at the helm.

On June 30, the ship dropped anchor off the atoll's northeast point, and a party went ashore. Permien later claimed that they "remained on the island for a few days, secured samples of the guano, and returned, after hoisting the American flag on Clipperton Rock, the highest point on the island, on July 4th, taking formal possession of the island in the name of the United States."[22]

Upon returning to San Francisco, Permien formally filed claim under the Guano Islands Act, submitting an affidavit dated July 30, 1892, to the Department of State "in the name of and as agent for the Stoningham Phosphate Company."[23] Although bureaucrats later acknowledged having received the document, for reasons never explained they took no action on the application for title.

A month later Permien returned to the atoll, this time with *Caleb Curtis*'s deck stacked high with lumber and supplies, which, because of the surf, were reportedly off-loaded only with considerable difficulty. Permien collected additional samples of guano before departing for San Francisco and left his son, F. W., Jr., and a carpenter, Harry Johnson, behind with instructions to erect dwellings in his absence. Once back in San Francisco, Permien submitted the samples to E. J. Wickson, acting director of the University of California's agricultural experiment station, who judged them to be "very high grade materials,"[24] comparable to Peruvian guano (or so Permien would later claim).

He even enlisted the services of a "Professor Shaw," identified merely as a Harvard-trained chemist from Washington state, who joined the third expedition to the island in September, this time aboard *Helen Merriam*. By the time they arrived, young Permien and carpenter Johnson had dutifully erected two stout wooden frame huts that protected them from the sun and, because they were slightly elevated, to some extent even from omnipresent crabs, which immediately set upon the structures with a vengeance. (Over time they devoured them splinter by splinter.)

The party remained on the island for twenty-seven days, surveying. Permien later swore under oath that the place was "covered to a depth of not less than six feet [in guano], and that in places it was ten to fifteen feet. What is known as Clipperton Rock," he asserted, "is a mass of hardened guano 1000 feet in circumference at the base and 100 feet high."[25] He also claimed that Professor Shaw assessed the atoll's commercial worth at $50 million. However valuable it might have been, Permien evidently left no caretaker there to replace his son and the carpenter when, with them aboard ship, *Helen Merriam* weighed anchor and sailed back to San Francisco, arriving in early October.

Stoningham Phosphate continued to press its claim. Permien filed yet another affidavit dated October 5, 1892, asserting that he had taken "possession of the island . . . 'for the benefit of himself, A. A. Cornell, P. J. Laflin, and John A. Magee, Jr.,' "[26] an application which State department bureaucrats "simply acknowledged [receiving] October 13, 1892."[27]

Perhaps because of the delay in perfecting title, or perhaps for other reasons altogether, about then the company ceased to exist, investors evidently abandoning their interest in the atoll to Permien. Then, on May 25, 1893, Melvin Chapman, representing the Oceanic Phosphate Company of San Francisco, wrote President Grover Cleveland "claiming an interest . . . derived by assignment from Frederick W. Permien, the alleged discoverer. . . ."[28] Chapman asked Cleveland to confirm U.S. jurisdiction over Clipperton island, and, of course, Oceanic's interest.

Cleveland referred Chapman's letter to the State department, and four months later a reply was addressed to Chapman by Acting Secretary of State Alvey Augustus Adee, whom renowned historian Thomas A. Bailey has described as "an able and permanent career" diplomat: "Deaf, retiring, unmarried, Adee would install a cot in his office when the pressure of work became intense. For some thirty years, scarcely a written communication went out from the Department [of State] that he had not passed upon or drafted with his facile red-inked pen."[29]

A Shakespeare buff, at the time the president asked him to address Chapman's query, Adee was carefully compiling and laboriously annotating *The Comedies, Histories, and Tragedies of Mr. William Shakespeare as Presented at the Globe and Blackfriars Theatres circa 1591–1623* for the Shakespeare Society of New York, which published the piece in 1906. A most exacting scholar regarding the Bard of Avon, Adee cared little about an obscure atoll in the eastern North Pacific, and consequently, he expended no effort whatsoever in researching its sovereignty.

After reviewing such correspondence relative to Clipperton island as the State department had received from Permien and Stoningham Phosphate Company, Acting Secretary Adee informed Chapman on behalf of President Cleveland:

> There is no assignment on file in this Department from either the Stoningham Phosphate Company or Frederick W. Permien and his associates, and [therefore] nothing to show how the Oceanic Phosphate Company derives an interest in the island.
>
> Moreover, it appears from Lippincott's Gazetteer of the World that Clipperton Island is claimed by France. Will you kindly advise me whether you have any information as to such claim by the French Government? If France has a prior claim to this Island, of course no action can be taken by this Department, in respect to the occupation and possession by citizens of the United States.[30]

Chapman was obviously unaware of the specious nature of the French claim to Clipperton island, otherwise he surely would have challenged Adee's astonishingly superficial investigation.

Regardless, an American corporation should have been able to expect better treatment by its own government, a competent investigation of its claim, and even a sympathetic hearing. Defending his as well as his department's inaction, Adee later said, "No reply appears to have been received from Mr. Chapman, and the above statement of facts throws all the light in the Department [of State]'s possession upon the subject."[31]

While it is unclear which edition of *Lippincott's Gazetteer* Adee cited, he must have consulted either the "new edition" (1883) or the "new revised edition" (1896), both of which stated merely that " 'Clip' perton Island' [is] an uninhabited annular coral island, claimed by France, in the Pacific. Lat 10°18' N; log. 109°10' W."[32] Previous editions either failed to mention the place (by whatever name), or, commencing with the 1863 version edited by Joseph Thomas and Thomas Baldwin (which was reprinted in 1876), avoided the issue of sovereignty, saying that "Clipperton Rock, [is] a low coral island in the North Pacific, N.W. of the Galapagos, in lat. 10°14' N, log. 109°19' W. It is about 3 miles in diameter. Both the existence and the position of this dangerous rock were doubtful, until ascertained by Captain Belcher, May 18, 1839."[33]

Far more perplexing than Adee's inadequate research is a more fundamental question: why did historian Bailey's able career diplomat completely ignore the Monroe Doctrine implications of French claim to the island? His bumbling would cost an American corporation title to the atoll and create problems for a future president, who would see considerable strategic value in this of all places.

Whatever Chapman may or may not have known about Clipperton island's past, for the next several years his company occupied and exploited the place as though title had been officially conferred.

Notes

1. France, *Mémoire,* p. 281. It is interesting to note that even though French mariner Michel du Bocage and hydrologist M. de Prudhomme named the atoll L'île de Passion in 1711, when Napoleon III asserted his country's claim to the place 150 years later, he identified it by its English name, Clipperton island.

2. Roberts, p. 3.

3. France, *Mémoire,* pp. 283, 301, 302.

4. *Ibid.*

5. *Ibid.*

6. *Ibid.* pp. 303–304.

7. *Ibid.,* p. 304.

8. *Ibid.*

9. *Ibid.,* pp. 304–305.

10. *Ibid.,* p. 285.

11. Detaille, quoted in *ibid.,* p. 306.

12. *Polynesian,* December 18, 1858, quoted in *ibid.,* p. 297.

13. *Ibid.*

14. France, *Mémoire,* p. 295.

15. James Monroe, "Seventh annual message (December 2, 1823)," in U.S. Presidents, II, 787.

16. U.S. *Code* (1978), 164, 11 Stat. 119.

17. U.S. Treasury, *Circular no. 1,* n.p. In 1872, Congress amended the original statute to guarantee American importers as minimum of $4 and a maximum of $8 a ton for guano "delivered alongside a vessel, in proper tubs, within reach of a ship's tackle. . . ." (U.S. *Code,* 164, 11 Stat. 119.) See also, U.S. State department, *Friendship and territorial sovereignty, passim,* regarding recent treaties with Tuvala, Kitibati, and Tuvalu, which relinquished American claims to those islands based on the Guano Islands Act.

18. Pease, p. 200.

19. Quoted in *ibid.*, pp. 200–201. Griswold's account is the earliest detailed description of the island, but nothing else of his 1861 guano-prospecting expedition is known. Pease's published account includes Griswold's description of Clipperton island, but it fails to note from whence the young explorer sailed or what other landfalls he prospected before returning to the United States for service in the Civil War.

20. *Ibid.*, pp. 200–201.

21. Quoted in "Claims the islet for Uncle Sam," p. 12.

22. *Ibid.*, pp. 200–201.

23. Quoted in Alvey A. Adee, Acting Secretary of State, Washington, D.C., to Melvin Chapman, President, Oceanic Phosphate Company, San Francisco, Calif., September 22, 1893, in U.S. State department Records, Record Group (RG) 59, 193 M[anuscript]s, Dom[estic] Let[ter] 489 (National Archives).

24. "Claims the islet for Uncle Sam," p. 12.

25. Quoted in *ibid.*

26. Adee to Chapman, September 22, 1893, in U.S. State department Records (RG 59), 193 MS. Dom. Let. 489.

27. Adee to John L. Thomas, Assistant Attorney General, U.S. Post Office department, August 13, 1895, in U.S. State department Records, 204 Ms. Dom. Let. 100.

28. "Claims the islet for Uncle Sam," p. 12. The terms of the assignment from Permien were never made public; however, years later, Permien alleged that he had been defrauded by Oceanic Phosphate.

29. Bailey, p. 9.

30. Adee to Chapman, September 22, 1893, in U.S. State department Records (RG 59), 193 MS. Dom. Let. 489.

31. Adee to Thomas, August 13, 1895, *ibid.*, 204 Ms. Dom. Let. 100.

32. *Lippincott's gazetteer* (1883), p. 498; *Lippincott's gazetteer* (1896), p. 912.

33. Thomas, *et al.* (1863, 1864), p. 467; Thomas, *et al.* (1866), p. 467;

Thomas, *et al.* (1876), p. 467. In fact, when the matter of Clipperton island's ownership came to be hotly disputed between France and Mexico, about the turn of the century, Lippincott's editors omitted any mention of territorial status; for instance, in its 1905 edition, the *gazetteer* gives merely the atoll's longitude and latitude and states that it is "an annular coral island in the Pacific Ocean." (See Heilprin and Heilprin, p. 431.)

4

Oceanic Phosphate Company
1893–1898

From 1893 through 1898, Oceanic Phosphate Company of San Francisco mined Clipperton island guano, but the operation was merely marginally profitable. Not only was its product inferior, but the fertilizer market was uncertain. Moreover, logistics—that is, the tasks of regularly provisioning both the digs with manpower and workers with supplies—constituted formidable problems that sorely strained the firm's resources.

Then, upon learning of these operations, the Mexican government challenged the company's title by asserting its sovereignty over the island, actually sending armed forces to stop the mining. At a time when the United States government was rapidly expanding its empire overseas, it uncharacteristically declined to defend the corporation's claim under the Guano Islands Act. Meanwhile, the miners had been virtually forgotten.

About the time Oceanic Phosphate head Melvin Chapman wrote President Cleveland, the company sent two employees, Charles Jensen and William Hall, to work the guano beds. Nothing of substance is known of either man. Times were hard in the United States during the early 1890s, and work was difficult to find. Throughout the decade, throngs of anonymous men such as Jensen and Hall labored in farfetched itinerant jobs. Their terms of employment with Oceanic Phosphate, including pay, are likewise unknown, but, as will become clear, they undoubtedly had some sort of incentive agreement with the company.

Oceanic Phosphate reportedly furnished the men with a mechanical condenser to collect fresh water in what was believed to be a desert climate similar to that of the guano islands off Peru, as well as provisions considered sufficient for a two-month stay. As it turned out, not only was Clipperton's lagoon water potable, if brackish, but it rained daily, sometimes in torrents; moreover, a relief ship did not arrive for more than four months. This was merely the first of several distressing episodes of both corporate and governmental callousness toward dependents on the isolated island.

Throughout much of their stay, Jensen and Hall hardly had time to worry about being resupplied, for they worked diligently. They erected another hut alongside the two constructed by young Permien and Johnson, near the northeast point and known anchorage.

Jensen and Hall also carted untold wheelbarrow loads of fresh feces from all about the oval atoll to a spot just south of the northeast point where, in the open, they piled it into a great gooey glob. Rain kept the malodorous mess moist and pungent. However repugnant this work, within four months they had erected an impressive mound of bird droppings. They also broke off several large, hundred-pound chunks of Clipperton Rock and hauled them to the point in the mistaken belief that the formation was petrified guano.

Although inadequately provisioned, the men never actually ran out of food because, from the outset of their stay, they supplemented their stores with fresh fish and terns' eggs. When a relief ship finally arrived in mid-September 1893, "Clipperton's two Crusoes" were found to be "in the best of health. . . . They had lots of reading material."[1]

Skippered by a Captain Dannevig, the schooner *Viking,* under a three-month charter to Oceanic Phosphate Company, had departed San Francisco fifteen days earlier, carrying six crewmen and eight passengers, one of them F. W. Permien. Sighting the huts, Dannevig located anchorage off the northeast point at fifty fathoms, upwind of the guano pile. The newcomers "had to surf everything ashore and aboard," one of the sailors later said. "We took the guano on board in sacks in a big boat, several tons at a time. . . . We laid there thirty-one days and put up two new houses. There were three before, so that makes five now. . . . This time we left seven men on the island, one of them being Chemist Bleh."[2]

Before sailing back to California, Captain Dannevig and Joseph Barth, the ship's carpenter, explored Clipperton Rock. "It is full of rooms, like halls," Barth later told a reporter, "and looks as if somebody—pirates maybe—had been living in it at some time. There are five halls in it altogether, with a dome-shaped roof; and there is a place that looks as if they kept a lookout on the ocean."[3]

Once aboard *Viking*, Hall complained bitterly that he and Jensen had been inadequately provisioned and poorly compensated by Oceanic Phosphate, but Jensen voiced no grievance. For certain, neither man at first could consume enough sugar to satisfy cravings for sweets; they had been sorely deprived of treats while on the atoll. When on October 30, 1893, *Viking* anchored off Meiggs wharf in San Francisco bay, her hold held "about 200 tons of guano," the San Francisco *Chronicle* reported, "which is worth about $40 a ton."[4]

Whether or not Oceanic Phosphate sold *Viking*'s cargo at that top market price is unknown, for corporate records apparently no longer exist. Whatever the revenues, company directors apparently believed in the project, because for the next five years the firm regularly mined Clipperton island—reportedly occupying the place continuously in the process, even applying for U.S. Mail service during the summer of 1895.

Information about much of the period is fragmentary and oblique. For instance, according to the U.S. Weather Bureau

> The hurricane of September 29–October 1, 1895, was at the time considered to have been one of the severest known in the vicinity of La Paz, [Baja California] where it caused considerable property damage and loss of life. It originated somewhere west and south of Clipperton Island, or near 10° N., 110° W., at which place strong southwesterly squalls were experienced by a vessel at anchor there on the 29th. The storm moved rapidly throughout its course. . . .[5]

The ship may well have been an Oceanic Phosphate transport, but if the storm caused damage to company property, none was ever reported.

Judging by later accounts, activity at the time of the storm was considerable. According to one source, since 1893 Oceanic Phosphate had "been steadily shipping guano to San Francisco and Honolulu, receiving from $10 to $20 a ton for it. In August of 1896 several shiploads were sent from the island. . . ."[6]

Details of life on the atoll are skimpy prior to September 30, 1896, when "the regular relief ship *Navarro*," chartered by Oceanic Phosphate, arrived with a skeleton work force consisting of Paul J. Hennig, Charles A. Johnson, and Joseph F. Moore, who replaced twenty-two men who reportedly had been laboring there since January. Whatever instructions may have been given the previous crew, the new men had "positive orders from their employers to prevent England from taking possession."[7]

Why the owners perceived a British threat to their operations, at least then, is unknown. In any case, *Navarro* lingered at the atoll for ten days, off-loading supplies and loading an undetermined quantity of guano. With a score of doubtlessly island-weary workers on board, it weighed anchor on October 10, setting course for San Francisco.

Little of Hennig, Johnson, and Moore's terms of employment is known. Even their rate of compensation is uncertain. Contemporary employees of the Navassa Phosphate Company of Baltimore, Maryland, then mining bird droppings in the Swan islands off Honduras's Atlantic coast under provisions of the Guano Islands Act, labored sixty hours a week to earn $24 a month, plus bunk and board.[8] It is likely Oceanic Phosphate of San Francisco paid similarly.

Whatever their wage rate, Hennig, Johnson, and Moore evidently passed most days shoveling fresh feces into wheelbarrows that they pushed to the northeastern point, piling up load after load for eventual export.

Paul Hennig later said: "We had plenty of provisions, and there is an abundance of fish and wild fowl there."[9] During free hours, Hennig—a naturalized American citizen from Germany who had resided in the United States since 1889—refined Belcher's chart of the atoll, which had been published by the British Admiralty in 1840. Hennig added to it sixty-six depth soundings in the lagoon, including one in the curious circular well-like hole in the Grand Reef, which he plumbed to a depth of 120 feet.

Also, to pass the time, Hennig kept a diary devoted to climatic observations. He recorded daily rainfall in October and almost as much in November, when thunderstorms were commonplace— some of them sudden, violent squalls. Rainfall tapered off in December, with little precipitation in January, but the climate remained oppressive—"hot and steamy"; the sun baked the coral rim to the point that it "blistered bare feet." Trade winds stiffened in February, making the climate "more pleasant." Thunderstorms resumed in March and continued through April, growing ever so slightly in intensity with each passing tempest.

Then, Hennig recorded in his journal:

> *Friday, April 30th—Wind N.N.S. Moderate breeze with squalls in the first part then gentle breeze with squalls and light rain, but mostly fair, hot, sultry weather. Heavy surf. At 8 A.M. stranger in W.S.W. in sight.*
>
> *Saturday, May 1st—Wind N.E. by E. Moderate weather, heavy surf. Stranger coming around east side of island, flying British colors. Proved to be ship* Kinkora, *Belfast, water-logged and bad steering. Beached at 5 o'clock. All hands saved.*[10]

The twenty-year-old, three-masted *Kinkora* had sailed from British Columbia on March 27, bound for London and carrying 1,700 tons of cargo—a million board-feet of raw lumber, includ- ing "huge pine timbers 150 feet long and 24 inches square. . . . Lumber [was] piled four feet high on her deck, secured by chains and skids. . . ." Skippered by Captain William McMurtrie, the ship labored virtually from the moment she cast off moorings at Burrard inlet, Vancouver, even requiring a tow to get clear of the Strait of Juan de Fuca. Off the Oregon coast, near Astoria, a storm sent a towering wave crashing over the deck; it carried away the starboard pump. Even so, the donkey engine, supplemented by crewmen on hand pumps, kept up with leaks until April 30, when *Kinkora* was about 600 miles west of Acapulco and perhaps 400 miles north of Clipperton island. There the ship again encoun- tered fierce weather. Powerful winds ripped away sails, leaving it adrift. When the storm finally passed, McMurtrie made for Clip- perton island, the "nearest available refuge,"[11] as best he could.

With much difficulty and the good luck of fair weather, the crew maneuvered the floundering ship within sight of the Rock at dawn on April 30 and to the atoll before dark on May 1, but McMurtrie could not find anchorage. He saw three men watching from the island, and he sent four sailors toward land in a lifeboat, but breakers were so violent that they turned back. A second, bolder crew surfed ashore, and they soon returned to the ship carrying Belcher's chart of the island, which showed offshore soundings. One of the island's caretakers, probably Hennig, reportedly even accompanied the seamen back to the ship to offer the captain advice.

The gesture was wasted, for *Kinkora* soon ran aground, "her starboard side to the shore." The ship's boats, already provisioned, were launched amid chaos, some of the crewmen hysterically throwing "their sea chests over the side in a vain effort to save their personal effects" while Captain McMurtrie grabbed the ship's log and a few instruments and clambered aboard a boat. The next day, Sunday, May 2, they tried to return to the beached ship, but the surf was too heavy. By Monday, the boat had settled, its port side under water; nevertheless, they salvaged some rations, particularly meats. Then two or three days passed "before the boats could revisit the ship. Meanwhile, the hull had again settled, and the deckload had washed off and the main deck ripped up. Finally the vessel broke amidship and also split longitudinally, the starboard side washing up on the beach"[12] near the northwest point, close to the mining camp.

According to the San Francisco *Chronicle,* "The appearance of such a crowd [of twenty-two persons] was hardly welcomed by the three islanders, whose provision supply was strictly limited."[13] Indeed, upon seeing the Union Jack flying from the mainmast of the floundering *Kinkora,* Hennig had run up the Stars and Stripes on a flagpole at the settlement, just as he had been instructed to do by his Oceanic Phosphate bosses. He further irritated the shipwrecked Englishmen by claiming for his employers, "the owners of the island,"[14] all the cargo that washed ashore from the shipwreck.

Whoever owned the lumber, the castaways soon appropriated it to build crude shelters to escape a searing sun and omnipresent crabs. One of the sailors later confided to a reporter, "It was a horrible place to live on, but a great deal better than a sinking ship. . . ."[15]

Hennig informed the shipwrecked Englishmen that he expected his company's regular relief ship at any time. Johnson and Moore were not so certain. Seven months of their contractual eight-month tour had elapsed without any contact whatsoever with their employer, and they feared that the relief ship would not arrive until their commitment was entirely up, which, considering loading-time requirements, would likely keep them at the detestable place another month, probably without compensation.

Beef and pork salvaged from *Kinkora* soon spoiled in the tropical heat, and along with Hennig, Johnson, and Moore, marooned sailors were quickly reduced to rations of fish, fowl, and eggs. Somehow, in the confusion of shipwreck, two live pigs that had been aboard were rescued and set free, with no one seriously proposing to slaughter them for food. The omnivorous swine scavenged, subsisting on eggs, chicks, weak or sick birds, and even pesky land crabs, which the island's human inhabitants gleefully applauded.

By mid-May, when no company vessel had arrived, all hands of *Kinkora* clamored to set out for Acapulco, 670 miles to the northeast. Both of the ship's boats were rigged with sails and launched on May 18, but one was immediately caught up in the surf and smashed to bits on the reef. Somehow everyone aboard made it back ashore safely. The other returned as well.

On the nineteenth, Captain McMurtrie sent his first and second mates, the boatswain, and three able seamen in the remaining boat for help. Their torturous voyage lasted sixteen days, and the weathered and worn mariners arrived in Acapulco on June 3. They cabled both *Kinkora*'s owners in Belfast and the Admiralty, begging relief for themselves and rescue for their sixteen shipmates left behind on Clipperton island.[16]

Ironically, not long after these heroic sailors had set sail from the atoll, a schooner appeared off the northwest point and, upon being signaled, dropped anchor. Hennig was reportedly so tired of his unwanted guests that, to arrange for their transportation, he jumped into shark-infested waters and swam beyond the surf line to a waiting dinghy that took him to *Twilight,* a vessel of American registry bound for the Galapagos.

The schooner's unidentified master demanded $1,500 to ferry the remaining castaways to Acapulco, information Hennig dutifully relayed to those marooned on the island. Somehow certain that his men would reach Mexico and therefore confident of rescue by Her Majesty's Navy, Captain McMurtrie considered the figure exorbitant and rejected it out of hand, whereupon the shooner's skipper lowered his price to $1,300, but McMurtrie still refused—Hennig wearily relaying messages back and forth between the two. *Twilight* eventually sailed away, presumably for the Galapagos.[17]

For those who remained behind on Clipperton island, boredom soon set it. When Captain McMurtrie "found his men pining away he invented [a] story of pirate gold and furnished his men with picks and shovels from the wrecked ship with which to dig. . . ." Sailors excavated great holes near the foot of the Rock, their attention diverted from a "ship which seemed never to come." Their search for treasure continued until rescue arrived, when, abruptly, they "were only too willing to forego . . . possible wealth in the certainty of getting back to their homes."[18]

A corvette carrying a crew of twenty-one and captained by Lieutenant Commander Henry P. Dyke, HMS *Comus* anchored off the northeastern point at 10:30 A.M. on June 27. "Captain McMurtrie wanted to hoist the British flag," but Hennig told him the island was American property and raised the Stars and Stripes for emphasis. Once ashore, Captain Dyke of *Comus* asked Hennig "by what right" he hoisted the American flag, asserting that if "the island . . . belonged to any one, [it] belonged to France." Hennig disagreed, saying "that if any one tampered with [the flag] there would be trouble."[19]

Despite Hennig's bluster, he and his fellow Oceanic Phosphate employees were admittedly sick of the place. Johnson and Moore especially complained of inadequate provisions and of tardy relief. Captain Dyke apparently thought the three looked peaked, and he asked the ship's surgeon, Thomas Kane, to examine them. The physician pronounced the guano miners to be slightly anemic but in no immediate danger. Dyke "offered to take them off, but they would not come as their contract time lacked a few days being up and they were afraid of losing 8 months' wages."[20] Before departing, Dyke gave them some supplies.

Comus weighed anchor at 4:00 P.M., setting course for Acapulco. Arriving there on the thirtieth, Dyke immediately cabled Oceanic

Phosphate Company in San Francisco, detailing the plight of its employees. Later that same day *Comus* picked up *Kinkora*'s six heroic crewmen, who had literally risked their lives to reach the mainland to summon help, and made for San Francisco, where the castaways were to be put ashore to await commercial passage home.

"When the news of the condition of the men on Clipperton reached the Oceanic Phosphate Company," the San Francisco *Call* reported on July 21, "the steam schooner Navarro was at once chartered and will sail this morning in charge of Captain Higgins. Governor [George D.] Freeth of the company will go down with the steamer, and besides the men a cargo of the fertilizer will be brought up."[21]

"Governor Freeth," reported the rival San Francisco *Chronicle,* "will take down a new gang of men who will relieve those there at present, as they are said to be suffering from blood poisoning or scurvy."[22] Just how much longer the company might have delayed relief, without prodding from the British Navy, is open to speculation—as is the nature of Freeth's governorship.

Navarro arrived off Clipperton island on August 2. Aboard was a new three-man work crew and four guests, John T. Arundel, R. A. Macondray, B. E. Holman, and Herbert N. Stone, representing the Pacific Islands Company, Ltd., of London. Arundel, the party's head, proposed to examine the "immense quantity of guano on the island."[23]

Before showing visitors around the island, Freeth oversaw the unloading of supplies and the loading of guano. Then, in an obvious attempt to provide residents a more nutritious diet, he proposed to plant several immature coconut palms that he had brought with him. Advised by Hennig, Johnson, and Moore that the plants would not last an hour under the relentless onslaught of land crabs, Freeth improvised with planking from the *Kinkora* shipwreck to build a "tree box," actually a large wooden frame approximately six feet by twelve feet by two feet tall—sufficient to keep out pesky crabs and rooting pigs. Workers filled the box with beach sand and guano and planted the palms.[24]

Work completed, Freeth showed the newcomers around. The Englishmen inspected a lone hopper car and a narrow-gauge steel track, which some previous work gang had laid to the landing place from the guano pile. Visitors then saw the camp and its five buildings before walking about the atoll to examine both its fresh guano deposits and its large beds of phosphatized coral rock. The Englishmen gathered several samples of each for laboratory analysis.

Freeth assured them that the island's product was valuable, or would be "as soon as fertilizer prices recovered." He said that Oceanic Phosphate had invested "large sums of money in its effort to make the island become a good commercial business, [but], seeing that its capital did not offer to give any prospect of remunerative profit soon, it would not [sic] manifest itself reluctantly to give up its claims to others who were in better circumstances to exploit it successfully."[25]

Arundel was obviously interested enough to inspect the lagoon thoroughly—so thoroughly that he took a series of new soundings. In what appeared to be "a perfectly round hole, . . . which looks very much like an old crater . . . we obtained as much as twenty fathoms. . . ." he wrote. "On the way from the circular basin, we took another sounding in what looked like a deep part [of the lagoon], but only obtained eleven fathoms."[26]

At the Rock, Arundel caught a lizard and, in the nearby lagoon, a fish, both of which he pickled in alcohol and, once back on the mainland, shipped to an acquaintance, the famed naturalist Alexander Agassiz, curator of Harvard's Museum of Comparative Zoology. Declared by one of Agassiz's graduate students, Samuel Garman, to be species new to science, the lizard (a skink) was named *Emoia cyanura arundeli,* and the equally unique fish (a goby) *Bathygobius arundeli.*[27]

There was yet another discovery. At the Rock, "in a crevice, out of reach of rains, . . . [the *Navarro*'s first mate, a Mr. Morey] stumbled upon an old oilskin, containing a copy of a navigator's manual, dated 1798, printed in the United States. It was falling apart from age and had to be handled with great care to prevent being destroyed after recovery. Mr. Morey [said he] will give the book to some museum or historical society."[28]

How the manual came to be there is unknown. Perhaps it was placed out of the weather by some poor anonymous shipwrecked soul who perished on the atoll, maybe someone from the disaster observed by Captain Belcher in 1838. More likely the book was simply hidden away for safekeeping by a member of the *Kinkora*'s crew as they dug "great holes" in search of pirate's treasure nearby. If so, it was probably forgotten when *Comus* hove into view.

On August 5, with all hands doubtlessly waving farewell to the new work gang, *Navarro* steamed for San Francisco with 200 tons of Clipperton island guano in her cargo hold. A midcourse change of heading took the vessel instead to San Diego, where it arrived on the thirteenth. Apparently eager to discuss terms with Oceanic Phosphate officials, Englishman John Arundel immediately disembarked and entrained for San Francisco.

He unquestionably recognized the marginal value of the atoll's product, for Oceanic Phosphate's method of dumping wheelbarrow loads of wet droppings into an open pile, where constant rainfall leached out valuable nutrients, resulted in a decidedly inferior fertilizer. Unlike Peru's highly valued guano, which desiccated on desert isles, Clipperton's was insipid, washed out long before it could be transported to the mainland; nevertheless, Arundel saw in "the broken coral rock of the atoll rim" much commercial promise. "In places [the coral rock] had transformed [by leaching] into large beds of calcium phosphate that . . . [could be] worked commercially."[29] This opinion he naturally kept to himself.

One of his associates, R. A. Macondray, was much more talkative. He told an interested reporter at the embarcadero in San Diego: "The island is supposed to belong to Mexico, but then it is not down on the map as included in Mexico's possessions. At any rate, once the English [Pacific Islands] Company secures the guano deposits, there will be no difficulty as to the island. It will be ready to pass into British control as a matter of course."[30]

Wire services throughout the United States picked up the story. Among them, the New York *Herald* reported "that the British flag would soon be hoisted over Clipperton island. . . ."[31] Mexico's minister to the United States read the article, clipped it, and sent it to his foreign minister, Ignacio Mariscal, in Mexico City.

Far closer to the true story—but with astonishingly little research (and much creative journalism)—the San Francisco *Examiner* disclosed:

> *By some oversight, Lord Clipperton, when he discovered it, forgot to hoist the English flag, and England has never acquired a title to the island. Geographically, the ownership should be vested in Mexico; but there is no precedent for a geographical distribution of the islands of the world, and Mexico has not asserted her claim.*
>
> *No nation has ever really wanted to own Clipperton island heretofore.*
>
> *Merchant ships bumped into the island at intervals, and finally some American mariners discovered, upon being shipwrecked, that the coral rim was rich in phosphates. The Oceanic Phosphate Company of this city was then organized, and since that time the island has been owned here and has practically been United States territory.*
>
> *The phosphate company has maintained a settlement there, having three or four men on the island at all times, and ships from this port have made frequent voyages to the island.*[32]

The *Examiner* predicted "another diplomatic dispute" with Great Britain if "the English plan . . . to add Clipperton to the British possessions"[33] was carried out.

The publicity prompted Captain Frederick W. Permien, retired in nearby Oakland and still robust at age seventy, to assert his claim. He filed a civil suit against Oceanic Phosphate Company, alleging that he had been defrauded of his lawful share of Clipperton's riches. He offered as evidence letters from the State department that acknowledged receipt of his application for title under the Guano Islands Act and even an 1895 communication from the U.S. Post Office that rejected his request for regular mail service to the island, citing inadequate need.

Permien eagerly told his story to the press. The San Francisco *Chronicle* ran a feature article on the old man's recollections of the place and his views of the impending litigation. It concluded: "The documentary evidence on file in Washington . . . seems to substantiate the claims of Captain Permien to Clipperton island, and it would also seem to prove that it is United States territory."[34]

Arriving in the Bay area on August 15 and soon thereafter being interviewed by the press, John T. Arundel dismissed Permien's claims. The Englishman said he had never heard of the old man, informing a *Chronicle* reporter that he dealt "entirely with the

Oceanic Phosphate Company," which was in possession of the island. "If we decide the guano deposits are worth anything and we wish to effect a purchase," he added, "it will then be time enough to determine who are the rightful owners of the property. If we decide to accept the offer of the Oceanic Phosphate Company, we shall expect the company to give us a clear title, or therefore [there will be] no purchase."[35]

Arundel questioned whether Permien had ever set foot on the remote, rarely visited atoll, noting that the old man had claimed in an interview "that the island is one mass of guano, and that a certain eminence, 1,000 feet in circumference at the base and 100 feet high, is a mass of hardened guano." Arundel said he could only infer that Permien was "ignorant of what guano really is." The English businessman asserted that the Rock, "some sort of a lava formation," was merely 64 feet tall. He laughed upon recalling that "Captain Permien or some one else [had] chopped off some big blocks of the Rock in the hallucination that it was hardened guano, and hauled them two miles across the lagoon [sic] to the place it was intended to ship the stuff. It lies there still. One might as well use cobble-stones for fertilizer as to use that rock."[36]

The Englishman added that the guano deposits on Clipperton island were "not by any means so rich as they have been made out to be." He observed that Permien said that Professor Shaw had estimated them "to be worth $50,000,000." Arundel claimed to be in correspondence with the professor on the subject, and Shaw had expressed doubts to him that "it would pay to transport it."[37] In any case, Arundel was confident that the samples he brought back with him and had already shipped to London for analysis would definitely answer that question.

As to the question of the atoll's allegiance, Arundel professed indifference, saying that his firm could deal with whatever government exercised control. Even so, he doubted that the place belonged to the United States. "I have never seen an American flag floating over the Rock. . . . So far as I know, there has never been any acceptance of the island [under the Guano Islands Act] by the American Government, and this is manifest from the records offered by Captain Permien in the proof of ownership."[38]

Five days later, reporting *Navarro*'s arrival from Clipperton island carrying Paul Hennig, Charles Johnson, and Joseph Moore, the San Francisco *Examiner* ran front-page excerpts from Hennig's journal, along with his pointedly chauvinistic version of events concerning the arrival of HMS *Comus*.[39] The story was headlined " 'Old Glory' Waves on Clipperton Island . . . Hoisted by Americans and Guarded by Shovels and Guns." The following day, the rival *Chronicle* published a smaller back-page follow-up account of Hennig confronting the British under the banner "New Territory Acquired for Uncle Sam." According to this article, Hennig was even willing to return to the atoll when his turn in rotation among company employees came up again.

Wire services readily picked up the *Examiner*'s feature of Hennig and the *Chronicle*'s follow-up, and newspapers throughout the country ran versions of both stories. The Los Angeles *Daily Times* headlined its one-paragraph Associated Press summary of events "Kept Old Glory Up: Americans Hold the Fort at Clipperton Island." The New York *Times* gave the tale two paragraphs under the banner "Clipperton Island American."

It should be recalled that the 1890s were a decade of press jingoism, an era in which skirmishes between competing New York newspapers for control of that city's lurid sensationalist market in part led to the Spanish-American War. It was an age in which West coast newspapers could demand and get the annexation of Hawaii by the U.S. government. Contemporary reports of American territorial expansion, real or not, were news.

Completely lost in the flap over the flag was the story of Arundel's negotiations with Oceanic Phosphate for ownership of Clipperton island. Before he departed San Francisco in September for the Orient, with stops planned in Hawaii and Australia, the Englishman purchased a year's option on the property. Depending on the results of sample analyses in London, he indicated that his Pacific Islands Company might be prepared to buy the place outright.[40]

Meanwhile, as Arundel resumed his odyssey across the Pacific in search of other guano deposits, and as Frederick W. Permien's claim to Clipperton island was being disputed in San Francisco, Theodore Gussmann, Frederick Nelson, and Henry Smith (Oceanic Phosphate's new work crew) quickly came to terms with the atoll.

Gussmann, a stout German emigrant who took seriously the responsibility of having been placed in charge by an American corporation, was remarkably like Paul Hennig—as subsequent events would demonstrate. Gussmann sported a handlebar mustache and wore a black, wide-brimmed felt hat to protect himself from the searing sun. Nelson, a cleanshaven Englishman, appears to have been of average height and build; he used a straw skimmer to shade his head. Despite an English-sounding surname, burly, walrus-mustached Smith reportedly was German; like his countryman Gussmann, he too wore a black felt hat.[41]

Little else about them is known, not even their ages, for, like most of the other workers who from time to time labored on the atoll, they are shadowy figures lost to history. Whoever they might have been, times were hard on the mainland, and like those who came before them, they probably agreed to live and work in the harsh environment for eight full months without relief.

By the time of their arrival, in early August 1897, the island sported five buildings, all of which were located on a spit of lagoon shoreline at the northeastern rim, near a 40-foot-high flagpole erected to signal vessels looking for anchorage and landing site, as well as to proclaim American sovereignty. A half-dozen feet above sea level, breezes there were fresh and life relatively pleasant, even if the offending odor from the guano pile frequently wafted by on the trade winds.

When Gussmann, Nelson, and Smith arrived on the island, three of its structures were used to store shovels, barrows, carts, and assorted stores; the other two served as dwellings. As boss, Gussmann appropriated one 16- by 16-foot hut for himself, and Nelson and Smith shared the other. Both structures were elevated about 18 inches off the beach to discourage crab cohabitation.

Similarly, Freeth's tree box effectively protected palm sprouts from crabs and pigs. Beach sand, guano, tropical rains, and warm temperatures fostered fabulous growth; within three months, the taller of two surviving palms topped 12 feet. Doubtlessly, Gussmann, Nelson, and Smith sincerely hoped they would soon bear fruit. Like everyone who had lived on the island for any length of time, they too suffered the privation of inadequate provisions.

Conversely, the two pigs saved from *Kinkora* shipwreck quickly adapted to life on the atoll and prospered.[42] Since it was the wet season when relatively few birds nested on the ground to provide easy pickings, the porkers caught crippled and sick birds, which they gobbled down—feathers and all, lest omnipresent crabs filch their meal. Over time these intelligent mammals learned to deal effectively with the crustaceans—to avoid their pincers and to crack open their hard carapace shells to get at the rather bland-tasting meat. Crabs thus died by the thousands, which initially made no dent whatsoever in the island's infestation.

For the first three months of their residence, the men labored diligently. As had those before them, they shoveled ton after ton of wet guano from all over the atoll, hauled it by the wheelbarrow load to the point, and, as directed by Freeth at Arundel's sugges-tion, scattered it liberally over the ground in an attempt to dry it prior to export. The men reportedly stood to earn sizable bonuses if they collected enough droppings during their eight-month stay. Nelson and Smith worked so tirelessly that Gussmann had no complaint.

Time passed apparently pleasantly enough, until the navies of two nations began dropping anchor off the point. First came a two-ship French flotilla, which arrived in late November. Upon sighting the warships, Gussmann immediately raised the Stars and Stripes.

Once it came to the attention of the French government that the United States flag was flying over Clipperton island, *Quai d'Orsay*, the foreign office, requested that the chief of naval operations in the Pacific inspect the place and report his findings. Arriving at dawn on November 24 aboard the cruiser *Duguay-Touin*, the officer "saw a group of houses whose inhabitants raised the American colors." He ordered a landing under the executive officer of the companion ship, *Terrier*, who found "three individ-uals presented as being employed to collect guano on the account of the Oceanic Phosphate Company of San Francisco. The exploi-tation . . . [was said to have] been in process for about seven years [sic]."[43]

A French sailor later wrote to his family: "We landed with the *Terrier*'s lieutenant. The island is covered with guano, which spreads an unbearable smell. The birds swarm. We easily walked up on broods; we brought back more than 2,000 [tern] eggs, enough to make omelets for three days."[44]

The naval officer had planned to stay the day in order to explore, but threatening weather caused him to cast off after an hour's stay. While there, the Frenchman did not raise the question of the flag, for "it seemed preferable . . . not to strike the colors of a friendly nation but to address oneself directly to the concerned government."[45] Its inspection complete, the French task force then sailed away.

Ten days later, on December 3—three months after the Mexican minister in Washington had sent the New York *Herald* clipping concerning British interest in the atoll to Mexico City—Alejandro Pezo, Mexico's war minister, telegraphed Mazatlán and ordered Captain Teofolio Genesta, commander of the gunboat *Demócrata*, to steam to Clipperton island to investigate American newspaper reports of British occupation. In a public announcement of this action released on December 16, Mexico promised stern diplomatic consequences should this be true, because, the government asserted, the island belonged to it.[46]

Meanwhile, on the evening of December 12, *Demócrata* had reached the atoll, anchoring for the night off the northeastern point. The following morning Captain Genesta lowered a boat, loaded it with fifteen parade-dressed and armed marines, and sent them ashore under the command of Lieutenant Rafael Pereyra; Eduardo Velasco, the ship's paymaster, who spoke English, went along as translator. As they approached land, turbulent surf caught their little vessel and smashed it against the reef, tossing all hands unceremoniously into the sea. The Mexicans washed ashore, drenched and lucky to be alive. All told, they lost seven rifles, three bayonets, three swords, and the Mexican flag.

A second boat, launched with a replacement flag, was almost swamped. The national pennant of Mexico "reached land thanks to the bravery of apprentice stoker Julián Santos, who went as a rower on the [second] boat and voluntarily leaped into water carrying [a tin] tube [containing the flag] around his neck; he swam across breakers, and as he was pursued by sharks that tried to attack him, he defended himself with the tube, without losing his nerve and landing in good condition, but almost exhausted."[47]

Through translator Velasco, Lieutenant Pereyra learned that the "colonists" worked for Oceanic Phosphate Company of San Francisco. Gussmann showed the Mexicans documents and disclosed that "property belonging to the Company valued at approximately $20,000 or more" was on the island, plus an "estimated 12,000 tons of guano that are stored and ready for shipment, which are calculated at a price of $16 in U.S. gold, or [in Mexican paper] at $32 a ton, totaling $384,000."⁴⁸

Pereyra informed Gussmann, Nelson, and Smith that they were in Mexican territory, and he ordered them to cease mining immediately. He told them they would be permitted to remain on the atoll in order to meet their contractual obligations and thereby collect their wages, but they might also return to the mainland aboard *Demócrata,* if they wished. According to the Mexican version of events, upon being informed of these facts the Americans voluntarily struck the Stars and Stripes, but by Gussmann's account, armed Mexican marines lowered Old Glory and, as the Los Angeles *Times* later sneered, "ran up 'the Buzzard and Snake.' "⁴⁹

Gussmann also charged that the Mexicans lured Nelson and Smith aboard the gunboat with promises of liquor—without disclosing how he too came to be drawn on board, all his documents of authority from Oceanic Phosphate in hand. In any case, he claimed that when he asked to be put ashore, Captain Genesta refused and instead demanded the surrender of his papers, announcing they would immediately weigh anchor and steam directly for Mazatlán.

Afraid he was about to be arrested and "taken in chains to a Mexican dungeon,"⁵⁰ Gussmann said he jumped overboard into shark-infested waters and made for the atoll. The Mexicans must have lost sight of him in the breakers, he later hypothesized, and "presumed [that he] drowned."⁵¹ On the other hand, Genesta later reported to his superiors that "at 4 P.M. on the 15th, after leaving Mr. Gosmann [sic] on the island, we left this port in good weather."⁵²

Thus, in neither account did Gussmann drown. He insisted that he made the swim of his life, "battling for hours in the breakers and eventually landing on the beach in an almost lifeless condition." Even when he recovered his strength, he said he did "not attempt to stand for fear the Mexicans would see through their glasses and send back" for him. Instead, he "lay flat on the beach until darkness came." He then crawled to his cabin, no doubt hastened along by nocturnal land crabs. "In the morning the Mexican cruiser was gone."[53]

Gussmann is the first person known to have been marooned alone on Clipperton island, and the experience almost drove him mad. "Days are all alike to me," he wrote in a touching letter to a friend that he penned to idle away time productively, at the outside chance it might somehow be dispatched. "I don't know Sunday from Monday, and sometimes think it is all a dream that I will wake out of very soon." He arose "each morning at dawn, often dreaming that it was the morning before." At first light he scanned the horizon for sails or smoke. Daily he threw more driftwood into a pile for a beacon fire, just in case. Meanwhile, all about him, "the breakers roar and the sea birds scream." The repetitious sameness of his life sometimes caused him to "neglect to eat, even though there is a plentiful supply of food and water on hand."[54]

He even considered building a raft from *Kinkora* debris and making for the mainland, but he did not because of his sense of obligation to his employer, or so he said. Danger doubtlessly dissuaded him as well. "And so the days pass, each so much like the preceding one that all becomes intangibly woven together," he wrote. "It is the same surf beating on the same beach, and the same sea birds scream monotonously. The days go on and the sun rises and sets, but life is at a standstill."[55]

Yet, when an unidentified ship sailed by, dropped anchor, and offered rescue, he declined. Instead, he dispatched two letters, one in German to a friend in San Francisco, describing his life, the other in English to Oceanic Phosphate Company, relating events and begging relief.

His correspondence arrived in San Francisco early in 1898. The San Francisco *Call* reported on February 13 that a "Captain Baettge is making efforts to get a schooner and go down after him." The newspaper also obtained limited use of Gussmann's letter to his German friend, as well as a "photograph taken last year by Newland Baldwin of this city" of Smith, Nelson, and Gussmann standing beside their pampered palm trees and "pigs saved from the Kinkora," and featured them as the "Strange Experiences of the Lone Man who is Defending Clipperton Island."[56]

Nowhere did the *Call*'s article acknowledge that Gussmann's uncorroborated claim of heroics in defying the Mexican Navy was at considerable variance with previously published accounts that placed him on the island alone, voluntarily, looking after the interests of Oceanic Phosphate. One of the newspaper's rivals, the *Chronicle,* certainly missed a superb opportunity to challenge its competition when it failed to point to a three-month-old dispatch from one of its correspondents in San Diego titled "Hauled Down the Stars and Stripes." That January 1, 1898, account by the *Chronicle*—based on information supplied by an unidentified passenger aboard *Albion* who claimed to have talked to either Nelson or Smith in Acapulco—had broken the news internationally of Mexican marines on Clipperton island. The newspaper reported that "the marines withdrew and notified the man who remained on the island not to allow any one to take away the guano under penalty of violating the Mexican law."[57]

Widely reprinted, the article was the first confirmation that the Mexican government was investigating reports of British occupation of Clipperton island.

News of Mexican troops landing on Clipperton island was headlined differently throughout the United States. The jingoistic Los Angeles *Times* on January 1 featured the story on its front page, under the banner "Hauled Down! Mexican Gunboat Strikes Old Glory: Buzzard and Snake Run Up in Its Place." The staid New York *Times,* carrying the item the same day, placed the piece on page nine under the heading "American Flag Displaced: Armed Mexican Marines Haul Down the Stars and Stripes on Clipperton Island; Three Americans Protested."

A page one New York *Times* follow-up story the next day disclosed that "The Department of State has heard nothing at all on the subject, but is not disturbed over the news." The *Times* explained that the Guano Islands Act permitted Americans to file claims on places such as Clipperton only if they were unclaimed, which appeared not to be the case. An unnamed diplomat informed a reporter, "It is simply a question as to the prior right of Mexico to title. . . ."[58] "Foggy Bottom," as the State department is sometimes known among detractors (because of the climatic peculiarities of its Potomac river basin locale), would soon revise that assessment.

Whatever the official American view as to Oceanic Phosphate's title to Clipperton island, on January 3 the New York *Times* editorialized:

> *If Mexico and the United States are looking for an excuse on which to found a quarrel, the incident reported from Clipperton Island will meet all requirements. . . . the question of ownership is utterly insignificant, and to nobody on earth does it make the slightest difference whether one flag or another flies there to scare the sea birds, . . . And how well our neighbors have laid the basis of their claim! "Clipperton Island," they say, "is Mexican territory." That "undoubtedly" is delightful, seeing that the island was not discovered by Mexicans, has never been occupied by them, and is not even off their coast, but far to the south of the Costa Rican frontier. In a few days we shall hear from France, which has long maintained a vague title to this speck of coral rock, and then there will be at least four parties to the dispute.*[59]

Three days later, the *Times* confirmed its prediction:

> *France has come forward with the expected and inevitable assertion of title to Clipperton Island, and now Mexico will not only have to explain why she pulled down an American flag that had been raised on that lonely reef, but she will also be asked to justify the raising of her own in its place. . . . Fortunately, it makes no difference who owns the island, so the warships can continue about their already sufficiently numerous businesses.*[60]

Far more lightheartedly, on January 27, under the banner "Personal," a *Times* editorial updated the story:

> *A new claimant for Clipperton Island has arisen in the person of one J. Russell Clipperton. This gentleman who lives near London, declares that the bit of coral rock about which Mexico, France, and the United States imagine they are having a little controversy, was discovered by and named after an ancestor of his who accompanied Capt. Cook [sic] in his famous voyage to the South Seas. "The little speck on the map," says Mr. Clipperton, "used to be pointed out to me as mine when I was a boy at school sixty years ago."*

This, at any rate, disposes of the French claim of having priority dating back only twenty-five years.[61]

Obviously anxious about the situation, Mexico moved quickly to head off possible confrontation with its powerful northern neighbor over what the press had labeled "the Clipperton island incident." On January 5—well before Theodore Gussmann's contrary version of events reached San Francisco—a high, unnamed Mexican diplomat was quoted by an international journalist as saying, "The American flag was found flying there, but the Americans themselves on hearing from the lips of Mexican officers that the island was Mexican territory hauled it down. . . ." The diplomat insisted that there "was no ill feeling or bitterness between the Americans found on the island and the expeditionary party. On the contrary, nothing but good-will and friendly disposition was displayed on both sides."[62]

As it turned out, Mexico had little reason for concern. Even though these events coincided with the apex of American imperialism—at a time when, in the words of diplomatic historian Julius W. Pratt, "the interests of the citizens of the United States were placed first"[63]—the State department refused to support the claims of the California corporation to the property, for diplomats had no interest whatsoever in the dismal little place.

On January 27, 1898, in answer to a query from Senator George C. Perkins of California concerning the title of his constituents to the obscure atoll, Secretary of State John Sherman cited summaries of events written earlier in the decade by Assistant Secretary Alvey Adee, who had relied on *Lippincott's Gazetteer* to ascertain sovereignty. Sherman said: "It is quite clear that the conditions prescribed by our statutes have not been complied with and that the Island cannot be considered as appertaining to the United States. There is no ground upon which this Government can intervene in the matter."[64] About this time an unnamed State department official also assured a *Times* reporter, "The United States has never had any basis for a claim to the island."[65]

Curiously, while the reporter's anonymous State department source earlier in the week had all but conceded the place to Mexico, Secretary Sherman thought it belonged to France. He informed Senator Perkins that "the French Ambassador at this capital [Jules Cambon had] called at the Department on the 6th instant and stated that his Government claimed Clipperton Island, its claim being based on the facts of discovery by a French captain in 1709 [sic], and the formal taking of possession of the Island by a French naval officer sent for that purpose in 1858."⁶⁶

The reasons why American business investment in the island was so casually written off by denizens of Foggy Bottom, or, for that matter, why the Monroe Doctrine was not enforced, are unclear. Throughout his tenure as *Quai d'Orsay*'s representative in Washington, Ambassador Cambon had "resolutely opposed the 'false' Monroe Doctrine."⁶⁷ With the Clipperton island issue, Secretary Sherman and the expansionistic McKinley administration missed an excellent opportunity to reiterate the Doctrine's principal tenet, "America for Americans!" by rejecting out-of-hand the French claim of sovereignty over the atoll.

There was ample legal precedent for the State department to have recognized Oceanic Phosphate's claim, however imperfect the company's filings. In the case of *Jones* v. *the United States* (1890), regarding the claim of the Navassa Phosphate Company of Baltimore to the Swan islands in the Caribbean, 125 miles off Honduras, the U.S. Supreme Court decided that an application for title under the Guano Islands Act was sufficient cause to presume American sovereignty and jurisdiction "over an otherwise unoccupied island, key or rock."⁶⁸

When Oceanic Phosphate's claim to Clipperton island was clouded by conflicting French and Mexican assertions of ownership, Paul J. Hennig, who had preceded Theodore Gussmann as caretaker of the atoll and was now captain of the steamer *Carlos* berthed at San Francisco, announced to the press that he owned the "100,000 [board] feet of timber which he collected from the wreck of the old *Kinkora* [on behalf of his employers]. . . . This lumber, which he values at about $3,000, he claims [now] belongs to him." Hennig sought to raise venture capital with which to salvage *Kinkora* flotsam and jetsam by arguing that because it is "650 miles from Acapulco, . . . Clipperton is out of Mexican waters."⁶⁹ Undoubtedly more ominous than a Mexican gunboat to Hennig was environment. He knew from experience that time, weather, and crabs would inevitably destroy the wood.

Meanwhile, poor Theodore Gussmann languished, alone. Despite Oceanic Phosphate's pronouncement in mid-February that his rescue was imminent, Clipperton's "second Robinson Crusoe" remained there as late as March 10, when the San Francisco *Call* reported that, because of the Mexican gunboat–enforced embargo, "Fred Gussman [sic], the man placed in charge of the island, . . . has absolutely no facility for getting back to civilization. He has repeatedly pleaded with the company to send for him, but owing to the fact that it will necessitate the hiring and equipment of a vessel they have refused to do so unless Gussman advances the $600, the amount necessary to send the relief."[70]

No one knows how (or when) he finally departed. He may well have been forced to remain there, in solitude, until a new party of miners employed by the Pacific Islands Company of London arrived in May 1898 to commence improvements. Unlike Hennig, Gussmann was apparently never tempted to return.

Notes

1. "Found them safe," p. 8.

2. *Ibid.*

3. *Ibid.* This is the first known published report of pirates on the island.

4. *Ibid.*

5. Hurd, p. 46.

6. "Mexicans demand an indemnity," p. 11.

7. " 'Old glory' waves," p. 1. Many questions concerning Oceanic Phosphate's operations on Clipperton island could be answered were its corporate records available for scrutiny.

8. See *Jones* v. *United States* (1890), 137 U.S. 202, 217, 222.

9. "New territory acquired for Uncle Sam," p. 7.

10. Quoted in " 'Old glory' waves," p. 1.

11. "Story of the Kinkora men," p. 2.

12. *Ibid.*

13. *Ibid.*

14. *Ibid.*

15. "Were stranded on Clipperton island," p. 8.

16. "Kinkora crew," p. 12; "The wreck of the Kinkora," p. 10; "Story of the Kinkora men," p. 2.

17. "Shipwrecked sailors here," p. 12; "Were stranded on Clipperton island," p. 8.

18. Edwords, p. 4.

19. "New territory acquired for Uncle Sam," p. 7.

20. "Were stranded on Clipperton island," p. 8.

21. "Shipwrecked sailors here," p. 12.

22. *Ibid.*

23. "Covets Clipperton island for England," p. 4.

24. A photograph of the protective boxes, along with Messrs. Gussmann, Smith, and Nelson, and the pigs, is contained herein. See Illustrations.

25. Mexico, *Isla de la Pasión,* p. 20.

26. Quoted in W. J. Wharton, p. 229.

27. See Garman, pp. 59–62, 63–64.

28. "Covets Clipperton island for England," p. 4. If Morey preserved the manual, its location has not been found.

29. Hutchinson, p. 197.

30. "Covets Clipperton island for England," p. 4.

31. "England to seize an island?" p. 3; cf., Mexico, *Isla de la Pasión,* p. 4.

32. "England's claim to Clipperton," p. 12.

33. *Ibid.*

34. "Claims the islet for Uncle Sam," p. 12.

35. "Permien's title is sadly clouded," p. 4.

36. *Ibid.* Even the Rock itself—contrary to assertions by Arundel—had been appreciably altered by chemical actions precipitated by bird droppings: "The original structure of the trachyte is still discernible, but the alkaline silicates have been replaced by phosphates of calcium, aluminum, and iron." See Owen, p. 2.

37. "Permien's title is sadly clouded," p. 4.

38. *Ibid.*

39. Hennig reportedly donated his journal and improved version of Belcher's chart to the U.S. Hydrographic Office in San Francisco. Hennig's map was published as H. O. Chart No. 1680, replacing Belcher's as the standard reference to Clipperton island, until the French survey of 1935. Both Hennig's journal and his original map were lost in the San Francisco earthquake of 1906. See Sachet, *Geography,* p. 6.

40. "Has an option on Clipperton island," p. 15.

41. Descriptions of Mssers. Gussmann, Nelson, and Smith are based on their photograph in Mexico, *Isla de la Pasión,* p. 21. See Illustrations, herein.

42. See Illustrations, herein.

43. France, *Mémoire,* p. 21.

44. Quoted in La Veyrie, p. 39.

45. France, *Mémoire,* p. 22.

46. "Clipperton island affair," p. 3; Mexico, *Isla de la Pasión,* p. 9.

47. Quoted in *ibid.,* pp. 12–13.

48. *Ibid.,* p. 14.

49. "Hauled down the stars and stripes," p. 1.

50. "Strange experiences," p. 21.

51. *Ibid.*

52. Quoted in Mexico, *Isla de la Pasión,* p. 15.

53. Quoted in "Strange experiences," p. 21.

54. *Ibid.*

55. *Ibid.*

56. *Ibid.* "The coconut palms are the only bits of vegetation on Clipperton island," the photograph's caption reads. "About a half dozen more were planted, but they were devoured by the voracious crabs that overrun and destroy every green thing on the island; only iron, rocks and boards escape them." The top half of the newspaper's fold is covered by a detailed drawing, said to have been based in part upon another Baldwin photograph, showing Gussmann as he "threw his papers overboard, jumped after them, and swam for the island," which was depicted in the distance, off *Demócrata*'s starboard bow, as a spit of sand on which there was a cluster of low, squat buildings.

57. "Hauled down the stars and stripes," p. 1.

58. "Clipperton island seizure," p. 1.

59. New York *Times,* January 3, 1898, p. 6.

60. *Ibid.,* January 6, 1898, p. 8.

61. "Personal," p. 6.

62. "Clipperton island incident," p. 2.; "Americans retracted," p. 2.

63. Pratt, p. 360.

64. John Sherman to Senator George C. Perkins, January 27, 1898, in U.S. State department Records, Record Group (RG) 59, 225 M[anuscript]s, Dom[estic] Let[ter] 17.

65. "No valid claim to Clipperton island," p. 2.

66. Sherman to Perkins, January 27, 1898, U.S. State department Records, RG 59, 225 MS. Dom. Let. 17.

67. Blumenthal, p. 201.

68. *Jones* v. *United States* (1890), 137 U.S. 202, 217, 222. Interestingly, this interpretation came on appeal of a homicide conviction that contested a Maryland state court's jurisdiction over Navassa island in the Swans. The Supreme Court held that under United States law (the Guano Islands Act), the Caribbean island was indeed an American possession; moreover, because its owner, Navassa Phosphate, was a Maryland corporation, that State had legal jurisdiction. The ruling upheld the conviction of Henry Jones, who had "murdered one Thomas N. Foster, by giving him three mortal blows with an axe, of which he died on the same day." *Ibid.* Jones, age 22, was hanged in his home town, Baltimore, on Christmas eve, 1890.

69. "Mexicans demand an indemnity," p. 11.

70. *Ibid.*

5

A Romantic Enterprise: English Entrepreneurs and the Mexican Concession 1897–1914

Well before the American State department decided not to defend business claims to Clipperton island, English entrepreneurs had commenced negotiations with the government of Porfirio Díaz of Mexico for rights to the atoll's guano. They soon signed an agreement that prevailed for the next two decades. The island's ownership was all the while contested by France, which pressed claims arising from the Second Empire.

Chartered in 1897, Pacific Islands Company, Ltd., of London was the product of a merger by John T. Arundel and Company with the "considerable interests in the Pacific" of Henderson and McFarlane, both of London. According to *The Times* of that city, Arundel and Company owned guano- and coconut-producing properties in the Fiji islands and held substantial investments in both Australia and New Zealand; Henderson and McFarlane, a partnership of British entrepreneurs, was engaged in similar ventures in the Gilbert, Marshall, and Samoan island groups. The "idea underlying the [new, diversified] company," the newspaper's financial reporter wrote, was "the fusion of large firms trading in the Pacific, in order to avoid unnecessary competition and to conduct the business with greater economy."[1]

Pacific Islands Company was unquestionably interested in Clipperton island. According to *The Times,* John Arundel, "a gentleman who is perhaps one of the better authorities, if not the best of those who presently know the guano business, has visited [the] island and . . . [is convinced] that if its deposits are exploited by persons who know the business well and may be ready to advance substantial sums which are probably needed, the acquisition would have great success."[2]

To be certain, before Arundel departed San Francisco in September 1897, he had shipped samples of the atoll's guano and phosphatized coral to London in care of Rear Admiral Sir William J. Wharton, hydrographer to the British Admiralty, who dabbled in geology. Wharton in turn gave specimens to several chemists, including J. J. H. Teall.[3] Teall's analysis, later published in the *Quarterly Journal* of the Geological Society of London, found Clipperton's coral to be "somewhat similar [to] phosphate shipped from Connétable Island off French Guiana,"[4] with a maximum of 38.5 percent calcium phosphate—a potential commercial deposit, depending on quantity. Subsequent and far more sophisticated analysis during the twentieth century would more than double Teall's estimate.

In return for an undisclosed cash consideration plus a royalty of seventy-five cents per ton of materials removed from the atoll, in October 1897 Pacific Islands Company acquired the interests of Oceanic Phosphate Company of San Francisco, then believed to be "the owner of Clipperton island,"[5] a title obviously predicated on United States sovereignty. When news broke worldwide that Mexican marines from *Demócrata* had seized the place, Pacific Islands Company moved promptly to protect its investment.

On January 11, 1898, company chairman Lord Stanmore (Arthur Hamilton Gordon) personally called at the Mexican legation in London and presented the chargé d'affaires, Carlos Romero, with a proposal for consideration by his government. Stanmore informed the Mexican that his firm had purchased Oceanic Phosphate's rights to Clipperton island "in good faith," but in the event the place proved not to belong to the United States, he proposed that Mexico sanction Pacific Islands's provisional control "in accordance with its contract with Oceanic" and that Pacific Islands pay, "as deposit, a royalty at a rate of 75 cents a ton [of product] that may be exported, the Minister of Mexico in this city or any other person the Mexican Government may name to be trustee in order to protect its interests."[6]

Stanmore predicted "that the Government of Great Britain will [not] dispute Mexico's claims [to Clipperton island], and in case the United States, France, and Costa Rica do not show any opposition to it, . . . then we will [seek from Mexico] the right to exploit the guano of the island, on payment of a suitable royalty, which will be determined later." If ownership were challenged by another power, Pacific Islands would place royalties in escrow, to "be delivered to the respective authorities when the dispute in question is terminated." Stanmore assured Mexico that his firm was completely "neutral to whatever question of nationality . . . may arise over ownership of the island."[7]

Interestingly, Stanmore's offer was actually the second overture Mexico had received regarding the atoll. On December 22, 1897, Tómas Terán, a "prominent Mexico City solicitor" acting for an otherwise unidentified "Sr. Alejandro R. Coney," had asked permission "to assess Clipperton island's guano and phosphate deposits" so that he might "submit an informed bid on the Clipperton island concession."[8] The government's response to the proposal, if any, is unknown.

In action uncharacteristically prompt for Porfirio Díaz's creaky regime, three weeks after Stanmore's presentation the Mexican government awarded the island to the Pacific Islands Company. It is unclear whether President Díaz, the absolute dictator of Mexico, wholly ignored Terán's request or whether, because of a notoriously dilatory bureaucracy, he was merely unaware of the alternative. Whichever was true, he personally approved Pacific Islands's offer, provided "75 cents will not be precedent for [any] future contingent contract."[9]

On February 2, Mexico cabled its conditional acceptance, and Stanmore promptly agreed in writing to the stipulation, presenting one copy to Mexico's London legation and telegraphing another to John T. Arundel in Mexico City. En route to England from Australia, Arundel had purposely returned through Mexico to sign "any necessary papers,"[10] which he did that afternoon. Four days later, on February 6, "Don Alejandro R. Coney requested that Clipperton island be granted to him," a petition Díaz "did not see convenient, now, to execute. . . ."[11]

On March 10, the Mexican government formally notified Oceanic Phosphate of San Francisco, the atoll's "current tenants," that it proposed to collect a $1.5 million indemnity "for unlawfully shipping guano from Clipperton Island," through American courts, if necessary. Moreover, "while the dispute of rightful ownership is in progress, the phosphate company [was told that it] will be prohibited from making further shipment of guano from the island and will have to keep entirely aloof from it."[12]

Curiously, two months later, President Díaz appointed George Douglas Freeth, the atoll's American "governor," as Mexico's "Interim Government Inspector on Clipperton island." Freeth was "to make sure that the Pacific Islands Company, which by concession of the Mexican Government, is exploiting guano from the said island, fulfill its obligations which the provisional agreement has imposed on it. . . ."[13]

Whether Freeth actually resided there is unknown, but he held the commission until October 30, when he resigned. Upon his recommendation, Díaz appointed Benjamin Edward Holman as replacement. Holman's role is likewise obscure.

As Stanmore had predicted, neither Costa Rica, nor Great Britain, nor the United States elected to claim the atoll, but the assertion of Mexican sovereignty was vigorously challenged by France, which had annexed the place from shipboard forty years before. *Quai d'Orsay* took on the Americans first. Late in 1897, when the commander of *Duguay-Touin* confirmed Yankee presence, France instructed its ambassador in Washington, Jules Cambon, to assert title to the atoll and to inquire as to the McKinley administration's intentions. On January 6, Secretary of State John Sherman in reply told Ambassador Cambon orally what he had just written to Senator George Perkins of California—"that the conditions prescribed in our statutes have not been complied with and that the Island cannot be considered as appertaining to the United States."[14]

Satisifed, *Quai d'Orsay* turned its attention to Mexico. On June 16, 1898, Hugues Boulard Pouqueville, French chargé d'affaires in Mexico City, personally conveyed to Mexican Foreign Minister Ignacio Mariscal his government's deep concern over the reported Mexican seizure of French property, namely "L'île Passion, sometimes called L'île Clipperton." Pouqueville informed Mariscal that

France intended to provide Mexico with documentation that definitively established French "title to the property in question . . . [and], in the meantime, that France reserves all the rights over the small island. . . ."[15] A month later, on July 15, Pouqueville dutifully presented copies of Victor Kervéguen's 1858 report of annexation and the subsequent public pronouncement of that action printed in Honolulu's *Polynesian,* as well as a list of published maps that had consequently ascribed French sovereignty to the atoll.

Porfirio Díaz at first apparently refused to deal with the French, who were despised throughout Mexico for having invaded in 1861 and for imposing Austrian Archduke Maximilian upon the country as Napoleon III's puppet-emperor. The old *jefe* doubtlessly instructed his foreign minister to reject *Quai d'Orsay*'s claim out of hand.

In any case, in a response dated September 30, Foreign Minister Mariscal dismissed French ownership of "Isla de la Pasión, sometimes called Isla de los Clipperton," as ludicrous. The Mexican said that the atoll had been an integral part of his country since colonial times. Noting its proximity to Mexico's west coast as circumstantial evidence of ownership, the minister cited more than a dozen popular maritime maps dating back more than a century—including one published in Paris in 1840—that placed it under *Mexican* authority.[16]

Even were that not the case, Mariscal contended that Lieutenant Kervéguen's belated declaration "without any act of possession or dominion accompanying or following it" had been grossly insufficient to lay valid claim. Furthermore, "It does not appear that any attempt was made [by the French] to notify any other State [than Hawaii], such as the Government of Mexico, whose coast is close to the Island, or the United States, which at that time had already undertaken the occupation of various islands for guano exploitation." Moreover, the "subsequent [French] abandonment [of the island] which lasted close to 40 years,"[17] Mariscal asserted, was tantamount to France unilaterally surrendering any and all claim to the place, tenuous or not.

The Mexican foreign minister informed Pouqueville that his country owned the island. Its agent, Pacific Islands Company of

London, was in physical possession. The Díaz government would not discuss the matter further.

France dispatched two follow-up notes to Mexico City concerning the island, both of which went unanswered. Thereafter, for a time, Paris likewise lapsed into silence.

Then, early in the century, as construction resumed on the Panama Canal, which promised to make remote Pacific products more readily accessible to North Atlantic customers, "a French company [became] interested in working the atoll's phosphates."[18] Therefore, in 1908 the French government dispatched the cruiser *Catinat,* attached to its Pacific fleet at Tahiti, to reconnoiter "the Mexican commercial pavilion" on Clipperton in the off-chance that "Mexico had abandoned the isle. . . ."[19]

Instead, the ship's captain found it to be "well occupied," and as he was under orders to "effect the mission with much discretion,"[20] he steamed on without attempting to land. Company employees nevertheless observed the cruiser as it slowly circled the atoll, and in due course they reported the incident to London, which relayed the information to Mexico City. News of renewed French interest prompted Díaz to place troops on the island, which he undoubtedly believed would fortify the Mexican claim.

Meanwhile, in Mexico City on October 10, 1906, French chargé d'affaires Peretti de la Rocca presented Minister Mariscal with a proposal to submit their dispute to binding arbitration. For inexplicable reasons, on November 15, the Mexican government accepted that proposition in principle, conditional on the two nations fashioning a suitable framework to define the issue and on mutual acceptance of an arbitrator. Those matters required two and one-half years of negotiations to settle.

On March 2, 1909, France and Mexico formally agreed to submit the question regarding "the sovereignty over Clipperton island" to binding arbitration. The respective governments then separately asked "His Majesty Victor Emmanuel III, King of Italy, . . . kindly [to] accept the role of arbitrator in order to give end to the dispute. . . ."[21]

Six months later, on August 22, the Italian monarch announced his "willingness to act as arbitrator in settling the question."[22] The two nations then compiled their documentation and composed their arguments, Mexico submitting its brief to the king late in the year, France following in 1912. However promptly Victor Emmanuel may have accepted this duty, he was to dawdle over his decision for more than twenty years.

Meanwhile, Pacific Islands Company had long since taken physical possession of the atoll. Actually, in 1901, a new chartered firm, the Pacific Phosphate Company, "was registered to carry into effect an agreement with the Pacific Islands Company (Limited), which was the owner of certain concessions in respect of phosphate deposits. . . ."[23] Pacific Phosphate's digs reportedly included the British rights to Ocean island in the Gilbert and Ellice group of Polynesian islands, the German rights to Nauru island in the Marshall islands protectorate, and, of course, the Mexican rights to Clipperton island, which, in 1906, were renewed for ten years.

While Mexican title to Clipperton island ultimately proved to be worthless, British and German concessions were quite valuable, enabling the British corporation as late as World War I to pay stockholders regular dividends of 30 percent annually. Such profits in 1912 led the financial editor of *The Times* to characterize the company's operation as "a romantic enterprise" in which "there is wealth beyond the dreams of avarice, wealth in the form of an inexhaustible supply of phosphate of lime, which may be unscientifically described as mineralised guano."[24] A company spokesman claimed that the firm had invested £50,000 in capital equipment on the Pacific guano islands, with only a small proportion of this outlay ever used to improve Clipperton island, most of it going instead to Ocean and Nauru islands.

The Times had reported in the spring of 1899: "In a short time it was expected that large, profitable, and continuous exportations of guano would be made"[25] from Clipperton island. Toward that end, the British firm had commenced capital improvements, among other things importing "considerable machinery for the concentration of guano. . . ."[26]

The company had, in fact, made numerous improvements, and the atoll became increasingly habitable. Along the southwestern coast—opposite anchorage a quarter mile offshore—employees of the English firm constructed a wharf out across the reef; however, because of relentless heavy breakers as well as the steep pitch of the atoll's mountainous submarine slope, they discovered it was impossible to build the pier "long enough to be of any use for landing purposes."[27]

Three hundred yards northeast of the wharf, near the best unexploited outcrop of phosphatized coral, Pacific Islands Company erected a large open-sided shelter containing heavy grinding equipment with which to reduce large chunks of bird-splattered coral cobble to gravel. Workers piled this into tall conical mounds along the western rim, north of the new settlement. Even with nearly incessant rainfall, over time these piles drained from the top down, the percolation improving the product, which was judged to be far superior to the raw, rather insipid guano sold by Oceanic Phosphate in San Francisco and Honolulu late in the nineteenth century.

Workers connected the island's warehouse to the pier with narrow-gauge railroad track, apparently moved from the northeast point, and the company added one hopper car to capital inventory. Intended primarily to haul product, it was also used to transport a 50-foot gasoline-powered launch between the pier and warehouse, where the longboat was stored in anticipation of delivering rock phosphate to oceangoing freighters.

The British completely abandoned Oceanic Phosphate's settlement and relocated across the island on the lagoon-side beach, at Pincer bay, near the new wharf and phosphate works. Workers dismantled three of the five Oceanic huts, hauled them across the island, and reassembled them. They also built several new structures that were covered with sheet metal to ward off crab attacks. By 1908, sixteen buildings stood along Pincer bay and served as storage facilities, community mess hall, and housing for workers and, later, for Mexican soldiers and their families.

Most capital improvements did little to improve the aesthetics of life on the remote, desolate atoll. At the new settlement, trade winds from the northeast regularly wafted across the stagnant lagoon, which reeked of ammonia during the dry season. Also, the constantly crashing surf—a sound inescapable anywhere on the atoll—was amplified enormously by the relentless pounding of heavy, current-driven breakers all along the southwestern coastline.

To its credit, the English firm tried "to save much hardship on the part of its employees. . . ." For instance, it imported "a shipload of soil" from the mainland with which to start a garden. The loam was spread out over a coral base, and seed was planted. The next morning the garden was alive with crabs, and within a week nothing remained, for the animals considered the soil as well as seeds to be delicacies, devouring everything. Then "they set in on the garden tools."[28]

Not to be outwitted by crustaceans, the men tried again. This time they erected a heavy, wooden-frame garden box on stilts, placing inverted tin pans at the top of the four-foot-tall legs in a fashion similar to that of farmers protecting corncribs from rats. Residents thus came to raise some vegetables, the cook going to the garden by means of a short ladder, "which he was compelled to remove as soon as used, for the crabs [soon became] as expert at ladder climbing as they were at eating vegetables." Ample rainfall produced prodigious crops, the animals quickly learning "that a visit . . . to the garden meant a feast for them. . . ." Whenever the garden was tilled, there was "always a swarm of crabs on the ground below, waiting for the weeds and surplus vegetables that are thrown over." Each time the cook visited the garden, he was "followed on his return to the kitchen, . . . the crabs stand[ing] in a circle about the door ready to feast on the refuse which they seem to know will come if they wait long enough."[29]

Workers likewise constructed Oceanic Phosphate–style "tree boxes" all along the southwestern shore, near the new settlement, and planted numerous coconut palms. They also built a small shed on Pincer bay in which they stored several rowboats; weather permitting, employees paddled about the lagoon for recreation and, during the nesting season, to reach the islands to gather delicious tern eggs. In time, as the colony on the atoll grew, raids on the Egg islands became increasingly frequent, sometimes out of sheer necessity. Even with improvements, human habitation was difficult.

Nor was the enterprise profitable. While the rock phosphate business overall was reportedly lucrative for Pacific Phosphate, company earnings came from large-scale digs in the South Pacific. By comparison, Clipperton island's deposits were inferior, neither high-grade nor in great quantity. In fact there was so little market for the product that the company apparently never exported any of it, stockpiling product instead on speculation that the Panama Canal—then being constructed and originally scheduled to open to traffic in 1915—would make the stuff competitive in the eastern United States and western European markets.

Clipperton's pitifully small phosphate reserves—estimated at no more than 100,000 tons—had never fared well in competition with much more commercially exploitable deposits throughout the world, including those of the United States. (The American industry actually dates to 1868, when 20,000 tons of low-grade rock phosphates were mined in South Carolina; by 1881, crude, labor-intensive pick-and-shovel operations nationwide yielded 200,000 tons annually—twice Clipperton's total reserves—with prices averaging $7 a ton, versus $10 to $20 a ton for Clipperton island guano, f.o.b. San Francisco. In 1888, even larger digs commenced along the Peace river in Florida, where huge deposits of phosphorite were located. Within the decade, laborsaving hydraulic mining techniques there produced more than 500,000 tons annually. Prices consequently tumbled, "to $2.50 [a ton] in the first seven years of operations in the Florida fields."[30] The Florida phosphates, "35% P_2O_5 [phosphorous pentoxide], the highest average content among all known United States deposits,"[31] were anemic by Clipperton's standards, which averaged 70 percent calcium phosphate,[32] but Clipperton's relatively small, almost inaccessible deposits could not be mined and delivered to the West coast of the United States as cheaply as Florida fertilizer.)

Global wholesale prices stabilized at about $4.50 a ton during the middle 1890s, when competing American companies created an oligopoly—that is, a monopoly shared by several firms, in this case six (sometimes nine) corporations that, following World War I, established a formal cartel, the Phosphate Export Association. The cartel divided the U.S. and export markets between cooperating firms, in the process driving up prices to about $7 a ton.

Artificially higher prices did not make Clipperton island's product competitive, nor did the earlier-than-planned opening of the Panama Canal. In fact, there is no evidence whatsoever that any of the atoll's rock phosphates were ever exported for sale to agriculturalists, or to anyone else; a relatively high calcium content rendered the deposits valueless as raw material in explosives, an industry then experiencing a considerable boom. It seems evident that fertilizer prices needed to rise well above $10 a ton to offer much prospect of profit on the atoll's phosphates.

Nevertheless, almost continuously from 1899 to 1910, Pacific Islands (and Pacific Phosphate) Company employed gangs of assorted nationalities (except Mexicans) to mine the atoll. About 1908, at the apex of operations, it may have employed as many as one hundred persons on the atoll, but since the firm shipped no phosphate, the venture yielded no revenue, and two years later English entrepreneurs ceased operations there altogether. Pacific Phosphate withdrew its work force, save for a lone caretaker assigned to look after its interests.

No corporate records survive, nor do published Mexican documents provide many details of life and labor on the island during this period. Instead, much of what is known of mining operations on Clipperton island is to be found in contemporary scientific literature.

Beginning with Charles Darwin in 1835, naturalists repeatedly visited biologically curious Pacific islands. Some scientists merely went on pilgrimage, especially to the Galapagos, to observe first-hand what Darwin had seen, while others set out systematically to add information to the body of knowledge. Over the years, some members of each group stopped off along the way at Clipperton island.

By the turn of the twentieth century, serious study of the Pacific coastal environment was centered in California, which was home to several aspiring academic institutions, such as Leland Stanford Junior University, founded in 1891. Its faculty organized "The Hopkins Stanford Galapagos Expedition of 1898–99," the fifth since Darwin's visit to the Galapagos, and the first ever to Clipperton.

The outing originated when financier Timothy Hopkins, adopted son of railroad magnate Mark Hopkins and a trustee of the university, put up the money "to transform [a] proposed sealing voyage, at least in part, into a naturalists' voyage."[33] Hopkins, who lived in Menlo Park, California, and dabbled in science, arranged with Captain W. P. Noyes, who commanded the schooner *Julia E. Whalen,* to take aboard two representatives of Stanford University, together with their equipment, and put them ashore on the various islands to allow them to collect plants and animals.

Dr. C. H. Gilbert, head of Stanford's zoological department, selected graduate students Robert E. Snodgrass and Edmund Heller, who had experience as collectors, to carry out the mission. Snodgrass and Heller "sailed from San Francisco on Oct. 25, 1898, touched at Guadalupe Island November 5, were at Clipperton Island November 23d and 24th, and reached the Galapagos Islands December 8, 1898."[34]

Robert Evans Snodgrass, then age twenty-three, eventually became a preeminent entomologist—*the* authority on insect anatomy. He would author two important books, one on insects in general, the other on honeybees in particular. After earning a doctorate in biology in 1901, he departed Stanford University to teach biology at Washington State College (presently Washington State University); seventeen years later he joined the Bureau of Entomology, U.S. Department of Agriculture, where he remained for the balance of a distinguished career as a scientist.

Edmund Heller, likewise twenty-three years of age in 1898, if anything was even more successful. In addition to the 1898–99 expedition that took him to Clipperton island, he served as field naturalist for a dozen major expeditions around the world, including the U.S. Biological Survey of Alaska (1900), Theodore Roosevelt's Smithsonian African Expedition (1909–10), the joint Yale University–National Geographic Peruvian Expedition (1915), and the Smithsonian's Cape-to-Cairo African Expedition (1919–20). Later, he directed the Milwaukee Zoo (1928–35) and San Francisco's Fleishhacker Zoo (1935–39), a post he held at the time of his death.

In 1898, fledgling scientists Snodgrass and Heller spent six months in the Galapagos and parts of two days on Clipperton island. Thus commenced scholarly study of the anomalous atoll. Years later they would report to the scientific community:

Boobies and terns inhabit the island in enormous numbers. The phosphates of their excrement, for they feed almost entirely on fish, have acted chemically on the calcium carbonate forming the coral surface of the island, and have in places transformed large beds of this coral into calcium phosphate. The island was leased from Mexico in 1898 by the Pacific Islands Company for the purpose of exporting this coral phosphate for fertilizing purposes. Where good formations are found the mixture is dug up, broken into small pieces, dried, stacked and shipped without further preparation [sic]. The chemist, Mr. F. T. Shepherd, told us that this exported product yields from 70 to 80 percent of phosphates.[35]

Snodgrass and Heller's description of "the only coral island of the eastern Pacific" is noteworthy, for it was the first time the place was scrutinized carefully by anyone except those with commercial interests. The young scientists found it to be a very unpleasant place: "Its climate is very hot and very humid. . . . The land fauna is very scant and . . . no land plant is native to this island, and the birds and crabs are everywhere so abundant that no plant could possibly grow there unless artificially protected."[36]

They speculated that flora and fauna had arrived naturally on the current, or, as in the case of pigs, artificially with man. Snodgrass and Heller collected 13 of their expedition's 284 species on or about Clipperton island: ants, cockroaches, fish, lice, lizards, and 80 species of birds—but, curiously, no specimen of land crabs.[37]

Upon their return to California in 1899, Stanford's zoology department announced that the expedition's collections of mammals, birds, reptiles, fishes, insects, mollusks, arachnids, crustaceans, echinoderms, and plants "are to be studied and reported upon by specialists and the results published. . . ."[38]

In 1905, R. H. Beck of Monterey, captain of the schooner *Academy*, carrying yet another American field trip to the Galapagos (this one sponsored by San Francisco's California Academy of Science), also stopped off at the atoll. Conceived by academy museum director Leverett Mills Loomis as an outing "that would have ample time to make an exhaustive survey [and] most extensive collections" from the Galapagos, the "result was an expedition that was organized and sent out, remaining in the field seventeen months and one day, and bringing back the largest and finest collections ever made on the [Galapagos] islands."[39]

The same may not be said of its survey on Clipperton island, where the Americans came ashore merely for part of a single day.

There, "sixty-five specimens [of the skink *Emoia cyanura arundeli*] were collected on [the] Rock. . . . "[40] Since the scientists did not remain overnight, they failed to observe the Rock's geckoes, or even to appreciate fully Clipperton's mostly nocturnal land crabs—which, on moonlit nights, carpeted the coral rim like an undulating orange blanket.

Even so, their brief visit provides a glimpse of life on the island. Beck recorded in the *Academy*'s log:

August 10: *Opened with clear weather and fair sailing breeze. When it came full daylight this morning we ran down before the wind and at 7 A.M. hove to off the wharf, sending the landing party ashore in two boats. The surf was quite heavy and we shipped plenty of water making the landing, as we had to go through three lines of breakers and enter a boat passage through the outer reef. Messrs. Larsen and Shultz, the two keepers on the island, were at the beach to help us land. They informed us that they had been on the island since December, 1904, as keepers for the Pacific Islands Co., this company holding a concession to work the guano deposits. We gave them some clay pipes, magazines, papers taken on board the day [June 28] we left San Francisco, a bottle of whiskey from the medicine chest, some soda, yeast, onions, and potatoes, the latter two articles being most welcome, as they never had any fresh vegetables [sic]. We found Clipperton to be a real coral atoll without a sign of vegetation, with the exception of a lone coconut palm growing by the house of the keepers and bearing about twenty nuts [sic]. . . . We were told that at one time several Japanese [sic] engaged in working the guano deposits died from drinking [brackish lagoon] water. We found the island to be infested with land crabs; they were to be found everywhere. It was necessary when collecting birds to be on the spot as soon as they hit the ground, as the land crabs would ruin them in seconds. . . . As it was unsafe to keep the vessel about the island owing to the squalls and sudden changes in the weather, the landing party gathered at the keepers' house early in the afternoon, prepared to say good-bye, and stood by to hail the schooner. Larsen treated us to some wine and cake made out of tern eggs taken off the islets in the lagoon. It was not bad at all. The cake was pinkish instead of yellow, owing to the color of the yokes, and had a rather peculiar though not unpleasant taste. When we had all gathered together and finished our good-bye, we made for the landing place and hailed the schooner. At 2 P.M. all hands were on board, having for the second time successfully negotiated the surf. Taking departure from Clipperton Rock, bearing N. by compass, distant three miles, we set our course for Culpepper Island, the most northern of the Galapagos group.*[41]

"Shultz" may actually have been Gustav Schulz, Pacific Phosphate's caretaker from 1910 to 1914, during the final phase of the firm's activities on the atoll. If so, he is said to have become insane, driven mad by the unending sameness of life on the isolated little island. Larsen has not been identified.

Whoever those men might have been, on or about September 11, 1906, Arthur James Brander, "a representative of the Pacific Phosphate Company, Ltd.," arrived at Clipperton island with Colonel Abelardo Avalos, "the Political Prefect of the island"[42] to relieve "Shultz" and Larsen, replacing them with a sixteen-man crew consisting of F. Angelis, G. Earditi, G. Franzone, Guillermo Foutg Gambi, A. Giovannetti, Celat Giscamet, A. Giusti, Joe Locatelli, S. Moltedo, Drago Morittimo, Lougi Nave, C. Paraviani, B. Schiaffing, P. Tasone, Selero Vallino, and Francisco Vittone.

These men (doubtlessly Italian immigrants working their way to the new world) were on the island when the French cruiser *Catinat* reconnoitered later in the year, and in due course news of that visit found its way to Mexico City. President Díaz thus decided to strengthen Mexico's claim to the atoll, sticking the British with the bill.

When its agreement with Pacific Phosphate expired in 1906, as cost of renewal Mexico required the company to cover the expense of establishing and maintaining "the presence of a detachment of federal service"[43]—at first merely a maritime beacon light but later an army garrison. Under the terms of the revised agreement, in addition to paying an undisclosed cash consideration to officials of the government, the company was to continue to deposit royalties of seventy-five cents (American) per ton of minerals shipped into a London trust account that would eventually go to whichever nation established sovereignty over the island, a question yet to be resolved. Little matter. No phosphates had been exported, and no dollars accumulated.

An engineer, Colonel Avalos returned later in the year aboard *Demócrata* with orders to place a maritime beacon atop the Rock, about seven stories above the coral rim. With the help of miners, Avalos's troops chiseled a flat surface into the pinnacle of the ancient volcanic extrusion. Atop it they nailed together a 12-foot-square wooden frame mold into which they poured wet concrete, laboriously lugged up from the beach below, to fashion a large battlementlike platform. To the center of this they affixed a six-foot-tall, three-foot-diameter metal and glass cylinder, the middle third of which held a 10,000-candlepower oil lamp manufactured by Henry and Company, Paris. Beside the beacon the Mexicans also erected a flagpole.

Because the light was difficult to reach, either by scaling the broken southwest face of the Rock, or by braving the bedlam of disturbed birds in caves that wound their way up through the formation to a point just below its summit, the army provided three wooden ladders. The first set of steps reached a notch in the Rock 30 feet or so above the ground; the second ranged upward a dozen or so more to a natural staircase that led in turn to a plateau in the Rock 50 feet above sea level; there, the last ladder provided direct access to the new platform at the pinnacle. Nearby, below the north face of the Rock, on the beach, workers also erected two wooden huts, one for a "light keeper" and the other for his supplies, including fuel oil for the lamp.

The identity of the first light keeper is unknown. No such person is mentioned by journalist Clarence E. Edwords, who, sailing by at about this time, stopped off to investigate "the strange island." Upon sighting it he observed what appeared "to be an immense swarm of bees hovering in the air," which upon closer approach proved "to be a great cloud of birds, which nest by the millions on this lone island." Upon landing, he discovered that the place was liberally covered with birds, "which give it its only value,"[44] and by ubiquitous land crabs.

Exclusively for the San Francisco *Chronicle*, he later wrote:

> *The land crab which literally infests the island, diabolical in appearance and persistent in activity, is a source of continued wonder. Though small in size, it gives one an uncanny feeling to see this little red crustacean gazing on him with malignant stare and*

causing him to feel as if some demon of the deep were watching him and waiting to drag him down to the depths and make a meal off his flesh. While the crab is no larger than a man's hand, and a majority not half so large, they are in such countless numbers as to give one an idea of their ability to do any amount of devilishness. They infest the whole island, are into everything unprotected, and will eat anything soft. To protect the [company's] stores from their ravages, it is necessary to build special crab-proof warehouses covered with sheet iron or tin, through which they cannot cut their way. . . . There is nothing the crab will not try to eat. Pieces of wood are gnawed until they are reduced to splinters. Clothing, especially shoes and leather belts, disappear in the night if left where the crabs can get at them.[45]

Edwords went on to describe the ingenious elevated gardens used by Pacific Phosphate to keep the crabs at bay. He said only the atoll's pigs, a half-dozen or so scrawny progeny of the *Kinkora* shipwreck, caused crabs to scamper away, lest the swine gobble them down. The journalist judged Clipperton island to be a dreadful place. "I often wonder," he wrote, "why the birds, which have wings, stay here."[46] Following a day-long tour, he left without hesitation or regret.

On the other hand, Alexander Agassiz, director of Harvard's Museum of Comparative Zoology, the man to whom John Arundel had entrusted specimens of the island's fauna, very much regretted that he was unable to visit the unusual landfall personally. A renowned naturalist acquainted with President Theodore Roosevelt, Agassiz had borrowed the U.S. Fish Commission steamer *Albatross* from the Bureau of Commerce and Labor and from October 1904 to March 1905 set forth to investigate the hydrography of the eastern Pacific, especially some of its deeper flora and fauna. Mostly the ship sailed parallel tracks across the ocean bounded by Acapulco, Easter island, and the Galapagos.

As they approached the atoll, Agassiz later wrote, *Albatross* "became greatly impeded by head winds in the region where we ought to have been in the full swing of the southeasterly trade. This led us to abandon with great reluctance all idea of further work when in the equatorial belt of currents; to give up our proposed visit to Clipperton; and, on account of our limited coal

supply, to make for Acapulco, merely [conducting depth] sounding[s] every morning."[47]

However much he wished to see this odd little atoll about which
he had heard so much, Agassiz never returned.

Notes

1. *The times,* April 20, 1899, p. 11e.

2. Mexico, *Isla de la Pasión,* pp. 22–23.

3. W. J. Wharton, p. 229.

4. Teall, p. 234.

5. Mexico, *Isla de la Pasión,* p. 20.

6. *Ibid.,* pp. 22–23. The youngest son of George Hamilton-Gordon (the fourth Earl of Aberdeen, British Prime Minister, 1852–55), A. H. Gordon served the Crown as colonial administrator in Trinidad, Mauritius, Fiji, New Zealand, and Ceylon before retiring in 1890, at which time Queen Victoria elevated him to peerage as the first Baron Stanmore.

7. *Ibid.*

8. *Ibid.,* p. 10.

9. *Ibid.,* p. 24.

10. *Ibid.,* p. 27.

11. *Ibid.,* p. 25.

12. "Mexicans demand an indemnity," p. 11.

13. Mexico, *Isla de la Pasión,* p. 31.

14. John Sherman to George C. Perkins, January 27, 1898, in U.S. State department Records, Record Group (RG) 59, 225 M[anucript]s, Dom[estic] Let[ter] 17.

15. France, *Mémoire,* p. 33; Mexico, *Isla de la Pasión,* p. 39.

16. Mexico, *Isla de la Pasión,* pp. 48–53.

17. *Ibid.;* cf., France, *Mémoire,* pp. 41–45.

18. "Ownership of Clipperton island," p. 10b.

19. France, *Mémoire,* p. 48.

20. *Ibid.,* p. 48.

21. *Ibid.*, p. 255; Mexico, *Isla de la Pasión*, pp. 68–69.

22. "Clipperton island case; Italy offers to arbitrate," p. 3.

23. "Bid of £575,000," p. 6b.

24. "Pacific phosphate, a romantic enterprise," p. 17d.

25. *The times*, April 20, 1899, p. 11e.

26. Morris, p. 33.

27. [Lieutenant (j. g.) Raymond Earle Kerr] Navigator, to [Commander Harlan Page Perrill] Commanding Officer, USS *Yorktown,* "Subject: Clipperton island," 18 July 1917, in U.S. Navy Records, Record Group (RG) 45, Subject File 1911–27, O[perational] S[ervices] USS *Yorktown* (National Archives).

28. Edwords, pp. 3–4.

29. *Ibid.*

30. Markham, p. 37.

31. Sauchelli, p. 52.

32. Obermuller, p. 47.

33. Snodgrass and Heller (1904), p. 363.

34. *Ibid.*

35. Snodgrass and Heller (1902), p. 504.

36. *Ibid.*

37. Between 1901 and 1905, the Washington Academy of Science published more than a dozen reports from the Hopkins Stanford Galapagos Expedition in its *Proceedings,* eleven of which mention Clipperton. Snodgrass and Heller authored or coauthored five of them—including the most detailed account of all, "The birds of Clipperton and Cocos islands" (1902), which they coauthored. In addition to pieces by Snodgrass and Heller, see separate articles by Banks and Richardson.

38. Snodgrass and Heller (1904), p. 363. This work evoked additional interest in the place. For instance, after having read "The birds of Clipperton and Cocos islands," sportsman–bird-watcher R. H. Beck of Monterey, California, wrote about a turn-of-the-century yachting trip that had taken him and several companions to the Galapagos. Along the way, "we stopped at Clipperton Island November 19, 1901, and went ashore for several hours." (Beck, pp. 109–110.)

39. Slevin, p. 5.

40. Van Denburg and Slevin, p. 150. In addition to R. H. Beck, "Chief of the party and Master of the vessel," the party included E. W. Gifford, an ornithologist, J. S. Hunter, an ornithologist and mammalogist, E. S. King, a herpetologist, F. T. Nelson, mate, W. H. Ochsner, a geologist, J. J. Parker, navigator, J. R. Slevin, a herpetologist, A. Stewart, a botanist, J. W. White, cook, and F. X. Williams, an entomologist.

41. Quoted in Slevin, pp. 20–22.

42. Mexico, *Isla de la Pasión*, p. 54.

43. *Ibid.*

44. Edwords, p. 3.

45. *Ibid.*

46. *Ibid.*

47. Agassiz, pp. ix–x.

6

The Mexican Garrison
1908–1917

On the eve of its arbitration agreement with France in 1908, Mexico stationed a regular army detachment on Clipperton island. Consisting of two officers and eleven enlisted men, the soldiers were ordered to repel any French force that might try to invade, to monitor the operations of the English fertilizer company, and to oversee the navigational light.

Eventually, mining ceased and the light was extinguished, but the tiny garrison remained. One of history's most isolated military posts, it came to be forgotten even by those who had established it, marooning residents and dooming many of them to death. As with so many aspects of the atoll's past, details are skimpy, but much of the story can be pieced together.[1]

Duty there was obviously a hardship, and officers and eventually even enlisted men—only a few of whom have been identified—were allowed to take their families. For much of the *presidio*'s early existence, soldiers seem to have been well provisioned. The gunboat *Tampico* called regularly, usually at four-month intervals, ferrying supplies and carrying people between the island and Acapulco.

Even so, life on the bleak, sultry, and bird-splattered remote speck of coral must have been miserable. However primitive, conditions actually were comparatively good so long as Pacific Phosphate Company maintained a work gang and provided fresh food, cooks, solid housing, and other creature comforts. When mining ceased in 1910 and the English withdrew all employees except a caretaker, existence became far more spartan for soldiers and their families.

The garrison's first and only *comandante* was Captain Ramón de Arnaud, a spit-and-polish career soldier of French extraction whose Austrian-style dress uniform (complete with an eagle-crested helmet) was absurdly incongruous to a smelly, seldom-visited island—a touch of comic opera destined to end in tragedy. He was "a highly educated [and] trained officer"[2] who doubled as Mexico's prefect.

When Arnaud established the garrison in 1908, he brought with him his twenty-year-old bride, Alicia Rovira. A patrician lady with regal bearing, she is said to have taken with her very stylish clothing and "enough diamonds to have obtained for her every luxury under different conditions."[3] Her jewels proved to be utterly worthless on the atoll, but her extensive wardrobe of high-neck, floor-length dresses became invaluable—shielding her as they did from a sizzling sun that literally scorched unprotected skin.

Alicia Rovira Arnaud resided on Clipperton island for nine years, during which she bore her husband four children. In the process she weathered from a lively, vibrant young woman into a tired old crone. One writer speculated:

> *What a strange adventure it must have been for Alicia de Arnaud . . . to abandon the security and the graceful formality of life in Mexican society, perhaps amongst the glamour of uniforms in kindly lighted ballrooms, beautiful frocks, the exciting attention of competitive males with many graces, and all the rest of it, for the low ring of coral, far out in the Pacific, with nothing upon it but a grove of coconut palms and the highest mountain of a peak in the ocean, and her husband, whom she no doubt loved, thus finding there a meaning far beyond all the glitter of the mainland.*[4]

For a time she and Frau Schulz, the otherwise unidentified wife of Gustav Schulz, overseer of Pacific Phosphate's interests on the atoll, may have been the only women there. Eventually, though, as many as six others came: Altagracia Quiroz, a young female who served Señora Arnaud as maid; Tirza Randon, whose status on the island is unclear; a Señora Irra, whose husband was a soldier in Arnaud's command; a Señora Nava, also an army wife; and, perhaps, yet another unidentified soldier's spouse and teenage daughter.

Although a decidedly unromantic place, the tropical island's population increased naturally. Frau Schulz may well have given birth while residing there, for, when she and her husband departed in 1914, they took a child with them. In 1909 on the atoll, Alicia de Arnaud unquestionably gave birth to a son, named Ramón for his father. Two years later she had a daughter, called Alicia for herself. Also that year Señora Irra was delivered of a son, Antonio. In 1913, Señora Arnaud's third child, a daughter named Lydia, was born.

A light keeper also resided on the island for much of this period. The navigational beacon that dictator Porfirio Díaz had ordered in 1906 to bolster Mexico's claims to the place reportedly illuminated surrounding waters intermittently over the years, but the identity of its first (and perhaps even a subsequent) attendant is unknown; however, by 1912 the job was held by a black man identified only as Álvarez—a mysterious, even somewhat sinister person whose nocturnal chores tending the beacon atop the Rock naturally kept him apart from the others. Even after a new government in Mexico ordered the light extinguished in 1914, reportedly for economic reasons, Álvarez remained on the atoll, keeping to himself. He lived in a hut at the Rock, almost two miles southeast of the abandoned mining settlement, where the soldiers and their families resided with the Schulzes. At first Álvarez apparently had few contacts with the others.

Dependent though Clipperton islanders might have been on the Mexican government, they were sometimes treated indifferently by those in power—to the point of callous disregard. Lapses in contact with the atoll had happened before often enough, but never with such dire consequences as those about to unfold. Oceanic Phosphate had repeatedly left employees there longer than contracted, and under the best of circumstances communication with the mainland was intermittent, so much so that shipwrecked castaways stranded on the island made for Acapulco rather than wait interminably for relief ships, public or private.

A distressing example of official Mexican indifference toward the atoll and its inhabitants occurred not long after the garrison was established: In 1909, an earthquake delivered a jolting shock of VIII on the Modified Mercalli Intensity Scale, or about 6.8 on the more modern Richter Scale. Detected in Washington, D.C., on July 30 at 5:56 A.M. by U.S. Weather Bureau seismographs, its epicenter was "about 2,800 miles south of Washington, possibly in Ecuador, or off the coast of South America in the Pacific ocean," scientists initially guessed, "with an actual movement of the ground at Washington of two-tenths of an inch."5

News reports soon disclosed that the quake's real focus had been Chilpancingo, Mexico, 2,500 miles southwest of Washington and 85 miles east of Acapulco. Chilpancingo was "partly destroyed," and Acapulco was "partly razed." In Mexico City, 120 miles to the east, cathedral "bells were rung." People as far away as the Gulf coast at Tampico, 220 miles to the northeast, felt the ground tremble. Early reports had half of Acapulco's stone-and-mortar buildings in ruins and half of its five thousand residents living in the streets, with hundreds missing and dead.

Middle Mexico rumbled repeatedly during the following three weeks. Within thirty hours of the initial tremor, persons as far away as the *distrito federal* had detected thirteen aftershocks. All told there were seventy-three—including one especially violent jolt situated somewhere off the Pacific coast on the thirty-first that sent a tidal wave crashing ashore at Acapulco. It flattened "what buildings the earthquake of Friday failed to raze. . . . [The city] now faces famine."6 On August 16 yet three more strong aftershocks rattled Acapulco—one of them also centered somewhere offshore in the Pacific basin. "The ocean dropped far below its usual level," one news service reported, "and along the entire shore line of the port the beach was exposed for a distance of thirty feet."7

On August 23, the Associated Press reported:

Dispatches from Acapulco to-day say that the people of that port believed that the Clipperton islands [sic] were swallowed up by the sea during the late earthquakes. No word of any kind has come from the islands and as the neighboring bed of the ocean is known to have been greatly disturbed, the port officials at Acapulco are urging the War Department to send out the gunboat General Guerrero to search for the islands. The claims of the Acapulcoans have not as yet duly impressed the War Department and no gunboat has so far been ordered in the quest.[8]

In fact, no government vessel ever went to investigate.

Completely unaware of the concerns of some persons on the mainland, the little colony merely waited patiently for regular relief, apparently oblivious to earthquakes nearby. Far from being "swallowed up by the sea," the atoll was altogether untouched by both tremor and tsunami. Indeed, there is no evidence whatsoever that anyone residing there so much as felt the ground shake, or observed any wave bigger than those that constantly battered the coral rim.

Geologically, Clipperton island is separated from the mainland by one of the earth's major discontinuities, the huge subduction fault popularly known as "the Ring of Fire" that encircles the entire Pacific basin, one segment of which parallels the whole American Pacific coast just a few miles offshore, from Alaska to Tierra del Fuego. Here the grinding collision of hard, westward-migrating continental tectonic plates with relatively soft, continuously eastward-spreading Pacific plates causes such events as the Chilpancingo quake of 1909.

By geological standards the earthquake's magnitude was quite modest, reportedly being felt no more than a couple of hundred miles inland without specialized scientific equipment. Therefore, there is no particular reason to believe that either the quake or its weaker aftershocks would have been noticed three times as far away on an island situated on an entirely different tectonic plate, the atoll actually being further buffered from disturbances on the continent by the great Ring of Fire discontinuity.

Moreover, it is quite likely that any tidal wave of 1909 went wholly unnoticed by Clipperton islanders, who were benumbed to a roaring sea by a constantly pounding surf. On open water, tsunamis flatten out in all directions—their energy dispersed over thousands of square miles. Great waves have crossed whole oceans undetected, passing peacefully under ships' keels to inundate coastal communities continents away. Only when disturbed water approaches the barrier of land does it stack up and take on tidal wave proportions. Such a slight impediment as a four-square-mile atoll, especially one that arises so abruptly from the sea bed, would little delay a surging tsunami.

Yet, these principles of geology and hydrography that protected Clipperton islanders had yet to be articulated by scientists, and no matter how oblivious to earthquakes and relatively safe from tidal waves the place may have been, Mexican officials knew merely that dependents were in possible danger. That politicians and bureaucrats declined to investigate the welfare of the colony—while simultaneously pressing their nation's international claim to the place—was reprehensible. That those same colonists were forgotten after 1914—when the country was swept by revolution and counterrevolution—is far more understandable.

In 1914, when the atoll's population numbered approximately thirty persons, out of the violent sea suddenly came a dozen castaways. Laden with lumber and bound for Peru, the American schooner *Nokomis* crashed into the reef one night in late February.

Owned by the G. E. Billings Company of San Francisco, the windjammer's voyage had been ill-starred virtually from the beginning. In early January, Captain Jens Jensen, accompanied by his wife and two children, had set sail from Seattle with a crew of nine. At sea on the fifteenth, well clear of the Columbia river, they encountered a horrendous storm. The Chinese cook was washed overboard, never to be seen again, and the ship was literally blown back into the Strait of Juan de Fuca and forced to take shelter at Port Townsend. Following repairs, as *Nokomis* was being towed clear of the sound by a tug, its lines fouled, yanking loose a part of the rigging, which necessitated repairs at sea.

The balance of the voyage was uneventful, until the night of February 27, when the vessel reached the vicinity of Clipperton island. Unbeknownst to Captain Jensen, not only had Mexico recently extinguished the light, but his maritime chart was dangerously dated; it showed the settlement at the northeast point, where it had been during the late 1890s, before the Pacific Islands Company moved everything to the southwestern shore. Thus, with no other reference to guide him, Jensen kept dimly flickering campfires at the settlement on his starboard quarter, and, thinking he had plenty of sea room, he sailed on southward just as the weather thickened, greatly reducing visibility.

"Early on the morning of February 28," the San Francisco *Chronicle* later reported, "the craft piled up with a crash on a reef jutting out from the north end of the island. A savage surf began to beat upon the doomed schooner, and it was with great difficulty that the boats were cleared away. . . . [Jensen's wife] and children were sent ashore in the first boat, which succeeded in getting safely through the surf only after a heart-breaking struggle on the part of the men who were manning the oars."⁹

All hands and some stores were saved, and a substantial portion of the ship's cargo of lumber washed ashore. Clipperton islanders advised the American castaways to be patient. Rescue would come, *mañana.*

Captain Arnaud undoubtedly explained that the gunboat *Tampico* called regularly, probably disclosing that he and his family had recently returned from a mainland holiday aboard the ship; therefore, he expected it again in April. Unbeknownst to Arnaud, a mutiny aboard *Tampico* merely four days before *Nokomis* plowed into the island had placed the warship in the service of revolutionaries who were fighting to overthrow dictator Victoriano Huerta. Relief was not on the way!

Based at Acapulco and assigned to coastal patrol, ten-year-old *Tampico* had been sitting at anchor in the harbor at Topolobampo in the Gulf of California on February 24, 1914, when, according to the New York *Times,* five junior officers clapped "Capt. Castellenes in chains. Lieut. Fernando Palacio was recognized by the mutineers as commander of the vessel. Col. Edouardo Hay, Chief of Staff to Gen. Huerta of Sinaloa, boarded the Tampico to-day [February 26] and formally took charge of the gunboat in the name of Gen. [Venustiano] Carranza, the leader [sic] of the Constitutionalists." The newspaper went on to speculate that "the Tampico probably will be used by the Constitutionalists in attacks . . . against the [loyalist ships] Guerrero and Morelos."¹⁰

Instead, under cover of predawn darkness on June 16, *Tampico,* which "was in no condition to fight," sneaked past the blockade and made for Mazatlán, 200 miles to the south. When the daring escape was detected at daybreak, the newer, faster, more heavily armed *Guerrero* gave chase, easily overtaking the rebels. At 8:20 A.M. they engaged in battle, and at noon "Tampico was sunk . . . in twenty-two fathoms of water, leaving the *Guerrero* the sole warship [sic] representing either faction on the west coast of Mexico." American destroyers *Perry* and *Preble,* along with the cruiser *New Orleans,* which had been watching the fray from afar, "were able to save many from drowning when the Tampico sunk and to give surgical aid to the wounded."[11]

Meanwhile, as islanders and castaways awaited a ship that lay at the bottom of the Pacific, Captain Jensen and his crew erected a lean-to shack with lumber salvaged from *Nokomis* to protect themselves from the searing sun, tropical downpours, and crabs. Otherwise there was little for the Americans to do to but wait.

Food was no immediate problem. The Mexican colony certainly had no supplies to spare, but, given salvaged stores from *Nokomis*, there was no imminent danger of starvation. Moreover, castaways could subsist for some time off the atoll's bounty, even if its natural diet was poor—consisting as it did merely of fish, birds, and terns' eggs. Fishy-tasting boobies were especially easy to catch. Palm trees also produced a dozen coconuts a month, but these were claimed by the island's regular inhabitants—the soldiers and their families, and the Schulzes.

A score or so of scrawny pigs also ran wild, progeny of a previous shipwreck, *Kinkora* in 1897. Apparently no porker had ever been slaughtered; nor did anyone molest chickens that Captain Arnaud had imported in January when he and his family had returned from the mainland with orders for Álvarez to extinguish the light.

Months passed, and no ship appeared. According to the San Francisco *Chronicle,* the Jensen children, Edith and Mary, both less than six years of age,

> became sick, and in despair Captain Jensen asked for volunteers to seek assistance from the outside world. Three hardy fellows—Gus Larsen, the second mate [sic], Herman Hendricksen, and Joe Oliver [both able seamen]—answered, and they set out on the [ship's] small boat upon the tempestuous seas headed for the port of Acapulco, 700 miles distant. That they ever reached there was a wonder.[12]

The rival San Francisco *Examiner*'s account of the heroics added: "The boat was provided with a leg-of-mutton sail but could not sail on the wind and the three men took spells at the oars almost the entire way."[13]

According to the *Chronicle*:

It took them seventeen days to make the hazardous voyage over the vast expanse of water, swept by black squalls at sea aglitter with the glistening fangs of sharks under the glare of a tropical sun in the daytime. The last three days of the voyage were made without food or water, and when the sea rovers reached Acapulco they were on the point of exhaustion.[14]

The *Examiner* further reported: "In Acapulco they could get no assistance and several days were lost in seeking a vessel that would go to the help of the survivors. Finally Rear-Admiral [T. B.] Howard was notified and he dispatched the cruiser Cleveland, which arrived at Clipperton Island on June 25."[15]

Perhaps; perhaps not. According to the official report of Commander George Washington Williams, captain of USS *Cleveland,* the warship was merely sitting at anchor in Acapulco's harbor on June 21 when one "J. Hansen, second mate [sic] of the American schooner *Nokomis*" reported a shipwreck and marooned people. Williams said, "I judged the conditions to be urgent and got under way for Clipperton Island the next morning, reporting to the Commander-in-Chief [Pacific Fleet, Admiral Howard] that I had done so." Before sailing, Williams had notified the British vice consul, and the "agents of the Pacific Phosphate Co., Ltd., of London, sent off two hundred packages of stores for their Agent on Clipperton Island, which . . . had to furnish the garrison consisting of two officers and eleven men of the Mexican Army and their families with food."[16]

A 3,100-ton, third-class cruiser sporting ten guns, *Cleveland* was attached to the Pacific Fleet and "alternated patrols in the waters off Mexico and Central America with reserve periods at Mare Island Navy Yard, Vallejo, California, between 1912 and 1917," according to U.S. Navy records, "protecting American lives and interests from turmoil of revolution."[17]

On a different sort of mission, the ship sailed from Acapulco at 0930 hours on 23 June 1914, setting course and speed to reach Clipperton island the following afternoon, "but owing to adverse currents and intense heat in the fire room," Captain Williams said,

I deemed it advisable to slow down so as to make the Island on the morning of the 25th, —the unreliability of the light made it

dangerous to approach during darkness. Due to cloudy weather on
the morning of the 25th the latitude on the morning of the 25th was
doubtful, and after arriving on the longitude of the Island and
steering to the southward when the ship was, according to reckoning,
within the range of visibility of the island high winds accompanied
by thick weather set in and the Cleveland *laid well to the leeward of*
the Island. Determining the position of the ship at daylight the 26th,
the Cleveland *made the Island at 11:00 A.M. . . .*[18]

The cruiser hove to in calm waters and sent its gig ashore with
supplies for the colony. If anyone from *Cleveland* told Comandante Arnaud about *Tampico*'s sinking, Captain Williams failed to
make note of it.

In any case, that afternoon the boat returned with "Captain
Jensen, his wife and children, First Mate C. Halvorsen, Second
Mate L. Hansen [sic], seamen J. Oliver, H. Henrikson, J. Halvorsen, W. Miller, donkeyman H. Brown, and cook H. Knowles . . .
together with a Mr. G. Schulz and his family, the Agent of the
Pacific Phosphate Co., Ltd., of London, E. C., consisting of three
people in all, passengers for Acapulco."[19]

Captain Williams reported to Admiral Howard:

There was one condition at Clipperton Island which was brought to
my attention in regard to Mr. G. Schulz, a German subject, who
has been stationed on the Island for a number of years as representa-
tive of the Pacific Phosphate Company, Ltd., of London, E. C.
The relations between himself and the Comandante of the Island
had reached such a state of antagonism which led the Comandante to
report to me that Mr. Schulz was, in his opinion, insane. Mr.
Schulz's statements in regard to the Comandante were of bitter
character.

Under the circumstances I deemed it advisable to take Mr. Schulz,
together with one woman and child who constituted his family, to
Acapulco. . . . The Phosphate Company has made no shipments
from the Island for several years. Mr. Schulz was simply residing
on the Island as a representative of the Company holding the
concession.

Upon inquiry it was found that the garrison was in no immediate
need, having on hand provisions for three or four months, consisting

of dried meats and hard beans, —it was said that these together with
the provisions landed from the Cleveland *will subsist them probably*
for five months.[20]

Ironically, when Arnaud expelled Schulz, he sealed the islanders' fate by inadvertently severing their last tie to the mainland.
With its employee removed, Pacific Phosphate obviously decided
that the moment had come to cut its losses, for it never sent
another caretaker to guard its stockpile of fertilizer from poachers.
Nor, apparently, did it even bother to notify Mexico that it was
abandoning the concession, and with it any further responsibility
for the island's inhabitants.

Little matter. Mexico was in chaos, and it is evident that no one
in authority cared about the isolated little garrison. To be certain,
after *Tampico* sank, no other gunboat, loyal to Huerta or not,
assumed its duties.

Mexico's failure to send relief may be understood by recounting
some of the revolutionary turmoil that gripped the country, a
condition far from new. Throughout the first half of the nineteenth century, especially following Mexico's independence in
1821 but preceding Díaz's dictatorship (1877–1910), the country's
internal politics often resembled anarchy. Mexico endured a succession of twenty-five different governments in fifty-five years,
most of them coming to power through armed insurrection.

The economy, lethargic under Spanish mercantilism, all but
collapsed during the early years of the republic. The Treasury was
systematically looted by a dozen presidents, including Antonio
López de Santa Anna three times—the national debt consequently
increasing annually. Poverty plagued the country, and armed
robbery was so widespread that all roads were unsafe.

Meanwhile, it lost three different wars (with Texas, France, and
the United States) and as a result saw its domain shrink by two-
thirds. Moreover, on four occasions since independence it suffered
the indignity of foreign occupation—by France (twice), Great
Britain, Spain, Texas, and the United States—and the humiliation
of an alien regime, Maximilian's empire, which was imposed
upon Mexico by the French in 1864.

Following the overthrow of Maximilian in 1867 by Benito
Juárez, who promptly had the Austrian pretender shot, sweeping

political, social, and economic reforms at the expense of the traditional power bases (the army, the clergy, and the landed aristocracy) created a political vacuum. When the charismatic Juárez died in office, disorder resumed.

Finally, in 1877, Porfirio Díaz came to power with the support of the army, the clergy, and the landed aristocracy. He brought order to Mexico by establishing a police state, offering the masses *pan o palo*—the choice of either bread or a club.

Díaz tried to transform Mexico's backward economy by developing natural resources. He seized much land, mostly from Indians, and sold it to foreigners, or gave it away to supporters and cronies who, like Díaz himself, became fabulously wealthy. Not only was the budget balanced for the first time in Mexican history, but large surpluses accumulated, which were used to buy off organized opposition.

American, British, and French firms purchased *ranchos,* built railroads, and acquired mineral deposits throughout Mexico— such as rights to the atoll which Díaz sold to Pacific Islands Company in 1898 for an undisclosed cash consideration, plus a royalty of seventy-five cents per ton of product exported. Little of this development benefited the majority of Mexicans, the impoverished masses.

In the case of Clipperton island, no benefit whatsoever was derived. Little if any of the "cash consideration" found its way to the Treasury. Nor did the atoll ever produce revenue for the state, for royalties were not collected because Mexico eventually lost title to the place, and the London escrow account was surrendered to the French in 1932. Island phosphates were not shipped to Mexico to enrich its soil. Nor did any Mexican find gainful employment working the atoll's phosphate beds, for all known company employees on Clipperton were either Europeans or Orientals.

Prosperous and tranquil though Mexico seemed because of the *Porfirista,* Díaz's aging dictatorship was easily toppled in 1910 by idealist Francisco Madero, a patrician reformer who craved democracy. Madero in turn was assassinated in 1913 by General Victoriano Huerta, an alcoholic notorious for outrageous public behavior who was little more than puppet of American Ambassador Henry Lane Wilson.

A cruel despot who ruled through stark terror, Huerta governed by whim and was immediately opposed by revolutionaries of all stripes: Emiliano Zapata, a charismatic Indian leader whose army controlled the states of Morelos, Guerrero, Oaxaca, Puebla, and from time to time, even parts of the federal district itself; Alvaro Obregón, a popular ex-factory hand who had raised an army in Sonora; Doroteo Arango, a notorious *bandido* better known as Francisco "Pancho" Villa, who ruled Chihuahua like a robber baron; and the scholarly appearing Venustiano Carranza, a cunning despot who, as governor of Coahuila, gripped the state with an iron hand.

Seemingly united in their desire for democratic government under a new constitution that would rid Mexico of tyranny, their armies together and separately converged upon Mexico City in 1914, but not before Huerta had fled for Europe, taking with him much of the national treasury.

Civil order completely collapsed. When Zapata, Obregón, Villa, and Carranza converged upon the capital in August, anarchy reigned nationwide, and rather than establish order, they conspired with and struggled against one another for power. For much of the next six years criminals and even some revolutionary soldiers pillaged, raped, and murdered with impunity.

Although Carranza served as president throughout much of that period, he enjoyed little support from his erstwhile revolutionary allies, and he exercised not much authority outside Mexico City, Veracruz, and the state of Coahuila, his home. To consolidate control, he even had Zapata murdered, and while Carranza did not cooperate with the United States, which sent a "punitive expedition" into Mexico in 1916 after the border-raider Pancho Villa, Carranza undoubtedly would not have been unhappy to see the old *bandido* captured or killed by *gringos*.

Pressured from all sides, in 1920 Carranza finally fled with trunkloads of gold and silver looted from the Treasury—only to be murdered by subordinates before he could reach Veracruz and sail for Europe. By then a reform constitution offered Mexico the hope of stability and progress.

Moreover, by then long-suffering Clipperton islanders had been rescued—no thanks to the Mexican government. "The reason the colonists were abandoned," their rescuer eventually speculated, "was that soon after the shipwrecked crew of the *Nokomis* was taken off, Huerta was deposed, and whenever it was suggested to the Carranza government that supplies be sent to the island, the answer was 'They are *Huerristas*. Let them die'."[21]

Whether or not Carranza's regime pointedly ignored the tiny garrison because of politics, Mexican officials certainly had not forgotten the place entirely. In late 1916 and early 1917, while women on the atoll were being brutalized by a sadist, statesmen at Querétaro, writing Mexico's new constitution, specifically listed the island as an integral part of national territory.

Obviously seeking to avoid a repetition of the Gadsden Purchase episode, in which a large part of Mexico had been sold to the United States by dictator Santa Anna, who pocketed the proceeds, and no doubt as a gesture of repudiation toward the defunct Díaz regime, which had submitted the dispute with the French to binding arbitration, the Mexican Constitution of 1917 precisely defined the national domain to include not only the states and territories of the federation, as had the Constitution of 1857, but also "the islands of both adjacent seas. These specifically include the islands of Guadalupe, the Revilla Gigedos, and Pasión [Clipperton], situated in the Pacific Ocean."[22] Thus, for Mexico ever to cede the place to another power, even as the result of international arbitration, a constitutional amendment would be required.

Mexican officials were obviously conscious of the atoll. Its status was a matter of ongoing international political concern.

Hence, when USS *Cleveland* weighed anchor on June 26, 1914, making for Acapulco, Clipperton islanders should have had little reason to expect to be forgotten. If Captain Arnaud was aware of *Tampico*'s fate, he surely must have believed that, in due course, the navy would send another relief ship.

Yet none came. For the next three years, the little garrison was mostly forgotten by those on the mainland. Thus unfolded a pitiful tale of privation, madness, rape, and murder.

Notes

1. Pacific Phosphate Company was bankrupted after World War I, and its records apparently no longer exist. Documents concerning the Mexican administration of the atoll were either misplaced or lost during the revolutionary turmoil that simultaneously swept the nation. General details of life and events on the island are therefore drawn from other primary and the best secondary sources: J. Y. Cousteau (1981), *passim;* Morris, 31–35; C. K. Perrill, 796–805; H. P. Perrill, 4–5; and from specific U.S. Navy Records, cited herein.

2. Commander Harlan P. Perrill, "Report of passengers carried," 23 July 1917, p. 2, in U.S. Navy Records, Record Group (RG) 45, Subject File 1911–27, O[perational] S[ervices] USS *Yorktown* (National Archives).

3. C. K. Perrill, p. 803.

4. P. G. Taylor (1948), pp. 173–74.

5. "Washington records shocks," p. 1.

6. "Acapulco total wreck," p. 1.

7. "More shocks at Acapulco," p. 4.

8. "Islands may have sunk into ocean," p. 2; "Fear islands are gone," p. 1.

9. "Babes cast away on lonely isle," p. 1.

10. "Mutineers took gunboat," p. 3; "Bottle up a gunboat," p. 2; "Gunboat to be dismantled," p. 2.

11. "Rebel gunboat sunk," p. 2.

12. "Babes cast away on lonely isle," p. 1.

13. "Mother, babies, sea castaways," p. 63.

14. "Babes cast away on lonely isle," p. 1.

15. "Mother, babies, sea castaways," p. 63.

16. Commander Geo[rge] W. Williams, captain, USS *Cleveland,* to CinPac [Commander-in-Chief, Pacific Fleet, subject:] "Rescue of crew

of American schooner *Nokomis* [sic]—wrecked, Clipperton Island, February 28, 1914, Conditions at," June 27, 1914, p. 1, in U.S. Navy Records, RG 45, Subject File 1911–27, OS USS *Cleveland*.

17. *"Cleveland,"* p. 129.

18. Williams to CinPac, June 27, 1914, p. 1.

19. *Ibid.,* pp. 1–2.

20. Commander Geo[rge] W. Williams to CinPac, "Passage afforded Mr. G. Schulz and family from Clipperton island to Acapulco, Mexico," June 28, 1914, p. 1, in U.S. Navy Records, RG 45, Subject File 1911–27, OS USS *Cleveland*.

21. H. P. Perrill, p. 4.

22. Mexico, *Constitución* (1917), pp. 37–38.

7

Marooned with the King
of Clipperton Island
1914–1917

When USS *Cleveland* sailed for Acapulco in June 1914, carrying
Nokomis castaways and the Schulzes, it left behind some twenty-
six persons—only nine of whom would survive. Yet, as the
Americans departed, "there was no apprehension of disaster."[1]

Captain Ramón de Arnaud apparently was confident that the
Mexican government would send a relief vessel in due course, even
though *Tampico* was then fully two months overdue. He did not
know that three years would pass before another ship would drop
anchor offshore. By then a terrifying tale had unfolded.

In June 1914, the atoll's resident population consisted of approximately fourteen men, six women, and six children. Arnaud's
household included his wife Alicia, age twenty-six, his three
children (five-year-old Ramón, two-year-old Alicia, and year-old
Lydia), and nineteen-year-old Altagracia Quiroz, an Indian chore
girl.

Arnaud's second-in-command, a Lieutenant Cardona, lived
with Tirza Randon, an apparently unattached nineteen-year-old
Indian female. She may have been the daughter of one of the other
soldiers, or perhaps a camp follower who somehow had gotten to
the island; whoever she was, she was two months pregnant with
Cardona's child.

Of the garrison's eleven enlisted personnel, only three have been
partially identified—soldiers known only as Irra, Nava, and Rod-

ríquez. Nava and Irra, probably noncommissioned officers, apparently lived with wives, for their children (Rosalia Nava, age twelve, and Francisco and Antonio Irra, ages nine and three, respectively) were eventually rescued. Another adult female and her adolescent daughter are also said to have resided there, but their identities have been lost to history. While it is possible that other soldiers likewise had dependents on the atoll, there is no evidence of such.

Also, at the Rock—living separate and apart from the others— was Álvarez, the light keeper.

When no relief ship had arrived by November 1914, supplies neared exhaustion. "I told [Captain Arnaud] the food was running out," Altagracia Quiroz later recalled. "The food was running out!"[2]

It had never quite happened before. Hennig, Gussmann, other island residents, and even castaways had never completely exhausted their stores; however, the garrison's rations finally ran out, and the twenty-six colonists were forced to subsist entirely off the atoll. Pacific Phosphate's elevated vegetable garden by all accounts produced a bountiful harvest for both workers and crabs, but by 1914 it no longer existed, having either fallen into disrepair after the company ceased mining in 1910—abandoned like rusting tools of the guano trade that littered the island's landscape—or destroyed by storm. In any case, crabs had long since devoured all traces of it—seeds, soil, and all.[3]

During three decades of human habitation, islanders had regularly supplemented canned food with fish, birds, and fresh eggs, but no one had been forced to subsist entirely off the island's natural resources, which provided a malnutritious diet. The atoll's half-dozen coconut palm trees between them reportedly produced no more than three nuts a week, which was insufficient vitamin C for everyone.

Early in 1915, after the last of the provisions had been eaten, scurvy broke out. Ramón Arnaud, Jr., later recalled, "There were fifteen deaths. The others were also dying, little by little. Then they got progressively worse, and the few medicines there, . . . well, they ran out."[4]

This ordeal by hunger actually lasted nine months. One by one the islanders died, soldiers mostly, apparently denied coconut meat and milk by the *comandante,* who evidently divided the precious fruit among the women and children, most of whom survived this crisis. The living dragged the dead to the wide expanse of beach along the southeastern lagoon shore, north of the Rock, and buried the corpses deep in the sand to protect them from crabs. Driftwood crosses marked the site, until the crustaceans devoured those.

Despite the hardships, new faces appeared on the island. In January 1915 Tirza Randon gave birth to a girl she named Guadalupe. By then, Señora Arnaud was again pregnant.

By September, the *comandante* may well have taken leave of his senses. An authoritarian figure under the best of circumstances, as Mexico's prefect in 1914 Arnaud had expelled Gustav Schulz, whom Arnaud had characterized to American sailors from *Cleveland* as "insane." If so, it probably was an island-induced malady, one that Arnaud likewise contracted, at least according to one source.[5]

The heat and the humidity were oppressive and inescapable. Years before, when Theodore Gussmann had been marooned here, he had believed that he too tottered on the brink of madness—an instability caused by the incessant cacophonous shriekings of millions of seabirds, by the constant deafening roar of crashing breakers, by an endless stream of identical days and nights, and by the unrelenting gaze of beady-eyed crabs that stood ready to eat the dead, the dying, and the weak.

Sane or not, "Captain Arnaud didn't wish to abandon his post,"[6] Altagracia Quiroz later explained. Besides, the 50-foot gasoline-powered launch, sitting idle in the warehouse, was useless without fuel enough for the voyage, and those soldiers remaining alive by September 1915 were far too weak from scurvy to pull at oars for 670 miles to Acapulco.

Then their predicament worsened. Ramón Arnaud, Jr., recalled sixty-three years later:

> We lived in the little house. My father had just finished his meal, and my sister was outside playing. Then she ran in and told him: "Papa, Papa. A ship." Then he ran out and saw it. He began to yell. "Cardona, Irra, Rodríguez, a ship. Let's go." They took the little boat, the ship's boat, and went. Standing near the high flag, my mother was watching with the telescope. The ship didn't carry a

flag. She watched and watched and watched. The little boat went back and forth in the waves until I think the men could not control it, or the oars broke. My mother started to tell us, [then] to cry. It was a tragedy—big emotions. We were all crying.[7]

Perhaps that is what happened. Perhaps not.

According to the first person to interview the survivors,

One day, imagining that he saw a ship a short distance off shore, [Captain Arnaud] compelled all the men, except the lighthouse keeper, to man a boat for the purpose of rowing him out to ask for help. The men obeyed to the extent of launching the boat through the heavy surf, but soon afterward, watching through her glass, Señora de Arnaud saw them begin to fight. They evidently had refused any longer to yield to the captain's whim, knowing full well that the ship existed only in his imagination. The boat overturned and she saw them disappear into the sea, which abounded in sharks.[8]

Within hours of the men's deaths, a hurricane suddenly slammed into the island, howling winds throwing up great towering waves that washed entirely across the little coral oval. Distraught women and children took shelter under the floor of the *comandante*'s house, which was the sturdiest structure at the settlement. Then, as the storm subsided, Señora Arnaud gave birth to a son, whom she named Angel.

When the skies cleared, the survivors saw devastation everywhere. All the huts had sustained some damage, the one under which they had taken refuge apparently suffering the least; nevertheless, to some extent "they [all] had to be rebuilt."[9] Many precious possessions were also lost in the tempest—either washed off the atoll by the storm surge, or scattered across the coral rim to become food for crabs.

Worst yet, the women's ordeal had just begun. Álvarez, the last man on Clipperton island, suddenly appeared from the Rock, gathered up all the firearms that remained from the garrison, and threw them into the lagoon—except for one Mauser rifle that he thereafter kept close by his side. He proclaimed himself "King of Clipperton,"[10] and he "brutally demanded the services of the women—raping and shooting a mother and daughter who refused him."[11]

His reign of terror lasted twenty-two months. "He hit us so much," Altagracia Quiroz later said, sobbing. "He beat us so much."[12] The first outsider to come upon the scene later reported, "He was a fiend incarnate, and the women were absolutely at his mercy. Whichever one his fancy chose, he would carry off to his hut and compel to live there just as long as he desired."[13]

Following the rape and murder of the unidentified mother and daughter, Álvarez forced twenty-year-old Altagracia Quiroz to move to his hut at the foot of the Rock. Eventually he tired of her, took her back to the settlement, and dragged away thirteen-year-old Rosalia Nava. She was followed by twenty-year-old Tirza Randon, who later swore that she would kill him someday.

A member of Mexico's lowest class by virtue of his race, the black man was apparently intimidated by Señora Arnaud's patrician manners. "He had a certain amount of respect for [her, and] she . . . [was] spared."[14]

Thus, when he finally tired or perhaps grew wary of fiery Tirza Randon, he started over with Altagracia Quiroz, who was followed by Rosalia Nava, and eventually by Tirza Randon once more. None of them, remarkably, became pregnant.

However brazen his actions, Álvarez openly feared what Señora Arnaud would tell authorities should help arrive. He threatened her repeatedly, saying "that she would never leave the island, that he would kill her the moment a ship was sighted. Often at night she awoke to find him standing over her with a dagger in his hand, evidently deliberating whether or not to carry out his threat. But something stayed his hand."[15]

However unpleasantly, life went on. They foraged for food, surviving on gulls' eggs and boobies, mostly. Since they had lost what little fishing gear they possessed in the storm, they fashioned hooks from the handles of oil cans in order to try to catch fish from the sea, which was an unreliable source. Finally reduced to a bodily size sustainable on a single weekly coconut, the colony experienced no more deaths from scurvy, but all the children suffered from malnutrition and were small for their ages. Tiny Angel de Arnaud developed rickets.

The women sewed garments for the children out of tattered

sailcloth salvaged from *Nokomis*. They even made a calendar to keep track of time. When help arrived, their calculations were off by two days.

In mid-July 1917, Álvarez tired of Tirza Randon once more. He took her back to the settlement and informed Señora Arnaud, "You are going to live with me." As he was armed, she did not reply. He told her to come to him the next morning. Later, after he left, Tirza Randon said, "Now is the time."[16]

Late the next morning, July 18, she and little Ramón accompanied Señora Arnaud to the light keeper's hut at the foot of the Rock. When they arrived, Álvarez was sitting in the shade of his doorway, overseeing a gull roasting on a nearby spit. Uncharacteristically sociable, he informed them that there was no need for anyone at the settlement to hunt, because he had gathered food enough for everyone, pointing as he spoke to a nearby pile of dead terns, obviously shot.

As Tirza Randon entered the house, Álvarez asked, "What are you doing here? Go do your thing." Instead, Ramón says, she

> *went to the corner by the trunk. She had left the hammer there, and she went back to get it. My mother told her to go ahead. Tirza struck, like this [a downward, crashing two-handed blow] with the hammer. Again. He fell. My mother shoved me away. I started to go inside, and then again he was standing. He took an axe and went at my mother. My mother grabbed him and held on. She yelled at me: "The Mauser!" The Mauser rifle was standing in the doorway. I grabbed the Mauser and turned around and ran. My mother yelled at me to go to the other side [of the hut] and bring petrol to burn Álvarez, but when I got over there I saw a ship. . . .*[17]

By then Tirza Randon had struck Álvarez again "with such force that Señora de Arnaud need have no fear of his ever carrying out his threat against her. Not content with the realization that she [Randon] had just killed him, she [grabbed a knife and] stabbed him repeatedly."[18]

She was hysterically slashing the dead man's face to ribbons when Ramón shouted the news. They ran to the nearby coral rim and saw a large, gray vessel still some distance to the northeast. They waved frantically, but at first no one on board saw them.

Still several thousand yards offshore, the ship began to circumnavigate the dangerous atoll. For more than an hour it steamed slowly around the place at a safe distance while, joined by the older children, the women kept pace along the low beach— alternately afraid of what might happen to them as a consequence of Álvarez's death, and then frightened that the strange ship might simply turn and sail away.

Meanwhile, apparently attracted by the smell of fresh blood, thousands of crabs swarmed toward the light keeper's hut.

Half a mile off the northeast point, the vessel stopped dead in the water and lowered a boat. Several men climbed aboard, and the gig made for the island—only to turn about abruptly just as it approached the shore. It returned to the ship.

On the atoll the women panicked. They "thought it was 'all up' and they were so desperate that one of them said she would go back to the settlement and kill the [younger] children, then the rest [of them] should walk out over the reef into the sea."[19]

Finally, the boat swung around once more and headed directly for the island. The surf was only moderate, and the gig rode the breakers effortlessly into the old Oceanic Phosphate landing place, which was marked on most maps.

Señora Arnaud rushed up to the men and, "greatly agitated," demanded to know "who they were and what they meant by landing on the island." Lieutenant (junior grade) Raymond Earle Kerr replied that they were from USS *Yorktown,* and he "assured them that no harm would come to them. She then broke down and begged him to bring them off. . . ."[20]

While another officer, ship's surgeon C. W. Ross, and two sailors accompanied the women to the settlement to collect the few belongings they could take with them, "Lieutenant Kerr went alone in the other direction to the lighthouse."[21] After visiting the Rock, he walked on to the settlement and joined the others.

Yorktown signaled recall, and everyone at the settlement began the journey back to the boat. Sailors pushed wheelbarrows piled high with belongings, and Francisco Irra, "who is nearly twelve years old [but] about the size of an eight-year-old child, . . . carried the youngest child of Señora Arnaud on his back from the settlement to the landing, a distance of more than two miles."[22] Everyone boarded the gig, and it made for the ship.

★ ★ ★

A gunboat assigned to the Pacific fleet, USS *Yorktown* had been searching for Germans on July 18, 1917, when it called at Clipperton island. Commissioned in 1889, it had long represented the interests of the United States along the West coast of the Americas, but it had never been to the atoll before. The rescue of women and children from the remote island would become the proudest moment in the ship's history, even if many of the details were suppressed for a time.

When the United States entered World War I, *Yorktown* was assigned general patrol duty off Central America. Then, early in the summer of 1917, Vice Admiral William Freeland Fullam, commander of the Pacific fleet's patrol force, lay a

navigator's ruler on the map from Honolulu to Panama. The island in question [Clipperton] came almost directly on the line, and it was decided that by no very great stretch of the imagination it could be considered as lying to the north of the ruler, and within the admiral's area of operations. Admiral Fullam and the members of his staff met in his cabin to plan the itinerary for the gunboat Yorktown, *which was to visit a number of islands adjacent to Mexico and find out if there was any foundation for the persistent rumors that the Germans, taking advantage of the strained relations between the United States and Mexico, had been able to establish radio stations and submarine bases in that part of the Pacific.*

In spite of the censorship and the utmost secrecy in regard to all ship movements, "scuttlebutt" rumor had it that the ship was to resume Mexican patrol duty, and no one, from the captain down, viewed with any pleasure the resumption of such duty. The memory of the deadly monotony of previous cruises in Mexican waters did not appeal to men of fiber, to whom the glamour of the airplane, the submarine, and the destroyer beckoned. Yet, before the cruise was over, the ship's log [sic] revealed a story which, as one of the officers remarked, "had Robinson Crusoe lashed to the mast," and which was some compensation for being deprived of the chance for active participation in the war.[23]

Skippered by Commander Harlan Page Perrill, a forty-three-year-old career officer who had commanded the ship for two years,

Yorktown dutifully inspected the Revilla Gigedo islands off Baja California and the Marías islands north of Puerto Vallarta before setting course for Clipperton, "the island in question."

On the day of the dramatic rescue, Captain Perrill wrote to his wife:

> *Having obtained such an unfavorable description of the island from the sailing directions, I decided not to attempt to make it before broad daylight. . . . Last night at 8:00 P.M. our position showed a slight easterly set, enough so that our course, prolonged, passed about five miles to the eastward of the island, but I did not change, for I was more than willing to miss it at that much, in case we were further along than we thought, and should happen to come up to it before daylight. The rain squall that struck us last night marked a turn in the weather.*
>
> *After an almost sleepless night, caused by excessive motion and heat, I got up when called at 6:00 A.M. and made my way to the bridge, finding a strong southwesterly wind, and a rough, choppy sea that gave us the motion. I also found that there had been repeated rain squalls that had driven all open air sleepers from the deck. It was so cloudy that the navigator was not able to get any morning sights. The head sea had knocked down our speed and instead of being up to it at 8:30 A.M. we were some distance from the island. About 9:50 the orderly reported that the masthead lookout had sighted land. It was a remarkable piece of work for the lookout, for we didn't get it on the bridge until at least fifteen minutes later. Meanwhile we altered our course and headed for it, and in due time picked up the rock and later the island itself.*
>
> *My first intention had been merely to make a circuit of the island without attempting a landing, on account of the heavy surf making boating hazardous, and if nothing appeared amiss to resume our journey. Later, however, I decided to make a landing if at all possible, if for nothing more than to ascertain for a certainty whether or not the light was working. Lieutenant Kerr [the navigator] said he would like mighty well to land and the surgeon [C. W. Ross, M.D.] decided to go with him. We had a boat's crew get early dinner and about noon the boat shoved off. Meanwhile, we had found that, in spite of heavy surf all around the island, it was comparatively quiet at the northeast side from which we had approached.*

We noticed some women walking along the beach and I remarked that the women of Clipperton Island evidently hadn't much to do when they could come down to the beach to watch every ship that came in. As our boat neared the shore we observed that the women were making frantic signals to its occupants. The boat seemed to be making a landing through considerable surf and there appeared to me to be a much better landing place nearer the ship. As they seemed unable to get our signals, I recalled them to the ship, and Kerr and I talked the whole procedure over again. The boat got away the second time about half-past one and finally succeeded in making a landing.[24]

Later that day Lieutenant Kerr reported officially in writing to Captain Perrill:

This afternoon I landed in the ship's gig on the sand beach at the eastern end of the island. The sea was moderate, from the south. A slight surf was breaking on the beach, but no trouble was experienced in making a good landing through it or in getting off again.

The remainder of the northern side of the island is not fit for landing on account of the very dangerous coral reef which extends completely along it about a hundred yards off shore.

The landing place is the one indicated on reference (a) [Hydrographic Office Chart No. 1680] above. It is further marked by a couple of small huts, the wreckage of an old sailing vessel, and, about 200 yards to the right, a tall, conspicuous coco palm. Referring to H. O. Chart #1680, the wreck of the Kingora [sic] shown there has disappeared as have also the houses on the northern part of the island. On the southwestern side of the island there is quite a collection of houses in the vicinity of the point marked "Flagstaff." A wharf extends part way across the coral reef but is not long enough for landing purposes. There is about 300 yards of small car track extending from the wharf to a large store house where a gasoline boat of fifty feet length is stored. There are a number of boats in a boat shed on the lagoon directly across from the wharf. There is also considerable machinery for the concentration of guano about the establishment. But all the houses, boats, and machinery are in dilapidated condition.

The light is established, as shown, on Clipperton Rock; but it

*has not been tended for a long time; and there is no keeper [sic].
There are three huts at the base of the Rock on the eastern side.*

*The island is nearly level, with the exception of Clipperton Rock.
The atoll is literally covered with nesting gannets. Four or five
different species were noted. Between the nests, and about the rim of
the lagoon, millions of land crabs crawl. At a distance they give the
lagoon the appearance of having an orange colored rim. It is
impossible to walk without stepping on crabs. On Clipperton Rock
thousands of noddies nest. The noddies are a sooty black species with
a white crown, supposed to be peculiar to the islands in this section
of the ocean. They lay their eggs in shallow depressions in the rock
that they first line with green algae. A single egg was all that was
noted in any of the nests and it was as large as a bantam egg. The
rock itself is an ideal place for birds to nest, since it is caverned and
caved and cleft and hollowed into innumerable shelves and depressions. Access to the light is easy by climbing the rock or by the series
of wooden ladders that have been rigged up the steeper places. The
light is fixed on a concrete pedestal a few feet high.*

*A dozen or more pigs roam the island. They seem to live
principally on land crabs, but in spite of the abundance of such food,
they are skinny and lean.*

*There are several cisterns on the southwestern part of the island
where the houses are. On the northeastern side of the island near the
boat landing there are several old metal boats sunk in sand for
catching water. They were full.*

*On the eastern side of the island, about midway between the
landing and the Rock, there is a cemetery with about twenty wooden
crosses in it. No grass grows on the entire island.*

The survivors of the party left there by the S.S. Korrigan II
*[sic], in January, 1914, three women and eight children, were
brought off to the ship.*[25]

Although his official report shaded the truth about the light and
its keeper, Kerr orally reported to Perrill everything he had seen
and done while on the island. Years later the captain acknowledged
that "Lieutenant Kerr had seen the body in the hut and knew he
had just been killed. There was no [convenient] way to bury the
body so he left it to the land crabs which had already begun their
work when Mr. Kerr made his gruesome find."[26]

Meanwhile, as Perrill later confided to his wife, while awaiting Kerr's return to the ship, he had gotten

under way to make a circuit of the island, and upon reaching the quiet water again, lay to till well after 4 o'clock. I thought it was then time to get our people back and took the ship in as close to the shore as I dared, and made the appropriate recall signals.

After a while we made out Lieutenant Kerr and Doctor Ross returning from the settlement, which was on the opposite side of the island from the place where the landing was made. They were followed by two bluejackets pushing wheelbarrows. Also I noted the women and some children gathering along the beach and you can imagine my surprise when the watchers on the bridge reported that they were getting into the boat. Speculation was rife. When Kerr got alongside and made his [oral] report, he revealed a tale of woe absolutely harrowing in its details.

The people he brought off were three women, one girl about fifteen years old, and seven smaller children, the sole survivors of the original colony. Not a man was left. They had not been visited by any ship since the Cleveland *was there over three years ago, at which time they were expecting a supply ship to arrive soon. Two and a half years ago their supplies gave out entirely and since that time they had lived on fish and the flesh and eggs of birds, with about one coconut a week to ward off scurvy. They have all had it in a mild way. The youngest child, two years old, is rickety and cannot walk.*

The widow of the captain, Señora de Arnaud, is the only white woman. Four of the children are hers, the youngest being the one with rickets. She is only twenty-nine, but looks forty. The other two women are only twenty-one [sic]. One of these women is the maid of Señora Arnaud and the other is the widow [sic] of the lieutenant of the party. The latter has a child about the age of Señora Arnaud's youngest child; the other three children are orphans of soldiers. With the exception of Señora Arnaud and her children they are all Indian, but I thought at first some of them were Negroes as they are so dark. The doctor says that, barring the child with rickets, they all are well, but I suspect they all need baths, and they certainly need clothes. Some of the children are wearing only coarse canvas slips.

Of course they had seen no Germans. They did not even know there was a European war. Their last paper was almost four years old. They were Huertistas and did not know that Huerta was not still President of Mexico.

After scurvy had caused so many deaths among them, the captain and the only men left, with the exception of the lighthouse keeper, put off from the island in a whaleboat, seeking relief, and were lost at sea. The lighthouse keeper proved to be a greater menace than starvation, for he was supposed to be insane and later killed one of the women [and her teenage daughter] and they were all desperately afraid of him. Only this morning one of the women killed him.[27]

. . . Before I forget, I want to tell you some of the things they brought off with them from the island. The most of the contents of the two wheelbarrows, which carried all they could bring away with them, consisted of clothing. They had conserved some of the clothing they had brought to the island with them, being able to do this by making clothes of the sails of the wrecked Nokomis. *You can imagine how poorly this adapted itself to the purpose, for the slip worn by one of the Indian boys is so heavy and coarse it can stand alone. A cake of Ivory soap was among their treasures. I presume their supply of soap did not last much longer than their supply of food and they had been compelled to use sand and canvas for cleaning purposes. They had two forlorn chickens when they got in the boat but one of them was drowned when the boat shipped so much water when being launched through the surf. I imagine the struggles for existence of these poor fowls on the barren island would make an interesting story in itself, and it seems rather too bad that after weathering all the vicissitudes one of them should find a watery grave with relief in sight. The other one is still on board and I presume will be landed with the other refugees. Certain that no one would be tempted to kill it and cook it, for it looks as if it might be one of the two originally owned by Noah.*[28]

Pandemonium accompanied the refugees as they boarded *York-town*, and Perrill was unable to question any of the women immediately. The Arnaud children commenced screaming "as they were passed out of the boat by the bluejackets, with their mother left in the boat. They evidently thought she was to be left behind. . . . Señora Arnaud . . . held up [well] until after she was taken to the sickbay, when she became hysterical."[29] Two days passed before the captain saw her again, and he was surprised by her improved condition and attitude. She clutched a "huge roll of bills [that] she had carefully cherished. This represented a huge fortune under Huerta's regime, but is now worthless."[30]

Upon being interrogated, she initially claimed that "the lighthouse keeper had died of scurvy, but Mr. Kerr had seen the body,"[31] and Perrill knew otherwise. Confronted with Kerr's account, she broke down and poured out the whole tragic tale of abandonment, starvation, madness, and death. She related how she had seen her husband struggle for control of a gun in the whaleboat and go overboard with the others into a shark-infested sea. She described how Álvarez had terrorized the women—his murders, and his repeated threats, beatings, and sadistic rapes. She explained how Tirza Randon, fed up with his outrages, had bashed in his skull with a hammer and, not satisfied, set upon his carcass with a knife—making "a perfect sieve of his face"[32] merely moments before *Yorktown* hove into view.

By then aware of Álvarez's repeated threat to murder Alicia Arnaud the moment rescue appeared imminent to prevent her from talking to authorities, Captain Perrill reflected, "What if we had been an hour earlier! It is almost certain that the man would have killed Señora Arnaud."[33]

Perrill also interviewed Tirza Randon, whom he described as "the most resolute-looking" of the islanders. She "doesn't seem to worry a great deal over the affair. She feels that she was simply the instrument employed to carry out the wishes of a Higher Power. She says she is sure the Good Lord never intended that the man should leave the island."[34]

However confident she may have been, Captain Perrill was not. Risking court-martial during wartime, he avoided any reference to Álvarez in the ship's log, its war diary, and his official "Report of Passengers Carried."[35] He later explained, "I was afraid of the effects it might have upon the fortunes of Tirza Randon."[36] He (and apparently all his shipmates aboard *Yorktown*) faithfully kept the secret for seventeen years, until Perrill himself broke the silence.

Soon after taking the women and children on board, he ordered a heading of 68°, toward Salina Cruz, a city on the Gulf of

Tehuantepec where many of the refugees had families. While en route, he transmitted a wireless message to William Wiseman, the British consul who handled American interests in the city, listing the names of the Clipperton islanders and requesting assistance in locating relatives; the consul was advised that *Yorktown* would arrive at Salina Cruz at 1600 hours on 22 July.

Yorktown's passengers initially suffered terribly from seasickness, which necessitated turning over "sickbay with its toilet facilities to them at night . . . , which would be dreadfully hot, [transferring] them to the quarter-deck in the morning."[37] To accommodate them further, Dr. Ross, who was treating two cases of mumps, set up a temporary isolation ward for the contagious sailors on the motor launch, which swung from a hoist.

The islanders quickly recovered from *mal de mer*. When the women and children were topside, a canvas screen was hung on the quarterdeck to afford them some privacy, but despite the screen and language barriers, they reportedly chatted amiably with their rescuers. In answer to one of the officers' questions, twelve-year-old Francisco Irra "said he did not like the island, but he did like the ship," Perrill told his wife. "The officers are all crazy about him and Lieutenant [(j.g.) Felix B.] Stump declares he would adopt him if the war were over."[38]

Perrill continued:

> *The men are all very much interested in the children and have given them a great many boxes of candy which they haven't the slightest notion how to use. I was amused watching the younger Indian boy [Antonio Irra, age six] trying to get the top off a box of marshmallows which had been given to him. When he finally succeeded, he went to the side of the ship, and taking the marshmallows out one by one, dropped them overboard into the sea then, replacing the lid, had a nice toy which rolled back and forth with the motion of the ship. The children have eaten very little of the food given them today, as they wanted their "bo-bo." The women, however, say they hope they will never have to eat another gull [sic] again as long as they live.*[39]

Sailors donated spare dress-blue blouses, which Tirza Randon altered to fit the older children (Ramón Arnaud, Francisco Irra, and Rosalia Nava); she also sewed garments for the younger ones out of cotton drill, which was in abundant supply in the ship's stores. The bluejackets also raised "a purse of about $200" for the refugees, an act which neither the captain nor the executive officer had encouraged, and although Perrill confessed that "he hadn't been approached [for money] . . . I'll gladly contribute. . . ."[40]

Precisely at 1600 hours, 22 July 1917, the *Yorktown* dropped anchor off Salina Cruz. According to its war diary, "Immediately after anchoring, the port Quarantine boat came alongside carrying among its passengers Señor Felix Rovira, father of Señora Arnaud of our passengers."[41]

Perrill described the scene for his wife:

As soon as they got on board I took Señor Rovira to the quarter-deck where his daughter was. One of the officers told me this evening that several of the men broke down and cried like children when they saw the reunion of the father and daughter. It was almost as if she had been returned to him from the grave. He had written letter after letter to the Mexican government inquiring as to her fate, and had always received the same reply—that all the colonists had perished. Later, when I joined them on deck, the father and daughter were still so overcome they could scarcely speak. On their way out to the ship, Señor Rovira had told the [British] consul [Mr. Wiseman] that he had never so much regretted his inability to speak English, as he so much wanted to tell us in our own language how grateful he felt to us for restoring his daughter to him. He insisted that he will take care of the whole crowd [of refugees] until other plans can be made for them.[42]

The fund "for the relief of the passengers . . . was turned over for distribution to Mr. Wiseman."[43]

"As they were coming off the ship," Captain Perrill later wrote to his wife, "Señor Rovira remarked to the Captain of the Port, 'They said they would be here at 4 o'clock and here they are just on time. That is the way the Americans do things.' "[44]

Captain Perrill soon closed the subject of Clipperton island in *Yorktown*'s war diary:

During the next afternoon [July 23] a delegation of Citizens etc. came on board to request that the departure of the ship be deferred

*long enough to permit them to give a dance to the officers and men of
the ship as a testimonial of their appreciation and gratitude toward
us for having rescued from Clipperton Island and restored their
fellow citizens to them. The manifesto to this party was issued in
the name of the Chief of Military Forces, the Mayor of the
Municipality, and a Social Club representing the best elements of
the citizens. The party was given at Hotel Gambrinus at 7 P.M.
and was attended by nine officers and thirty-five men. Every where
was evident extreme cordiality. The incident was undoubtedly added
to the American prestige in the vicinity of Salina Cruz, and it is
hoped that it will gain sufficient publicity throughout Mexico to
accomplish similar results elsewhere.*[45]

Captain Perrill's greatly abridged official report of the dramatic
rescue received some attention from a world press caught up in
the wrenching events of World War I. For example, on August 13,
1917, the New York *Times* ran the story on page eighteen,
featuring it in the center column, top fold, under the banner,
"Marooned 2 Years on Isle: Naval Commander Reports on Rescue
of Mexican Women and Children." In full, that account reads:

*The Navy Department made public tonight the report of the
American warship commander who rescued from Clipperton Island,
the Pacific, some time ago, three women and eight children who were
the last remnants of a party of Mexicans who went to the island
with Captain Ramon De Arnaud of the Mexican army to develop
its guano deposits.*

*For military reasons the name of the American vessel and its
commander were not made public. The Commander's report shows
that the women and children who were rescued had barely escaped
starvation, while Captain De Arnaud lost his life at sea in the small
boat in which he started out for help, and that the other members of
the party died of starvation and scurvy.*

*It was not until the number of women and children left alive on
the island had been reduced to the limits of the small supply of
coconuts that the ravages of scurvy ceased. For more than two years
these survivors were forced to subsist on the flesh and eggs of gannets
and gulls, and occasionally fish.*

The officers and crew of the warship raised a fund of $200 for the relief of the refugees, who have been landed at a Mexican port.[46]

Had Perrill not sanitized his reports and included titillating details of Álvarez's reign of terror, including his violent end, and had the Navy released those details, the story undoubtedly would have received far greater attention.

However much the gallant naval officer may have wished to spare Tirza Randon and other islanders public scrutiny regarding Álvarez, "that macabre chapter in the history of the island [soon was] freely told in towns up and down the Mexican coast between Salina Cruz and Acapulco. . . ."[47]

Notes

1. Commander H[arlan] P. Perrill, "Report of passengers carried," 23
  •July 1917, p. 2, in U.S. Navy Records, Record Group (RG) 45, Subject
  File 1911–27, O[perational] S[ervices], USS *Yorktown* (National Archives).

2. Quoted in J. Y. Cousteau (1981), n.p.

3. There is inconclusive evidence that the elevated garden had fallen into
  disuse as early as 1905, because, when Joseph Slevin visited the atoll that
  year aboard *Academy,* he reported that Pacific Phosphate employees
  "Shultz and Larsen . . . never had any fresh vegetables." See Slevin, p.
  23.

4. Quoted in Cousteau, n.p.

5. *Ibid.*

6. *Ibid.*

7. *Ibid.*

8. C. K. Perrill, pp. 804–805.

9. *Ibid.,* p. 804.

10. Morris, p. 32.

11. Cousteau, n.p. The identities of Álvarez's first victims are unclear.
  They may have been the wife and daughter of Irra, or of Nava, or of
  someone different altogether. In any case, precisely what happened to
  Señoras Irra and Nava is unknown.

12. Quoted in *ibid.*

13. C. K. Perrill, p. 804.

14. *Ibid.*

15. *Ibid.*

16. Quoted in Cousteau, n.p.

17. *Ibid.*

18. C. K. Perrill, p. 804.

19. *Ibid.*, p. 801.

20. *Ibid.*

21. *Ibid.*

22. *Ibid.*, p. 802.

23. *Ibid.*, p. 799.

24. *Ibid.*

25. [Lieutenant (j.g.) Raymond Earle Kerr] Navigator, to [Commander Harlan Page Perrill] Commanding Officer, USS *Yorktown,* "Subject: Clipperton Island," 18 July 1917, in U.S. Navy Records, RG 45, Subject File 1911–27, O[perational] S[ervices] USS *Yorktown.*

26. H. P. Perrill, p. 5.

27. C. K. Perrill, pp. 800–801.

28. *Ibid.*, p. 803.

29. *Ibid.*, p. 802.

30. *Ibid.*, p. 803.

31. H. P. Perrill, p. 5.

32. *Ibid.*

33. C. K. Perrill, p. 804.

34. *Ibid.*, pp. 804–805.

35. U.S. Navy Records, RG 45, Subject File 1911–27, OS USS *Yorktown.*

36. H. P. Perrill, p. 5.

37. C. K. Perrill, p. 801.

38. *Ibid.*, p. 802.

39. *Ibid.*

40. *Ibid.*, p. 805.

41. USS *Yorktown,* "War diary," 22 July 1917, in U.S. Navy Records, RG 45, Subject File 1911–27, OS USS *Yorktown.*

42. C. K. Perrill, p. 805.

43. USS *Yorktown,* "War diary," 22 July 1917.

44. C. K. Perrill, p. 805.

45. USS *Yorktown,* "War diary," 23 July 1917.

46. "Marooned 2 years on isle," p. 18.

47. Morris, p. 32.

8

The Pen and the Sword
1922–1938

For a quarter-century following the dramatic rescue of women and children from Clipperton island, it was uninhabited once again; however, this time it was not entirely forgotten. Its name was repeatedly in print throughout the 1920s and 1930s, mentioned by scholars interested in its unique ecology or its curious place in history, by popular writers fascinated by rumors of a sensational past, and by journalists covering such disparate events as Victor Emmanuel's arbitration award and visits by Franklin Delano Roosevelt. Finally, in 1935 the government of France belatedly landed representatives on the island to take possession formally.

Foremost among these events was the decision regarding the island's sovereignty. However "utterly insignificant"[1] this may seem today, as the New York *Times* has editorialized, the atoll's ownership was once vigorously disputed. While five nations—Costa Rica, France, Great Britain, Mexico, and the United States—possessed seemingly plausible claims to the place, one by one all but France and Mexico dropped out of the contest for title. Then, early in the twentieth century, they agreed to submit the issue to arbitration, the results becoming a noteworthy case in international relations, one frequently cited in academic treatises and casebooks.[2] (The situation may also have been a little-known instance of Fascist intrigue.)

As previously noted, on March 2, 1909, following more than a decade of dispute, France and Mexico agreed to submit the issue of the island's ownership to binding arbitration, and the following August 22 Italian King Victor Emmanuel III accepted that task. The claimants consequently compiled their documentation and composed their arguments, Mexico submitting its brief in 1909, France in 1912. Two decades passed before the Italian monarch rendered his decision—one that many contemporary observers considered tainted.

Practically the last ruler ever produced by the house of Savoy, by nature Victor Emmanuel was indecisive and unprincipled. Often described benignly by historians as a tractable constitutional monarch, he was in fact a shallow weakling whose "appearance has been mentioned in scientific discussions of physical degeneration through inbreeding."[3]

The grandson and namesake of the Sardinian nobleman under whom Italy had been unified in 1861, Victor Emmanuel ascended the throne in 1900 at age 31, upon the assassination of his father Humbert I, an authoritarian imperialist who had joined in a Triple Alliance with the Hohenzollerns of Germany and the Hapsburgs of Austria-Hungary. As monarch, Victor Emmanuel was easily swayed by politicians holding forth the promise of imperial aggrandizement. This led him to support war against Turkey in 1911, as well as Italian entry into World War I in 1915 on the side of Great Britain, France, and Imperial Russia and against his father's allies, Austria and Germany.

Then, when the Italian parliamentary system was sorely strained by that "Great War" and by the disorder which followed, Benito Mussolini rose to prominence. The king might easily have prevented a Fascist takeover in 1922 merely by signing a martial law decree laid in his hands by Prime Minister Luigi Facta. Instead, Victor Emmanuel—believing that such a regime "strengthened the prestige of the Crown which the troubles of 1919 to 1922 had seriously shaken"[4]—appointed Mussolini premier. Thereafter, for the following two decades, the monarch was little more than a figurehead whose appetite for titles was appeased by "Il Duce's" aggression, Victor Emmanuel becoming Emperor of Ethiopia in 1936 and King of Albania in 1939. Even so, he once warned a confidant, "Be careful what you say to me, for I must tell everything to Mussolini."[5]

That the king took an inordinate amount of time to decide such a relatively uncomplicated issue as the Clipperton island case, and then that his dilatory decision was apparently influenced by international politics, should not be surprising.

The positions of Mexico and France were clearly delineated but spottily supported by documentation. Mexico's *Isla de la Pasión, llamada de Clipperton* (1909), was ninety-six pages of scanty evidence. The document bulked with the details of mining operations since 1897, when the government of Porfirio Díaz first learned of Americans on the atoll and sent in the marines.

Unaware that it had likely been discovered by Ferdinand Magellan in 1521 (persuasive evidence of such would not appear in print until three years after Victor Emmanuel's decision), Mexico claimed title by right of succession from Spain, into whose half of the world, as defined by Pope Alexander VI's encyclical *Inter Caetera Divinae* (1493), the atoll unquestionably fell. Even so, Mexico produced no incontrovertible evidence that the place had ever been sighted, much less formally claimed, by any Spaniard prior to 1711, when Frenchman Michel du Bocage named it *L'île Passion*.

Mexican bureaucrat Antonio García Cubas, who compiled Mexico's evidence, asserted that the lonely atoll was undoubtedly seen repeatedly by early Spanish mariners who regularly sailed south seas waters. As to the lack of documentation, Cubas asserted: "One [is] not to be surprised . . . by the impossibility of obtaining indications of such island in the personal relations of the first Spanish explorers, if one pays attention to its little importance, since it consists of a single rock, surrounded by breakers and coral reefs which developed through the years into an atoll with guano deposits. . . ."[6]

As evidence that it was known variously over the years, Mexico reproduced a sixteenth-century chart from the archives of the Royal Geographical Society of *Nueva España,* or Mexico; on it in the actual vicinity of Clipperton was an "*I. Pasión.*" Other period maps located islands of various names about the area of the lone atoll. Mexico also traced the voyages of Saavedra Cerón (1527), George Anson (1742), and José Camacho (1783) to provide circumstantial evidence of general maritime familiarity with the place, which conclusively proved, Mexico contended, that Spanish *Pasión* and French *Passion* were identical and therefore Mexican property. Curiously, included among the government's exhibits is yet another chart, "copied from the archives" by García Cubas, that clearly shows "*Isla Pasión descubierta en 1715,*" thereby giving credence to France's claim of prior discovery.

Nowhere in its wordy, 518-page *Mémoire défensif présenté par le gouvernement de la République Française dans le litige relatif à la souveraineté de l'île Clipperton* . . . (1912) did the Republic of France challenge Mexico's assertions of prior sighting by Spanish explorers. France acknowledged that many sailors had seen the place, including "the famous English pirate whose name was sometimes attached to it," but *Quai d'Orsay* argued that inasmuch as the atoll had not been formally claimed nor actually occupied by any power, it was "*territorium nullis,*" that is, unowned on November 17, 1858, when Lieutenant Kervéguen formally annexed it on behalf of Emperor Napoleon III. *L'île Passion,* better known as Clipperton island, therefore was French territory.

Far larger than the Mexican brief, France's *Mémoire* was hardly more substantive. A third of it comprised French-Mexican correspondence relative to the dispute (in double translations), commencing at the outset of the affair in 1898 and concluding with French-Spanish translations of the arbitration agreement. Twenty-five percent related to Bocage's "discovery" in 1711 and to Kervéguen's purposeful expedition in 1858 to claim the place, among others in the Pacific; interestingly, included among these documents was Lieutenant Kervéguen and Captain Detaille's separate candid appraisals that Clipperton island was utterly worthless.

The balance of the French brief consisted of assorted supporting material: a lengthy geographical description of the atoll; a treatise on Spanish claims (which concluded that while numerous Spaniards likely saw it, there was no evidence whatsoever that anyone ever claimed it); translations of the 1885 arbitration award by Pope Leo XIII relative to the German-Spanish dispute over the Caroline islands in the western Pacific (which the French somehow believed relevant); and the complete English text of the U.S. Guano Islands Act of 1856 (with double translations). Nowhere did France mention that its 1858 claim to Clipperton contravened the American Monroe Doctrine, a matter that conceivably might have tipped the balance toward Mexico.

Some of Victor Emmanuel's twenty-two years of indecision

Clipperton Rock, viewed from the southeast. FROM W. J. WHARTON, "NOTES ON CLIPPERTON ATOLL," GEOLOGICAL SOCIETY OF LONDON QUARTERLY JOURNAL (1898)

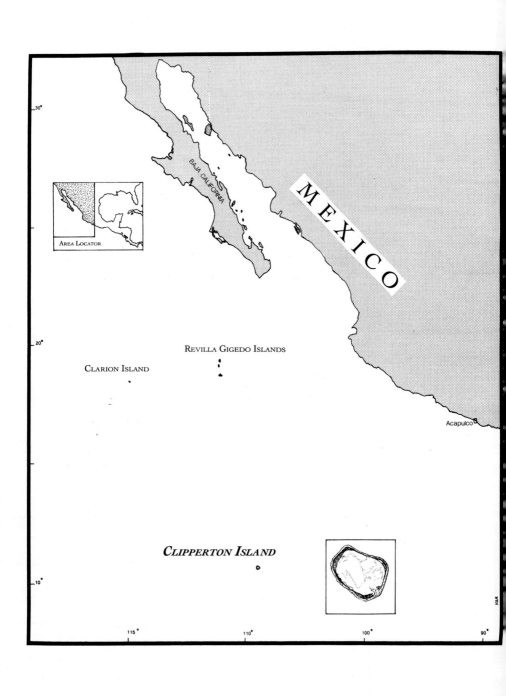

30°

AREA LOCATOR

BAJA CALIFORNIA

MEXICO

20°

REVILLA GIGEDO ISLANDS

CLARION ISLAND

Acapulco

CLIPPERTON ISLAND

10°

115°   110°   100°   90°

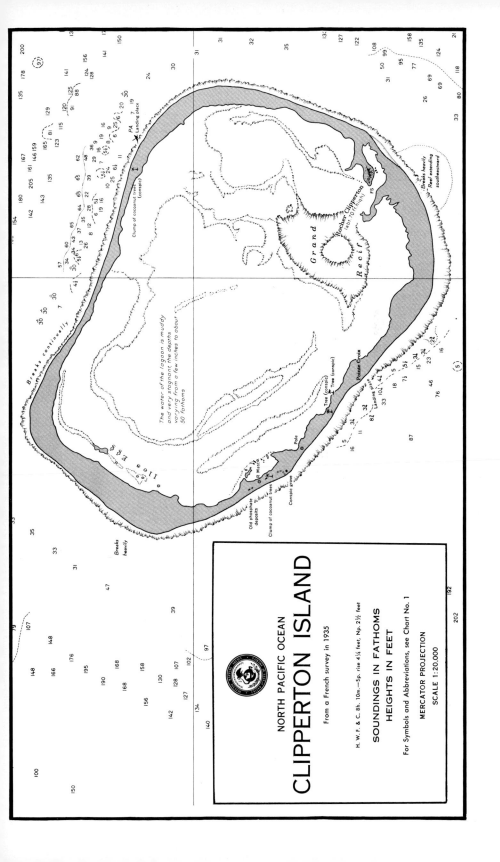

NORTH PACIFIC OCEAN

CLIPPERTON ISLAND

From a French survey in 1935

H. W. F. & C. 8h. 10m.—Sp. rise 4¼ feet, Np. 2½ feet

SOUNDINGS IN FATHOMS

HEIGHTS IN FEET

For Symbols and Abbreviations, see Chart No. 1

MERCATOR PROJECTION

SCALE 1:20,000

Grand   Recif

Rocher Clipperton
(abt. 70 high) FS

Breaks heavily
Reef extending
southeastward

Pointe Croix

Tree (conspic)
Tree (conspic)

Conspic grove

Pole

R Mast

Old phosphate
deposits

Clump of cocoanut trees

Breaks
heavily

The water of the lagoon is muddy
and very stagnant, the depths
varying from a few inches to about
50 fathoms

Breaks continually

Clump of cocoanut trees
(conspic)

PA
Landing place

Landing place

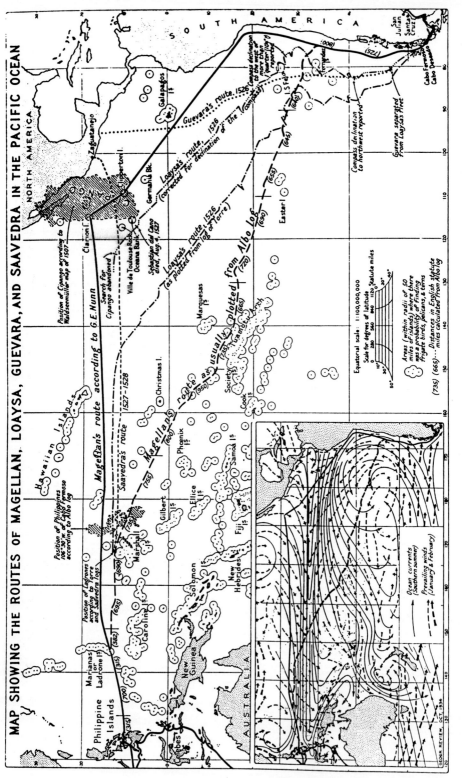

"Map showing the routes of Magellan, Loaysa, Guevara, and Saavedra in the Pacific Ocean." FROM GEORGE E. NUNN, "MAGELLAN'S ROUTE ACROSS THE PACIFIC," *GEOGRAPHICAL REVIEW* (1943)

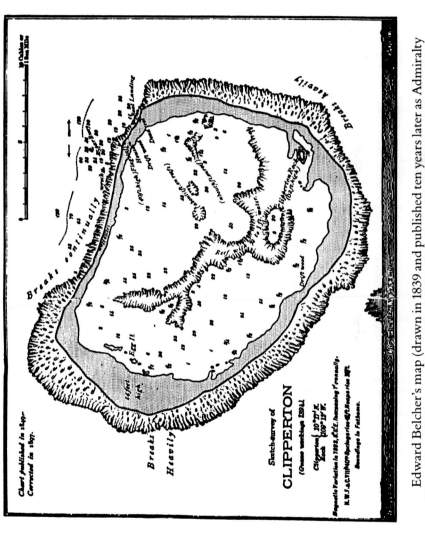

Edward Belcher's map (drawn in 1839 and published ten years later as Admiralty Chart No. 1936), as improved by Paul J. Hennig and John T. Arundel. From W. J. Wharton, "Notes on Clipperton Atoll," *Geological Society of London Quarterly Journal* (1898)

"The Rock was earth, on a rim of coral that belonged to the ocean." FROM P. G. TAYLOR, *FORGOTTEN ISLAND* (1948)

"Standing amongst some stones was an old iron cross." Note the Rock in the distance. FROM P. G. TAYLOR, *FORGOTTEN ISLAND* (1948)

"Clipperton island—the steamship *Navarra* [sic] anchored offshore; foreground, the remains of the *Kinkora*," c. 1897. From Mexico, Isla de Pascón (1900).

"Clipperton island—a place near the Rock [sic]—guano miners, Mr. Gosmann, the boss, on the right; Henry Smith (center); and Frederick Nelson (left)." Notice both the island's pigs and the crab-proof tree box protecting precious coconut palms. FROM MEXICO, *ISLA DE PASIÓN* (1909)

In 1906, the Mexican government erected a maritime beacon light atop Clipperton Rock to strengthen its claims to the remote island. The light illuminated surrounding waters intermittently until 1914, when it was permanently extinguished. FROM CHARLOTTE K. PERRILL (ED.), "FORGOTTEN ISLAND," U.S. NAVAL INSTITUTE *PROCEEDINGS* (1937).

On Clipperton island (left to right) Alicia Arnaud, Altagracia Quiroz, and Triza Randon. The photograph was taken by an unidentified member of the landing party from the USS Yorktown, which rescued them. From Charlotte K. Perrill (ed.), "FORGOTTEN ISLAND," U.S. NAVAL INSTITUTE PROCEEDINGS (1937)

Safe aboard USS Yorktown. Left to right (back row) Tirza Randon, Alicia Arnaud (senior), Atlagracia Quiroz, Rosilia Nava; (on laps) Angel Arnaud, Guadalupe Randon, Antonio Irra; (bottom) Alicia Ramón (junior), Ramón Arnaud (junior), Francisco Irra, Lydia Arnaud. FROM CHARLOTTE K. PERRILL (ED.), "FORGOTTEN ISLAND," U.S. NAVAL INSTITUTE PROCEEDINGS (1937)

"*LST-563*, broached on Clipperton island, circa 22 December 1944."

THE WHITE HOUSE
WASHINGTON

SECRET

July 29, 1943.

MEMORANDUM FOR

THE SECRETARY OF THE NAVY

I have your letter of July twenty-sixth, enclosing another report of the General Board on the subject of island bases between the Americas and the Southwest or Middle Pacific. I note that all of their suggestions are based on the assumption that 2100 sea miles is the longest single leg that can be flown with profitable pay load on board.

That may be and probably is true today but the consideration of these bases must take into account the probability that the development of planes will increase this distance by many hundreds of miles in the reasonably near future. It is probably safe to say that the profitable distance twenty years ago was not much over 500 miles.

Therefore, I do not want the committee of civilians who are to make a study of this route to be

---

SECRET — THE WHITE HOUSE
WASHINGTON

-2-

bound by existing profitable distances. Also, I do not want them to devote much time to the extreme southern route touching Easter Island. It is worthwhile to make rough surveys but we must remember that commercially this route will have little advantage for very many years to come, and that Easter Island and Juan Fernandez present difficult climatic conditions.

I note also that the northern route is based on a flight from the Canal Zone to Clipperton Island and thence to the Marquesas. This is a round-about flight. It should be based on a flight across Mexico to some place on the west coast of Mexico, and thence to Clipperton Island.

In the same way, the Canal Zone will become commercially a crossroads with much commerce, and the route from there via the Galapagos and the Marquesas to Australia should be studied. It could also pick up passengers and freight from Colombia and Ecuador.

I do not quite know why the General Board takes no interest in the Central and South Pacific Islands from the naval point of view. Two

---

SECRET — THE WHITE HOUSE
WASHINGTON

-3-

years ago we took no interest in the Solomons or Bora-Bora, from a naval point of view, but I understand we are now doing it.

F. D. R.

In a secret 1943 memorandum to the Secretary of the Navy (Frank Knox), President Roosevelt explains what he has in mind for Admiral Byrd and his "committee of civilians" who were to study a new air route to Australia via Clipperton island. NATIONAL ARCHIVES

Visiting the island with Jacques Cousteau in 1980, Ramón Arnaud, Jr., stands beside a cross erected in memory of his father. © THE COUSTEAU SOCIETY, A MEMBER-SUPPORTED, NONPROFIT ENVIRONMENTAL ORGANIZATION

Ramón Arnaud, Jr., stands below the Rock, near where Alvarez had lived. There the light keeper died at the hands of those he terrorized. © THE COUSTEAU SOCIETY, A MEMBER-SUPPORTED, NONPROFIT ENVIRONMENTAL ORGANIZATION

A Clipperton island crab, one of many now that the atoll's feral pigs have been exterminated. © THE COUSTEAU SOCIETY, A MEMBER-SUPPORTED, NONPROFIT ENVIRONMENTAL ORGANIZATION

A booby nests among World War II munitions, seemingly unconcerned that some of the shells might still be live. She has more pressing problems with the crab that has taken up a relentless vigil. © THE COUSTEAU SOCIETY, A MEMBER-SUPPORTED, NONPROFIT ENVIRONMENTAL ORGANIZATION

U.S. Navy debris litters the landscape all along the atoll's southwestern coast. Notice the proliferation of palm trees, no doubt beneficiaries of the time when pigs dominated. © THE COUSTEAU SOCIETY, A MEMBER-SUPPORTED, NONPROFIT ENVIRONMENTAL ORGANIZATION.

may have had an academic basis in the diametrically opposing conclusions of Italian scholars who became interested in the atoll's discovery because of their monarch's arbitration duties. In the 1917 *Bolletino* of the Royal Italian Geographical Society, Royal Navy Commander C. Roncagli, a respected lay maritime historian, examined Mexico's evidence in the case (including the administrative map of New Spain, showing *Isla de la Pasión* in the province of Soconizco, which he dismissed as inconclusive) plus such secondary documentation as was readily available to him, and he judged that there was no definitive proof of Spanish discovery.

He also made a heroic assumption: that the atoll had been completely unknown to early Spanish explorers. Because it lies along the boundary of the west-flowing north equatorial current and the east-flowing countercurrent, a zone generally unfavorable to sailing vessels because of variable winds and calms, Roncagli asserted that the place likely was never sighted by early mariners, who, he contended, steadfastly avoided such waters. Even if they did occasionally sail by, he believed that the island's low altitude would have rendered it invisible, except at very short distances— where its sailcloth-shaped rock likely would have been mistaken for a ship, perhaps a privateer, which would have been dangerous to investigate.

While he reiterated the assertion of ninetenth-century pirate authority and popular writer James Burney that the island probably was sighted by English buccaneer John Clipperton in 1705, hence its popular name, Roncagli correctly pointed out that there was no firsthand evidence of such; therefore, he stated the obvious, that the "first firmly established discovery is that by Du Bocage . . . in 1711. . . ."[7]

Two years after these views appeared in print, University of Bologna geography professor Antonio Renato Toniolo categorically disputed Commander Roncagli's findings in an article featured by the prestigious *Rivista Geografica Italiana*. Toniolo reexamined the question of currents and winds in the northeastern Pacific ocean and concluded that, far from lying off the probable course of early Spanish mariners, the low-lying atoll was almost certainly on the track both of Manila galleons during the dry season, when Spanish ships were accustomed to sailing westward from Acapulco, and of vessels engaged in the year-round coast-wise trade between Mexico and Peru. Toniolo believed that Span-iards were well acquainted with the place, pointing to "*Isla de la Pasión*" on the very sixteenth-century Mexican map that Roncagli had superciliously dismissed as inconclusive. Toniolo asserted, "Roncagli was wrong."[8] He believed that the map constituted persuasive circumstantial evidence.

Contradictory interpretations may have led Victor Emmanuel to dawdle another dozen years before rendering judgment. Then again, perhaps academic disputes did not delay him. Some writers have charged that instead he was "influenced by Italy's desire for Mediterranean naval concessions from France."[9]

Whatever his reasoning, on January 28, 1931, the king an-nounced "that the sovereignty over Clipperton Island belongs to France, dating from November 17, 1858."[10] Key to the award was his decision

> not [to] confer official character upon . . . a geographical map printed from the Archives of the Mexican Society of Geography and Statistics, where the island figures as comprised within the 'Political and Military Governments of Spain in North America,' . . . because it is not certain that it was drawn by order and under care of the state, . . . [and] because the manuscript memorandum which one reads there, namely, that it was used at the Royal Tribunal of the Consulate of Mexico, does not confer official character upon it.[11]

Given the "impossibility" of obtaining much early documentation on the island because of its "little importance,"[12] Mexico thus lost its only evidence that *Pasión* preceded *Passion*. That Victor Em-manuel chose to discount the provincial map of New Spain, dismissing it as unofficial, undoubtedly reveals bias. Without that key ruling, the Clipperton island award to France would not have been possible.

Because the king ruled that there was no evidence of Spanish colonial ownership, he therefore judged "that, when in November 1858, France proclaimed her sovereignty over Clipperton, the island was in the legal situation of *territorium nullis,* and, therefore, susceptible of occupation." Moreover, he asserted that "if a terri-tory, by virtue of the fact that it was completely uninhabited, is, from the first moment when the occupying state makes its appearance there, at the absolute and undisputed disposition of that state, from the moment of the taking of possession must be considered as accomplished, and the occupation is thereby completed [sic]."[13]

Although France had admitted that its sole authorized representative, Lieutenant Victor le Coat de Kervéguen, had never set foot on the island, the king apparently judged that the Frenchman had done enough by reading the official proclamation of annexation from the rolling deck of *L'Amiral*. Logic insists that if such an absurdly ritualistic exercise in international protocol could have been performed adequately from shipboard, it might as well have been done inside *Quai d'Orsay* in Paris.

As to Mexico's counterclaims that through inaction over the years France had abandoned its title, however tenuous, and that only Mexico had ever legally occupied the place, the king answered, "There is no reason to suppose that France . . . [had] subsequently lost her right by *derelictio,* since she never had the *animus* of abandoning the island, and the fact that she has not exercised her authority there in a positive manner does not imply the forfeiture of an acquisition already definitively perfected."[14]

The king's reasoning was fatally flawed. By no known standard of international law or practice had France exercised "effective possession." The Tricolor had never flown from atop the Rock, or anywhere else on the island, as had banners of both the United States and Mexico. Unlike Mexican marines who took possession at the point of wet bayonets in 1897, French merchant marines who had gone ashore forty years before (unlike contemporary American citizens) were not authorized to act on behalf of their government. Their presence constituted neither *de jure* nor *de facto* occupation, in the way that Oceanic Phosphate's presence conceivably did for the United States. In the absence of an American claim to Clipperton, Mexico's was the stronger.

Victor Emmanuel nevertheless awarded sovereignty to France.

Trying to explain the king's convoluted logic, Edwin D. Dickinson, professor of international law at the University of California, told readers of *The American Journal of International Law* in 1933 that the decision was a "significant application in novel circumstances of the principle of discovery and occupation. . . . The award is significant, in its legal aspect, chiefly for what it contributes to the development of the doctrine of occupation. . . . In effect, it is held that the occupation which is required is such an occupation as is appropriate and possible under the circumstances."[15] Dickinson failed to speculate why Victor Emmanuel subjected Mexico's claim of "occupation" to a stricter test than France's.

Nor has the reason for taking twenty-two years to reach a decision ever been explained. If the award was truly intended to curry favor so that Mussolini's fleet might call in French Mediterranean ports, as was widely alleged at the time, corroboration has not been found; however, oblique evidence seems supportive.

Writes Alan Cassels, an expert on Fascist Italy interested in diplomatic questions far weightier than ownership of an obscure, bird-splattered Pacific atoll: "King Victor Emmanuel repaid Mussolini for his . . . conversion to monarchial principles by accommodating his visits, invitations, and general relations with foreign royalty to suit Fascism's diplomacy."[16] Surely the king would have been equally pliable over the relatively unimportant Clipperton island case.

If indeed Victor Emmanuel's arbitration decision was a Fascist ploy to further Italian military interests in the Mediterranean, it failed miserably. One writer says that "when count Manzoni, then Italian Ambassador to France, called at the *Quai d'Orsay* to inform the French Government of the decision finally reached by King Emmanuel—after twenty-three years [sic] of deliberation—he had difficulty finding any official who had ever heard of Clipperton!"[17]

Following the public pronouncement of the decision, the New York *Times* reported: "This island has been disputed principally because of its position on the trade routes followed through the Panama Canal toward the Pacific archipelagoes and because of its possible value in the future as an aviation base."[18]

Whatever its actual or potential value, Mexicans balked at accepting the decision. "The Association of Genuine Soldiers of the Revolution started a drive to hold up transfer of the island to France, which they said had been made by 'Mussolini's First Citizen.' "[19] Many Mexican legislators also objected, some of them even arguing that the transfer of territory anywhere in the western hemisphere to a European power was a violation of the

Monroe Doctrine—an American foreign policy heretofore vehemently denounced south of the border.

On December 29, 1931, the Mexican Congress created a blue-ribbon panel to study the Clipperton island case. Luminaries such as Fernando Gonzalez Roa, an international jurist and Mexico's delegate to the League of Nations, Eduardo Suarez and Manuel J. Sierra, both career diplomats, and International Law Professor Juan Manuel Álvarez del Castillo of the University of Mexico scrutinized Victor Emmanuel's ruling for a year before reluctantly concluding that, however illogical and unjust the decision, Mexico was obligated under the terms of the 1909 arbitration agreement to accept it. There was no mechanism for appeal.

The commission recommended that the Mexican Congress ratify the award by amending the Constitution of 1917, which specifically included *Isla de la Pasión* as part of the national domain. Mexican Foreign Minister Manuel Téllez also urged ratification "as a matter of national honor. . . ."[20] Eventually, the Mexican Senate foreign relations committee likewise concluded "that, although not agreeing with the King of Italy's decision, Mexico is honor bound to live up to an agreement made . . . when Porfirio Díaz was dictator to abide by the decision."[21]

Consequently, on December 14, 1932, Congress ratified the arbitration decision and enacted the necessary legislation to amend the Constitution. Two days later, "the Senate unanimously approved the proposal of Senator Ruben Ortiz of Chihuahua that Mexico, although recognizing the award of the King of Italy, holding Clipperton island in the Pacific Ocean to be French territory, offer to buy the islands [sic]. Funds for the purchase would be provided by a levy of one day's salary on government workers."[22] Ortiz proposed to have "an uninterested third power" fix a price that would be agreeable to both France and Mexico. Nothing came of the notion.

As to reaction north of the border, *Newsweek* reported in 1933: "There has been talk in France of the possibilities of [using] the small lagoon as a hydroplane base, for planes bound from the French island of Tahiti to the American mainland. Whether such a base would conflict with the Monroe Doctrine, from the American point of view, has not yet been decided."[23]

To the contrary, the U.S. Department of State had long ago

reached a conclusion regarding the atoll, a position set in cement irrespective of fact or Doctrine. Indeed, much of *Newsweek*'s story was incorrect. According to the magazine, the Mexican garrison had been established in 1897 and later, during one of the country's frequent revolutions, had been forgotten: "With the exception of one emaciated man who met the relieving ship, the garrison starved to death. . . . Clipperton Island is [now] uninhabited, and guano phosphates and tortoises are its only products of value."[24]

Neither in 1931, when some Mexicans pleaded with Washington to invoke the Monroe Doctrine, nor in 1933, when France was said to have been contemplating the conversion of the island into a military base, did the State department so much as issue a press release on the matter—despite innumerable requests for action. The New York *Times* reported from Mexico City on November 15, 1932: "There has been considerable discussion here as to what attitude the United States would take in applying the Monroe Doctrine, which Mexico does not recognize, to the possession of a European power of an island only 600 miles out in the Pacific which would be suitable for a naval or aviation base. Also there has been much opposition to the award, made on Jan. 28, 1931, on the grounds that it was influenced by an Italian desire for Mediterranean naval concessions from the French."[25]

The reason for State department silence on the subject is unclear. Perhaps diplomats deemed the obscure, generally worthless little place to be sufficiently insignificant to serve as an object lesson—a chastisement of Mexico for failing to toe the Yankee line on the Monroe Doctrine, as well as payback for other grievances dating back to the days of Pancho Villa. More likely, the Latin American section probably did not question Alvey Adee's original judgment.

Obviously, as Otto Holstein asserted in the 1931 issue of the *Geographical Review,* a publication of the learned American Geographical Society, "In the hands of a first-class power, on the direct steamer route between Japan, the Hawaiian islands, and the Panama Canal, with a still-water lagoon, and within easy distance from the canal, Clipperton Island takes on strategic importance."[26]

Such seems to have escaped denizens of Foggy Bottom. Diplomats were even unaware that United States military war planners had long considered the place to be within their defense perimeter.

In fact, during World War II the U.S. Navy even secretly occupied it, giving diplomats ample cause to regret repeated refusal to apply the Monroe Doctrine to the island when provided the opportunity.

However reluctantly, Mexico ultimately accepted Victor Emmanuel's decision. On January 10, 1934, the *Diaro Oficial* in Mexico City announced: "The Congress of Mexican states, and with the approval of the majority of the State Legislatures, declares amended Article 42 of the Political Constitution."[27] Thus, *Isla de la Pasión* became *L'île Passion*, even though the world—including both the Mexicans and the French—continued to call it Clipperton island.

Interest in the atoll seemingly peaked between the two world wars. Scholars frequently studied the place, but mostly from afar. Several mentioned it in general treatises of geology and natural history of the Pacific basin.[28] More significantly, two expeditions actually attempted field research there, only one successfully: an effort cosponsored by the University of Southern California failed, while one undertaken in the name of the Smithsonian Institution in 1938 was in the news internationally—not because of the discoveries made on the remote atoll, but rather because President Franklin Delano Roosevelt went along.

The first expedition, cosponsored by USC and the Allan Hancock Foundation, visited the vicinity in 1934. A wealthy Californian and an avid yachtsman who eventually earned "the necessary papers to permit him to take command, as Master, of ships of any size on any ocean,"[29] in 1930 George Allan Hancock commissioned the Craig Shipbuilding Yards of Long Beach to build *Velero III,* a diesel-propelled, steel-hulled, 195-foot-long cruiser designed specifically for oceanographic research. It was an unusually sleek ship for its day, replete with a rakish flying bridge; and in addition to "regular equipment such as nets, seines, townets, diplets, diving helmet, harpoons, and fishing tackle," it also had "two sizes of dredges, a beam trawl, a sounding machine (as well as the fathometers in the pilothouse), 6 reversing water bottles, 12 deep-sea thermometers, several types of bottom samplers, and bottom 'core' apparatus."[30]

Captain Hancock took delivery of the new vessel in 1931 and personally conducted sea trials off southern California. Satisfied with the ship's performance, he took aboard several USC scientists, and on December 3 they set sail southward toward the Galapagos islands. They returned to Los Angeles two months later, having finished merely the first of ten Hancock-USC expeditions.

Velero III did not call at Clipperton on its maiden voyage; however, on its third excursion (December 30, 1933–March 14, 1934), Captain Hancock purposely placed the atoll on the research vessel's itinerary. "The 1934 Expedition," chronicler McLean Fraser says, "took quite a different route [from those previous], although it covered little new area. The first stop was made at Socorro Island (in the Revilla Gigedos), and the second in Clarion in the same group. From Clarion the course was set to Clipperton Atoll. . . . On the occasion of the only visit to this island [January 6, 1934], the surf was too heavy to attempt landing. Dredging was attempted to the east of the atoll, but the slope was so steep and the bottom so rocky that the attempt met with little success."[31]

The expedition settled for a single wide-angle photograph of the island, featuring the Rock and, quite some distance to the southwest, a lone palm tree. *Velero III* then sailed on to the Galapagos. However disappointed shipboard scientists may have been that they were unable to set foot on the remote anomalous atoll, only Waldo Schmitt among them ever returned, and, through him, numerous naturalists became acquainted with the place.

Born in Washington, D.C., in 1887, Waldo LaSalle Schmitt had joined the U.S. Department of Agriculture at age twenty as an "aid in economic biology," being promoted to scientific assistant with the U.S. Bureau of Fisheries three years later. In 1913 he became a naturalist with the U.S. National Museum's Division of Marine Invertebrates. In 1915 he was named assistant curator of the division and in 1920, curator. Meanwhile, attending college mostly part-time, he earned a B.S. in zoology at George Washington University in 1913, an M.A. at the University of California in 1916, and a Ph.D. at George Washington University in 1922.

Alternating curatorial duties with field research, in 1924–25 and again in 1930–32, Schmitt worked at the Smithsonian's Tortugas Marine Laboratory off the Florida keys to study crustaceans, his specialty. From 1925 to 1927, he was the Smithsonian's Walter

Rathbone traveling scholar in South America. From 1931 through 1935, he sailed with Hancock-USC Pacific expeditions, in 1937 with the Smithsonian-Hartford expedition to the West Indies, and in 1938 with Franklin Delano Roosevelt who, while "vacationing from the heavy cares of the Presidency,"[32] made his second trip to Clipperton island.

An "old salt," Roosevelt, who had been Woodrow Wilson's assistant navy secretary, thoroughly enjoyed the sea—sometimes taking the presidential yacht *Potomac* as far south as the Bahamas on weekend cruises. Crippled by polio and his strength increasingly sapped by the heavy demands of office, he alternated therapeutic visits to Warm Springs, Georgia, with refreshing deep-sea fishing excursions to tropical climes aboard U.S. Navy vessels. For instance, the previous May he had cruised the Caribbean aboard USS *Philadelphia*.

However unlikely it may seem, like Schmitt of the Smithsonian, President Roosevelt had previously been to the atoll, but not for scientific purposes. Accompanied by his sons John and Franklin, Jr., during the summer of 1934, FDR sailed "almost 12,000 miles through the Caribbean and to Portland, Oreg., by way of Hawaii."[33] Along the way, according to an unidentified Associated Press reporter on board, "The President scanned the map of the Pacific and noted that his course took him near Clipperton Island, where the deep-sea fishing is reported to be excellent. He ordered that the [USS] *Houston* head for this little dot of land in the ocean, and present plans are to anchor near it Tuesday afternoon. If the weather permits, he will try the fishing."[34]

Clipperton Rock was sighted dead ahead on Tuesday, 17 July 1934, and Roosevelt "came on deck and viewed the approach with great interest . . . [but] because of the heavy seas the President did not undertake any fishing." Nevertheless, the ship launched two boats, and those aboard soon discovered "that there are even more fish around Clipperton than there had been found at Cocos. The catches were heavy but in many instances sharks caught the fish before they could be landed." Franklin, Jr., hooked two large tunas "but lost all but the heads to attacking sharks—this in spite of a Marine rifleman who did effective work whenever a shark came near the surface." As the boats were recalled at midafternoon, young Roosevelt was caught up in a "fight with a shark which was believed to be a tuna until brought to the surface. The resulting delay caused some concern on board [the cruiser *Houston*] for fear . . . [young Franklin's] boat had broken down in [the island's] heavy surf."[35]

Houston reached Hawaii on the twenty-fourth and returned to the mainland a week later, the president on board. By then he had seen strategic value in the atoll, and not long afterward he asked the navy to investigate its possible use.[36] Seeing little value in the idea, the Navy department dragged its feet.

However significant it would later become to him and his administration, Roosevelt failed to return in October 1935 when, again aboard *Houston,* he sailed nearby on a voyage between Seattle and Charleston, via the Panama Canal, with a party that included Interior Secretary Harold Ickes and WPA boss Harry Hopkins, whom FDR had dragged along "to compel the quarrelsome boys to learn to fish and to love each other."[37] They wet lines together off Baja California and Cocos island, both regular Roosevelt haunts, but not off Clipperton—at least not in 1935.

Thereafter, the president's involvement with this most curious of places increased steadily until, at the time of his death, it occupied an inordinate amount of his time and energy. It all began casually enough.

In 1938, Roosevelt purposely sailed to the island, taking with him a naturalist to inspect it and other biologically curious landfalls, such as the Galapagos, which they also planned to visit. Of this outing James Roosevelt, the president's oldest son and sometime cruisemate, reported:

Father was sensitive to the public relations aspects of these long cruises. . . . On his 1938 cruise aboard the Houston, *Father took along a scientist, Dr. Waldo L. Schmitt, and turned collector for the Smithsonian Institution. He provided the Smithsonian with a rare specimen of* Seriola dumerili, *alias the Great Amberjack, and many new species of fish and plant life. A number of items were named after Pa, which tickled him as much as if he had carried a hitherto Republican county in an election. Among these were* Pycnomma roosevelti *(a fish);* Merriamium roosevelti *(a sponge);* Thalamita roosevelti *(a crab);* Neanthes roosevelti *(a worm);* Octopus roosevelti *(a mollusk); and even a new species of royal palm which became* Rooseveltia frankliniana.[38]

The cruise commenced on July 16, 1938, at the conclusion of a western whistle-stop tour to lend a hand to New Deal Democrats running in the primaries. Roosevelt boarded *Houston,* this time at the San Diego Navy Yard, and as commander-in-chief ordered the cruiser and its escort vessel, USS *McDougal* (an *O'Brien*-class destroyer), to put to sea, bound for Florida by way of the Panama Canal. Along the way, *Houston* became America's third warship to land an armed force on Clipperton island—after *Cleveland* in 1914 and *Yorktown* in 1917—and far from the last to do so.

The president's official party included assorted acquaintances, aides, bodyguards, cronies, reporters, and, of course, one lone scientist—Schmitt of the Smithsonian.[39] The president and his companions trolled for albacore, bonito, marlin, sailfish, and wahoo—wagering modestly among themselves as to who was "kingfisher." As the task force steamed southward toward the Galapagos, their ultimate objective in the Pacific, *Presidente* Lázaro Cárdenas greeted Roosevelt by radiogram, granting the American flotilla unrestricted anchorage in Mexican waters. The government of Costa Rica similarly extended the courtesy of a visit to its Isla del Coco, as had been requested weeks earlier by the State department. Curiously, permission from the French to land at Clipperton island was apparently neither sought nor offered—foreshadowing future Roosevelt policy toward the atoll.

Over the course of a week, the flotilla anchored near Cerros island, off Baja California and off Socorro island in the Revilla Gigedos, before setting course for Clipperton. At each of these places fishermen sallied forth in the ship's boats to test the waters, and their luck was good. "Basil O'Connor, a frequent fishing companion of the President's, got tired of hauling 'em in and secretly had his hooks straightened out. . . . Not so the President. He loved to drag in fish," Secret Service chief Michael Reilly said. "I saw him fight for two and three-quarter hours to land a 250-pound shark. The rest of us just cut our lines when we were unlucky enough to hook into a shark, but the Boss was determined about his fishing as he was about everything else."[40]

Houston reached Clipperton island on 21 July, the atoll "sighted [at] about 1000 [hours] just as it emerged from a curtain of rain deposited by a passing squall." Because of a lack of charted soundings, both *Houston* and *McDougal* spent about an hour in search of bottom before finding anchorage off the northeast point. "Despite a somewhat choppy sea and moderate swells the Presidential Party took to the fishing boats shortly after luncheon. . . . Hardly had the President's boat shoved off from the *Houston* before he had hooked and landed a 60-pound shark—a forerunner of the type which played havoc with fishing tackle and spoiled, after a fashion, the day's sport. For, hardly had one hooked a Grouper, Jack or Yellow Tail before it was snatched bodily by a voracious Shark."[41]

Since some money and much pride were at stake, "much argument ensued at the dinner table this night as to whether or not a shark was, in reality, a fish, and should or should not count in the day's catch as to size and quantity." Colonel Edmin M. Watson, FDR's army aide-de-camp, "contended that the 'revolting Shark' was not *edible* (none contested that statement!) and therefore should not be counted. Arguments pro and con were settled when the President," who had caught several of them, "announced his decision that now and henceforth Sharks *would* be counted as part of the day's catch."[42]

Meanwhile, as the presidential party fished, "Dr. Schmitt, accompanied by a large voluntary party of officers and men," including Reilly of the White House, "had landed on the Island through the surf and conducted a bit of scientific exploring. Among the trophies brought back by this party were a small black and young pig, which fell to the unerring marksmanship of Lieut[enant]-Commander [T. J.] Kelly,"[43] *Houston*'s executive officer. Schmitt pickled assorted specimens of the island's regular flora and fauna for future scrutiny, but "the wild pig," Roosevelt later informed Eleanor, "we duly ate!"[44] It was the first of *Kinkora*'s progeny known to have been slaughtered.

Considering "the calamitous loss of a large amount of fishing gear" to "omnipresent sharks . . . all hands were pleased when, at 1719 [hours] this day the Presidential Detachment got under way and headed southeastward for the Galapagos Islands."[45] However much Roosevelt's fishing cronies were delighted to sail on— because the "sharks . . . [had] utterly ruined the fishing, . . . not only . . . destroy[ing] the few fish that were hooked, but . . . [also] the tackle as soon as it was put into the water"[46]—Schmitt of the Smithsonian later reported to the scientific community that he considered his landing on "this isolated and seldom-visited coral island . . . [to be] one of the high lights of the cruise. . . ."⁴⁷

For the navy, Roosevelt's fishing excursion to the atoll had not been entirely a lark. An unidentified journalist reported to readers on the mainland that "Three seaplanes piloted by Aviation Cadets W. C. Jakeman, J. P. Jones, and A. J. Dugan made a two-hour survey flight over the island and surrounding waters" for intelligence purposes. According to the reporter, the skipper of *Houston* even "discovered an error in Clipperton's present charted location. Captain [George Nathan] Baker, taking astronomical observations, said Clipperton Island apparently was one mile southeast of the position shown on [Navy] charts. Uncertainty of its location long has made the island a menace to boats."⁴⁸

The presidential party reached the Galapagos on July 24. They fished and explored thereabouts for a week before sailing back northward to Cocos island for a two-day visit. On August 5 *Houston* and *McDougal* passed through the Panama Canal, entered the Caribbean, and set course for the Gulf coast of the United States. On 9 August, at the conclusion of the 5,888-mile cruise, they docked at the Pensacola Navy Yard, Colonel Watson being declared winner of the fishing derby.

Upon his return to Washington, Schmitt of the Smithsonian shared specimens of plants and animals with colleagues around the country who identified and classified them, writing up the results of their studies. During the next several years these investigations were serialized in *Smithsonian Miscellaneous Collections*. All told, fourteen monographs resulted, ten of which mention the atoll.⁴⁹

About then, professional and lay historians likewise became interested in the place. Foremost among these was George Emra Nunn, who, while a graduate student at the University of California, had studied Ferdinand Magellan's reported route across the Pacific.

A pioneer in the arcane field of historical geography, Nunn was fascinated by such seemingly trivial details as precisely what did Columbus know before he set sail for the Orient, and exactly where did Magellan go on his epic voyage? Nunn's doctoral thesis at the University of California, "The Geographical Conceptions of Columbus," was published in 1924 by the prestigious American

Geographical Society. Ten years later the Society's quarterly ran his article-length study of Magellan's route. As previously mentioned, in it Nunn concluded that Magellan's "San Pablo and Tiburones [islands] may be identified with Clipperton and Clarion islands. . . ."⁵⁰

Six months after Nunn's findings on Magellan appeared in print, *New Outlook* published C. Edward Morris's article, "The Island the World Forgot," which the magazine correctly touted as "the first time in detail the story of a tragic incident when for a little while the island was completely forgotten."⁵¹

Apparently while vacationing in Mexico, Morris had heard about the atoll and its sensational past. On returning to the United States, he researched the tale as best he could, even securing from the U.S. Navy copies of relevant reports from *Cleveland* and *Yorktown*—including those authored by Captain Harlan P. Perrill and Lieutenant Raymond E. Kerr.

Inexplicably, both failed to confirm the salacious tales he had heard in Mexico. Morris wrote:

> *Commander Perrill does not mention that a month [sic] after Captain de Arnaud and his companions were drowned a tropical hurricane swept over Clipperton, destroying many of the flimsy structures in which the colonists lived. Too weakened by hunger, disease and despair to rebuild extensively, the colonists lived largely in the open for some time thereafter, foraging for food and shelter almost like wild animals.*
>
> *Nor does his report refer to a period toward the end of the survivors' ordeal during which the 3 women finally were forced to do the bidding of a half-mad despot, a Negro lighthouse keeper, the last adult male survivor, who made himself King of Clipperton by cornering all of the firearms and forcing the others to obey his every command.*
>
> *But that macabre chapter in the history of the island is freely told up and down the Mexican coast between Salina Cruz and Acapulco, the homes of the families whose relatives are buried on Clipperton.*
>
> *The local version is that before the arrival of the Yorktown, one of the women, mastering her fear of the Negro, crept to the hut where the tyrant slept and crushed his skull with the blunt end of an axehead. Whether that lurid detail is true or not the writer does not*

know, and at this distance, measured in miles and years, it is difficult to check upon its authenticity. There is no record in Salina Cruz of any criminal proceedings against the woman who the story says swung the axe.[52]

Critical of Perrill's version of events though he may have been, Morris quoted it and Kerr's companion report extensively in his seven thousand-word effort to tell "the whole story of the atoll" from the time of its discovery "by one of Cortes's captains in 1523" to the present, 1934, when, according to Morris, Mexico still balked at accepting Victor Emmanuel's arbitration decision.

Relying principally on newspaper accounts, Morris pieced together some of the island's history, including fragments of its early exploitation by American and British capitalists and even a few details of Mexican occupation since 1897; however, as with the tale of Álvarez's demise, much of Morris's version of events was incorrect. For instance, regarding the visit of the French cruiser *Duguay-Touin,* he wrote: "The Stars and Stripes were lowered and the tri-color of the French Republic raised in their place."[53]

Morris could not explain "Exactly how and why the Clipperton colony came to be abandoned to a terrible doom by those who established it, and who were responsible for its welfare on an island more than 600 miles offshore from Mexico's Pacific coast, which was known to be quite incapable of supporting human life. . . ."[54]

Captain Harlan Page Perrill could, and did. Retired and living in Point Loma, California, when that issue of *New Outlook* hit newsstands, he happened upon Morris's article and immediately wrote the editor of the magazine to "congratulate you upon your success in printing it." Perrill asserted, "I consider that rescue of the colonists from the desolate island one of the highlights of my naval career."[55]

In answer to Morris's questions, Perrill reported: "The reason the colonists were forgotten was that soon after the shipwrecked crew of the *Nokomis* were taken off, Huerta was deposed, and whenever it was suggested to the Carranza government that supplies be sent to the island, the answer was, 'They are Huertistas. Let them die.' " As to his omission of the "lurid details" regarding Álvarez, Perrill admitted: "The most dramatic part of the story was not stressed [sic] in my official report as I was afraid of the effects it might have upon the fortunes of Tirza Randon."[56]

Although he unquestionably knew that Morris's version of events was riddled with errors, Perrill challenged not one word; instead, he merely confirmed that Álvarez had brutalized the women and that Tirza Randon had finally killed him. Perrill added that there were no doubts whatsoever as to events. "Lieutenant Kerr had seen the body in the hut and knew he had just been killed."[57] Perrill also failed to mention in his letter to *New Outlook* that his omission of those facts from his official reports was contrary to navy regulations and that, had it been discovered at the time, he might well have been court-martialed.

Possible repercussions did not deter Charlotte K. (Mrs. Harlan P.) Perrill from sharing with the world her husband's correspondence concerning the dramatic story. Her interest in publication doubtlessly stirred by Morris's article, she penned an introduction to five of her husband's letters (18 through 21 July 1917), the whole piece aggregating about four thousand words, and submitted it along with photographs of the women and children "taken by the rescuing party" to the *Proceedings* of the Naval Institute at the U.S. Naval Academy, which published it in 1937. Those letters have languished there ever since, for the most part overlooked by researchers.

Karl Baarslag, a popular writer who published *Islands of Adventure* (1941), certainly did not know of their existence. Otherwise he likely would have used them to spice up his skimpy, error-filled six-page version of "The island the world forgot, [whose] brief history is surely one of the strangest and most tragic of all the isles beyond the horizon."[58] This version appears to have been entirely based on Morris's account.

About this time an anonymous journalist understandably confused the light keeper story and the island's historical names. On January 19, 1935, the Associated Press reported that French cruiser *Jeanne d'Arc* would soon depart Los Angeles "to take formal possession of the tropical Isle of Passion, 1,300 miles west of the Panama Canal, as a naval landing field in the Pacific. The desolate, coral-ringed formation, about one mile square [sic], has in its center a lagoon ideal for use by seaplanes."[59]

As it ran in the New York *Times,* the story reported:

> *Called Clipperton Island on the maps, it was the scene years ago of a weird tale from which it derived its name, "the Isle of Passion."*
> *A mad Negro reputedly proclaimed himself king of the island after all the other male inhabitants had perished. He decreed that all women on the island become his harem. One night one of the women crushed his skull with a hammer.*
> *The United States gunboat* Yorktown *stopped there in 1917 and discovered the tragedy. The body of the "king" remained unburied. Twenty rude crosses marked the graves of other inhabitants.*[60]

At that time, such details as "twenty rude crosses," a "hammer" as the murder weapon, and Álvarez's unburied remains could have come only from Morris's article and from Perrill's epilogue, both of which had appeared in *New Outlook* the previous fall—sources not attributed by the nameless reporter who, understandably, linked "Isle of Passion" with the light keeper's sexual appetites rather than historical names associated with both the French and the Spanish.

And if the pen frequently skipped over Clipperton island, the sword sometimes wavered. Under orders "to present itself off the island and place at the summit of its famous Rock the French flag and an official seal" that had been specially minted in Paris to commemorate Victor Emmanuel's arbitration award, French man-of-war *Jeanne d'Arc* had sailed from Panama in 1934 with Captain M. Y. Donval in command. "Alas!" reported French passenger and journalist Jean La Veyrie early in 1935, "Neither Commander Donval nor any other person among his crew was able to land. Strong wind gusts created crashing, foamy breakers making access to the shore absolutely impracticable. They got as close as possible with the boats and rafts, [but] it was a waste of time: an impossible 'barrier' forbade one to insist on passing the obstacle. So, no French[man] was able to disembark in the inhospitable 'colony,' although for two days they tried everything they could."[61]

Her mission not accomplished, *Jeanne d'Arc* returned to Clipperton island two months later. Years afterward, Lieutenant M. L.

Gauthier, the ship's executive officer, reported to readers of the French journal *Annales Hydrographique:*

> Jeanne d'Arc *pursued its cruise along the coast of California and Canada and then returned to the island on the morning of January 26, 1935. Big rolling waves of almost three meters in height crashed against the north coast, but a landing place was found on the southwest coast [near the abandoned Pacific Phosphate pier]. The same day the national flag [of France] was raised atop the Rock and a [new] bronze plaque sealed in a fault on the east face of the Rock; the date on the plaque [2 Decembre 1934] refers to the first passage of the vessel in sight of the island. The 27th of January was devoted to hydrographic work, but the operations of the officers who landed on the island were limited by a short stay, from 10 A.M. to 4 P.M.*[62]

Gauthier said that the landing party took three astronomical fixes while on the atoll to refine "the American map by Henning [sic], Master Mariner"; collected several specimens of vegetation, guano, rocks, and lagoon water for later analysis elsewhere; and snapped a few photographs, including one showing the Tricolor atop the flagpole, beside the long-extinguished, French-made beacon at the very apex of the Rock. The landing party then returned to the ship. The following day, "*Jeanne d'Arc* completed three complete tours of the island by measuring the depths with the help of an acoustic sounder. . . ."[63]

Meanwhile, on June 12, 1936, in Paris, French President Albert LeBrun had proclaimed Clipperton island to be an integral part of French Oceanica. Four years later, "just prior to the fall of France," the République awarded "exclusive and exceptional rights" on the atoll to one Charles Michelson, lasting for "thirty years after the conclusion of the present war."[64] Michelson apparently never exercised his rights, exceptional as they might have been.

Notes

1. "Clipperton island flag," p. 1.

2. For examples, see works by Fenwick; Gross; Hackworth (1940, 1943); and McDowell. For a contemporary evaluation of the case by an eminent Latin American historian, see Hackett, pp. 466–67.

3. "Victor Emmanuel III," p. 791.

4. *Ibid.,* p. 789.

5. Quoted in *ibid.*

6. Roncagli, p. 821.

7. Mexico, *Isla de la Pasión,* pp. 32–36.

8. Toniolo, p. 100.

9. Morris, p. 35.

10. Victor Emmanuel III, "Arbitral award," p. 394; or, Victor Emmanuel III, "Decision," p. 98.

11. Victor Emmanuel III, "Decision," p. 96; Victor Emmanuel III, "Arbitral award," p. 303.

12. Mexico, *Isla de la Pasión,* pp. 32–33.

13. Victor Emmanuel III, "Decision," p. 97; Victor Emmanuel III, "Arbitral award," p. 394.

14. *Ibid.*

15. Dickinson, p. 131.

16. Cassels, p. 381.

17. Morris, p. 33.

18. "Awards Pacific isle to France," p. 10.

19. "Seeks delay on island," p. 6.

20. "Cession urged on Mexico," p. 5.

21. "Senators of Mexico accept loss of isle," p. 6.

22. "Mexicans vote to buy isle," p. 12.

23. "Mexico; France to get almost forgotten island," p. 16.

24. *Ibid.*

25. "Cession of island to France delayed," p. 14.

26. Holstein, p. 489.

27. Quoted in U.S. State Department, *Foreign relations of the United States; diplomatic papers, 1945: Europe* (1968), IV, p. 786. In fact, the names of all offshore islands were struck from the Mexican Constitution, leaving Article 42 to read: "The national territory comprises the integral parts of the federation and also the adjacent islands in both seas." See Mexico, *Constitution of . . . 1917,* Section II, Article 42.

28. See works by Chubb; Davis; and Owen.

29. Fraser, "Historical introduction," p. 22. As a young man early in the twentieth century, Hancock thoroughly explored the waters off southern California and the Baja peninsula. After World War I he had custom-constructed *Velero II,* a 125-foot, 195-ton diesel-powered cruiser. "With [it] in commission, a much more extensive expedition was soon initiated. Calls were made [in 1922] at Guadalupe Island, Cerros Island, Magdalena Bay, Cape San Lucas, Clarion Island, Clipperton Island, several points in the Gulf of California, Mazatlan and other points on the mainland coast of Mexico. . . ." (*Ibid.,* p. 21.) Nothing else of the 1922 visit is known.

30. *Ibid.,* p. 41.

31. *Ibid.,* pp. 51, 71. In addition to the captain and his crew, aboard ship were University of British Columbia zoologist C. McLean Fraser, who specialized in hydroids; Hancock Foundation zoologist John S. Garth, an expert on arthropods (insects, crustaceans); University of Nebraska zoologist Harold W. Manter, who studied fish parasites; ship's physician Edwin O. Palmer, M.D.; United States National Museum of Natural History (Smithsonian Institution) zoologist Waldo L. Schmitt, an authority on crustaceans (crabs, shrimp); University of Michigan botanist William Randolph Taylor, an expert on algae; and Hancock Foundation field collector Fred Ziesenhenne, who studied echinoderms (starfishes, sea urchins, sea cucumbers).

32. "Presidency; wahoos for McAdoo," p. 7.

33. *"Houston,"* III, 374.

34. "Roosevelt heads for Clipperton island," p. 34. See also, "Roosevelt stops at Clipperton," p. 1; and "Roosevelt watches naval 'hide and seek,' " p. 3.

35. USS *Houston,* "Presidential log," July 17, [1934], in Franklin D. Roosevelt Papers as President, O[fficial] F[ile] 200, Box 69, "USS *Houston,* July–Aug., '38" folder. See also USS *Houston* "Deck log," in U.S. Navy Records, Records Group (RG) 24 (National Archives).

36. F[ranklin] D[elano] R[oosevelt], untitled memorandum, December 3, 1942, in Roosevelt Papers as President, Personal File "PSF: Navy."

37. Sherwood, p. 78.

38. James Roosevelt *et al.,* p. 228.

39. Other presidential guests included Frederick B. Adams, a director of the Air Reduction Corporation and FDR's cousin by marriage; Commander (soon to be Captain and eventually Rear Admiral) Daniel J. Callaghan, U.S.N., FDR's naval aide; Stephen K. Early, FDR's personal secretary; Captain (later Vice Admiral and Surgeon General of the Navy) Ross T. McIntire, M.D., FDR's personal physician; D. Basil O'Connor, FDR's onetime New York law partner; Colonel (later Major General) Edwin M. "Pa" Watson, FDR's army aide; eight Secret Service agents, including Michael F. Reilly, head of the White House detail; H. M. Theurer, a postal inspector; and an unknown number of mostly anonymous correspondents serving as media pool, of whom only George E. Durno of the International News Service has been identified.

40. Reilly, p. 112.

41. [Daniel J. Callaghan], "The inspection cruise and fishing expedition of President Franklin D. Roosevelt on board USS Houston, 16 July 1938–9, August 1938," pp. 4–5, in Roosevelt Papers as President, O[fficial] F[ile] 200, Box 69, "USS Houston, July–Aug., '38" folder.

42. *Ibid.*

43. *Ibid.* In addition to Lieutenant Commander Kelly, *Houston* crew members that went ashore included Seaman Jack Barron, who served as Schmitt's assistant, and R. B. Thompson, "of the paymaster's clerical force, an experienced amateur photographer, [who assisted] . . . in taking pictures. . . ." (Schmitt, "Decapod," pp. 2, 4.) Neither Reilly nor McIntire mention the atoll in their published memoirs.

44. [F. D. Roosevelt], *F.D.R.; his personal letters,* IV, 799.

45. [Callaghan], "The inspection cruise," p. 5, in F. D. Roosevelt Papers as President.

46. Schmitt, "The presidential cruise," pp. 7, 10.

47. *Ibid.* Afterward, Schmitt would investigate the natural economy of Alaskan king crabs for the U.S. Fish and Wildlife Service (1940); and he would accompany Smithsonian expeditions to South America (1939, 1941–43), the Belgian Congo, Egypt, and the Sudan (1955), the Caribbean (1956, 1958, 1959), Tahiti and the Society islands (1957), Yucatan (1960), and the Bahamas (1961). From 1943 to 1947, he served as the Museum of Natural History's head curator of biology, being head of zoology from 1947 until his retirement ten years later, when he was named research associate of the Smithsonian Institution.

48. "Roosevelt lucky off Clipperton," p. 19.

49. See works by Bartsch and Rehder; A. H. Clark; Hartman; Hyman; Killip; Schmitt (1939, 1940); Shoemaker; W. R. Taylor; Wetmore; and G. W. Wharton. The first crustacean authority ever to visit Clipperton island, Schmitt collected numerous specimens and, once back in his laboratory in Washington, personally identified ten species—two of which were new to science. One, actually a subspecies of a marine crab common to tropical North Pacific waters, he called *Crangon hawaiiens clippertoni;* the other Schmitt named *Thalamita roosevelti,* and he included a detailed description of it in his monograph on decapods. However unique such Clipperton island flora and fauna as *T. roosevelti* might have been, only one of the Smithsonian's presidential cruise monograph series was devoted exclusively to it—or, more precisely, to its birds. See Wetmore.

50. Nunn, "Magellan's route," p. 633.

51. Editor's note, in Morris, p. 31.

52. Morris, p.32.

53. *Ibid.,* p. 35.

54. *Ibid.,* p. 31.

55. H. P. Perrill, p. 4.

56. *Ibid.*

57. *Ibid.,* p. 5.

58. Baarslag, p. 295.

59. "Macabre isle of passion," II, 1. See also, "Barren reef may be international pawn," p. 7.

60. "Macabre isle of passion," II, 1.

61. La Veyrie, p. 39.

62. Gauthier, p. 8.

63. *Ibid.*, pp. 10–11. "Petrographic studies," Gauthier says, "were performed according to the plan established by M. Alfred Lacroix" and resulted in "samples brought back to him, which the eminent mineralogist analyzed," (*Ibid.*, pp. 11–12) along with similar samples from Easter and Pitcairn islands of the South Pacific. Lacroix published the results of these analyses in 1939. In the case of Clipperton island, he confirmed the 1898 study by English chemist J. J. H. Teall, which had identified the Rock as a trachyte. Like his countryman Victor Kervéguen, whose evaluation of the atoll had preceded him, Lacroix concluded that the coral beds (a sample from which he found to be 78.09 percent calcium phosphate)—given the island's isolation and resultant high transportation costs—were insufficiently pure to be valuable commercially. Perhaps because of Lacroix's negative report, no Frenchman called at Clipperton island again until World War II. By then, it had been occupied by the U.S. Navy.

64. R. L. Connolly, "Memorandum for the Chief of Staff," December 18, 1942, in Roosevelt Papers as President, Map Room Collection, Box 162, "Air Base, Clipperton Island" folder.

9

The Clipperton Island International Airport: A Tale of War and Commerce 1942–1944

However much the United States Department of State had ignored Clipperton island over the years, the nation's military strategists had not. Since the turn of the century, war planners had recognized the atoll's strategic significance—so near the Panama Canal—and consequently included it within their defense perimeter. That posture propelled the gunboat *Yorktown* there in 1917; afterwards, visits by American warships became routine. In time, the island's placement in an otherwise empty ocean made it valuable to aviators wishing to establish a new air route across the Pacific ocean; those economic possibilities rekindled President Roosevelt's interest in the place.

During the 1920s, military strategists in Washington envisioned the worst possible threat to American security as being posed by naval powers that might bring war to hemispheric waters, perhaps even invading them. In the Atlantic, only the navy of Great Britain (called "Red" by planners) was sufficiently large to pose significant danger, real or imagined, to the eastern U.S. seaboard; however, in the Pacific, the Japanese ("Orange"), who owned that ocean's largest fleet, obviously menaced many U.S. interests scattered in and around the Pacific. A Red-Orange alliance, however remote that possibility, offered a far graver danger to America and its Pacific empire. Consequently, strategists were directed "to develop a new plan which should provide . . . for an initial '*position in readiness*' along the west coast and the strategic triangle formed by Alaska, Hawaii, and Panama."[1]

Planners devised five scenarios, dubbed "Rainbows." These ranged from the United States fighting alone, to its being part of a great alliance. Rainbow Five (eventually renamed Plan Dog) essentially became American (and Allied) strategy during World War II: "the United States, Great Britain, and France . . . [would act] in concert to effect the defeat of Germany and Italy. A strategic defensive was to be maintained in the Pacific until success against the European continental Powers permitted the transfer of major forces to the Pacific for an offensive against Japan."[2]

Unlike World War I, when the atoll technically fell 100 miles outside of the Hawaii-Panama leg of the strategic triangle, Rainbow Five (aka Plan Dog) embraced everything north of 10°S latitude. Thus, Clipperton island became an American protectorate.

Its location and sovereignty accorded the atoll special significance. As far as the U.S. Army was concerned, "Panama, like Hawaii, feared attack mainly from Japan. To the east was a protective screen of islands extending from Florida to South America. There was no such barrier in the Pacific. The only islands on which defenses could be built were the Gálapagos, Cocos, and Clipperton."[3]

Least useful of these, according to Major General David L. Stone, commanding the Army's Panama Canal Department, was "Clipperton Island, which jutted up out of the open Pacific 2,000 miles to the northwest of Panama; but the fact that it was a European possession made it of interest."[4]

Perhaps; perhaps not. In September 1940, when the United Press wire service reported that Secretary of the Navy Frank Knox wanted to establish defenses on offshore Pacific islands such as Cocos and Clipperton, Roosevelt told journalists at an off-the-record ("on background—not for attribution") press briefing that he had seen to it that the wire service withdrew the story, implying that it had not been in the interest of national security. "It is something we don't want to talk about," the president explained, observing that the "other press associations did not carry it."⁵ Roosevelt said that his personal visits to those islands had convinced him that neither was truly suitable for military use.

Cocos, he said, "is a little bit of an island, with no harbor, and it comes straight out of the ocean, with these cliffs all around it. You couldn't possibly put a flying field on the island, it is physically impossible." As to the other place, he said "I suppose you cannot land on Clipperton Island more than a hundred days a year. The surf is too great. It is a litty bitty of a coral atoll, with a shallow pond in the middle of it, too shallow [sic] for airplanes to land on. . . ."⁶

The Japanese attack on Pearl Harbor changed everything, and American interest in and activity on and about the island increased markedly thereafter. In February 1942, navy brass recognized it as "strategically placed to cover trade routes along the coast of Mexico and Central America," but decided that the "physical characteristics of Clipperton Island render it unsuitable for any naval purpose of the United States."⁷

When informed of that opinion, President Roosevelt "remarked he could not 'wholly go along with it.' He stated that he recognized that it[s occupation] probably could not be done at the present time, but that we should keep in mind establishing a PBY [patrol bomber seaplane] patrol from there at such time as the plane situation would permit."⁸

Prior to such an establishment, the navy kept an eye on the atoll, just in case. The island's presence off the Central American coast obviously posed the possibility of a wide range of clandestine Axis uses, from submarine base to weather station. While the former was very unlikely, the latter was a real possibility. Reliable weather forecasts were of great significance to both sides during World War II. For example, the Germans "managed to set up an automatic weather station at the northern end of [Jan Mayen] island [a little-known dot of land in the Norwegian sea, north of Iceland], but it was soon destroyed. The Nazis set up these automatic stations in other remote places as well, and some of them went undetected. Remnants of a tiny unmanned station, planted by a U-boat in 1942, were discovered in 1981 on the Labrador coast. It [the station] had been used to transmit weather information to Nazi submarines in the North Atlantic."⁹

Early in 1942, USS *Atlanta*—a recently commissioned light

cruiser en route from the Canal zone to Pearl Harbor, under the command of Captain S. P. Jenkins—was diverted to Clipperton island to investigate the possibility of just such a secret Axis station operating on the remote atoll. At 0954 hours on 17 April, *Atlanta*'s deck watch sighted Clipperton Rock at a distance of 13 miles, bearing 308° true, and the warship changed course and made directly for the promontory. Eleven minutes later the watch spotted a two-masted schooner lying to off the northeast point, and Captain Jenkins ordered "General Quarters," or preparation for any contingency, including combat.

Battle ready, *Atlanta*'s log says, the warship "Changed course to 265° T to intercept [the] schooner . . . [which] hoisted American colors." A boarding party under Lieutenant P. T. Smith soon set out in the number two whaleboat "to visit and search [the] schooner," *Atlanta* meanwhile securing from General Quarters. Within half an hour, Smith and his party had returned and reported to Jenkins that the little ship was the "*Skidblanir* out of San Pedro, California. Master: R. H. Walsh. Crew 5; cargo, Shark Liver. Seamen and cook aboard, captain, mate, and seaman ashore on Clipperton Island."[10] Precisely what they were doing there was not reported.

Atlanta reconnoitered by steaming around the island at a safe distance, seamen carefully scanning the coral ring with binoculars. Finding "no suspicious conditions,"[11] Captain Jenkins resumed course for Pearl Harbor, and for the war. Later that year his warship participated in the battles of Midway and Guadalcanal, being so severely damaged in the latter that it was scuttled.

Meanwhile, late in 1942, Clipperton's importance to the U.S. government increased markedly when the Australian Legation in Washington, D.C., approached the State department "concerning air routes across the Pacific." Citing the vulnerability of "present communications by air with New Zealand and Australia across the Pacific," which were dependent on "a single air route . . . by way of Hawaii . . . in the vicinity of Japanese occupied territory," the Australian government proposed to investigate

an alternative route across the Pacific . . . hundreds of miles south of the present route . . . from a point to be chosen upon the West Coast of North America (e.g., Acapulco) to Clipperton Island, a French possession some 700 miles off the coast of Mexico. From there the route lies through the Marquesas Islands (2,160 miles), thence to Tahiti in the Society Islands (750 miles), thence to Aitutaki Island in the Cook Islands (620 miles). From the Cook Islands the route lies to Auckland (1,680 miles) and thence to Sydney (1,200 miles). Although by this route the distance across the Pacific is slightly longer than by way of Hawaii, the total distance from Washington by way of Miami and Clipperton is approximately 800 miles less.[12]

The Australians acknowledged that most of the necessary bases and facilities for such an alternative route did not yet exist, and they requested American cooperation in surveying the sites to assess feasibility. The State department forwarded the request to the White House, which sent copies for evaluation to the army chief of staff, General George C. Marshall, and to the chief of naval operations, Admiral Ernest J. King.

On October 2, 1942, while the navy studied the matter, the War department informed the secretary of state that "the project was not justified at this time."[13] Two months later, Captain R. L. Connolly of Admiral King's staff concurred:

> *The question as to the establishment of a trans-Pacific air route via Clipperton Island and the Marquesas is not a new one. It first saw the light of day as a result of a thorough independent study on the part of the Bureau of Aeronautics, who rejected the route as infeasible [sic].*
>
> *. . . in February, 1942, this [same] route [had been] recommended to Mr. [Frank] Knox [Roosevelt's Navy secretary] through political channels. It appears that Mr. Charles Michelson has exclusive and exceptional rights on Clipperton which he obtained just prior to the fall of France and which extend for a period of thirty years after the conclusion of the present war. As a result of an investigation following the offer of Mr. Michelson, the Director of Plans Division recommended against the acquisition or use of Clipperton Island.*
>
> *. . . it develops that the [Australian] project was the proposal of one Captain T. [sic] G. Taylor, an Australian long connected with commercial aviation. . . .*
>
> *Without wanting to stress the post war air transportation question,*

it can be pointed out that the British have made many attempts to get
us to build them an air route between the British Isles and Australia
which would by-pass the United States.[14]

King forwarded Connolly's report to the White House, adding:
"There is serious doubt as to the feasibility of constructing any
kind of air base on Clipperton Island. . . . I therefore recommend
that the Australian Legation be informed . . . that it is deemed
best to decline the offer to share the responsibility with them and
with other Governments, for the survey and preparation of their
proposed trans-Pacific air route via Clipperton Island and the
Marquesas."[15]

However much sailors, like diplomats, preferred to ignore the
smelly, offbeat little atoll, ultimately President Roosevelt ordered
otherwise. Visualizing "that some kind of international police
force will come out of the war," in December 1942 he directed
his joint chiefs of staff to determine where " 'International Police
Force' air facilities [should] be located throughout the world . . .
without regard to current sovereignty."[16] While that study was
under way, he amended the assignment to include a list of "what
island bases we should seek to control after the war."[17]

Prodded by persistent presidential pressure, the navy's General
Board, which was responsible for overall Pacific strategy, within
the week forwarded to the White House through Navy Secretary
Knox a series of interim reports that it believed adequately addressed both subjects, "although the matter of post-war commercial aviation was not emphasized. . . ."[18] With respect to postwar
"International Police Forces and Air Bases," the General Board
recommended Clipperton island as one of several "tentative sites
for bases . . . to cover Panama."[19]

Ironically, Admiral King had meanwhile advised Admiral William D. Leahy, Roosevelt's wartime White House chief of staff: "It
appears that the proposition to develop a British all air route from
Great Britain to Australia, which will include stops at Bermuda,
Clipperton Island and the Marquesas, is being revived." After
pointing to his memorandum on the subject and to Connolly's
report, King concluded, "I do not believe the establishment of
such a route would contribute to the war effort."[20]

Whatever King's evaluation, Roosevelt clearly understood the long-term economic threat posed by a British air monopoly to the southwest Pacific. He confided to Secretary Knox in 1943 "that we should make up our minds now which individual islands, because of their geography and location, promise to be of value as commercial airports in the future, [and] . . . a board of commercial aviation experts should actually visit the islands we select as having possible value in the future." Furthermore, Roosevelt suggested, "It seems that Admiral [Richard E.] Byrd's experience would make him a particularly valuable member or head of the expedition."[21]

Richard Evelyn Byrd, Jr., was one of America's most celebrated contemporary heroes—a man of extraordinary accomplishments and seemingly selfless dedication to his country. In 1928, officially retired from the navy because of a wartime disability, he led the first major aerial survey of the South Pole. Cosponsored by the National Geographic Society and numerous wealthy patrons, Byrd put together a sophisticated expedition of scientists, engineers, mechanics, dogsled drivers, and aviators. For thirteen bitterly cold months, they lived and worked along the Ross sea at a base camp Byrd named "Little America." He personally flew several surveys, during which he discovered and mapped vast regions never before seen by man, areas that he formally claimed for the United States. In 1929, he and his crew were the first to fly over the South Pole. A few days later, an appreciative Congress by special act promoted him to the rank of rear admiral.[22]

When America entered World War II, the fifty-three-year-old retired admiral wrangled transfer from his billet as a consultant with the War department to the navy's Bureau of Aeronautics, where he believed he might make a contribution to the war effort, perhaps even fight. The fleet was still reeling from the devastating blow delivered by the Japanese at Pearl Harbor, and navy brass early in 1942 considered using air bases to leapfrog across the Pacific in order to carry the fight to the enemy—a fast, economical alternative to the huge outlay required to build sufficient ships to battle all the way to Tokyo bay. "What was needed," says one of Byrd's biographers, "was a survey of the islands of the south by some responsible and competent senior officer who knew an aileron from a rudder and a good island air base from a bad one."[23]

Byrd was naturally selected for the job. During the late spring and early summer of 1942, he and eight fellow officers had concluded a similar inspection of proposed bases at Palmyra, Tutuila, Upolu, Wallis, Tongatabu, Suva-Nandi, Efate, Nouméa, and Bora Bora in the South Pacific. On his return to Washington, the admiral penned a secret report and awaited action, but nothing happened. Then, "In the spring of 1943 President Roosevelt's active imagination seized upon the subject of postwar air routes across the Pacific, and he asked Secretary of the Navy James V. Forrestal [sic] to find out what islands of the southeast Pacific would be of special value as air bases."[24]

Actually, late in July 1943, the navy's General Board had finally concluded its own separate study of postwar Pacific island air bases and commercial aerodrome sites, originally called for by President Roosevelt in 1934, and the report was dutifully if belatedly forwarded to the White House. Having been advised by civilian aviators "that 2,100 sea miles is the longest single leg that can be flown with profitable pay load on board," the navy study concluded that

> there are two possible trans-Pacific air routes along which lie islands, within the above limits of commercial transport planes. . . . The northern route, and perhaps the more important under existing commercial trends, utilizes Clipperton island as an essential stop, with any American continental terminal. . . . The importance of . . . [Clipperton's] position is manifest; it provides the only point on the northern route from which the Marquesas can be reached in continuous flight. . . ."[25]

Roosevelt was not entirely satisfied. On July 29, he replied to Navy Secretary Knox that

> the assumption of 2100 sea miles is the longest single leg that can be flown with profitable pay load on board . . . probably is true today but the . . . development of planes will increase this distance by many hundreds of miles in the reasonably near future. . . . Therefore I do not want the committee of civilians who are to make a study of this route to be bound by existing probable distances. . . . I also note that the northern route is based on a flight from the Canal Zone to

Clipperton Island and thence to the Marquesas. This is a round-about flight. It should be based on a flight across Mexico to some place on the west coast of Mexico, and thence to Clipperton Island.[26]

Being "available to act as senior member of the group of air transport experts appointed to make the study,"[27] Byrd met personally with Roosevelt "to settle the confusion arising from the uncertainty as to just exactly what the President desires." The explorer learned "that the President wants a comprehensive survey made of the Pacific from the standpoint of postwar security and commercial aviation. . . . We will carry the ball," the admiral assured FDR's naval aide-de-camp Rear Admiral Wilson Brown, following the conference with the president, "getting under way and finishing this job as soon as practical."[28]

On the eve of his departure for Panama to meet the survey party, Byrd suddenly became concerned that the British, whom he knew to be interested in just such a trans-Pacific air route, might somehow learn of his mission. He telephoned Admiral Brown to clarify the matter of secrecy. Brown replied: "I had heard the President say repeatedly that . . . the islands of the Pacific should be open to commercial use by all nationalities and that, therefore, I believed that there was no need for secrecy about what we were doing, but that, on the other hand, we, of course, do not want any publicity."[29] Whatever Brown's impression of Roosevelt's intentions, details of Byrd's expedition remained top secret until 1959.

On 1 September 1943, Admiral King officially ordered Byrd "to assume direction of a survey and investigation of certain islands in the East and South Pacific in connection with national defense and commercial air bases. . . . This survey will include investigation of the air bases and prospective air base sites and routes from the standpoint primarily of National Defense and also of commercial use. After departure from Balboa [Panama] your approximate itinerary will be: GALAPAGOS, CLIPPERTON, MARQUESAS, TUAMOTU ARCHIPELAGO, HENDERSON ISLANDS, EASTER ISLAND and return to Balboa."[30]

Five days later, USS *Concord* (an *Omaha*-class light cruiser) sailed from Balboa carrying maps, charts, assorted tropical clothing, surveying paraphernalia including photographic equipment, camping gear, rubber boats, outboard motors, two jeeps and trailers, a landing craft vehicle (LCV), and a J2-5 observation airplane. In addition to Admiral Byrd, the survey board consisted of thirteen army, navy, and civilian air transportation experts.[31]

However serious the American government might have been about this mission, for the six civilians (nominated by the Airlines Committee for United States Air Policy and personally approved by the president), the survey was mostly a lark. American Airlines executive (later, Chairman of the Civil Aeronautics Board and Under Secretary of Commerce for Transportation in the Truman administration) D. W. Rentzel would insist that his company "wasn't interested in the Pacific." Instead, he later asserted that he and the others

> *were picked by President Roosevelt [to go along] for various reasons. None of us was particularly nautical minded, but we had vaulted positions on the ship. The captain was just completely submerged. The admiral ran the ship and everything on it.*
>
> *We used to eat up in the admiral's quarters nearly every night, and we talked about a lot of different things, but not necessarily about the trip. He would start the conversation by making some startling remark about an event of some kind, which really got everybody all riled up. We'd all talk big, and he enjoyed it. He liked that.*
>
> *And of course we'd advise him. For example, one day he said, "Well, do you think we ought to fly today?" The meteorologist [E. O. Meyer of American Airlines] would wet his finger, hold it up as if he were measuring the air to gauge the velocity of the wind, and say "Yep, let's go." So Byrd said to the captain who was all but suffering a nervous breakdown because of this trip, "Okay, put the aircraft on the water and take off."[32]*

On the night of 8 September 1943, *Concord* anchored in Aeolian bay, at South Seymour island in the Galapagos, and the following day Byrd's board inspected army and navy air bases already operating there. Work finished, *Concord* then set course for Clipperton island, arriving there at 0815 hours, 14 September.

The cruiser dropped anchor off the northeast point and, apparently unaware of the atoll's well-deserved reputation for danger, prepared to send a party ashore. An LCV loaded with surveying equipment, camping gear and supplies, and enlisted men, along with a whaleboat carrying the admiral and his official party, surfed ashore without incident at the old Oceanic Phosphate landing site. An ensign in the naval reserves who, for the duration of the secret mission, held the temporary rank of lieutenant commander, Rentzel was "armed with two six-shooters [and wore a] hard hat because we didn't know what [or who] we would find there, but of course we didn't find anything."[33]

While the survey team poked about the atoll's northeastern rim, the LCV returned to the ship for equipment, twice ferrying jeeps and rubber boats ashore. On its third trip, "the LCV bent a propeller shaft on a rock while backing off the beach, seriously enough to require hoisting aboard the cruiser for repairs."[34] Worse, "a seaman was nearly drowned when he was knocked off his feet by the heavy surf during the landing of supplies and jeeps. Byrd took over. He ordered a line anchored [offshore], which would be used to hold off the boat when it came near the beach and then to ease it into shore. Then he personally directed the landing of the LCV with the jeeps aboard."[35]

They explored the island thoroughly, both by foot and by jeep, and took soundings throughout the lagoon from a rubber boat, those efforts requiring fully two days' work. They laid out several possible airplane landing strips with flag markers and photographed the proposed runways from both land and air with still and motion-picture cameras. At twilight of the first evening, five sailors remained on shore overnight to observe the tide while the remainder of the party, including Byrd and his civilian experts, returned to the ship.

The next morning, as navy personnel resumed work and as "the admiral did his own thing," the civilians toured the atoll, walking around its perimeter counterclockwise. Rentzel and his companions inspected debris from shipwrecks, what remained of assorted human habitation, the mound of phosphates piled high by fertilizer companies anticipating global markets, and the Rock and its passageways.

Along the southwestern coast, between the Rock and the ruins of the Pacific Phosphate settlement, they encountered a stretch of beach that reached entirely across the coral rim from oceanside to the lagoon. There, stuck upright in the middle of the sand, was a six-foot-tall iron cross that "looked like it had been there a while, longer than ten years."[36] No grave site was discernible, and unaware of the story of the light keeper and his violent end, they did not investigate further.

Their mission completed, the survey party made preparations to depart. Byrd later wrote:

> The high surf pounding the landing place made embarkation hazardous. It was found that the breakers on the beach could be forecast by observing the time the breakers broke on a point a mile to the northwest. Sixty to 70 seconds elapsed between the time of break at this point and the time they reached the landing beach. Shortly before sunset on 16 September, practically all equipment had been disembarked by the use of rubber boats on a messenger line or by being towed through the surf to the LCV. In maneuvering into a more favorable position to evacuate personnel from the boat, the LCV parted the messenger line. Several attempts to carry the line out from the beach by rubber boat were prevented by unusually heavy surf capsizing the boat. It was then decided that the 15 members of the party ashore should remain overnight. The party had ample food and water, but no protection, other than an open fire, from the steady wind which blew through the night.
>
> On the morning of the 17th, the cruiser, which stood out to sea during the night, returned and lowered the whale boat to bring the personnel and the remaining gear on board. The surf was still running high, but by using a messenger line and rubber boats, all men and equipment were brought safely off. All was secured, and the ship set course for CLARION Island.[37]

Wind and swells were too heavy for landing at Clarion, so Byrd ordered *Concord* to San Diego, where it took on fuel and supplies sufficient for the long trek to the Marquesas. On 5 October, the ship anchored in Nuku Hiva's beautiful Taiohae bay, made famous by Herman Melville's *Typee* (1846). Resplendent in dress whites, Admiral Byrd went ashore to seek the cooperation of French authorities, but the administrator was absent, and his wife threatened to notify the Vichy government by radio of *Concord*'s arrival. Ignoring her protests, Byrd had the island's wireless transmitter disabled to prevent any lurking Japanese submarine from tuning in on their mission. Without permission, he also surveyed the place.

On 7 October, as they prepared to depart, *Concord* was rocked by a tremendous explosion, apparently caused by fumes from improperly stored aviation fuel, which somehow had ignited. Three sailors were blown overboard, one of whom was never found; all told, twenty-two men, including *Concord*'s executive officer, either died in the explosion or in fighting the fire that followed. To save the ship, the captain ordered its magazines flooded. No member of the special mission was injured.

Its steering severely damaged, *Concord* limped on to Anaho bay for temporary repairs, which required almost two weeks. Meanwhile, the survey party lounged comfortably in Tahiti. Their respite on that tropical paradise, amid lovely, relatively uninhibited native women, who catered to the Americans' every delight, was all too brief. Life was so pleasant that "not even Admiral Byrd wanted to leave."³⁸

Eventually, though, the top-secret survey resumed and was completed, *Concord* returning to Balboa 24 November. There the admiral wrote a detailed report that plotted six possible air routes across the Pacific, to either New Zealand or Australia, three of which would use the atoll: Clipperton–Nuku Hiva ("the most efficient of all southern routes, and more efficient than the present Hawaiian route to Auckland, [and] after Route 4 [South Seymour–Easter–Henderson island], the shortest critical leg"); Clipperton–Puka Puka ("with New Orleans as the eastern terminal, this route is more efficient than 4 and less than 2 [Clipperton–Nuku Hiva]"); and Clipperton–Fangahina ("the most inexpensive combined land-plane and seaplane route except for Route 5 [South Seymour–Fangahina]."³⁹

While observing that Clipperton was "French-owned," Byrd—perhaps still chafing from his encounter with obstructionist Vichy French on Nuku Hiva—made no mention whatsoever of possible diplomatic consequences of U.S. occupation. Leaving that to others, he evaluated the place solely for aviation purposes.

Byrd noted that although the atoll "lies within the intertropical front from July to November, during which period low ceilings, poor visibility and turbulence may be expected," experience elsewhere had shown that operations were feasible in areas similarly affected. Byrd stated that three land runways could be constructed on Clipperton: "one prevailing wind runway, 5,300 feet long by 300 feet wide, along an approximate NE-SW bearing, could be located along the northwestern part; a second prevailing wind runway in the southeastern part of the island, 7,000′ × 500′, azimuth 50°; and a 'no-wind' runway, 9,600 feet long by 300 feet wide, at approximately a 110° bearing, could be located on the northerly shore." He added that it was "not possible to construct a 10,000-foot runway in the direction of the prevailing winds. . . ."[40]

The lagoon could provide both shelter for ships and landing site for seaplanes, but at considerable cost to the unique island. Byrd noted: "Considerable dredging will be necessary to provide a 10-foot depth . . . [for safe seaplane operations], but the materials so obtained can be used as fill for landplane runways." Moreover, since there was no channel into the lagoon, a passageway needed to be cut through the rim of the island to move a dredge and other equipment into place. "By deepening and widening this pilot channel to accommodate supply ships and tankers, discharging may be done in the quiet of the lagoon."[41]

While the creation of a combined landplane and seaplane base at Clipperton island would be a major undertaking, Byrd concluded, it was certainly possible—provided the government was prepared to pay the bill. He calculated the cost of a seaplane base at $3,640,000, and that of a combined land-sea operation at $21,906,000. In the latter case, construction "would require 3 years."[42]

Byrd's five-volume "Report of Certain Pacific Islands by Special Mission" (December 1943) was submitted to Admiral King, who passed it without comment to Navy secretary Knox, who left it on his desk to be handled by his successor, James Forrestal. Apparently unaware of the president's personal interest in the matter, Forrestal neglected to forward it to the White House until the following June, almost six months later, suggesting in his cover note that its contents should forever remain "secret."[43]

Meanwhile, in a separate "Dear Franklin" letter—penned in mid-April because the admiral was well aware of Roosevelt's "great interest in what islands and other areas we should get control of after the war"—Byrd wrote the president:

My study shows that you were right—that you were years ahead of all of us, even those concentrating on the overall aspects of post-war strategy and commerce.

Not until I had made a thorough analysis of the whole problem did I fully comprehend the reasons that brought you to consider this matter of such transcendent importance to the future of this nation.

My findings (arrived at objectively, I can assure you) show that you were entirely correct about Clipperton and the strategic and commercial value of certain key islands in the Tuamotu, Marquesas and Society Groups, as well as about the feasibility of new air routes to the Southwest Pacific. There can be no question about this.[44]

Precisely what Roosevelt had been "entirely correct about" with regard to Clipperton island is unknown, but as events would demonstrate, White House involvement with the offbeat atoll was steadily increasing.

Perhaps because of Secretary Forrestal's dawdling, Byrd also personally "brought to my office," Admiral Leahy later recalled, "for transmission to the President [a copy of] his survey of both military and commercial aviation possibilities in the Pacific. It was an all-inclusive document of great value in the planning of postwar defense of America and in postwar arrangements for international commercial air traffic."[45]

The tardy official copy of Byrd's report from Forrestal's office finally arrived at the White House in October on the heels of a separate, independent study by the Joint Strategic Survey Committee, composed of diplomats and warriors who independently judged the atoll to have strategic significance. JSSC members thought that Clipperton island was one of two dozen places, mostly in the Americas, that had special value. In fact, they believed that its postwar occupation was "required for [the] defense of the Western Hemisphere; . . . [therefore the] U.S. [should] have military rights on a participating and, if necessary, reciprocal basis."[46]

Roosevelt forwarded JSSC recommendations to Secretary of State Cordell Hull and ordered him, "as a matter of high priority, to initiate negotiations with the governments concerned to acquire permanent or long-term benefit of the bases, facilities and rights required, at the earliest possible moment."[47]

By then it was abundantly clear that the British intended to use Clipperton island as an air base, which Roosevelt was determined to prevent. It might be necessary to move promptly and occupy the place; obviously, it would be better to proceed with French blessings than without.

Meanwhile, in recognition of his secret wartime visit to Clipperton and other tropical islands, Byrd received the Legion of Merit with one gold star and a special letter of commendation from Secretary Forrestal. The admiral's last mission ever in a combat zone, it seems an odd ending to an extraordinary career.

Notes

1. Morton, pp. 11–18.

2. Quoted in *ibid.*

3. Dod, p. 8.

4. Con, *et al.*, p. 304.

5. Franklin D. Roosevelt, Press Conference Number 678, September 6, 1940, p. 4, in Franklin D. Roosevelt Papers as President, "Press Conference," Vol. 16, pp. 193–94.

6. *Ibid.*

7. "Clipperton Island, study in reference to," memorandum, February 27, 1942, in *ibid.*, Map Room Collection, Box 162, "Air Base, Clipperton Island" folder.

8. Captain John L. McCrea [Naval Aide to the President] to [Admiral Ernest J. King], Commander-in-Chief, U.S. Fleet, March 8, 1942, in *ibid.*

9. Osing, p. 13.

10. USS *Atlanta*, "Deck log," 17 April 1942, in U.S. Navy Records, Record Group (RG) 24 (National Archives).

11. *Ibid.*

12. Australian Legation, Washington, D.C., "Memorandum concerning air routes across the Pacific," December 9, 1942, in Roosevelt Papers as President, "Air Base, Clipperton island" folder.

13. Quoted in R. L. Connolly, "Memorandum for Chief of Staff," 18 December 1942, in *ibid.*, "Air Routes" folder.

14. *Ibid.* "Mr. Charles Michelson and one via Paul Winkler [a Hungarian journalist with the Washington *Post* who had served in Paris before the war] wrote Secretary of the Navy [Frank] Knox offering to turn over Michelson's rights to the development of Clipperton Island to a privately owned organization which would be controlled by the United States Navy. Secretary Knox wrote Mr. Michelson [on] March 4, 1942, thank-

ing him for his generous action in putting the rights of the Island to the disposal of the United States Navy." See Enclosure 2, "Present status of Clipperton island," an attachment to Navy General Board Memorandum No. 450, "Post-war air routes from the Panama Canal and South America to New Zealand and Australia," 21 July 1943, Serial 246, in U.S. Navy Records, RG 80 (National Archives).

Curiously, when the French vehemently objected to American occupation of Clipperton island in 1944, the United States government failed to cite the Michelson concession as possible authorization for its action.

Michelson has not been positively identified. If he was *the* Charles Michelson—FDR crony, speech writer, and onetime chairman of the Democratic National Committee—his memoirs, *The ghost talks* (1944), fail to mention either the island or any concession from the French.

15. E. J. King, "Memorandum for the President; air route across the Pacific," 20 December 1942, in Roosevelt Papers as President, "Air Base, Clipperton Island" folder.

16. John L. McCrea to Admiral [William D.] Leahy, December 28, 1942, in *ibid.*

17. Franklin D. Roosevelt to Secretary of the Navy [Frank Knox], June 12, 1943, in *ibid.*

18. Admiral A. J. Hepburn to Secretary of the Navy [Knox], 18 June 1943, in *ibid.*

19. Navy General Board, Memorandum 450, 21 July 1943, Annex A.

20. King to Leahy, 3 April 1943, in Roosevelt Papers as President, "Air Base, Clipperton Island" folder.

21. Roosevelt to the Secretary of the Navy [Knox], June 30, 1943, in *ibid., "*Air Routes" folder.

22. Byrd returned to Antarctica three times, once almost dying of carbon monoxide poisoning when, alone at an advance camp, his hut was entirely buried by snow. Forced to use his stove to keep warm while he awaited rescue, he was near death from asphyxiation when help arrived. He may well have suffered brain damage, his biographer has speculated; for certain, Byrd's personality ever afterward was affected.

23. *Ibid.,* pp. 349–50.

24. *Ibid.,* p. 351. Frank Knox was Secretary until 1944; he, not Forrestal, ordered the navy to carry out Roosevelt's survey of certain Pacific islands.

25. Navy General Board, Memorandum No. 450, 21 July 1943.

26. Roosevelt to Knox, July 29, 1943, in Roosevelt Papers as President, "Air Base, Clipperton Island" folder.

27. A. L. Gates to Roosevelt, 11 August 1943, in *ibid.*, "Air Routes" folder.

28. R. E. Byrd to Wilson Brown, 1 August 1943, *ibid.*

29. Wilson Brown, "Memorandum for Collection," 27 August 1943, *ibid.*

30. Richard E. Byrd, "Report of survey of certain Pacific islands in connection with national defense (primarily) and commercial air bases and routes, by special mission," December 15, 1943, Book 1, p. 3 (copies in Modern Military Branch, National Archives, Washington, D.C.; Operational Archives, Washington Navy Yard, Washington, D.C.; and Roosevelt Papers as President, "Air Routes" folder).

31. M. H. Anderson, vice-president, Northeast Airlines; Lieutenant Peter N. Heintskill, Fifteenth Naval District, Balboa, Canal Zone, representing the Bureau of Yards and Docks; Captain Allan F. Hubbard, an Australian engineer who served as aide to Admiral Byrd; R. M. Huber, superintendent, airways and support engineering, Transcontinental & Western Air, Inc.; T. Johnson, assistant vice-president and Pacific operations manager, United Air Lines, Inc.; Lieutenant James W. Jordan, a Navy engineer; Lieutenant Colonel Robert A. Logan, an Australian attached to the U.S. Army Air Corps, representing the Air Transport Command; F. MacKenzie, airport engineer, Pan American Airways System; E. O. Meyer, chief of dispatching and meteorology, American Export Airlines, Inc.; Delos W. Rentzel, director of communications and radio, American Airlines, Inc.; Lieutenant Commander Edward C. Sweeney, a logistics specialist representing the Navy Planning Division; Colonel William M. Wanamaker, district commander, Army Corps of Engineers, Denison, Texas, who served as senior army engineer and mission chief of staff; and Colonel Harry C. Wisehart, commanding officer, Pecos Army Airfield, Texas, senior army aviator.

Enlisted personnel: Chief Yeoman Fred Crammer, Chief Carpenter's Mate Lester K. Barnard (surveyor), Chief Carpenter's Mate Felix J. Rabito (surveyor), Photographer's Mate (first class) Otto G. H. Ellerman, Photographer's Mate (first class) Gerald P. Pully, Photographer's Mate (first class) F. D. Farmer, Technical Sergeant (third grade) John L. Irvine (photographer), Aviation Machinist Mate (first class) Edward C.

Saxe, LCV Coxwain John A. Harris, and LCV Fireman (first class) Eugene J. Shields.

32. D. W. Rentzel, Oklahoma City, Oklahoma, to JMS September 9, 1985 (interview).

33. *Ibid.*

34. Byrd, Book II, p. 4.

35. Hoyt, p. 353.

36. Rentzel to JMS.

37. Byrd, Book II, pp. 4–5.

38. Rentzel to JMS.

39. Byrd, Book I, pp. 84–85.

40. *Ibid.,* pp. 22–24.

41. *Ibid.*

42. *Ibid.,* p. 25.

43. James Forrestal to Roosevelt, 19 June 1944, in Roosevelt Papers as President, "Air Routes" folder.

44. Byrd to Roosevelt, April 14, 1944, in *ibid.*

45. Leahy, p. 243. Leahy remembered Byrd's visit to hand over a copy of his report as early June 1944, at least six months after the original had been submitted to King; within days of Byrd's visit, Forrestal forwarded the tardy report to the White House.

46. Joint Strategic Survey Committee, "U.S. requirements for post-war bases; military air base requirements—period I," map, ca. 7 October 1943, in Roosevelt Papers as President, "Air Routes" folder.

47. Roosevelt to Secretary of State [Cordell Hull], January 7, 1944, in *ibid.;* cf., U.S. State department, *Foreign relations of the United States; diplomatic papers, 1944* (1967), pp. 546–47.

10

Hurricane at
Clipperton Rock
1944

During the late 1930s, not long after President Roosevelt conceived of Clipperton island as a link in a chain of trans-Pacific airports, Australian aviator Patrick Gordon Taylor reached a similar conclusion—that, given the flying range of contemporary airplanes, the atoll was vital. Like Roosevelt, Taylor would visit the dangerous place twice—the second time almost costing him and his companions their lives.

Born in Sydney in 1896, Taylor had served with the Royal Air Force during World War I; he was a combat ace who won the Military Cross, merely the first of many laurels that would culminate in knighthood in 1954. "Between the wars he became one of the big figures of Australian aviation," a biographer says of this tall, thin, dashing flyer, "with an impressive record as an airline pilot, as a contract flier on his own account, and as a pioneer of long-distance trans-ocean flights."[1]

As Qantas Airways' chief pilot, in 1938 Taylor tried to establish a transoceanic route from Australia to Mexico, "an alternative to the [United States–controlled] Hawaiian line by the North Pacific." He selected his proposed sites by looking westward across the Pacific, from North America to Down Under: "from Acapulco in Mexico to Clipperton Island, the Marquesas or Tuamotus, the Society and Cook Islands; and thence to New Zealand. Little was known of this route from the air aspect. Aircraft had not yet crossed the South Pacific and most of the islands on this line either had not been seen from the air, or a few had been viewed briefly from a small seaplane flying locally from a ship at sea."[2]

War in Europe forced cancellation of his survey of these sites, planned for the fall of 1939, but he did not abandon the idea. Recalled to active duty, he readily understood that Australia itself was an inevitable target of the Empire of the Rising Sun, and he lobbied his government for a string of "emergency air bases in the Pacific" that would more securely tie Australia and New Zealand to the Western world during such perilous times. As previously mentioned, his idea was formally advanced by the Australian Legation in 1942 but rejected by the United States government as unnecessary; however, unbeknownst to Taylor, he had provoked President Roosevelt into ordering a U.S. Navy survey, the Byrd mission.

Transferred about then to London and duty with the R.A.F.'s high command, Taylor seemingly forgot the idea for the duration of the great global conflict. Then, in 1944, "when the war in Europe was obviously in its final stages . . . [and] the diversion of R.A.F. operations to assist in finishing off Japan after the defeat of Germany was now in sight, and a convenient ferry and communications route to the Pacific was being considered,"[3] he sparked interest in his pet project among the British high command.

In January 1944, the British Joint Staff Delegation in Washington informally broached the subject of a trans-Pacific survey to Pentagon officials, who still claimed to see no wartime value in such an initiative. The British refused to be discouraged, and in May they formally asked Admiral Ernest J. King, chief of naval operations, to approve a British flight over American-patrolled waters, including departure from Acapulco and two flights to Clipperton island (with a week's stay there, all told), as well as stops at Bora Bora, Aitutaki, Tonga, Auckland, and Sydney. King replied that the proposed flight and survey seemed "not in the interest of the war effort."[4] He also advised the White House of the British request.

Meanwhile, evidence from Mexico City, where the R.A.F. had sent a delegation to secure Mexican cooperation, confirmed King's suspicions. American intelligence officers at the U.S. embassy reported that while the British survey flight was being posed "for immediate war purpose[s, it] is actually being considered for postwar commercial uses."⁵ Moreover, "The French have not been informed about [British] plans to use Clipperton . . . [and indications are] that [the] British have no intention of doing so."⁶

Throughout the summer, the British pressed for U.S. approval. In June, Air Marshal Sir William L. Welch, chief R.A.F. representative on the Joint Staff Delegation, again petitioned Admiral King for American naval cooperation; in August, Welch insisted on cooperation. King asked the White House for guidance, but since "President Roosevelt was out of Washington at the time, he was not immediately consulted." Repeatedly pestered by Welch, on 1 September King asked for presidential authorization to reply affirmatively. Inasmuch "as the only help the British wanted was 3,000 gallons of fuel and 100 gallons of oil at Bora Bora, [King] did not feel that we should refuse it to them as the war effort depended upon the cooperation and mutual assistance in many theatres."⁷

Rear Admiral Wilson Brown, Roosevelt's naval aide, passed along King's recommendation, adding that the "refusal to provide the fuel requested might be misinterpreted."⁸ Roosevelt agreed. On 3 September, the admiral notified the British of American approval, finally.

P. G. Taylor and his crew, who had been prepared and ready to depart Canada for Mexico since May, were beginning to despair of ever conducting their survey. By the time King's okay arrived, they knew they had missed the most favorable possible weather.

Taylor had planned otherwise. Thinking that his idea was unique and with the rubric of the British high command in his pocket, the previous spring he had flown to Bermuda, where JX 275, a lend-lease Catalina flying-boat (PBY) normally used for flight instruction and for communications (the only type of aircraft in the whole British inventory capable of making a trans-Pacific survey), had been detached to stand by for the mission. He christened it *Frigate Bird,* ordered it stripped of all but essential equipment, and flew it to Consolidated Aircraft Corporation facilities in Elizabeth City, New Jersey, where priority clearances got oversized fuel tanks installed promptly. Afterward, he piloted the modified aircraft on to Montreal for final preparations.

With cramped living conditions aboard a PBY in mind, Taylor handpicked men from the R.A.F.'s Atlantic Transport Command whom he believed to possess harmonious temperaments. He minimized their number to save weight for fuel but covered each critical aircraft function with at least two persons in case someone became ill. Once they departed Clipperton island, they would be on their own for 3,000 miles—all the way to Bora Bora in the Societies.

Each man was a qualified pilot from Down Under. Flight Lieutenant Norman Birks, a large, affable Australian serving with the R.A.F., was second captain. Flight Lieutenant "Hendy" Henderson, a New Zealander who was dispatching officer at Bermuda, navigated and, in a pinch, could handle the wireless. Serving as signalman was Flying Officer Len Bligh, an experienced radioman and descendant of the infamous Captain Bligh of HMS *Bounty* fame. Flying Officer Jock Hogg was engineer, mechanic, and cook. Both Bligh and Hogg, like Taylor and Birks, were Aussies.

When word from Washington finally arrived, another PBY (JX 532), captained by Wing Commander L. L. "Slim" Jones, preceded *Frigate Bird* to Mexico "to make fuel, diplomatic and other arrangements." This second amphibian, Taylor says in his memoirs, "was also [detailed] to stand by for any emergency till after we had left Clipperton Island for Bora Bora."[9]

Frigate Bird would need every drop of fuel it could carry to reach the Society islands, thirty hours flying time to the southwest, especially the 200 gallons of petrol Taylor planned to stockpile on Clipperton island. Without topping off tanks at the atoll, the airship would surely run out of fuel short of the Marquesas and crash into an endless sea. There was no fuel and probably little welcome at such Marquesas islands as Nuku Hiva. They must reach Bora Bora.

As much as anyone who ever visited Clipperton island, Taylor and his crew would be at its absolute mercy. Clearly, they did not fully appreciate the atoll's awesome potential for disaster.

To his credit, Taylor researched the subject as well as he could, given the press of wartime. "The first report I could find of it," he wrote, "was as a pirates' base, from which it is said to have received the name of Clipperton. . . ." He also read accounts by Edward Morris and Karl Baarslag that told "the grim story of . . . [the] inhabitants of Clipperton island, . . . [and] of an immense negro . . . [who] conceived a plan to kill the rest of the men, enslave the young women . . . , and make himself king of the island." More to the point of his mission, Taylor located charts that indicated that the "water of the lagoon is muddy and very stagnant, the depths varying from a few inches to 50 fathoms."[10]

Adequately informed or not, Taylor took *Frigate Bird* aloft from Acapulco Airport at dawn 9 September 1944 and set course for the atoll. Hinting of events to follow, the weather thickened midway there, and just before they reached the island's vicinity, a squall line slammed into the PBY, heavy rain further obscuring visibility. Taylor was beginning to fear they had missed the place altogether when, through the wet, he caught sight of what appeared to be "the strange ethereal shape of a full-rigged ship far away on the horizon. Her sails were white, and through the glasses she seemed close-hauled to the wind, her spanker hard on and her mainsail and foresail, topsails, top gallants and royals reaching up in a single tower. . . . We had seen it in the old *Sailing Directions* in the National Geographic Society's Library in Washington. . . . Clipperton Island [was dead] ahead."[11]

They watched wordlessly as the lagoon came into view. It was "not muddy and stagnant, but flashing with colour," Taylor later recalled. "I went no further in my dream. The lagoon appeared as a place of horror for the pilot of a flying-boat. Around the shore were wandering shadows in the blue that told of coral, some of it reaching to the surface."[12]

He dove to 1,000 feet for a closer look, disturbing life on the island. Clouds of panicked seabirds filled the sky, and out his window Taylor caught sight of "some dark creature . . . running awkwardly in furtive rushes, seeking cover to escape from this sudden thing of terror."[13] He pulled up into a tight turn and looked down the wing to see pigs scurrying about.

Lower still, the aircraft zoomed across the island northwest to southeast, past a coconut grove off the starboard wing tip, beyond which Taylor and the men observed remnants of a settlement. As they whizzed by the Rock, thousands of terrified terns abandoned their heretofore safe roosts, scattering chaotically into the morning sky. By then, Taylor had seen "a shred of hope." No longer certain that all of the dark shadows in the lagoon were coral, he gained altitude and looked more closely at what he at first had thought to be reefs in the middle of the lagoon. "This was something different from ordinary coral," he thought. "Some of it was brown, spreading too evenly across the bottom for coral. . . . I could not tell from the air."[14]

The situation was critical. He still believed that the place might be used, but if he flew back to the mainland without landing and surveying on foot, he feared that no one "would believe my conclusion that I still regarded the island suitable for development. . . . We had to get in somehow and investigate."[15]

He selected a landing course and flew over it several times to fix it firmly in mind. He then passed control to Birks, who flew *Frigate Bird* while Taylor, Henderson, and Bligh individually photographed the island, just in case it became necessary to abort landing at the last moment and, for whatever reason, to make haste for the mainland. Picture-taking finished, Taylor resumed control of the airship and ordered Bligh to radio Slim Jones at Acapulco that they had arrived and were preparing to land; however, at Taylor's express orders, Bligh was not to mention any danger they faced.

Taylor piloted the PBY around the island's perimeter one last time before turning by the Rock onto a final heading of 315°. Flying low over the outer edge of the atoll, he aimed the airplane at the Egg islands, adjusted its trim, and eased off the throttle. As the airplane lumbered 100 feet above the Grand Reef, he saw the light yellow stain of shoals at the edge of the reef and, just beyond, blue water. He cut power and allowed the ungainly *Frigate Bird* to glide toward what he hoped was deep water. Land at the far end of the placid lagoon rushed toward them as the keel of the flying boat brushed the surface, the drag of water becoming an ever-harsher sound as it braked the plane. Taylor signaled Bligh with two quick blasts of the Klaxon to deploy drogues, or water anchors, and the amphibian came to rest near the interior reef, off the Egg islands.

Birks killed the engines as Taylor opened the roof hatch above his head. He stood up in his seat to survey the scene before him, he later said, in the realization that they were committed, "for better or worse. . . . The morning was dead calm and perfect with solitude. . . . there [was] only the deep echo of the surf on the reef and the far cry of a sea bird to accompany the music of silence . . .

[which in time] became a discordant noise."[16] Thus commenced an interrupted six-week stay on the atoll, all but a week of which was unscheduled.

That first day Taylor carefully checked the flying boat's anchorage to assure himself that "disaster was unlikely in a blow" before the crew set out in a rubber dinghy to inspect the lagoon. He had originally planned to taxi *Frigate Bird* close inshore, lay empty barrels out on the beach, and using an electric pump, defuel into them from the aircraft's hull and wing tanks, but on seeing from the air the dangerous reefs that paralleled the lagoon shore, he knew he must find safe passage.

The men discovered that most of the interior shoreline was paralleled by submerged and exposed reefs; only the lagoon's middle was deep and entirely free of coral. Taylor considered himself fortunate to have landed the PBY safely. The longest stretch of open water, at a mile and a half, ran generally north-south. The only alternative, his actual landing course of southeast to northwest, was a quarter of a mile shorter. He would surely need the longer runway for takeoff with a full load of fuel.

The southeastern quadrant of the lagoon, including the Rock, was dominated by the Grand Reef—much of it covered by merely an inch or so of water. In the southwestern quadrant, off Pincer bay, parallel reefs—much of them exposed, as though in fair warning—lay 100 to 1,500 feet offshore. All along the northwestern shore, near the Egg islands where the amphibian was anchored, the reef was entirely submerged but clearly visible from the surface. And throughout the northeast, off Oceanic Phosphate's campsite, shallows stretched far out into the lagoon. The only entrance to sheltered western lagoon waters lay between the reefs in the southwestern quadrant.

No safe anchorage existed anywhere close inshore. "One touch of the thin duralumin plating on any of these [coral] heads," Taylor later wrote, "would have holed the bottom and probably brought irretrievable disaster to us." He therefore concluded that anchorage off the reef was acceptable and, since gasoline was lighter than water, calculated that even with the added weight of the thin steel barrels they "could make a raft of the tanks with the filler-spouts up, lay it alongside and defuel into . . . [the] fuel barge, then moor it in a sheltered position and bring it up alongside for refueling when we returned to the island."[17]

They found plenty of planking ashore, "evidently the last remains of an old hut,"[18] and by afternoon they had lashed together a raft of boards and empty barrels. Within another couple of hours they had pumped 200 gallons of gasoline into the improvised fuel barge and, singing "The Song of the Volga Boatman," Birks and Henderson foot-paddled it to a spot midway between the Eggs and the northwestern shore, where, using several lengths of anchor chain, they secured it between the reef and the lagoon islands. By dusk they were done.

Taylor recorded in his diary:

> *Bligh elected to sleep ashore this night. In the morning we found he had awakened in the darkness to find an immense tusker hog looking into his face. He didn't seem much concerned about this experience, which I thought rather horrifying. We did not yet know what creatures were on the island, nor definitely whether it was uninhabited by man. We did not expect some frightening reincarnation of the murdering lightkeeper . . . but there was no getting away from the impression that this was a strange place where somehow one expected unusual things to happen. Apparently Bligh so shook the morale of the pig when he sprang up out of his sleep that it gave one hideous scream and ran off into the night and never appeared again.*[19]

The next day, they examined the coral rim "concerning the suitability of the island for development of land-based aircraft." With the sun shining, the temperature in the mid-seventies, and fresh southeastern trade winds keeping gnats at bay, Taylor and Bligh stripped to the skin and enjoyed a sunbather's tour of the place; however, they soon discovered that "the coral was too sharp even for the toughest bare feet, so shoes of some sort were necessary except when over on the beach. . . ."[20]

Walking counterclockwise around the atoll, they "passed some mounds which may have been graves . . . probably those of the inhabitants who died of starvation and beri beri [sic]." Next they encountered a large pile of phosphates and rusted rails leading to the twisted remains of a steel jetty on the edge of the reef. One hundred meters farther south, along the lagoon shore near the coconut grove, they came upon the ruins of a settlement, which were overgrown with coarse grass and weeds. "Strewn on the ground were many thin, wide boards which must have been the covering of the buildings. Some were netted to the ground and creepers had grown over them through the years, but others were lying tumbled as they must have fallen. They were spread about loosely, probably by the wind."[21]

They paused at the grove to eat fresh coconuts, which Taylor judged good. Then, abruptly,

a number of pigs . . . ran out, looked at us with blank astonishment, and trotted off into the grass. I noticed that the birds were very hostile to them. Any pig which started fossicking towards the shore of the lagoon, which was lined with nesting gannets and noddies [sic], was immediatly attacked from the air, and after making a futile display of irritation and ferocity was eventually driven off in confusion. It must have been difficult for these animals to make a living and to breed successfully through all the years they had been there. They evidently sought to supplement their meagre diet of roots and scrap vegetation with sea birds' eggs, of which there must have been thousands on the island. I began to feel some respect for these pigs. They had succeeded where man had failed, with all his resources, to live on this island. . . . Apart altogether from the fact that these pigs were rather gaunt and tough, I could not have brought myself to kill one of them unless we had needed food and could not otherwise get it. . . .[22]

The men resumed their tour. Midway between the grove and the Rock, on a "stretch of white sand," they encountered "an iron cross, apparently marking a grave. Looking across the bare rim of the island to the gaunt Rock," Taylor wrote, "I had an impression of utter desolation, and I wondered why anybody should have been buried in such a place. Perhaps it was the grave of the light-keeper, hurriedly put down in the sand. The cross, originally of heavy iron, was now hanging in flakes of rust. Somebody touched it and a piece fell off, like a sign of the fallibility of all things, into the sand. . . ."[23]

At the Rock they discovered "distinct tracks where the gravel was pressed down, tightly packed by some wide-tyred vehicle.

There was some speculation, since they were about the track-width of a jeep. [Taylor] . . . wondered whether somebody had been to look over Clipperton when the imminence of this survey flight had suddenly stirred up interest in the island."[24]

The men searched for a way to the summit of the Rock, where they might see for some distance. At the base of the escarpment, Taylor was "startled by a sudden commotion in the scrub almost at my feet, by a wild panic-stricken shriek from moving bushes. The hunched figure of a great spotted hog disappeared, screaming, into a tunnel in the base of the Rock. I looked in, but the tunnel ended in darkness and a lifeless silence."[25]

They entered, blundering into bedlam. The "eerie and objectionable" cavern "stank of birds," its narrow passages glazed slippery white with guano. Thousands of nesting birds objected to the men's presence—squawking, pecking out in protest, panicking, and madly fluttering into flight in the confines of the narrow fissure. Taylor later recalled, "We dared not look up for the droppings which rained upon us."[26]

Then, abruptly, he found himself eye-to-eye with a pig. "I was standing on one leg," Taylor wrote, "hanging to a ledge of slippery rock and trying to step over the gannets without breaking their eggs when I saw this apparition about three feet away under the rim of my sun helmet. It shot at me a whinnying scream with a wild expression of insane malevolence, hesitated for a moment, then swung round and was spirited away into The Rock. It was like a sudden nightmare. I leapt over the gannets and hurried round a rock straight into the piteous squeal of a noddy which flew out of its nest at my face."[27]

Finally, they emerged into the open near a ladder leading to the top of the Rock. It was too rotten to use, and they climbed up the final few feet by hand. Shrieking protests merely once or twice, terns nesting at the very pinnacle seemed less distressed by the men than had their neighbors, the cave birds.

Holding onto tarnished brass stanchions that still held the light's lens for support against brisk trade winds that whistled by, Taylor and Birks looked across the lagoon to *Frigate Bird* laying at anchor. From that vantage point Taylor was even more convinced than before that the atoll might be developed for flying boats.[28]

Part one of their mission completed, the next morning, 11

September, Taylor piloted a defueled and considerably lighter *Frigate Bird* off the lagoon without incident. They returned to Acapulco, refueled to capacity, and with R.A.F. PBY 532 continuing to stand by, on 22 September took off for Clipperton island once more, "now in a position to leave there with [enough] fuel for the 3,000 nautical miles flight in unknown winds to Bora Bora."[29]

Taylor had scheduled a week's work on the atoll to study the lagoon carefully. Not only did he need to determine the longest possible runway across it, which the *Frigate Bird* would surely need to get airborne with an unusually heavy fuel load, but he also wished to know precisely where the interior reef must be blasted away to make the place safe for regular seaplane operations.

Hurried along by a 25-knot tail wind, the ponderous PBY reached Clipperton island in merely six hours. As it approached, weather threatened; the sky was ominously dark to the southwest. Taylor circled the atoll, and all aboard saw evidence that a tempest had recently raked the place. Fresh green pond weed, uprooted throughout the lagoon, had washed ashore in great tangles all along the northeastern shoreline. Perfectly placid on their previous visit, the lagoon's surface was now choppy, whitecaps running to windward.

The fuel barge was missing. They searched frantically, finally spotting it aground in shallows hundreds of feet off the Oceanic Phosphate campsite, near the lagoon's northeastern shore but across the lagoon from the Egg islands, where it had been moored. It was completely covered with weed, and one barrel lay separate from the others, along the edge of the shore, washing to and fro in agitated water. Taylor later confessed to "a sick feeling inside— not to know whether it was still holding the fuel."[30]

At 1445 hours Acapulco time, he carefully landed, taxied through the channel between the reefs to a point midway between the Egg islands and Pincer bay, which he thought offered better shelter, and switched off the engines. He opened the roof hatch, stood up in his seat, and looked around, drawing in a deep breath of fresh air as he did. "The smell of birds came on the wind from the phosphate mound to the windward," he later wrote. "It was sour, but it was the island. . . ."[31]

The men anchored the amphibian securely and set out in a

rubber dinghy for land. The breeze was fresh, the water choppy, and paddling the raft was difficult against the wind. After depositing Bligh, Hogg, and Henderson ashore at Pincer bay to make camp, Taylor and Birks set out across the lagoon somewhat on the wind to assess damage to the barge. They reached the separated gasoline drum first, and it proved to be undamaged, with no loss of fuel. Now more optimistic, they towed it to the weed-entangled barge. The barge's anchor chain had somehow snagged on an offshore reef, keeping the rest of the raft's precious contents just out of harm's way. Taylor breathed a sigh of relief.

Because of threatening weather, he and Birks hurriedly untangled the barge from weeds and pushed it to shore, then disassembled it. Laboriously, they levered and rolled individual barrels up onto the beach and secured them before nightfall.

The weather worsened. Overnight, winds upwards of 25 knots blew up out of the southwest, the opposite of Taylor's expectations. At dawn the skies were overcast, and conditions quickly deteriorated. Winds stiffened to 35 knots, with gusts of 45, which kept the men off the lagoon. Evening came without relief, and they passed a sleepless night ashore, watching the aircraft, regularly checking its anchors. At dawn, rain squalls commenced and lasted fully twenty-four hours. Following yet another sleepless night, they were too exhausted to take advantage of somewhat improved conditions on the twenty-fifth to study the lagoon. Then, the next day, the winds freshened again. Unable to raise Acapulco by radio because of freakish atmospheric conditions, Bligh instead reached the R.A.F. base at Dorval, Quebec, nearly 4,000 miles away, and explained that they were very likely socked in for several days.

Taylor had not added an outboard motor to his equipment list in Acapulco because he believed he needed its weight equivalence in fuel to reach Bora Bora, and his frugal nature would not allow him to abandon it on the island when done, even if the Crown picked up the tab. Besides, when he had previously visited the atoll, the weather had been calm, and the lagoon waters were placid and easy to ride.

Even so, as Taylor noted, "A rubber dinghy is unlike an ordinary boat. It sits on the surface, with practically no grip of the water. It wants to stop after each stroke of the paddles. . . . Some way of giving it a grip of the water had to be devised."[32]

Since an effective mast and sail could not be fitted into a rubber raft without poking a hole in its bottom, they improvised. "The Clipperton Island Construction Company" fabricated a wooden frame, like an outrigger, from weathered lumber gathered around the island; Henderson even found a pile of galvanized nails at the settlement, and while those on the surface were eaten away by rust, underneath were sufficient good ones for their needs. In a day Henderson sewed together a sail from spare canvas and rigged it to a mast fixed to the frame.

The crew endured another week of inclement weather before testing their craft. When they did, it sailed well before the wind and, with the lee board down, it could even be coaxed windward. It was blundering but manageable in moderate breezes. On its maiden voyage they resumed their survey of the lagoon, at first failing to find a way through the main reef. They discovered the coral belt to be so narrow in places that they might easily have broken through with a crowbar, but it would take weeks and much labor to cut a channel sufficiently large for the flying boat to taxi through safely. When subsequent voyages confirmed the extent of the lagoon's interior reef system, Taylor began making mental calculations for an unorthodox, somewhat desperate style of full-load takeoff, if necessary.

Meanwhile, they had set up camp. Since it was evident that they were in for a prolonged stay, Hogg built a cook house from materials salvaged from the old phosphate settlement. He accumulated a stockpile of coal from a plentiful supply he found scattered about in the grass. Birks and Bligh also erected a primitive but effective lean-to as a communal shelter from the weather; it fronted on the lagoon. Birks found an old Doulton filter at the coconut grove and used it to purify lagoon water to conserve supplies; he placed layers of stones and sand in it and produced potable water. Over the ensuing weeks, they added such creature comforts as a table and benches where they might sit to eat. There, early each morning, Taylor maintained his log, lounging "in comfort, with a view over the lagoon to the aircraft."[33]

He wrote: "The birds are nesting round our camp. One, a gannet [booby], is within five feet of the cook house, and sits on its egg, looking at us with an expression of interest and confidence now that it knows us and has suffered no harm." Hogg talked soothingly to her almost constantly, working "out a lot of his cooking problems with her, asking her advice about unusual fish we brought which might be poisonous, and consult[ing] her generally about affairs of importance." Everyone fed her to the point that she gave up hunting altogether, the bird merely sitting on her egg and regularly squawking for handouts, Taylor wrote, "stretching her neck at us and telling us to hurry with her meal. Then she would make a great show of her appreciation. She was a decent bird whom we liked to have with us."[34] A noddy tern also nested nearby, but she never became comfortable in the presence of men. She shrieked at them often and flew off whenever anyone came too close, accepting neither handouts nor verbal reassurances.

Pigs also rooted about the camp. Taylor wrote: "they are gaunt creatures, very unattractive. Apart from any humane feelings toward them, we have not been tempted to eat one."[35] There was fresh food enough to supplement their ample stores of canned and preserved rations without resorting to pork. The coconut grove yielded plenty of nuts for their needs, and they even discovered a green plant that, when cooked, tasted like spinach.

Their preferred source of food was the sea. Fish swarmed among offshore reef waters at high tide, and the men were able to get many. Taylor said that fish "were not interested in bait, not in any lure that we had, but we shot them and speared them with iron rods from the ruins. Birks was a good shot with a revolver. . . ."[36]

They harvested crayfish from the offshore reefs, locating the delicious animals in shallow water by spotting their whiskers protruding from hideaways in the rocks, the men wading among coral heads to capture them. Taylor lost some enthusiasm for this sport when, as he prepared to capture a crayfish, a moray eel swam up to him and assessed his right foot with relish. "Springs in my legs," he wrote, "shot me up to the rock, and reaction drove down the spear. [The eel] gave a convulsive heave, bent the iron rod like a piece of wire, and tore away from the barb."[37]

One day, when their survey was almost complete, Hogg commenced a scheduled tune-up of engines in preparation for takeoff and the long flight westward. Spark plugs, which had been put in new in Canada, needed to be replaced to improve fuel economy on the most critical stretch of their flight, but Hogg quickly discovered that several of his tools were missing, including the special spanner, or wrench, needed to remove the plugs. Bligh repeatedly tried to contact Apaculco by radio, but atmospheric conditions jammed the airwaves; instead, he raised Dorval, Quebec. He requested that news of their predicament be relayed to PBY 532 so that it might bring tools.

Ten days passed before help arrived. As it turned out, Wing Commander Jones had fallen ill and could not fly, so the R.A.F. sent Squadron Leader Paddy Uprichard from Bermuda to take command. With him came Captain Al Torrey, "a C-47 captain [who was] to examine the runway at Clipperton."[38] Then, just as it was preparing to depart Acapulco, PBY 532 developed engine problems of its own, and a new airplane had to be requisitioned from Elizabeth City, New Jersey. Dorval radioed Taylor and his crew to be patient. Little matter. Throughout the interim the weather had been uncooperative, making it doubtful that another PBY could have landed safely on the lagoon anyway.

While awaiting assistance, Taylor oversaw preparations for departure. One day, when the weather cleared, he had the aircraft refueled. They rolled the barrels back into the water and lashed them together, and Birks and Henderson paddled the awkward raft more than a mile westward across the lagoon to the Catalina, which lay at anchor north of Pincer bay. All hands laid the barge alongside *Frigate Bird* and pumped up the fuel, leaving the port tank about 100 gallons down and the starboard slightly less than full to allow for heat expansion in the sun. That done, they moored the barge nearby, leaving it handy for topping off tanks before departure.

The next day, Taylor declared a holiday. They had been working strenuously each day since arrival at the island, and some relaxation was needed. He could see that "there was some clash of temperament between Henderson and Bligh. . . ." Henderson, "whose unremitting and effective handiwork in every aspect of our life on the island was valuable to us all, . . . was being irritated by Bligh's nonchalant and lighthearted manner, which Henderson misinterpreted . . . as derision"[39] directed at him. Taylor hoped a day off would help. When it did not, he assigned them to an isolated work detail in the belief that, alone, they would work it out. They did.

On the day of rest, Taylor visited the Rock "to examine [it] more closely for [signs of] past habitation. . . ." Alone, Taylor says, "I was very conscious of its sinister former inhabitant, the murdering keeper of the light. Standing below it, . . . I had to convince myself that time had not turned back to the grim last days of the survivors at the island, and that the mad eyes of the lightkeeper were not now fixed upon me from some hiding place. Close behind me there was a quick rustle in the bushes and a pig ran screaming into The Rock."[40]

Taylor discovered "a deep fissure, a flat-floored cavern," the existence of which "was concealed from the isthmus leading from the rim of the island by a peculiar fold in the walls." Inside he found what he believed to be evidence of Álvarez: "A sloping trough had been cut in the side of a steep wall, and at the end of it had been shaped to a lip from which water was now seeping and dripping, from a beard–like deposit in stalactite form, to the floor of the cavern. There, partly buried, was some wooden arrangement which I found to be the remains of a well-made barrel bound with brass hoops. This apparently had been his water supply. . . ."[41]

Taylor climbed up to the light, "through the same uproarious clamour of gannets and noddies, . . . pecking and complaining as I tried to step over them and avoid breaking their eggs. . . ." Sitting atop the Rock, he "made a more detailed drawing of the reefs. . . ." Later, he climbed down and, below the Rock, literally stumbled on the remains of the light keeper's shack. "It was in some low scrub, and covered with grass and creepers. Only the old timber and some twisted iron were there. . . ."[42]

He walked on, beyond "remains of a large wooden sailing vessel," its mast "well preserved under the crinkled gray surface where weather had worn the softer grain," to the oceanside northeastern coast and its offshore reefs. Carrying a six-foot-long iron rod with a barb on one end and a line tied to the other, Taylor ventured out away from land, stepping from one exposed coral head to another. The sea "was clear and brilliant, flashing with colours of the reef, . . . rockfish country." He soon spotted "an immense rockfish, like a blue grouper, his fins gently fanning the water to hold his position . . ." as he awaited smaller prey. Taylor "moved back out of his sight for a moment, put [his] spear in position, . . . aimed for behind his head, and let go."[43]

The rod struck home, and the man jumped into waist-deep water to subdue the stunned fish, which he quickly dragged back up on the exposed coral head. There, as he finished off the fish with his knife, Taylor wrote, he "looked up and saw the fin of a shark cutting through the water towards the rock. It came on lazily, slipping easily through the surface, and circled my perch on the reef. In a few minutes another arrived. This was unwholesome. . . . those dusty *Sailing Directions* came back to me again, 'The water is infested with sharks which are a ferocious variety and swarm in great numbers close to the island.' "[44]

The smaller of the two, a six-footer, swam in so close by the Rock that Taylor "could see the coldly murderous look that is always in the eye of a shark as, with an easy flick of his tail, he slid in and turned to steer away." Holding tightly to its line, Taylor hurled his spear as hard as he could at the shark, nearly overbalancing and falling into the sea. "For a moment," he later recalled, the iron rod "stood like a raised periscope, stiffly out of the water, fast in his head. I dropped to the rock and grasped the edge, holding the line, trying to hold the shark and save my spear. It must have struck the fish in the bone or the tough part of his head. There was a whizzing vibration through the water, and the line came away free in my hand with only the dead weight of the spear."[45]

Panic-stricken as a thin streak of red streamed from its forehead, the wounded shark dove headlong for the safety of deep water, beyond the edge of the precipice. Its larger companion turned and followed, suddenly accelerating toward the trail of blood; it abruptly disappeared into the depths. The reef seemingly empty of man-eaters, Taylor quickly made his way to the atoll's rim. There, on solid ground, he cleaned the rockfish, "throwing the guts in the water. They drifted about, washing along the edge of the beach. While finishing the job," he said, "I saw splashing in the water a few yards away. It was the tail of a shark stranded for a moment in his rush in for the innards of the fish. I was learning more about the reef and its inhabitants."[46]

At sunset he reached camp with the fish, which was enough to feed everyone. As it cooked, Taylor noted, "Hogg was greatly disturbed." The booby had left, apparently on one of her now-rare fishing expeditions seaward, and had not returned. Hogg insisted that "her absence was a bad omen, with something in store for us," but Taylor sensed nothing amiss. The weather was calm, the sky clear, and the temperature pleasant. *Frigate Bird* rested motionlessly, "shining white in the glitter of the moonlight, and the island was silent, with the sea whispering caresses to it."⁴⁷

After dinner, Taylor strolled to the nearby palm grove to be alone. There, he said he

saw something in the grass, bent down and picked it up. It was a small, flat, metal object which I saw from the light of my torch was a locket. I managed to pry it open, and found the miniatures of a man and a young woman looking out to me with frank eyes from a beautiful and intelligent face. I was touched lightly by a sense of intrusion. I switched off the flashlight, closed the locket and held it in my hand, not knowing at that moment what to do with it. . . . The solitude was absolute. Nothing existed but the island and the ocean.

Presently I seemed to become aware of the presence of other people—that I was standing without material presence myself, watching a scene in which I had no part. In the vision of my mind was a small fire glowing on the top of the coral bank by the grove, its light shining on the leaves of the coconut trees. Round the fire a group of people were gathered, reclining in various attitudes of rest and singing some haunting song to the accompaniment of two men standing with guitars. I could hear the song very clearly.

I watched, fascinated, and presently a young man and a girl in an evening dress, soft in the moonlight, passed me. They strolled slowly on and stood by the shore where the others were singing. She looked up to him, then turned, and I heard her voice join with the song, very softly at first, but clear and true. Gradually the others stopped their singing, and listened, with me, to this voice of infinite sweetness melting into harmony with the night and the quiet breaking of the ocean.

Standing there, I was spellbound and knew nothing but the voice,

till the fire began to fade and with it the sight and sound of what had
come into the night before me. I found myself looking over the empty
shore by the palm grove and out over the sea, unable to believe for a
while that I was alone.

The locket was still in my hand, warm and smooth now with the
touch of the metal case which held the miniatures. I walked back to
where I had found it, scraped a hole in the coral, and put it down to
the ground. Then I covered it over with sand and left it there.

I didn't tell the others of this experience. It impressed me too
much at the time, and seemed too fantastic for repetition.[48]

The next day, PBY JX 603 arrived from Acapulco bearing tools,
supplies, and a surprise. As the Catalina flew by overhead, Taylor
radioed landing advice to Squadron Leader Uprichard, and "in a
few minutes the two boats were lying together quietly on their
anchors off our camp." Taylor noted, "I saw in this other aircraft
the next step towards the establishment of the base at this island."[49] In time, he would see in 603's very presence a threat to
the island's tranquility and well-being.

There were ill omens from the outset. PBY 603's surprise
proved to be a wooden dinghy and an outboard motor, but just as
the newcomers tried to hand the gasoline engine to Taylor's
appreciative crew, they dropped it irretrievably into 20 feet of
weed-entangled water. Taylor nevertheless put the wooden boat to
good use, paddling it with relative ease about the lagoon, thereby
allowing them to deflate the rubber dinghy and stow it away. It
was beinning to show signs of wear and would surely be needed if
they had to ditch somewhere in the vast Pacific—provided they
ever got off Clipperton island.

PBY 603 also brought a new tool kit that inexplicably failed to
contain a spark plug wrench, and Hogg had no choice but to use
the one from the other Catalina, thereby causing it to linger
longer on the atoll than anyone had anticipated. Eventually, Hogg
encountered a plug that was practically welded into the engine
head and broke it off with the spanner. Taylor signaled Dorval for
spare parts and for permission to send 603 back to Mexico to fetch
them.

By then he was eager to be rid of the newcomers. PBY 603
contained ten people, some of them incapable of fending for

themselves. They stood about in driving rain, "wet and bedraggled," until others erected shelters for them. A few were even bent on violent fun. Equipped with gelatinite for blasting away coral reefs, as well as rifles and ammunition, "some of the 603 party planned to set out on a delicious orgy of slaughter on the island— of the pigs, the birds, and the fish on the reef." Taylor discovered this "in time to stop . . . the actual destruction of trees in the grove where each one was a priceless asset to anybody who might be on the island, including ourselves."[50]

As soon as Al Torrey surveyed possible C-47 landing strips, Taylor sent them all back to Acapulco to await parts for *Frigate Bird*. Having kept 603's wrench, the following day Hogg broke off yet another spark plug. Taylor was thankful he had also ordered two new cylinder heads as well as a spare set of spark plugs. Even so, he instructed Hogg not to attempt to loosen the starboard engine's three remaining plugs, all of them installed in Canada and similarly stuck, for fear they too might snap off. With Birks assisting and with a canvas catchment rigged below the motors, just in case, Hogg instead removed the starboard heads, which contained stubborn plugs, "with the ever-present danger of dropping a vital part into the water."[51] On dry land Hogg quickly removed all but one spark plug; it proved to be welded to the metal by engine heat. The entire head would have to be replaced.

With heavy, dark clouds threatening, PBY 603 returned on 8 October, this time commanded by a Captain Spinks, his crew having "come prepared to fend for themselves."[52] Hogg, Birks, and a man named Hicks, engineer from the second plane, immediately set to work to fix *Frigate Bird*. While they worked, Taylor grew more apprehensive about the weather and set another anchor at a different angle, just in case. It was good that he did. Soon after they retired for the night, a storm slammed into the island from the southwest. What had been a light breeze hardened into a sustained 35-knot wind, with gusts of 50, accompanied by a drenching downpour. Through a sheet of rain, Taylor saw both Catalinas move. Their anchors were losing grip of the bottom, and both amphibians drifted toward sharp coral heads—and disaster.

All hands made for their airplanes. Like canoeists running rapids, Taylor and his crew rowed the wooden dinghy on the wind to *Frigate Bird*. They grabbed hold of the PBY just as the wooden dinghy skittered by on the gale, and, once aboard, Birks and Henderson ran forward and let out slack on both lines, working anchors by hand in attempts to grab hold of the bottom. Hogg stood by to start the one serviceable engine, should anchors fail to check their drift, but one anchor soon snagged hold, then the other.

By then Taylor had lost sight of 603, which sailed on in the storm. He tried to raise his companions with signal lamps, to no avail. At daybreak he spotted the PBY, aground on the lee shore. "While we were watching her," Taylor later wrote, "I was astonished to see her engines start and the boat taxi very slowly out from the shore. She came on, and up the lagoon. Miraculously, she must have drifted back in the darkness, dragging her anchors wrapped in weed, passing safely through the coral heads, and rested against the shore with her tail in the grass. . . . She taxied on up to the windward shore, twice walked away with her anchor, went up again with her engines, and finally held in a good sheltered place."[53]

The blow continued unabated throughout the day, and all hands remained aboard their craft. "It was a miserable day," Taylor later remembered. Winds subsided that evening, the tempest passing by dawn. Wishing to reposition *Frigate Bird* within easy paddling distance of shore to facilitate work, Taylor tried to start the good engine, but he failed. Hogg quickly located a defective coil and replaced it, whereupon the electrical starter refused to engage. Ultimately, the mechanic had to hand-crank the engine. Then, when they commenced to haul in an anchor, its chain snapped in two. Taylor taxied under power to a spot 300 feet off Pincer bay and reanchored the flying boat, using rope in place of broken chain.

Lest they face another storm before they could take flight, Taylor directed all hands to moor *Frigate Bird* securely. Among property abandoned by Pacific Phosphate Company were the rusted remains of two rail cars and, nearby, in the grass, several heavy iron chains that, although quite oxidized, seemed strong enough to hold. It took all day to haul the heavy, unwieldy cars to the water's edge near the PBY where, one at a time, they were hauled aboard a wooden-framed rubber dinghy out to the Catalina and dumped overboard, one chain and three ropes attached to each. These the crew secured to the aircraft, mooring it against any possible drift in another tempest.

Reassured, that night Taylor slept peacefully for the first time in days—until awakened at dawn by a "flapping bird caught in the aerial, . . . panicking, trying to free itself from the wire. . . ." It took Bligh much of the day to repair the aerial. The incident was fair warning. The longer they tarried, the more problems they encountered. Hogg, Birks, and Hicks of the 603 resumed work, replacing the cylinder head by day's end. Only a few connections needed to be made in the morning before the engine might be started. "We could run up for a test on the lagoon," Taylor believed, "and, if everything proved satisfactory, top up the tanks and be off at noon if the wind was suitable for any of the more feasible take-off plans and the . . . forecast was favorable."[54]

That night, Bligh radioed Dorval to inquire about the weather. Meteorologists in faraway Canada using primitive methods tried to do the impossible: predict atmospheric conditions halfway around the world, between Clipperton and Bora Bora. They forecast generally favorable weather along the entire 3,000-mile-course for the next two days.

Taylor awoke at dawn and checked the sky; it was dark and threatening. A fresh, 20-knot breeze blew from the north, exactly opposite of what he wished for takeoff. "There was something sinister in this weather," he thought to himself. He rowed out to the PBY and consulted its altimeter, finding the barometric pressure to be 29.85 inches of mercury, which was on the low scale of recent daily readings but no lower than he had seen before, elsewhere. "I decided to go ahead with preparations for departure," he later wrote, "and to keep an eye on the barometer and the weather." With 3,000 miles of uncertain weather ahead, he decided that nothing was to be gained by staying at the atoll because of tempests they might quickly fly through. Nevertheless, "fair weather in the beginning was desirable while the aircraft would still be heavily overloaded with fuel. . . ."[55]

As both crews sat down to a final Clipperton island breakfast of porridge, cornflakes, and canned fruit, a storm suddenly broke, and they forgot about food. Through a howling gale men ran to check mooring and anchorage on 275 and 603. Taylor saw 603 begin to move on winds he estimated to be in excess of 50 knots. "I stood," he later recalled, "my feet fixed to the rock, fascinated by the inevitability of disaster, unable to do anything to avert it. And then the aircraft, drifting for a moment half across the wind as she began to bear away, suddenly swung up, and stopped. The line from her bollard stretched tight like a rod straight to the water ahead, as though suddenly taken by some enormous fighting fish and held fast where the anchor had caught on the coral."[56]

PBY 603 was safe, for the moment at least, held securely by a taut line, and 275 rode "rock solid at her mooring." No matter. The men were powerless to act. With the wind came drenching rain, and they took such shelter as they had, holding onto the lean-to for dear life lest it and they blow away. The wind hardened into a steady blow that commenced to break things. "It sizzled over the water and rushed through camp, taking with it anything that was loose about the place. . . . The camp itself began to disintegrate round us as the wind, instead of passing, rose steadily in violence."[57]

Soon, only the cook house remained, and Taylor moved to it. He braced its walls with his body, trying to shield the charcoal cook fire, which he desperately wanted to keep going. It might well prove to be the difference between life and death. Already he was chilled to the bone by cold rain. Even the "birds had left," Taylor observed, "except for a few who now could not escape. Where they had gone I do not know, because we did not see them leave, but I suspect it was to The Rock, where there was shelter in the caverns and fissures from the weather." Then, a powerful gust of wind took the cook house. Taylor dropped to the ground to avoid going with it. Exposed to the gale, the fire momentarily became "a shower of flame and sparks, like a comet, till in a few seconds it was extinguished by the rain."[58]

The wind abruptly abated, dropping to no more than 30 knots, and Hicks, the 603's engineer, jumped into the wooden dinghy and rowed frantically for his aircraft, which lay some 150 feet from the shore and was "still holding precariously on one anchor." The man reached the plane, scrambled aboard, and shoved the dinghy away from the thin-skinned Catalina. The boat washed toward shore, but before it could reach the beach, the wind had swung abruptly eastward and shrieked down on the island even more fiercely than before. "Hicks disappeared into the aeroplane," Taylor wrote, "and closed the blister. We saw no more of him as she hung there, shrouded in rain and driving spray."[59]

Those ashore caught the dinghy as it reached land, "before she could smash herself on the rocks," and "against a hail of tiny bullets" of spray hauled it out of the water. As Taylor again made for shelter he saw a young gannet, "wet and bedraggled, but alive" among the rocks; he found it a shelter in "a dry spot behind a rock." Without much hope for the bird's survival, he dashed on to join others at camp, which was being totally demolished: "things now [were lifting] . . . off the ground and blow[ing] away." Taylor began "to think beyond the aircraft, to a question of [his own] survival. . . ."[60]

Taylor had "no doubt about the nature of this turmoil. A hurricane was passing over the island, and, because of the rapid shift of wind," he judged, "we could not have been far from its centre." About then he heard something "roaring towards us, down the lagoon. The Rock was blotted out and the lagoon was sweeping towards us in a wall of water like spray from many hoses, reaching from shore and leaving no definition between sky and lagoon. It was a fantastic sight, as though the ocean was folding up like a carpet, and rolling down in some cataclysm of water torn and driven in blinding showers by the wind. *'Mountainous seas sometimes sweep right over the island.'* Again I heard the words of the old *Sailing Directions*."[61]

The men were helpless, powerless to protect themselves from a solid, ten-foot-tall wall of water that crashed down upon them. "There was nothing to do but crouch there and try to breathe, each breath being dealt with systematically as a separate operation which had to be completed deliberately as a lead to the next. Suddenly everything had become very simple. There was just the question of breathing; a single purpose in some strange dream." The storm surge actually passed quite quickly, and through it all Taylor saw *Frigate Bird* "lifting and swaying like a ghost aircraft flying through turbulent air—and like a ghost she stayed there, flying but neither advancing nor fading into the background of her shroud."[62]

That either plane had survived struck him as miraculous, but his heart sank when, through the rain, he saw 603 being driven backward, toward the rocks and destruction. Then, through the mist, he "saw first one propeller swing over and spin, splattering the air with a circle of spray, and then the other." As though an "invisible hand had reached down to rescue the aircraft, she suddenly stopped, and began to move away from the shore." Above the howl of wind he heard the roar of engines. Spellbound, he watched Hicks power his way "through the chaos, out from shore—out, for water where he could hold her with the engines facing up to the wind, . . . obviously pushing the wheel hard forward as squalls of incredible violence struck her, threatening to lift her out of the water and throw the twelve tons of aircraft like a moth against the land. A Catalina will fly at 70 knots. These squalls must have been more than a 100. Only the suction on the hull and the tail raised high by the elevator to stop the positive lift on the wing was keeping her in the water."[63]

Noon approached without relief. As the sea crept ever higher up the coral crown, the men ashore carried such supplies as they could salvage and made for the palm grove, which harbored pigs and even some birds that had taken refuge from the storm. Prepared to shinny up the trees if the water rose further, the airmen huddled together against the storm. At about 1500 hours, the sky lightened, and the wind eased slightly; it continued to "be a screaming gale, but the unbelievable violence had gone out of it."[64]

Incredibly, both aircraft still sat upright on the lagoon, 275 secure on her mooring and 603 facing the wind, propellers turning smoothly. *Frigate Bird*'s starboard engine cover had been torn half off; it was threshing about wildly in the wind, threatening irreparable damage. Seeing the urgency of the situation, Birks dove into the lagoon and tried to swim to the Catalina, but he was soon ensnared in a veritable jungle of storm-tangled weed and very nearly drowned before struggling back to shore. The rest of Taylor's crew rigged a stern line to the wooden dinghy and carried it overland to a point precisely upwind from the Catalina, where it was launched with Henderson in the stern and Taylor up front, maneuvering with paddles, to reach 275. Taylor wrote: "The voyage of 100 yards down on the wind to the aircraft was an adventure for me no less than the flight to the island."[65]

They grabbed a wing strut and climbed aboard through the

starboard waist bubble, abandoning the dinghy to a stern line tended by those ashore. Inside, the plane smelled damp, but its hull was dry and warm. It was also remarkably stable, swaying very little in the still-shrill wind. They went forward and out through the roof hatch to reach the starboard engine. Although buffeted by brisk breezes, they secured the cowling in a few minutes and immediately returned inside. "After that," Taylor wrote, "there was nothing more to do now but wait for the hurricane to pass, which it appeared to be doing."[66] They went aft and changed into dry clothing, and afterward Henderson brewed coffee on the plane's cook stove. Meanwhile, Hicks continued to keep 603's nose into the wind and her engines revved up enough to hold fast.

By 1700 hours, the winds had subsided to 40 knots, and Birks, Bligh, and Hogg took to a rubber dinghy, which, tied down to some vine roots, had ridden out the storm, and set out for *Frigate Bird*. They skittered about the surface of the lagoon on the wind, their paddles flaying the water wildly as they tried to maintain direction. Finally, they came alongside the Catalina, grabbed the starboard strut, and climbed aboard, tying off the dinghy to the airplane. Soon afterward the crew of the 603 similarly reached it, Hicks continuing to hold the PBY against the wind.

Neither airplane had been seriously harmed by the storm. Nor was the fuel barge, securely anchored nearby and so entangled with vegetation that it appeared "merely as a lump in the surface weed," in any way damaged. "Everything ashore was wrecked, but the canned provisions were mostly intact," Taylor says, "and I felt that if the night held fine we should soon be well established again."[67]

Winds moderated to 30 knots during the night, and all hands relaxed and slept in the comparative comfort of their aircraft. At dawn, a gentle shower drifted overhead on light southerly breezes. When it passed, the sky was absolutely clear. Taylor ordered cowlings removed to permit the engines to dry in the sun. That done, the men went ashore. Taylor found the young gannet he had rescued during the hurricane; it was very much alive but still trapped in its improvised shelter. He freed the chick just in time for it to be reunited with its parents, who flew home as though nothing had happened. Soon the atoll was covered with boobies, frigates, and terns, apparently all of them having come back—"all except Hogg's bird, which never returned. He attributed all . . . setbacks to the disappearance of this bird, which was a bad omen. 'It's yon burrd,' he said. 'I knew when she didn't come back that we were in for trouble.' "[68]

By evening Hogg had completed repairs, and Taylor ran up the engines. He let them warm slowly, the Catalina still fast on her moorings. He resolved to sit there, tied up snugly, until he was certain about the weather. That night Bligh handed Taylor a radio message from Dorval. Two Dakotas (C-47s) were being loaded in Canada with engineering equipment. Taylor wrote in his log: "There is great satisfaction in the knowledge that our work is to be followed up by this early development of a base at Clipperton Island."[69]

At dawn, 14 October, the sky was clear, with a light southerly breeze. Dorval's latest forecast from Clipperton to Bora Bora, received the night before, was favorable—"similar to the last."[70] Taylor was determined to depart at noon. Believing that nothing would be gained with a separate engine test on the lagoon, which would necessitate taxiing the Catalina in again through the coral reef to top off its tanks, he planned to run up the engines as a part of the regular preflight check; therefore, his men brought up the gasoline barge, fueled *Frigate Bird,* and bid farewell to 603's crew.

Taylor tried to crank the port engine, but its starter refused to engage. Hogg wound up the inertia starter on the main batteries; Birks scampered out onto the wing and tripped it by hand; and the recalcitrant engine started and ran smoothly. Taylor then cranked the starboard engine without difficulty. He signaled his fellows to let go all lines, and he carefully taxied the plane out away from its moorings and into clear water, carefully steering the fuel-heavy Catalina through the narrow channel in the reef. In the middle of the lagoon he circled slowly, warming the engines in deep water. Then, as he switched to the backup magnetos as part of the preflight check, the starboard engine misfired, vibrating violently. Reluctantly, he taxied back to the sheltered bay by the camp.

There Hogg located three cold spark plugs and changed them. In less than an hour, *Frigate Bird* was back on open water, its engines running smoothly. Then, when Taylor again tested the backup magneto, the starboard engine misfired as badly as before. He switched on both magnetos and revved the engine to full power to clear it with backfire; it banged loudly, and he cut power.

As he taxied along, Taylor wrote later that he

put into effect a decision I had made when we left the mooring the second time. . . . I purposely deceived the others, except Birks, who could see what was happening, anyhow. I turned her and ran up the engines again, this time taking care not to run the starboard on the left magneto alone. Everything was splendid. . . . This decision screamed at me in outrage of my own principle against the acceptance of avoidable risk in the air. But . . . I was convinced that if we didn't leave now we would never leave. For weeks we had struggled with an assortment of adverse influences, and had managed to keep afloat and a jump ahead of each. But I now had a strong impression that the aircraft was gradually bogging down in the insidious effects of wind and weather and something that inhabited the island, and that failure to extricate her now, in what favorable circumstances we could command, would be the end of it.[71]

Beginning the run near a red flag marker he had set at the edge of an Egg island, Taylor pointed *Frigate Bird* toward Grand Reef, a mile and one-quarter away. If he saw that they could not be airborne because of the extraordinary fuel load, he planned to over-run around Grand Reef, toward the Rock. He only hoped that this little, half-mile-long channel would prove to be sufficient to arrest the flying boat's momentum before it ran out of water, slid up onto the sand, and crashed into the Rock.

At Taylor's signal Birks advanced the throttle, and the Catalina commenced to gain speed, smashing rhythmically through the water as it went and sending cascades of spray up over the wind screen, obscuring vision. As *Frigate Bird* strained to be free of the water, Taylor wrote, "I took a light tension on the control column and lifted her away. She was heavy in the air, but flying securely, as I held her down for speed. . . . I called for Birks to reduce power, as we swept low over the sea, and leaned her into a turn to come back and fly over the camp where the others were standing, watching the take-off. . . . I pulled down over the lagoon and, in a steady turn that she would take with the heavy fuel load, saw them waving up to us."[72]

Free of the atoll, Taylor reflected: "All that happened at Clipperton Island seemed suddenly to become condensed and unimportant and, as I looked down for the last time on the island, to sink with its strange past into the blue depths of the crater. Now there was no reality but the aeroplane. . . . Everything was as it had been, before the dream from which I seemed now to have awakened."[73]

Soon after PBY 275 was airborne, 603 likewise took off for Acapulco, its first stop on the way to Dorval.

Within a week of departure, Taylor's mission had been completed. The PBY reached Bora Bora in twenty-seven hours, where it was thoroughly serviced. Two days later they resumed their journey, inspecting sites for R.A.F. bases at Bora Bora, Tahiti, Aitutaki, Tonga, New Zealand, and Australia, their ultimate destination. Later, back at Dorval, Taylor nominated Hicks for the George Medal for his heroics during the typhoon, the citation being awarded some years afterward. Meanwhile, confident that the atoll would soon be a British air base, Taylor and the others were quickly caught up in the war.

So too was Clipperton island.

Notes

1. Hetherington, p. 181.

2. Taylor (1948), p. 10.

3. Taylor (1963), p. 162.

4. Ernest J. King, Chief of Naval Operations, to Air Marshal Sir William L. Welsh, Royal Air Force Delegation, Washington, D.C., 25 May 1944, in Roosevelt Papers as President, Map Room Collection, Box 162, "Air Base, Clipperton Island" folder.

5. Quoted in George M. Elsey, "Memorandum for Admiral Brown; Subject: Clipperton Island," 19 January 1945, p.3, in *ibid*.

6. "Alusna, Mexico City," to Chief of Naval Operations, [Admiral E. J. King], 7 June 1944, in *ibid*.

7. Elsey, "Memorandum," 19 January 1945, pp. 4–5, in *ibid*. Apparently no one in the American government ever learned that Taylor's stay on Clipperton island was lengthier than scheduled.

8. *Ibid*.

9. Taylor (1948), p. 42.

10. *Ibid*., pp. 72, 74.

11. *Ibid*., p. 83.

12. *Ibid*., pp. 83–86.

13. *Ibid*., p. 86.

14. *Ibid*., p. 87.

15. *Ibid*., pp. 87–88.

16. *Ibid*., pp. 91, 93, 101–102.

17. *Ibid*., pp. 103–104.

18. *Ibid*., p. 104.

19. Quoted in *ibid*., pp. 106–107.

20. *Ibid.*, p. 111.

21. *Ibid.*, p. 112.

22. *Ibid.*, pp. 113–14.

23. *Ibid.*, p. 115. Who might have buried Álvarez a mile and a half from the spot by the Rock where he was killed by Tirza Randon is open to speculation. Perhaps the cross marked someone else's grave, but inasmuch as no one else is known to have died there since 1917, it is another Clipperton island mystery. No visitor since World War I has reported seeing any portion of Álvarez's remains—and it is not likely that any would have survived the ravenous assault of both crabs and pigs.

24. *Ibid.*, p. 116. It seems evident that Taylor never learned of Admiral Byrd's secret 1943 expedition to Clipperton island.

25. *Ibid.*, pp. 121–22.

26. *Ibid.*, p.123.

27. *Ibid.*

28. *Ibid.*, p. 124. Before climbing down, Taylor said: "We examined the lamp, which was a thing of great beauty, obviously made by some craftsman among makers of lamps. . . . I [looked] for the name of the maker of the lamp—found it in letters stamped into the heavy brass casing that held the lens. The name, like the light, had endured through many years of weather on this lonely peak. After a little rubbing, it was still clearly marked: *Socte des Etablissement Henry—Le Paute—*Paris." *Ibid.*, pp. 125–26.

29. *Ibid.*, p. 166.

30. *Ibid.*, p. 150.

31. *Ibid.*, p. 151.

32. *Ibid.*, pp. 158–59.

33. *Ibid.*, p. 161.

34. *Ibid.*, pp. 154, 164.

35. *Ibid.*, pp. 154–55.

36. *Ibid.*, p. 162.

37. *Ibid.*

38. *Ibid.*, p. 169.

39. *Ibid.*, pp. 171–72.

40. *Ibid.*, pp. 173–74.

41. *Ibid.*, pp. 175–76.

42. *Ibid.*, pp. 176–77.

43. *Ibid.*, pp. 177–84.

44. *Ibid.*, pp. 185–86.

45. *Ibid.*, pp. 186–87.

46. *Ibid.*, pp. 187–88.

47. *Ibid.*, p. 188.

48. *Ibid.*, pp. 188–90.

49. *Ibid.*, p. 197.

50. *Ibid.*, pp. 201–202.

51. *Ibid.*, p. 207.

52. *Ibid.*, p. 212.

53. *Ibid.*, p. 215.

54. *Ibid.*, pp. 221–22.

55. *Ibid.*, pp. 224–25.

56. *Ibid.*, pp. 226–27.

57. *Ibid.*, p. 227.

58. *Ibid.*, p. 228.

59. *Ibid.*, p. 229.

60. *Ibid.*, p. 230.

61. *Ibid.*, p. 231.

62. *Ibid.*, p. 232.

63. *Ibid.*, pp. 230–34.

64. *Ibid.*, pp. 241–43.

65. *Ibid.*, p. 245.

66. *Ibid.*, p. 247.

67. *Ibid.*, p. 248.

68. *Ibid.*, pp. 251–52.

69. Quoted in *ibid.*, p. 253.

70. *Ibid.*, p. 254.

71. *Ibid.*, pp. 256–57.

72. *Ibid.*, p. 261.

73. *Ibid.*, pp. 254–61.

11

Snafu at Island X
1944–1945

The British failed to establish an aerodrome on Clipperton island because Franklin Delano Roosevelt personally stopped them. P. G. Taylor, who died in 1961, never learned that within six weeks of *Frigate Bird*'s last flight from the coral-rimmed lagoon, the president of the United States had ordered his navy to seize the place, maintaining facilities there until 5 October 1945, well after the war's end. Had Taylor known details of that operation, he probably would have sympathized with the mighty Yankee fleet, which perpetually faced problems on and about the remote atoll. Classified top secret until 1967, the proud service's experiences with "Weather Station No. 1" on "Island X" are best described by that unofficial navy acronym of the age, "Snafu"—Situation Normal, All Fucked Up!

On 16 October 1944—four days after *Frigate Bird* flew away, bound for Bora Bora—British Vice Air Marshal R. P. Willock advised the U.S. Navy that "the preliminary survey of Clipperton Island has now been completed, and . . . the prospects . . . for both a small seaplane base and suitable land strips for two runways would appear reasonably good. Further and more detailed survey of the Island is however necessary. . . ." For that purpose, he said, an engineering group was prepared to visit the island for about one month. Willock assured the Pentagon: "There is no intention of going beyond the detailed survey of Clipperton Island until the final return of the reconnaissance aircraft from Australia and preparation of the report on the operation."[1]

Admiral E. J. King promptly replied that he still considered the proposed "route via Clipperton Island to the Southwest Pacific . . . [to be] of no military value" and advised Air Marshal Willock that as far as he was concerned the topic was "a policy matter [suitable] for discussion and decision between your government and those of the United States and Mexico and the French authorities."[2] Willock disagreed, insisting that the "desirability of surveying the Island has already been agreed to. . . ."[3] To clarify matters, he requested a personal interview with the admiral, which King denied.

Instead, on 4 November Willock saw Vice Admiral Richard S. Edwards, King's deputy chief of staff, and "stressed the 'urgency' of the British survey with more vehemence than his letters had shown. . . . [He] explained that the survey party was [already] in Mexico awaiting [American] approval."[4] The next day, King notified Willock in writing: "I consider that there is little to be gained from further discussion. . . . I await instructions from my government before taking action."[5]

British tactics changed. Following "a lull in the Clipperton Island discussions," on November 21 Lord Halifax, British ambassador to the United States, asked Secretary of State Edward R. Stettinius the status of the British request regarding the atoll. Stettinius replied that neither the air route nor the island was important to the war effort, an exchange he promptly reported to the White House.

There "the suspicion [persisted] that the British might be proceeding [secretly] with operations in Mexico and Clipperton." Thus, President Roosevelt directed Rear Admiral Wilson Brown to "find out what the British are doing at Clipperton," but, since there was no practical way of accomplishing that short of sending troops to the island, Admiral Brown "recommended on 27 November that a weather station be established at Clipperton, pending future discussions with the British, French and Mexicans, [and] the President ordered it done."[6]

The following day, as a matter of "top secret—priority," Admiral Brown informed Admiral Edwards that the president "wanted a plane sent to Clipperton at an early date to investigate whether or not any [British] survey operations are under way. . . ." Moreover, he said that Roosevelt ordered the establishment of a weather station on the island "as soon as practicable." When Edwards asked whether the navy was "to consult the French about this," Brown replied, "No . . . these steps are being taken as necessary war measures and the question of ownership would be discussed later."[7]

Admiral Edwards dutifully relayed presidential orders to Admiral King, who immediately instructed Rear Admiral Howard F. Kingman at San Diego, the naval facility closest to the scene, to reconnoiter the atoll. Kingman in turn directed Captain Duncan Curry, skipper of USS *Detroit,* to conduct an aerial photographic reconnaissance.

An *Omaha*-class light cruiser assigned to routine West coast patrol duty in waters no longer considered dangerous, *Detroit* zigzagged its way to the island, arriving early on the morning of 2 December. At 0718 hours, its crew catapulted both ship's airplanes into flight, one armed in case of trouble, the other sporting a camera; both planes were recovered within three hours, and the warship departed the island seventeen minutes later. En route to California for other duties, Captain Curry reported by radio in code that the mission had been completed and that there were "no personnel present."[8] A copy of that transcription was promptly forwarded to the White House.

Also in response to White House orders, on 28 November Admiral King had directed Admiral Royal E. Ingersoll, Commander, Western Sea Frontier, to "Establish at [the] earliest practical date [an] expeditionary aerological station on Clipperton island," its personnel complement to consist of one officer, "an aerologist," and six enlisted men. Toward this end, King ordered Ingersoll to arrange for a construction crew, transportation, supplies, and facilities for refueling seaplanes. Above all else, King directed, "Preserve secrecy [about] this project."[9]

Within the hour, Admiral Ingersoll had directed USS *Nevada* to conduct another aerial reconnaissance, this mission preliminary to the establishment of the clandestine station. A World War I vintage battleship, *Nevada* was part of "Task Unit 12," then patrolling Pacific waters off North America, in the Western Sea Frontier. Immediately upon receiving the priority dispatch from Ingersoll, the ship detached and set course for the island.

On 4 December, Captain Homer L. Grosskopf, Sr., *Nevada*'s

skipper, dispatched two "fully armed" OS2U aircraft to reconnoiter, as ordered. Lieutenant P. F. Ickes, the ship's intelligence officer, went along in one aircraft as observer, and on his return, he reported to Grosskopf that he had "sighted . . . five or six markers which appeared to have been made of white sand or gravel and flush with the ground. . . ." Located on the northwest rim, they were situated about 150 yards apart and extended for a total distance of about 1,000 yards. On the beach of the lagoon, northwest of the southernmost Egg island, were what appeared to be "soccer goal posts." On the lagoon, near a large mound of phosphates, "was located a lean-to" that "appeared to be constructed of driftwood with the roof and 3 sides covered, and the fourth side open, facing the lagoon. Inside the lean-to was a table and several benches. . . . There was a raft pulled up out of the water onto the grass on the left side of the lean-to. The raft appeared to be made out of 2 long cylindrical tanks which had been lashed together. Around the lean-to were 8 or 9 black pigs."[10]

Aside from a small American fishing boat, *Sea Lion,* a quarter-mile off the atoll's west end, there were no other signs of human activity. Captain Grosskopf dutifully radioed these findings to Western Sea Frontier headquarters in San Francisco, and *Nevada* steamed westward toward war, to employ the devastating firepower of her 13.4-inch guns in support of U.S. Marines on Iwo Jima.

Admiral Ingersoll then directed his chief of staff, Captain G. M. Lowry, to see to the establishment of the top-secret base. Lowry in turn instructed a Lieutenant Barr, captain of USS *Argus* (a German yacht confiscated by the government and converted by the navy into a patrol craft stationed in San Francisco), to "establish and maintain on Clipperton Island an expeditionary aerological station."[11] Lowry said that prior to *Argus*'s departure from San Francisco, an aerological party consisting of one officer and six enlisted men would report to Barr for transportation to the atoll.

Cautioning about the probability of heavy weather and of difficulties in going ashore, Captain Lowry urged Lieutenant Barr to give "due consideration to safety of personnel." In any case, sailors were to land with "rifles, machine guns, and ammunition, . . . [to] maintain a beach party ashore, [and to] . . . erect a flag pole and fly a United States ensign in accordance with U.S. Navy Regulations. . . ." Lowry ordered Barr to "report to Com[mander]West[ern]SeaFron[tier, Admiral Ingersoll], by secret priority dispatch arrival date, date of establishment of weather station, location on island, [and the] practicability of beaching an LST [Landing Ship, Tank]. . . ." Afterward, Barr and *Argus* were to "remain on station until after [the] arrival of a vessel with permanent shore equipment, rendering such assistance as may be necessary in establishing a permanent base on shore." Finally, in accordance with Admiral King's directive, Lowry told Barr to "preserve utmost secrecy of this movement, project, and destination."[12]

The day Captain Lowry sent *Argus* to sea, bound for the atoll, he also ordered Lieutenant J. B. Hockswender, commander of *LST-563*, to Port Hueneme, California, to load "the construction personnel, equipment, provisions and supplies as designated by Commanding Officer, Advanced Base Office, Pacific, and [to] transport this equipment to Clipperton Island. . . ." Lowry told Hockswender: "If necessary you may inform the Commandant 11th Naval District and Port Director [at] Port Hueneme that you are sailing under special secret orders including routing issued directly to you by Commander, Western Sea Frontier. You are directed not to divulge destination. . . ." Lowry further advised Hockswender, as he had Barr on *Argus,* to be alert for tropical storms in the vicinity of the low-lying island, ominously adding that "there is a heavy surf."[13]

Captain Lowry specified that a "permanent aerological base," commanded by Lieutenant M. S. Savere, was to be constructed under the direction of Lieutenant Commander Luke W. Dufresne, an engineer and the officer in command of operations in the island's vicinity. Once construction had been completed, Hockswender was to "report to Commander, Western Sea Frontier, by secret priority dispatch . . . [the] probable date . . . [of departure from] Clipperton Island for San Diego. . . ."[14]

It would seem that among the brass only Captain Lowry appreciated the formidable task facing the navy. What was doubtlessly envisioned by admirals Brown, Edwards, King, and Ingersoll to be a routine assignment proved to be a difficult job, and a disaster of some magnitude.

At first, events proceeded routinely. On the morning of 11 December, *Argus* arrived at the island and landed an armed force without difficulty. As ordered, the shore party raised the American flag—the first time Old Glory had been unfurled there since 1897. The men then pitched tents along the southwestern beach, where the meteorological station would eventually be situated, and Lieutenant Barr reported to Admiral Ingersoll by coded radio message that one officer and six enlisted personnel were on "Island X." A week later, 19 December, the Western Sea Frontier followed extraordinary procedure by informing the White House directly that a "special secret"[15] base now existed.

Then things began to go wrong. *LST-563* arrived late on the afternoon of 20 December, carrying Seabees and construction equipment with which to build a naval base. As the newcomer searched for anchorage, it steamed across *Argus*'s anchor chain, causing the little patrol craft to lose hold of the bottom. Informed by Lieutenant Barr that he knew of no other shallow water in the vicinity, Lieutenant Hockswender was forced to "remain under way all night on leeward side of the island. . . ."[16]

The following morning, Hockswender searched for a suitable landing place for his "Landing Ship, Tank," one of 1,051 specialty cargo ships constructed (at a cost of $800,000 each) during World War II to provide both oceangoing and beach delivery of tanks and other large vehicles. LSTs were 328 feet long and sported 14-foot-wide bow ramps; they had large ballast systems that were flooded for ocean passage and pumped dry for beaching. Workhorses of the navy, these versatile vessels repeatedly demonstrated their worth from North Africa to the South Pacific, but *LST-563* proved to be inadequate to the task of landing at Clipperton island.

Thinking he had found a suitable spot along the southwestern coast, Lieutenant Hockswender carefully nosed his ship ashore in what appeared to be shallow water. When the bow grounded, he ordered the ramp lowered and the first vehicle in line, a jeep, unloaded. As a sailor drove it over the ramp, "high surf capsized her and it was necessary to make a recovery and bring the car back on board." Fortunately, the driver was not hurt. Dissatisfied with the location, Hockswender tried another at the northeastern point, the Oceanic Phosphate landing site, which appeared to him to be

more sheltered. "The ship proceeded to beach cautiously at reduced speed," Commander Dufresne later reported. "Suddenly
she stopped and full speed astern had no effect on her. She
apparently was pivoted on a rock. This coupled with the wind
and surf broached her. An attempt was made to pass a line to the
USS *Argus* but the messenger cable parted. At sunset any further
attempts [at pulling the ship free] were discontinued as heavy seas
were running."[17]

For the next several weeks, activities at Island X were divided
between efforts to refloat the ship and construction of the permanent weather station. By dawn, 22 December, the surf had swung
the LST about, so that its ramp pointed away from land, preventing off-loading of cargo. In an attempt to float the ship off the
rocks, sailors rigged pontoons, but "excessive high surf caused
lines and cables to part, [and] the men were being constantly
washed overboard from the pontoons and working under great
difficulties." As this labor was under way, Hockswender and
Dufresne visited Barr to discuss the situation, taking with them
"two officers and several men from the USS *Argus* who had been
stranded ashore for ten days as the USS *Argus* was unable to return
them to ship due to lack of boats."[18]

Dufresne directed Barr to pass the stranded ship a line attached
to a 1,000-pound anchor, which *Argus* was to drop well out to
sea, off the LST's stern, in the hope that it would bite bottom and
allow the beached vessel to wrench itself free of the island.
Unfortunately, the anchor did not hold until 450 feet of line had
been played out, and then not firmly enough for the LST to yank
itself loose.

The following day, "all lines to the pontoons parted" in a
violently surging surf, the floats being smashed to bits on the
atoll's offshore reefs. Because of the violent sea, "no attempt at
refloating the ship [was] made all day—or the next." On Christmas morning, all hands turned out for work details. One group
of sailors set new pontoons on either side of the ship. Another
commenced to off-load by hand small equipment, including
emergency rations and dynamite. A third party filled and then
placed two thousand sandbags under the LST's open ramp, which
was stuck three feet in the air and at a 45° angle to the coral rim;
thus they built a bridge over which the larger of two bulldozers

aboard ship was driven ashore. When the other bulldozer refused to start, the first climbed back up into the ship and pulled its stubborn junior ashore. Once the bulldozers were off-loaded, "the men were given their Christmas dinner."[19]

When sailors prepared to resume work the next morning, Commander Dufresne says, they discovered that "the pontoons were 3 feet astern of the bow and the sand ramp had been washed away." He ordered them to reset in anticipation of floating the ship up off the reef at the moment of a pull by offshore ships. To coordinate efforts at the critical moment, he ordered the weather station ashore to devote one of its radio transmitters to serve as a communications link between atoll, *Argus,* and *LST-563;* however, heavy surf continued to batter the island for the next several days, forcing repeated postponements. Meanwhile, "the LST lost one LCVP [landing craft, vehicle and personnel] caused by [a] rudder striking a rock. This boat was broached by the surf and broken up."[20]

Problems compounded. Informed by Dufresne of mounting difficulties, Captain Lowry ordered USS *Seize,* a new salvage ship on shakedown cruise under command of Lieutenant Norman B. Conrad, to assist. Arriving on 29 December, *Seize* tied a line to the beached vessel and "pulled until the forenoon of 30 December when she finally beached directly ahead of the LST and it was found that she had several turns of towing cable around her starboard propeller." Attempting to free *Seize,* "the LST lost 3 more boats (LCVPs)."[21]

Commander Dufresne pressed Seabees who were constructing the weather station into a work party to unload the second grounded vessel to make it lighter. He also advised San Francisco by radio of the latest development. "Begun with such great secrecy that the island had been dubbed 'Island X' in early designations," the navy later noted, its identity, "while still a guarded secret, fell from 'Top Secret' grace into a slightly lower category of mystery when the *LST-563* and the *Seize* went aground. . . ."[22]

Captain Lowry ordered additional vessels to the scene, the region's radio waves by now crackling with communications regarding the clandestine base. On 4 January 1945, USS *Tenino,* a new oceangoing tug on her maiden mission, Lieutenant Forrest L.

Van Camp commanding, arrived carrying Commander Arthur E. Genereaux, a salvage officer sent by Lowry to take charge of operations. Upon his arrival, Genereaux immediately convened a conference ashore, receiving rude welcome to the island when the LCVP in which he landed "lost her rudder on hitting a rock near the beach. This boat had a line secured to another LCVP which pulled her off. The disabled boat was then turned over to the USS *Argus* for towing but sank."[23]

Commander Genereaux had Seabees bulldoze a new roadway from the beach to the LST's ramp, still suspended in midair, in order to remove a heavy generator and a large crane; with those items ashore, he theorized that the LST might be light enough to float free of its impalement. *Seize,* now rather ironically named, appeared to be less of a problem; Genereaux believed that it could be pulled free of the reef once sufficient power was available to achieve the task.   More help arrived on 7 January in the form of *Viking,* a *Lapwing*-class minesweeper sent by Captain Lowry to lend a hand. The next day *Tenino* and *Viking* rigged lines to *Seize* and tugged, pulling it around about 7°, but the effort was a failure. On 9 January, Lieutenant Van Camp of *Tenino* advised Lowry that "*Seize* was [also] impaled on the rocks and that it would be necessary to lighten the vessel [further] before another attempt at refloating would be made."[24] By 12 January, 109 tons of equipment, ammunition, and engine spare parts had been off-loaded onto the island from both ships.

Meanwhile, during high tide, *Tenino* and *Viking* had pulled on *LST-563,* moving it about 80 feet, but because of heavy swells outside the reef, they could not yank it free. By then fully appreciating the enormity of the task, later that day Commander Genereaux "requested additional help in order that salvage of both the ARS-26 [*Seize*] and *LST-563* might be hastily completed."[25]

Accordingly, Captain Lowry ordered *ATR-37,* a rescue tug stationed at San Diego, to the island; however, before it arrived, *Tenino* and *Viking* had freed *Seize* from the reef. Its hull was pierced, but damage-control measures were effective, preventing it from sinking. Disabled, the vessel was promptly taken in tow by *Argus,* pending the arrival of *ATR-37,* under whose sway *Seize* would return to San Diego.

Salvage operations then focused on *LST-563.* On 15 January,

Commander Genereaux estimated that it would take four days to prepare it for the next pull. Toward that end he had two beach gears fixed on the grounded ship and "hawsers" (cables used in towing or mooring) run between it and *Tenino* and *Viking* so that they could tug with the next tide. With a calm sea and a low tide running on the nineteenth, they pulled mightily, swinging the ship around 9 degrees, but no real progress was made in freeing it.

Supplies neared exhaustion. On 22 January, Commander Genereaux advised San Diego that *Viking* and *Tenino* had only enough fuel and provisions to last until February. If the grounded LST had not been refloated by then, he would have no choice but to send salvage vessels to port. Three days later, he added that the grounded LST had "a flooded generator room, no power, no lights, except from an auxiliary generator, and cooking had to be done ashore. However, there were no major casualties."[26]

Problems multiplied. Seamen aboard *Tenino* made four unsuccessful attempts to haul a hawser to the LST before finally securing a line on 29 January. Then, as the tide swung the LST five feet seaward, *Tenino* pulled once more, only to lose "all her salvage gear when her No. 3 starboard set of bitts was torn away from her bulwarks. Water poured into the engine room through the opening left by the bitts and the holes around the loosened rivets. The tug then proceeded to the lee side of Clipperton Island to effect damage control measures."[27] Lieutenant Van Camp "advised San Diego of the loss and damage of salvage equipment during these operations and urgently requested replacements."[28]

Heavy seas the following day tossed the grounded LST back up on the beach, farther onto land than ever before, forcing a reassessment of the situation—"bad." To maintain the ship's position and, he hoped, to avoid further damage, Genereaux ordered the LST's ballast tanks flooded. With *Tenino* damaged and *Viking* unsuited to salvage operations alone, he requested permission for all ships to return to San Diego for repairs and replenishment of stores. Lieutenant Hockswender, captain of the beached LST, also recommended that four of his officers and sixty of his men return to base with them, leaving himself on the island along with his engineer, communications officer, and fifty men to stand by the grounded vessel. "It was estimated that they could subsist for about 3 weeks on available food and supplies."[29]

Two days later, on 1 February, Captain Lowry authorized *Tenino* and *Viking* to return to San Diego and to bring back all personnel except those essential for the safety of the grounded LST and those assigned to the weather station. Lowry also directed Lieutenant Van Camp to take aboard *Tenino* "a seriously injured officer," hurt in a fall from a cargo net, "and two other patients," one with a "broken wrist" and the other with a "punctured knee vein," who required prompt medical attention. *Tenino* was to steam with all deliberate speed to Magdalena bay at Socorro island in the Revilla Gigedos, where a seaplane with a physician aboard would meet it and fly the men on to San Diego for treatment. Lowry also "indicated that in light of present conditions surrounding the *LST-563*'s plight, a discussion of possible abandonment of the project would be in order."[30]

Accordingly, on 8 Feburary, the Western Sea Frontier notified Lieutenant Hockswender that salvage operations were to cease. In a subsequent report to the navy's Bureau of Ships, Admiral Ingersoll stated that the grounded vessel was beyond repair: "18 tanks, engine and generator room[s] holed and flooded; all frames and plates on bottom and port side buckled, bent, or broken; salvage plans abandoned. Vessel being stripped of all valuable material, instruments and equipment. Upon completion of that task, all personnel being returned to San Diego." Ingersoll recommended "that *LST-563* be stricken from the list of Navy ships inasmuch as the salvage of the grounded vessel had been declared no longer practicable. The beached vessel's value to the Navy . . . would not be commensurate with the cost, even if salvage could be accomplished."[31]

On 16 February, the frigate *Grand Island* arrived from San Diego to rescue *LST-563*'s remaining crew members, who had been idling away the war. Aboard ship was Lieutenant Louis Etienne Jampierre, a French naval officer detailed to inspect American operations on behalf of his government. Jampierre was said to have engaged in "no patriotic or heroic displays of the French flag." In fact, he reportedly "did not think much of the possibilities of developing Clipperton as a base of any kind."[32] Instead, he severely sunburned his nose, which led him to pronounce the climate insufferable. He happily departed the following day, when *Grand Island* sailed for San Diego.

By then, Clipperton's "permanent weather station" had been constructed, and without serious damage to the environment. At first, Seabees considered establishing the base at the southeastern end of the island, near the Rock, but "after much thought it was decided to be unsuitable owing to the great number of pinnacles and cavities and [because] there was not sufficient dynamite to flatten it."[33]

Instead, the Seabees selected a site along the southwestern shore, beside Pacific Phosphate palm trees. Even so, the location was far from perfect, there being no landing place nearby; supplies had to be trucked around the atoll. In fact, the secret base's principal problem proved to be logistics. To maintain the place adequately, Captain Lowry theorized in faraway San Francisco, it would be necessary "to knock a hole in the reef" in order to give ships safe access to the atoll's lagoon, "and get some kind of anchorage inside there . . . [but that] would take a lot of money and I don't believe that it is justified."[34]

Fortunately for the atoll, its reef survived intact. Weather Station No. 1, laid out by Seabees in a semicircle, consisted of two 20-by-50-foot ammunition huts and four 12-by-56-foot Quonset huts, all set on concrete slab floors. One ammunition hut actually held munitions in case of invasion by a foreign power, enemy or ally. The other hut, which housed the weather bureau and radio station, was topped by a signal tower replete with two 12-inch searchlights and a flagpole from which the U.S. ensign flew daily. Nearby, Quonset huts served as galley and storeroom and as officer's, petty officer's, and crew's quarters.

Seabees also constructed a latrine, the first sanitation facility ever on the atoll. The navy's "head" consisted of a "concrete floor enclosed in a side-screened hut. Flushing [was] obtained by rise and fall of tide. . . . Officer's and CPO's [chief petty officer's] and crews huts have hot and cold water."[35] Three 85-gallon-per-hour water distillers, two storage tanks with 9,000 gallons total capacity, and even an electric washing machine were included in the equipment list as drawn up by the Advanced Base Office for Weather Station No. 1 on Island X, by then also known as "Navy Unit 950." Another washing machine, salvaged from *LST-563,* was also set up in the head when it came to be needed by as many as 150 naval personnel either stationed or stranded there.

Five generators (three on the equipment list and two salvaged from *LST-563*), the largest being 50-kilowatt, provided ample electricity for this most sophisticated human habitation of Clipperton island ever. There was need for much power. In addition to the washing machines, naval personnel enjoyed electric lights in all six buildings, a 150-cubic-foot refrigerator in the galley, and in the crew's quarters, a phonograph and an AM radio capable of receiving commercial broadcasts from the mainland, when atmospheric conditions were just right.

Also requiring much power were Island X's sophisticated weather station and radio broadcasting facilities, which consisted of two transmitters, each capable of output on two high- and two low-frequency bands, and four radio masts (two 90-foot broadcast towers with V antenna directed at San Francisco, and two 40-foot receivers). Thus were weather reports transmitted four times daily (at 0030, 0630, 1230, and 1830 hours, "zebra," navy-ese for Greenwich mean time), all messages to and from the island being encoded.

Navy records fail to disclose the significance of any of these meteorological reports, but inasmuch as no truly spectacular storms scoured the region during the whole ten months of the station's existence, they were undoubtedly limited in intelligence value. Nor did sailors stationed there ever have to repel invaders, friend or foe.

Lieutenant Savere, the aerological officer in charge, eventually commanded as many as twenty-two enlisted personnel (four of whom were "aerographers"), including a chief petty officer. Navy records also fail to disclose their identities.

Perhaps to occupy idle time, between 29 March and 10 May Savere ordered his men to survey the place as a possible airplane base, the third such study in the atoll's history. As had Admiral Byrd and Captain Taylor before him, Lieutenant Savere judged that a 9,000-foot runway might be constructed along the northwestern coral rim, using as fill the material dredged from the lagoon. After observing that the base could only be resupplied by small boats, which "continually require maintainance [sic] due to mishaps incurred when passing through the surf," he suggested that a "channel [be] dredged into the lagoon. . . ." Either that "or a breakwater and jetty appear to be the only solution to this difficulty and would be essential to large scale activity."[36] Nothing came of the survey.

For recreation, the men played baseball. They also "fished, shot sharks and moray eels, and swam in the deeper portions of the lagoon, . . . away from a moss . . . regarded as possibly injurious to swimmers."[37] They anchored a makeshift raft toward the center of the lagoon, which was reached with one of six boats on the island—two LCVPS, two LVTs (landing vehicle, track), a dinghy, and a punt, all salvaged from *LST-563.*

Lieutenant Savere reported that the atoll had "few insects and no mosquitoes. Flies have almost been eliminated through insecticides, and the use of screens." To be on the safe side, "A supply of food and first-aid material has been cached on Clipperton Rock as a precaution against the possibility of high seas washing across the island during a hurricane." He also noted that a "number of pigs were found on the island, some of which could be fattened for food."[38]

U.S. Navy personnel assigned to Island X never had to resort to such measures. *YP-419,* a patrol craft, made one round-trip monthly between San Diego and the atoll, carrying personnel, supplies, and mail. Unlike the Mexican garrison before it, Weather Station No. 1 never missed a shipment. Nevertheless, duty there was sheer drudgery. Before departing in early February, his work done, Commander Dufresne said that even though base discipline was "excellent" and even though sailors enjoyed plenty of free time for recreation, he believed a maximum tour of six months was long enough.[39]

As Lieutenant Savere's survey was in progress, President Roosevelt died, forever fading whatever the future might have held for the atoll. The navy did not consult President Harry Truman about Weather Station No. 1; apparently, he never learned of American operations on Island X or its peculiar place in the mind of his predecessor. Little wonder: as vice president, Truman had been unaware of atomic bomb research; for him to have been privy to Roosevelt's personal plans for this of all places would have been a ludicrous twist to an unlikely tale.[40]

On 14 August, five days after the bombing of Nagasaki, Navy

Secretary James Forrestal advised Secretary of State James Byrnes that "In view of the changed military situation in the Pacific, the Navy Department desires to withdraw the naval personnel now occupying Clipperton Island." Forrestal requested that Byrnes inform French authorities of impending American withdrawal and, following that notification, advise "the Navy Department [of] the earliest date at which the personnel appropriately may be withdrawn from the island."[41]

More than a month passed before Acting Secretary of State Dean Acheson replied:

> *I regret the delay in replying to your letter of August 27, 1945, indicating the intention of the Navy Department to withdraw naval personnel from Clipperton Island at an early date. The delay was due to a clerical error, as a result of which your letter did not come to the attention of the appropriate officers of the State Department until September 18.*
>
> *In compliance with your request, the Ambassader of the French Republic [Henri Bonnet] is being immediately informed of the Navy Department's intention to withdraw naval personnel from Clipperton Island at an early date in view of the changed military situation in the Pacific.*
>
> *In requesting the State Department to inform the Navy Department concerning the time when naval personnel can appropriately be withdrawn from Clipperton Island, I assume you have in mind the effect which the maintenance or withdrawal of these men might have on any future negotiations with the French concerning the ultimate use of the Island. As you are aware, the presence of American naval forces has been a source of friction with the Provisional Government of the French Republic, and the State Department is of the opinion that any future negotiations would be aided rather than harmed by the immediate withdrawal of our forces now that their military mission has been accomplished. In the circumstances, I would strongly recommend that all American naval personnel be withdrawn from Clipperton Island as quickly as possible, and I shall appreciate being informed when this has been done.*[42]

Accordingly, on 19 September, Secretary Forrestal instructed Admiral King to close the base and abandon the island. In the idiom of the navy, the weather station was "disestablished on 5 October 1945."[43] Admiral Ingersoll "was advised . . . that the evacuation of all personnel and equipment, except that of value not commensurate with the cost of salvage, from Clipperton Island had been completed and that the above had arrived in San Diego 21 October."[44]

United States presence on Clippteron island was rather expensive for the navy, and for American taxpayers. The total cost of top-secret Weather Station No. 1 on Island X has never been calculated officially, but it easily exceeded a million dollars.

In addition to medical expenses related to personnel injuries and other intangibles, such as the value of lost time to ships, equipment, and manpower needed elsewhere, many tons of war materiel were abandoned on the atoll as not being worth the cost of salvage. Additionally, the fleet lost one capital ship *(LST-563)* and five LCVPs outright and sustained considerable damage to three other ships of the fleet, *Seize, Tenino,* and *Viking,* which, according to the latter's official history, "suffered damage from heavy seas and put into San Diego for repairs soon thereafter."[45] Added to these are the considerable costs of construction of a weather station and the maintenance of its personnel for the duration of its existence.

Whatever the atoll's potential value to postwar commercial aviation, the existence of Weather Station No. 1 on Island X shortened World War II not one tick in time. Judging the situation from San Francisco, Captain Lowry remarked of the whole operation: "I can't think it is worth it. . . . I don't know what is behind all this but politics."[46]

Notes

1. Vice Air Marshal R. P. Willock to Vice Admiral R. S. Edwards, 16 October 1944, in Franklin D. Roosevelt Papers as President, Map Room Collection, Box 162, "Air Base, Clipperton Island" folder.

2. Admiral E. J. King to Willock, 24 October 1944, in *ibid.*

3. Willock to King, 1 November 1944, in *ibid.*

4. George M. Elsey, "Memorandum for Admiral Brown; Subject: Clipperton Island," 19 January 1945, p. 3, in *ibid.*

5. King to Willock, 5 November 1944, in *ibid.*

6. Elsey, "Memorandum," pp. 9–10.

7. Wilson Brown, "Memorandum for file," 28 November 1944, in *ibid.*

8. [Duncan Curry, captain], USS *Detroit* to CINPAC [Commander-in-Chief, Pacific, Admiral C. W. Nimitz], 2 December 1944, in *ibid.*
The reconnaissance plane was piloted by Lieutenant J. M. Holladay, and the camera was operated by Photographer's Mate (second-class) Frederick La Tour. Enclosed with Curry's report were twenty-three aerial photographs of the island, ranging in altitude from 100 to 1,600 feet and representing all principal points of the compass. The navy has since misplaced the photographs. See Duncan Curry, USS *Detroit,* to CNO [Chief of Naval Operations, Admiral King], "Subject: Aircraft photographic reconnaissance of Clipperton Island," 2 December 1944, in U.S. Navy Records, World War II Command File, Western Sea frontier (WSF), Box 27 (Operational Archives).

9. King to Commander, Western Sea Frontier [Admiral R. E. Ingersoll], 2 December 1944, in Roosevelt Papers as President, "Air Base, Clipperton Island" folder.

10. H. L. Grosskopf, USS Nevada, to CNO [King], 4 December 1944, in Navy Records, World War II Command File, WSF, Box 27 (Operational Archives). Along with his report, Captain Grosskopf attached an unspecified number of developed photographs of the island and of the cabin cruiser, their negatives, an undeveloped roll of 16mm film, and an overlay of Hydrographic Office Map No. 1680, with sites marked. These photographs, like those of *Detroit,* have disappeared.

11. USS *Argus,* Operation Order, 4 December 1944, in *ibid.* Lieutenant Barr's full name is not to be found in these records.

12. *Ibid.*

13. *LST-563,* Operation Order, 4 December 1944, in *ibid.*

14. *Ibid.*

15. R. S. Edwards, "Memorandum for the naval aide to the president," 19 December 1944, in Roosevelt Papers as President, "Air Base, Clipperton Island" folder.

16. Luke W. Dufresne to Commander, Western Sea Frontier, "Subject: Weather Station Number One—establishment of," 9 February 1944, p. 1, in Navy Records, World War II Command Files, WSF, Box 27 (Operational Archives).

17. *Ibid.,* p. 1.

18. *Ibid.,* p. 2.

19. *Ibid.*

20. *Ibid.*

21. *Ibid.,* p. 3.

22. "Excerpts from war diary of Commander, Western Sea Frontier [re: Clipperton island]," January 1945, p. 1, in *ibid.*

23. Dufresne, "Weather Station No. 1," p. 3.

24. "Excerpts from war diary," January 1945, p. 2.

25. *Ibid.* "It is interesting to note," Ingersoll's war diary comments, "that, with the *Seize* (ARS-26) aground and the *Tenino* (AFT-115) engaged in an important role in salvage operations, ComServPac [Commander, Service Fleet, Pacific] directed a communication to ComWestSeaFron [Commander, Western Sea Frontier] on this same date, asking when both of these vessels would complete their respective shakedowns and be available for transfer. . . ." *Ibid.*

26. *Ibid.,* p. 3.

27. "USS *Tenino,*" in U.S. Navy, *Dictionary,* VII, 86.

28. "Excerpts from war diary," January 1945, p. 4.

29. *Ibid.*

30. *Ibid.*, February 1945, p. 1.

31. *Ibid.*, p. 2.

32. Wallace M. Beakley, U.S. Fleet, Officer of the Commander in Chief, "Memorandum for Admiral Edwards; subject: Visit of French naval officer to Clipperton island," 23 February 1945, in Roosevelt Papers as President, "Air Base, Clipperton Island" folder. As suggested by Admiral Ingersoll, the Navy officially struck the grounded LST from its list of commissioned ships, the beached vessel becoming a breakwater on the island.

33. Dufresne, "Weather Station No. 1," p. 2.

34. G. M. Lowry to Capt. Lassing, 2 February 1945, in U.S. Navy Records, World War II Command Files, WSF, Box 27 (Operational Archives).

35. Dufresne, "Weather Service No. 1," p. 4.

36. Quoted in [Lieutenant M. S. Savere], "Clipperton island," Enclosure A, p. 4, attached to "Excerpts from war diary of Commander, Western Sea Frontier [re: Clipperton Island]," p. 3.

37. *Ibid.*, pp. 3–4.

38. *Ibid.* The fact that Savere failed to mention Clipperton island's heretofore large crab population was probably related to the atoll's growing swine herd. The impact of pigs on the environment is discussed in Chapter 13.

39. Dufresne, "Weather Station No. 1," p. 5

40. President Truman's involvement with the atoll is discussed in Chapter 12.

41. James V. Forrestal to James F. Byrnes, 14 August 1945, in Navy Records, World War II Command Files, WSF, Box 27 (Operational Archives).

42. Dean Acheson to Forrestal, September 19, 1945, in U.S. State department, *Foreign relations of the United States; diplomatic papers, 1945: Europe* (1968), IV, 793–94.

43. No specific date is to be found in the Western Sea Frontier's Clipperton island file. The date used herein was provided by F. Kent Loomis,

Department of the Navy, Office of the Chief of Naval Operations, in a letter to Charles F. Harbison, 15 December 1958 (Harbison Papers).

44. "Excerpts from war diary," October 1945, [p. 1].

45. "USS *Viking*," in U.S. Navy, *Dictionary*, VII, 521.

46. Lowry to Lassing, 2 February 1945.

12

Franklin Delano Roosevelt and American Designs on Clipperton Island 1944–1947

During the final four and one-half months of Franklin Delano Roosevelt's life, obscure little Clipperton island, far from center stage in World War II, was of considerable interest to the president and, consequently, to his government. It was a point at issue between the United States and Great Britain, its status ultimately determined at the highest level. Moreover, its seizure by American armed forces precipitated a diplomatic flap with the French.

As Roosevelt's health deteriorated and his strength waned on the eve of the Yalta Conference—what many critics contend was the most serious and least competent of his dealings with Winston Churchill and Joseph Stalin about the future of the world—the president was increasingly distracted by this island. Unlike its occupation—he allowed Admiral E. J. King's navy to handle that matter, the White House receiving some (but not all) reports of goings-on thereabouts—the president took personal charge of American foreign policy vis-à-vis the atoll, altering the State department's historical hands-off position. He even proposed to transfer its ownership to Mexico to facilitate permanent U.S. occupation. Although he clearly foresaw the day when the place would become "much less significant as aircraft ranges increased after the war,"[1] as previously mentioned, he was convinced that, for the moment at least, it was vital to trans-Pacific aviation, and he meant to guarantee its use by American corporations, which might well be denied landing rights if the British acquired total control.

This paternalistic gesture toward business by the Roosevelt administration was actually part of a larger economic issue in contention between Great Britain and the United States—global commerical aviation. Since American companies owned the world's largest commercial air fleet, Roosevelt naturally preferred that international airlines "compete for traffic in a free market. The British, hoping to hold onto their share of the market, advocated pooling arrangements whereby commercial carriers would be guaranteed a portion of the business."[2]

Outright control of Clipperton island would automatically afford Great Britain a monopoly in any new air route to the southwest Pacific. Accordingly, on November 27, 1944, to prevent seemingly imminent British occupation of the atoll, President Roosevelt secretly ordered his navy to seize the place. That very day he also wrote Prime Minister Churchill:

> *In mid-October Air Vice Marshal Willock informed our Navy Department of his intention to survey Clipperton Island in compliance with instructions from British Air Ministry and we understand that a survey party is now at Acapulco, Mexico. Having in mind the Monroe Doctrine, air agreements now under discussion and American public opinion, I suggest that any plan of development of military bases on Clipperton or any other territory in or near American waters be discussed by the Governments concerned rather than by the Armed forces. I request that you cancel any instructions by your people about a further survey of Clipperton until you and I can discuss it. [Admiral] King is sure he can work out a schedule of your planes through Hawaii to meet military requirements. I have personally visited Clipperton twice.*[3]

The following day, Churchill replied: "I had not heard of this, but of course all action will now be suspended till you and I have discussed the matter."[4]

Six weeks later, on January 10, Churchill responded more completely to Roosevelt's original communiqué:

I have now looked into the matter of Clipperton Island survey and am relieved to find that the Air Ministry here did not issue any instructions in this matter until our delegation in Washington had received full approval in writing from the Navy Department for this survey to be carried out. The Navy Department, furthermore, provided facilities in the form of gasoline and oil at Bora Bora. The survey was then carried out, and the results communicated to the Navy Department.

The question of further flight to complete the survey was being discussed with the Navy Department and the State Department at the time your telegram was sent. I mention this to correct any impression which may be in your mind that the Air Ministry acted high-handedly.

I entirely agree that we should leave the whole matter till we meet.[5]

White House aides criticized Churchill's explanation. A staff report on the island states: "The Prime Minister's dispatch is not completely accurate. What Roosevelt had objected to was the plan for an extensive survey of Clipperton, and the Prime Minister confused the issue" by referring merely to approval of P. G. Taylor's reconnaissance flight. Moreover, the report asserted that Churchill "was wrong when he said 'the further flight to complete the survey' was under discussion when the President's message was sent. . . . Secretary [E. R.] Stettinius had told Lord Halifax on 21 November [a survey] must wait until after the war."[6]

Whatever qualms his aides may have had, Roosevelt was satisfied with Churchill's response, the president replying that "I feel sure that we will be able to work out a solution that will be satisfactory to all concerned."[7]

Meanwhile, Roosevelt had anticipated diplomatic consequences of military action, once word leaked of Clipperton island's occupation, and he moved to shift blame to the Pentagon. He undoubtedly believed that Churchill would recognize American seizure for what it was, a power play to perpetuate its civil aviation advantage in the postwar world. Moreover, even though ten months earlier he had specifically asked Secretary of State Cordell Hull to secure French cooperation regarding the atoll, Roosevelt must have anticipated that unilateral American action would result in a vehement protest by Charles de Gaulle, with whom relations were already strained.

Roosevelt therefore had his staff concoct a cover story. On December 19, a week after the Navy occupied the atoll, presidential aide Vice Admiral Wilson Brown advised Admiral King's staff that "The President thinks it would be well if a representative of the Navy Department could inform [Vice] Admiral [Raymond] Fenard [naval representative at the French mission in Washington] orally that we have established a weather station at Clipperton as a necessary war measure."[8]

By special courier that same day, Admiral Brown sent Admiral E. S. Edwards, Admiral King's assistant, the draft of a version of events that the White House proposed to give the British, the French, and the Mexicans; it blamed the navy for the island's seizure. Edwards returned the scenario to Brown several days later, saying that Admiral King "concurs in the ideas expressed in the draft" and was "quite willing"[9] to accept full responsibility should the British or anyone else object.

Addressed to the secretary of state, with copies for both War and Navy Departments, the note would have the president say:

> On December 11, 1944, the Commander, Western Sea Frontier [Admiral Royal E. Ingersoll] established an armed observation party and a weather reporting station at Clipperton Island. This action was taken as a matter of military urgency concurrently with an increase in Japanese operations in the waters of the Western Sea Frontier. The Navy had notified the head of the French Naval Mission, Vice Admiral Fenard, orally, of the establishment.
>
> Please inform the British Ambassador [Lord Halifax] of the establishment of this station and of the fact that Admiral Fenard has been notified. Also please let the Mexican Government know of the action we have taken. It should be brought to the attention of the British and Mexican Governments that the aerological station has been provided with armanent in view of possible Japanese raids, and that proposed visits by British and Mexican vessels or aircraft should be cleared with the U.S. Navy Department in order that there be no incidents resulting from mistaken identity.
>
> My message to the Prime Minister dated 27 November requested him to cancel any instructions to the Royal Air Force about a further

survey at Clipperton until matters can be discussed between us. This he has agreed to. The ownership and development of Clipperton Island are matters which I regard of significance to the United States because of the strategic location with respect to the Panama Canal. Mexico has long contested the claim of France to this island and the Mexican argument has not been without substance. It would be to our advantage that the United States, in the absence of direct ownership, should obtain base rights on Clipperton Island on long-term lease through Mexican ownership.[10]

Roosevelt signed Brown's draft on January 1, 1945, and sent it to Secretary Stettinius, thereby misleading even his own State department as to the reason behind American action at the atoll.

The explanation—increased Japanese operations in the waters of the Western Sea Frontier—was patently false, which should have been obvious to all nations concerned. The closest the Japanese surface fleet ever came to Clipperton island was to attack Pearl Harbor. Interestingly, after World War II French writers stated that there had been unauthorized "stopovers there by Japanese boats between the two world wars,"[11] and that during the war the atoll was "visited by Japanese submarines,"[12] thereby explaining, perhaps even justifying, American occupation.

However unlikely it was that civilian or military vessels of the Rising Sun had frequented the place between the wars, there is no evidence whatsoever that Imperial Japanese submarines ever came closer than Santa Barbara, California (2,100 miles north-north-west), which was shelled by a Japanese U-boat's deck guns early in 1942. In fact, with tropical waters about Clipperton island rarely (if ever) menaced by Japanese submarines (and never by the emperor's surface fleet), U.S. Navy brass saw no reason to occupy the strategically placed atoll, until ordered to do so by the White House.[13]

Farfetched cover stories notwithstanding, FDR's aides fully expected the incident to be a sore point with the British when Roosevelt and Churchill met at Malta in early February 1945, preliminary to the Yalta Conference with Stalin. A White House staff report judged that the American "objective [with respect to the atoll] has been achieved, . . . to forestall British occupation." The report stated that because the island was destined to play a large role in postwar Pacific aviation, "if for no other reason than that the British are determined to develop it," with reference to the Malta conference "it would seem advisable for the President to reiterate to the Prime Minister . . . that the development of this Island is not feasible now, [but that] the President might agree to a thorough survey of Clipperton immediately after the war. This would be a concession of sorts to the British and would give the appearance of a compromise whereas in reality we would be yielding nothing."[14]

Perhaps Roosevelt reiterated this position to Churchill at Malta on February 2 when they met. Perhaps not. The record is incomplete. During a formal session with their combined chiefs of staff to hammer out differences before facing Stalin, Clipperton island was not mentioned, according to the minutes of these meetings. Little wonder: it was irrelevant to Soviet-Western relations; however, it may well have been discussed at either (or both) of two lesser sessions when Roosevelt and Churchill (joined only by their foreign ministers and closest advisors) dined together. No notes of those encounters survive; neither do Churchill's memoirs deal with the matter, nor do those of anyone else who was present.[15]

Perhaps no one broached the subject. The prime minister, whose personal involvement with the atoll was evidently minimal, likely considered it to be inconsequential. Rather than irritate Roosevelt, who obviously felt quite strongly about it, Churchill probably did not raise the matter as an agenda item. If so, Roosevelt, who already had ample diplomatic problems over the place with the French, as well as with his own State department, undoubtedly would have been delighted to allow the British aspect of the issue to die quietly.

At least since 1943, denizens of Foggy Bottom had been resisting the president's efforts to alter established policy regarding the island's sovereignty. In April, while meeting President Ávila Camacho in Monterrey, Roosevelt stunned his own diplomats when he "mentioned to [Ezequiel] Padilla, the Foreign Minister of Mexico, his own thought that Clipperton Island be given to the Mexicans."[16] Advisors apparently dissuaded him from discussing the issue further, at least then.

Couched as a Good Neighbor Policy gesture, Roosevelt's real motivation obviously had been his desire to control the place, which he believed would be easier to achieve were it Mexican than French. It is evident that he never learned the specious basis of French title, nor even of actual American corporate occupation under law, or surely he would have overruled his State department, declared Napoleon III's claim of 1858 to have been in contravention of the Monroe Doctrine, and proclaimed U.S. sovereignty over it.

On December 9, 1944—two weeks after he first wrote the prime minister about the island, and two days before armed sailors from USS *Argus* landed to take possession—the president met his ambassador to Mexico, George S. Messersmith, who was in Washington for consultations. Although Roosevelt failed to disclose impending naval action, he did tell Messersmith "that in his opinion Clipperton should be under Mexican sovereignty. Of course, when it was returned . . . the appropriate arrangements should be made so that we, the British and others could use Clipperton as a base for commercial air operations."[17]

He also said that "he knew Clipperton very well, . . . [that] he had been there several times. It had real importance in connection with certain air routes. . . ." Observing that it belonged to the French, he stated that they "would probably not want to give it up, . . . but it remained his opinion and intention that Clipperton should return to Mexican sovereignty. He said that at the appropriate time he would take this up with the French."[18]

While never openly challenging Roosevelt's evaluation of Clipperton's geopolitical or economic significance, American diplomats who had recognized French sovereignty since 1898, when Alvey Adee read about the French claim in *Lippincott's Gazetteer,* resisted any alteration in their traditional hands-off policy. Over the years, American diplomats had mostly ignored the bird-splattered speck of coral—despite its obvious Monroe Doctrine implications, as Roosevelt pointed out to Churchill—save when some aspect of its existence conveniently fitted departmental needs.

For instance, in 1940 Acting Secretary of State Sumner Welles had cited Victor Emmanuel's Clipperton island arbitration award to refute Honduran assertions of ownership of the Swan islands in the Caribbean, which, like Clipperton, had been claimed and occupied by Americans under the Guano Islands Act.[19] Otherwise, fastidious diplomats mostly avoided the bird-splattered little place until, their noses repeatedly rubbed in it by Roosevelt, they were forced to deal with the odious atoll.

Even so, the Department of State's handling of American interests remained far from circumspect. As previously noted, following a 1943 study by the interdepartmental Joint Strategic Committee, which listed Clipperton island among some two dozen places "required for the defense of the Western Hemisphere" in a postwar world, in January 1944 President Roosevelt ordered Secretary of State Cordell Hull "as a matter of high priority, [to] initiate negotiations with the governments concerned to acquire permanent or long-term benefit of the bases, facilities, and rights required, at the earliest possible moment."[20] In ill health, Secretary Hull failed to take up the matter of Clipperton island with the Vichy government.

Nor did his successor, Edward Stettinius, ever discuss it with the provisional government of the French Republic, which, following the liberation of France (and preceding the occupation of the atoll), the Roosevelt administration had formally recognized. These oversights would sorely strain relations with the French.

Later in the year, when at President Roosevelt's request the navy notified Admiral Fenard of American presence on the atoll, the Frenchman "reacted with shock and dismay." *Quai d'Orsay* was even more distraught. Annoyed "that the U.S. was flaunting French Sovereignty over Clipperton, . . . as a test case to re-assert French Sovereignty and to discover the scope of U.S. activities," it directed its representatives in Mexico City to investigate. Accordingly, Garreau Dombasle of the French Legation organized "an expedition of Mexicans and Americans who planned to leave Acapulco for Clipperton . . . for 'shark fishing.' "[21]

Captain A. S. Hickey, naval attaché at the U.S. Embassy in Mexico City, reported to superiors that a Major Dives, the French military attaché, had informed him of the outing, saying that he had hired "a small sailboat, the property of a Mr. Spratling, an American citizen," and that a party of eight planned to sail it from Acapulco "on or about the 7th or 8th of January [1945] under the charge of Mr. Martin Durand, . . . an advisor experienced in shark fishing. . . ." Major Dives asked Captain Hickey to "notify the proper Naval authorities of the United States, informing them of the proposed expedition and requesting that the Naval authorities on Clipperton Island be notified so that the expedition would not be mistaken for an enemy (he said, for Japanese)." The French officer explained that a French firm was interested in the commercial exploitation of "shark livers at Clipperton island, [which] were twice the size of the livers elsewhere."[22]

Ambassador Messersmith was incredulous. "I have small faith in the real desire of the French Government to promote a shark fishing industry on Clipperton Island," he advised Secretary Stettinius. "I fail to see what food the sharks in the vicinity of Clipperton feed upon so that they have livers twice the size of those on the Pacific Coast and in the Gulf of California. It would seem that the French Government and the French Legation in Mexico are showing a strange interest in Clipperton after a complete lack of interest for so many years."[23]

After consulting the White House, Secretary Stettinius instructed Ambassador Messersmith to inform "the President of Mexico [Á. Camacho] and the Foreign Minister [E. Padilla] that in view of certain circumstances vessels and planes leaving Mexican territory for Clipperton Island should give previous notice before leaving for that destination, such notice to be given to the Commander of the Western Sea Frontier of the United States Navy at San Francisco. . . ." Messersmith complied and soon thereafter advised Washington that "the Mexican Government has taken the appropriate steps which we have indicated are desirable."[24]

Accordingly, a week later, "Mexican naval authorities" at Acapulco detained *Pez de Plata,* formerly *Lucky Lady,* "until [a] satisfactory high seas navigator [could be] employed. [Martin] Durand [was reportedly] on board but replaced as Captain by Rodney Satlier, an English citizen."[25] Mexican port officials also informed the new captain that special permission was required from the U.S. Navy to visit the atoll.

Meanwhile, upon learning of the expedition, Admiral King had ordered Admiral Ingersoll, under whose aegis the atoll fell, that, "In the event [of] unannounced visits, British, French or Mexican personnel should be allowed to land but only for a stay of temporary duration. . . . [All interested parties] have been informed of existence of weather station through diplomatic channels and advised to seek clearance from Navy Dep[artment] or from you but this may not suffice to stop Durand party."[26]

About then, Comte Jean de Caraman, a representative of the French Legation in Mexico, called at the American embassy in Mexico City to see Captain Hickey, asking if Major Dives and his assistant, a corporal, might be permitted to land on Clipperton. Caraman disclosed "that he had visited the Mexican Ministry of Marine and had seen [an] Admiral Blanco who told him that he did not wish to give permission for the vessel [*Pez de Plata*] to sail until he was assured that the American authorities would permit a landing to be made at Clipperton, or words to that effect." Caraman insisted that there was a capable crew on the ship and that Mr. Durand "was familiar with shark fishing."[27]

Hickey replied that "the Commander of the Western Sea Frontier did not wish such a visit as that planned by the *Pez de Plata* to take place at this time. . . ." Hickey suggested that Caraman "communicate with the French Embassy in Washington on this matter." The Frenchman then inquired "whether or not it would be possible to have one of our vessels take Commandant Dives on board on a possible voyage to Clipperton" but was again referred to the French embassy in Washington. In his report on the incident, Hickey observed: "there must be some other reason, other than shark fishing, for visiting the island in view of the desire of the French minister to obtain permission for his military attaché to visit the island on board an American man-of-war."[28]

U.S. intelligence reports the following day disclosed that "Mexican immigration authorities in Acapulco have detained Martin Durand because he lacks citizenship papers. . . ." He was said to have claimed Mexican, Peruvian, French, and American citizenship at various times, and Major Dives expressed an unwillingness to sail without Durand. As a result, "*Pez de Plata* is still anchored in the harbor at Acapulco."[29]

Such unprecedented Mexican cooperation no doubt stemmed from the belief that the United States government had belatedly decided to champion Mexico's claim to Clipperton. President Roosevelt had indicated as much to President Camacho in 1943.

Unable to learn anything of substance in Mexico, the French turned to Washington and pointedly asked for an explanation. On January 15, 1945, Under Secretary of State Joseph C. Grew (serving as Acting Secretary while Stettinius was en route to Yalta) reported to the president that on January 11 a Monsieur Baudet of the French embassy in Washington had telephoned the State department to inquire "about the United States Naval establishment on Clipperton Island."[30]

Grew said he gave the Frenchman the same general information as the department had provided the British and the Mexicans, according to Roosevelt's instructions of January 1; moreover, Grew told Bidault that the U.S. Navy had already fully informed Admiral Fenard of American action. Grew reported that "Baudet inquired whether the French flag was still flying over Clipperton Island. We told him frankly that we did not know here whether or not the French flag is flying over Clipperton Island but that if one was flyng when our forces arrived, he could be sure it was still there. Mr. Baudet appeared to be satisfied with this and although he had spoken of a note to us, we have heard nothing further from the French Embassy on the subject."[31]

Referring to Roosevelt's January 1 assertion "that Mexico has long contested the claim of France to the island," Grew further informed the president that the Mexican Congress in 1934 had ratified Victor Emmanuel's arbitration award. Even were that not the case, if the United States wished to secure rights to the atoll, as recommended by the joint chiefs in 1943, it was the State department's opinion "that it would be much easier . . . [to get the rights] from the French Government than it would be for us to obtain such rights from the Mexican Government. This view is strengthened by the attitude which the Mexican Government has taken during the present war in which Mexico, is, of course, a co-belligerent, in respect to similar questions."[32]

On January 12, the day following Monsieur Baudet's visit to Foggy Bottom to inquire about American naval presence on the atoll, "an officer of the French Embassy called on Mr. John Hickerson [deputy director] of the State Department['s Office of European Affairs] . . . to inquire why Clipperton Island was occupied without previous notification. [When] answer[ed] military necessity, the French Officer likened the U.S. to Hitler in method."[33]

Six days later, Rear Admiral L. A. Davidson of Admiral King's staff called Hickerson to say that Admiral Fenard was on his way to see him regarding the shark fishing expedition, which was still on hold in Acapulco. Davidson asked whether the State department would object "to his telling Admiral Fenard perfectly frankly that the Navy Department did not wish to have civilians unnecessarily visit Clipperton in view of the military installation there. He said that he would like to say further to Admiral Fenard that the Navy would of course have no objection to the visit of a bona fide French military man if a French officer wished to visit the island."[34]

Hickerson endorsed Davidson's tact, and later in the day Davidson called again to report on Fenard's visit. Davidson said the French admiral had "appeared unhappy over the Clipperton Island matter." Fenard had asked "whether the Navy Department would be prepared to instruct the U.S. Naval officer in command at Clipperton Island to erect a small flag pole and run up a French flag and also to provide accommodations for a French officer to be stationed on the island." Davidson replied that if Fenard insisted, he would take the matter up with his superiors, who would doubtlessly see it as casting aspersions on American intentions. Fenard consequently withdrew the request but "left in an unhappy state of mind."[35]

Davidson asked Hickerson for his opinion, and the diplomat replied that the navy was perfectly correct in not wanting civilians on the island but that the French "were entitled to send an officer out there if they wished." Hickerson therefore suggested that the navy offer "to provide transportation to Clipperton for any French army or naval officer they wish to send to look the island over briefly and return, perhaps by plane." Davidson said he would pass the suggestion along and get back to him to "discuss it further."[36]

Before they could "discuss it further," France seized the initiative. On January 22 in Paris, French Foreign Minister Georges Bidault personally handed American Ambassador Jefferson Caffery an undated note, saying as he did: "This is very humiliating to us. We are so anxious to cooperate with you, but sometimes you do not make it easy."[37]

Aware of U.S. presence on Clipperton island, "no previous authorization having been requested of the French Government," and frustrated in its independent attempt to investigate from

Mexico because of objections to a visit raised by the American navy, Bidault said his government "finds itself compelled to protest against such methods so contrary to international usage and to which it is all the more sensitive since they are employed by a friendly nation." Reserving the right "to send to Clipperton, by the means at its disposal, such personnel as it may appear useful to it to send and maintain there," Minister Bidault nevertheless expressed a willingness to maintain on the island "in liaison with the United States Navy [such] meteorological services [as are] necessary to the war effort, . . . [especially] in the defense of French possessions in the Pacific and to contribute to the struggle against Japan to the full measure of its possibilities."[38]

On January 26, Acting Secretary Grew telegraphed news of the formal French protest to President Roosevelt aboard USS *Quincy,* which was steaming for Malta and the pre-Yalta meeting with Churchill. Even though the "Clipperton Island situation [is] deteriorating rapidly," Grew recommended that the United States continue to "refuse to permit vessel [*Pez de Plata*] to proceed to Clipperton from Mexico but offer to take French officer designated by French Naval Mission here on [a] visit of inspection. This should materially ease present tension." Grew further suggested that in its reply to the French note the American government ignore the overture "of a joint meteorological service, stress[ing instead the] emergency character of our station on Clipperton, . . . [and indicating] that our action does not affect question of sovereignty over Island and that we will expect to enter into discussions [with the French] later regarding [the] use of Island in connection with post-war security."[39]

Grew regarded the controversy as "extremely urgent." The situation could easily "lead to an incident which, because of the basic weakness of our position, could seriously and needlessly impair our relations with the French, at a time when they are exceptionally sensitive to all matters affecting their sovereignty, and provide our enemies with an additional propaganda weapon."[40]

The diplomat believed that Franco-American relations were strained enough at the highest levels. Already miffed with Roosevelt for not having promptly recognized his Free French as the *de jure* authority in France, Charles de Gaulle was furious when he was not invited to attend the conference at Yalta as the equal of Churchill, Roosevelt, and Stalin. Were de Gaulle to learn that Roosevelt had personally ordered the island's seizure, likely the episode would become a convenient *cause célèbre* for the new regime.

Roosevelt wired his conditional approval of Grew's proposal, provided the department made "no commitment with respect to the eventual sovereignty of Clipperton Island."[41] The president obviously intended to thrash out that issue with Foggy Bottom once and for all upon his return from Yalta.

Meanwhile, James C. H. Bonbright, the department's assistant chief of western European affairs, had briefed a Monsieur Lacoste, counselor at the French embassy, on the matter. Bonbright assured Lacoste "that the whole question was under review and that . . . we would be in a position to give him something more definite within the next few days." Bonbright asked Lacoste to "keep the lid on his own people so that we would not be faced with an incident." Lacoste promised to do his best. Bonbright reported to superiors that "Lacoste was very friendly throughout." The Frenchman even told the American that he had been disappointed to learn that his government had presented the United States a formal communiqué on the subject, believing such to be overreaction. Lacoste "took the line that the whole matter was a result of excessive zeal on the part of the [American] military, and that he did not for a moment believe we had an ulterior motive or any designs on French territory."[42]

On February 3, 1945, under instructions from Secretary Grew, Ambassador Caffery in Paris replied to the French government that, because "an increase in the Japanese operations in the waters of the Western Sea Frontier suggested the desirability of establishing a weather reporting station and armed observation party on Clipperton Island, . . . the necessary action [had been] taken by the United States Navy without prior consultation with any civilian agency. . . ."[43]

For reasons of military necessity and to avoid any incident that might arise "through mistaken identity," Caffery said his navy had forbidden any civilian visits to the atoll, such as the proposed "shark fishing expedition" from Mexico. Nevertheless, the military service would "be happy to furnish transportation for a

French officer, designated by the Naval Mission in Washington, for a visit to Clipperton Island. If this offer is accepted, the French officer will be afforded every opportunity to familiarize himself fully with the measures taken by the United States Navy." Probably unaware that his government's response was a blend of half-truths and outright lies, Caffery expressed the sincere hope that it would "place this entire question in its proper perspective."[44]

A month later, on March 15, Secretary Stettinius reported in writing to a worn and weary president, recently returned from Yalta, that Ambassador Caffery had communicated with the French regarding "security measures taken by the United States Navy on Clipperton Island." Also, in Roosevelt's absence, a French officer, Lieutenant Louis Jampierre, had visited the atoll, and "while there are various indications that the French are still unhappy over this situation," Stettinius stated, "we have thus far heard nothing further from them." As the president had ordered, the issue of postwar sovereignty had not been broached with the French; nevertheless, Stettinius implored: "I cannot urge too strongly that we handle the question of obtaining the right to establish a post-war military base on the Island solely with the French, and leave the Mexican Authorities out of the picture entirely."[45]

However reluctantly, Roosevelt gave in, returning the memorandum to his secretary of state the following day with the terse note "OK, F.D.R."[46] scrawled across it. Consequently, on March 21, Stettinius informed Ambassador Messersmith in Mexico City that "the President has approved [the] Department's suggestion that we should not endeavor to obtain any change in the present sovereignty of the island, and that we should handle the question of a post-war military base solely with the French."[47]

Three weeks later, Roosevelt died. Whatever postwar plans he—and, for a time, his joint chiefs—might have had for the atoll, clearly the State department had none. On April 13 (the day after his death), when Assistant Secretary of the Navy for Air John L. Sullivan suggested that "the Secretary of State initiate action to acquire ownership of Clipperton Island for the United States as part payment for French Lend-Lease obligations,"[48] diplomats rejected the idea out of hand.

They stated that throughout World War II the U.S. government had repeatedly pledged to support "the re-establishment of the integrity of French territory"; that, since the atoll "is normally uninhabited, . . . base rights obtained under long lease would present substantially the same advantage as would be obtained by outright annexation"; that "in view of the unusual sensitivity of the French Government . . . [it] would find it easier to lease base rights to the United States than to relinquish sovereignty"; and that "annexation of the Island by the United States would have undesirable ramifications not only in connection with our relations with Mexico but with all the American Republics."[49]

Moreover, following FDR's death, denizens of Foggy Bottom deftly deleted the atoll from the nation's list of priorities, even though Harry Truman stated in his first Cabinet meeting, "I want to do everything just the way President Roosevelt wanted it."[50] Secretary Stettinius's written summary of relations with France, given to President Truman on April 13, failed to mention either American naval presence on the island or his predecessor's insistence on maintaining control of the place after the war. Stettinius did say, "The best interests of the United States require that every effort be made by this Government to assist France, morally as well as physically, to regain her strength and her influence." While the French "from time to time put forward requests which are out of all proportion to their present strength . . . it is in the best interest of the United States to take full account of this psychological factor in the French mind and to treat France in all respects on the basis of her potential power and influence rather than on the basis of her present strength."[51]

Curiously, even though the atoll was a matter of ongoing contention between the United States and France, it apparently failed to arise as a topic on May 18 when Truman received French Foreign Minister Bidault to discuss "a number of problems of primary interest to France and the United States."[52]

Had the new, plain-speaking president been fully apprised of American involvement with the island, he might well have judged the navy's occupation of the place to be preposterous and ordered it ended forthwith; however, such a decision was never his to make. Rather, it appears that this curious chapter of United States history ended quietly in a conspiracy of silence between Pentagon brass and Foggy Bottom diplomats, both of whom cut the new chief executive out of the decision-making process.

As previously mentioned, on August 14 (five days after the bombing of Nagasaki), Navy Secretary James Forrestal wrote to new Secretary of State James F. Byrnes, saying that sailors wished to depart the island. Forrestal's note arrived while Byrnes was in London, attending the Foreign Minister's Council meeting, and more than a month passed before Under Secretary Dean Acheson acted in Byrnes's stead, agreeing that American personnel indeed should be removed promptly.

A career diplomat no doubt well aware of his department's view of the atoll, Under Secretary Acheson wasted no more time. He immediately informed Ambassador Henri Bonnet "that, in view of the changed military situation in the Pacific, instructions are being issued by the Navy Department for the withdrawal of American naval personnel from Clipperton Island."[53] Two and one-half weeks later, on October 6, Bonnet replied that "the French Government welcomes the decision taken by the American authorities and has duly appreciated the communication which has been made to it on this subject."[54]

On November 7, in what diplomats must surely have believed to be the final note on the subject, Secretary Byrnes informed the French chargé d'affaires that the U.S. Navy had withdrawn all personnel from Clipperton island. American occupation had ended.

Yet, the U.S. government was not quite done with the place. Across town that very afternoon, the "State-War-Navy Coordinating Committee" (SWNCC), relying on the latest Pentagon advisory, which showed the atoll to be garrisoned by American armed forces, judged that its occupation (along with some two dozen other foreign-owned spots around the globe) was "required"[55] for the security of the United States. On receipt of SWNCC policy recommendations, the joint chiefs asked the State department to negotiate a minimum of joint occupation with France.

Two months later, on February 11, the joint chiefs inadvertently omitted the place from the revised list of required locations—"the rights for which should be obtained . . . for military rights of air transit and technical stops"[56]—which, of course, prompted the State department to drop it from its list of sites acquired from

France in the "Air Transport Services Agreement," signed at Paris on March 27. That accord granted the United States limited military and commercial landing privileges in Algiers, French Guiana, Guadeloupe, Hanoi, Marseilles, Martinique, New Caledonia, Paris, and Saigon, but not Clipperton.

On June 5, the joint chiefs "recommended a reduction in the category of certain bases,"[57] this time purposely striking the atoll from its "required" list of twenty-three bases worldwide. By then, the place was no longer needed as an aviation stepping-stone to the southwest Pacific; technology had so advanced flight that the Marquesas cold be reached nonstop from the North American continent. Even so, on September 9, 1947, the joint chiefs officially designated Clipperton island, "in addition to such obvious [places] as Northwestern Europe, United Kingdom, and South America," as a *"Strategic Area . . .* for which surveillance is particularly necessary with the object of denying or restricting the development of military potential either directly or indirectly by possible enemy powers."[58]

French property or not, the atoll had not seen the last of the United States Navy.

Notes

1. W. F. Kimball, III, 504.

2. *Ibid.*, 404. See also, U.S. State department, *Proceedings, passim.*

3. Franklin D. Roosevelt to Winston S. Churchill, in Franklin D. Roosevelt's Papers as President, War Room Files, Box 162, "Air Base, Clipperton Island" folder; cf., W. F. Kimball, III, 417. This communication contains the only known application of the Monroe Doctrine to the atoll to be found in U.S. government records.

4. Churchill to Roosevelt, November 28, 1944, in *ibid.;* cf., W. F. Kimball, III, 422.

5. Churchill to Roosevelt, January 10, 1945, in *ibid.;* cf., W. F. Kimball, III, 504. Historian Warren Kimball contends that Churchill may well have been far more conversant with P. G. Taylor's mission than he ever admitted. Writes Kimball: "Given the tension which had arisen over the Civil Aviation Conference and the extension of lend-lease, Churchill chose not to press the British plan to survey Clipperton Island." (Kimball, III, 422.)

6. George M. Elsey, "Memorandum for Admiral Brown; Subject: Clipperton island," 19 January 1945, pp. 11–12, in Roosevelt Papers as President, "Air Base, Clipperton Island" folder.

7. Roosevelt to Churchill, January 19, 1945, in *ibid.;* cf., W. F. Kimball, III, 505.

8. Wilson Brown to E. S. Edwards, 19 December 1944, in Roosevelt Papers as President, "Air Base, Clipperton Island" folder.

9. Edwards to Brown, 30 December 1944, in *ibid.*

10. *Ibid.*, attachment, n.d., in *ibid.;* cf., Roosevelt to E. R. Stettinius, Jr., January 1, 1945, in U.S. State department, *Foreign relations of the United States; diplomatic papers, 1945: Europe* (1968), IV, 784–85. A copy of the original memorandum is also on file in the U.S. Navy Records, World War II Command File, Western Sea Frontier (WSF), Box 27 (Operational Archives).

11. Bourgau, p. 69.

12. Sachet, *Geography*, p. 7.

13. All told, during World War II the U.S. Navy sank 146 Japanese submarines, 141 of them going down in Oriental (western Pacific) waters; of the 5 sunk in the eastern Pacific ocean, none were in Western Sea Frontier waters—the closest incident being in the Marshall islands, 5,800 miles west-southwest of Clipperton, where on 24 March 1944 USS *Manlove*, a destroyer escort, sank *Inamoto*, an I-class submarine. See, "Japanese submarine casualties," in U.S. Navy, *United States submarine losses*, pp. 175–77.

14. Elsey, "Memorandum," p. 12.

15. See U.S. State department, *Foreign relations, the Malta and Yalta Conferences*, pp. 459–546. In *Triumph and tragedy*, Churchill writes (p. 295) merely that "the future campaigns in Southeast Asia and the Pacific" were discussed.

16. U.S. State department, *Foreign relations, 1945: Europe*, IV, 783.

17. *Ibid.*, pp. 784–85.

18. *Ibid.*, p. 784.

19. See U.S. State department, *Foreign relations, 1940: the American republics*, V, 936–37.

20. Roosevelt to Cordell Hull, January 1, 1944, in Roosevelt Papers as President, Map Room Collection, Box 162, "Air Routes" folder; cf., U.S. State department, *Foreign relations, 1944: the American Republics*, VII, 546.

21. Elsey, "Memorandum," p. 12.

22. [Captain] A. S. Hickey, [Naval Attaché], Mexico City, to Chief of Naval Operations [Admiral E. J. King], 6 January 1945, in Roosevelt Papers as President, "Clipperton Island" folder.

23. George Messersmith, Mexico City, to Secretary of State [Stettinius], January ?, 1945 [date obliterated], in *ibid.*

24. Messersmith to Secretary of State [Stettinius], January 9, 1945, in *ibid.*

25. Alusna [?], Mexico City, to Chief of Naval Operations [Admiral King], 16 January 1945, in *ibid.*

26. Chief of Naval Operations [Admiral King] to Commander, Western Sea Frontier [Admiral Royal Ingersoll], 3 January 1945, in *ibid.*

27. U.S. Naval Attaché [Captain Hickey], Mexico City, to Chief of Naval Operations [Admiral King], 23 January 1945, in *ibid.*

28. *Ibid.*

29. Alusna, Mexico City, to Chief of Naval Operations [Admiral King], 24 January 1945, *ibid.*

30. U.S. State department, *Foreign relations, 1945: Europe,* IV, 785–86.

31. *Ibid.*

32. *Ibid.* Grew might also have cited as evidence that Mexico had abandoned all claim to the atoll in a 1940 letter from Eduard Hay, Mexican minister for foreign affairs, to Paul C. Daniels, then United States ambassador, regarding Mexico's recent expropriation of American petroleum interests in that country and Mexico's willingness to present the whole matter of compensation to binding arbitration. Hay asserted that Mexico's acceptance of Victor Emmanuel's Clipperton island arbitration award was indicative of the way his country "has always scrupulously fulfilled the arbitral decisions, even in those cases where the award had been adverse. . . ." *Ibid., 1940: the American republics,* V, 1022.

33. "Memorandum by Rear Admiral Davidson," 12 January, 1945, in Roosevelt Papers as President, "Clipperton Island" folder.

34. U.S. State department, *Foreign relations, 1945: Europe,* IV, 787–88.

35. *Ibid.*

36. *Ibid.*

37. *Ibid.,* pp. 788–89.

38. *Ibid.*

39. *Ibid.* pp. 789–90. Curiously, nowhere in his two-volume memoirs, *Turbulent era,* does Grew mention the rapidly deteriorating "Clipperton island situation," which he termed "extremely urgent," even though the president eventually accepted Grew's recommendations regarding the atoll. Perhaps, for the sake of economy, Grew (or his editor, Walter Johnson) judged the tiny place to be of such little significance that the petty affair was omitted from the diplomat's voluminous reminiscences.

40. U.S. State department, *Foreign relations, 1945: Europe,* IV, 789–90.

41. Quoted in Stettinius to Roosevelt, March 15, 1945, in Roosevelt Papers as President, "Air Base, Clipperton Island" folder; cf., U.S. State department, *Foreign relations, 1945: Europe,* IV, 792–93. Roosevelt's "telegram of January 28" was not printed by the State department, nor is it to be found in the White House's Clipperton island file.

42. U.S. State department, *Foreign relations, 1945: Europe,* IV, 790–91.

43. *Ibid.,* pp. 792–93.

44. *Ibid.*

45. Stettinius to Roosevelt, March 15, 1945; cf., U.S. State department, *Foreign relations, 1945: Europe,* IV, 792–93.

46. The Roosevelt Library's copy of Stettinius's letter of March 15, 1945, carries the following notation: "Carbon initialed 'E.R.S. Jr. OK F.D.R.' and returned to the Secretary of State, 3/16/45. elb."

47. U.S. State department, *Foreign relations, 1945: Europe,* IV, 793.

48. Memorandum from the State department," 19 April 1945, in Roosevelt Papers as President, "Air Base, Clipperton Island" folder.

49. *Ibid.*

50. Quoted in Morganthau diaries, April 12, 1945, II, frame 1,547.

51. Quoted in Truman, I, 25.

52. "Statement on France," p. 7. Clipperton island does not appear as a subject in President Truman's "War Room Messages," which, like Roosevelt's Map Room File, dealt with weighty issues of war and peace.

53. U.S. State Department, *Foreign relations, 1945: Europe,* IV, 794.

54. *Ibid.,* p. 795.

55. *Ibid., 1946: general* (1972), I, 1,117. "Required places" were Tarawa, Funafuti, Talara, Canary Island, Morotai, Blak, Guadalcanal-Tulagi, Espíritu Santo, Nouméa, Viti Levu, Christmas, Bora Bora, Clipperton, Edmonton-Whitehorse route to Alaska, Fort Chimo–Frobisher Bay route to Greenland, Goose Bay, Upolu, Salinas (Equador), Batista Field (Cuba), St. Julian–Lafe (Cuba), Curacao, Surinam, Casablanca–Port Lyautey, Dakar, Monrovia, and Formosa.

56. *Ibid.,* p. 1,142.

57. *Ibid.,* 1,175.

58. *Ibid., 1947: general* (1972) I, 769.

A Potpourri of
L'île Clipperton
1947–1980

Neither France nor the United States has officially occupied Clipperton island since October 5, 1945, when the American Navy "disestablished" its top-secret weather station, but from time to time both nations have landed military personnel there, primarily for research purposes in support of assorted postwar scientific expeditions. Actually, since World War II, hundreds of diverse persons have set foot on the remote anomalous atoll, with permission and without, and the resulting reports of their visits, including analyses of the island's flora and fauna, have greatly expanded the body of knowledge about it and fundamentally altered its ecology.

Clipperton island experienced its fourth documented maritime disaster when, on May 19, 1947, the American fishing boat *Thistle* out of San Pedro and under hire of California Marine Curing & Packing Company of Terminal Island, was shipwrecked on the atoll. Although the exact circumstances were never fully reported, it seems that Captain William Noble and crewmen Charles E. Warren, Gilbert B. Stethe, Robert Marchall, and Walter Richards were marooned for six weeks on what they characterized as the "Isle of Thirst," subsisting "on salvaged rations from their wrecked boat."[1]

They were finally plucked from the lonely atoll on June 29, when the tuna clipper *Normandie,* bound for South American fishing waters, happened upon the scene, took them on board, and notified the U.S. Navy. Because the Eleventh Naval District headquarters in San Diego had no warships in the immediate vicinity, Vice Admiral J. B. Oldendorf, commander of the Western Sea Frontier, asked *Normandie* to continue on to the Galapagos to meet a U.S. Navy vessel from Panama, which would ferry the castaways home. They were reportedly in "fair condition" even though "their clothing [was] in rags and their bodies [had been] blackened by tropical sun." Upon learning the location of the shipwrecked *Thistle,* long since given up as lost at sea, the Terminal Island cannery president, M. J. Gorby, expressed utter amazement. He claimed that the little fishing boat's "normal crising range was only about 700 miles and that she must have been blown to Clipperton out of control."[2]

Numerous others have since landed, mostly fishermen passing by, such as those on *Normandie,* but the atoll's most significant modern visitors have gone ashore purposefully, primarily to explore in order to understand this unique north Pacific landfall better. The French Navy has repeatedly called there since World War II, but mostly to cement national claim to the place. While France has never made details of these visits public, bronze plaques fastened to the Rock's face and to palm trees attest to four occasions that the Tricolor has flown in the tropical breeze above the island: "*La Commandant Charcot* on 23 April 1951, *La Jeanne-d'Arc,* 11 February 1952 (with a plaque identical to that of 1934–35), *La Moqueuse,* 6 August 1952, [and] *Le Dumont-d'Urville,* 23 August 1957."[3]

According to A. Goua, captain of the frigate *La Commandant Charcot,* French sailors "solemnly came to reaffirm French sovereignty." They affixed a plaque, raised the flag, and looked the place over in response to a call by "the Seventh South Pacific Scientific Congress, meeting in New Zealand, [which] suggested that meteorological and seismologic stations be immediately installed in the South Pacific [sic], notably on Easter Island, Clipperton, Marcus Island, etc., in support of trans-oceanic flight—an act desirable in terms of French prestige."[4]

As had numerous people before him, Goua concluded that both land plane and seaplane facilities could be developed, but at considerable cost. Considering that the nearest French base was

4,000 miles away, at Tahiti, logistical problems likely would prove to be overwhelming. He believed that any French occupation of L'île Clipperton would in all probability be as transient as that of the United States—all traces of which were steadily being "ruined . . . [by the atoll's] hot, humid, and salty climate. . . ."[5] Before long, Goua predicted, no reminder of the humiliating American occupation would remain on the lonely French possession—not even the rusting hulk of *LST-563*.

While a permanent base was desirable "in terms of French prestige," nothing came of the proposed meteorological station. Two years later, the French cruiser *La Moqueuse* visited, again largely for ceremonial purposes. A landing party "surfed ashore through shark-infested waters," nailed a plaque to a palm tree near the Rock, and raised the Tricolor. According to Captain A. Bourgau, "The ceremony is moving in its simplicity: no honor guard, no chinstraps, no bugle, but simply four sailors in fatigues with faces more or less tanned by the ocean air in the course of a voyage in its fifteenth day and which is still far from over. The moment is short but solemn, and the gesture symbolic in its brevity. . . . Only the goal counts and in this instance, it was attained: France's [reassertion of] right over this far away and rarely visited isle."[6]

However much the République may have successfully defended its title to the little out-of-the-way atoll following World War II, linguistically purist Frenchmen the world over who vehemently object to the intrusion of any and all alien words into their language must surely have been especially galled that the name of an English pirate had stuck like wet guano to their offbeat possession. Even in France, what once had been known as L'île Passion was invariably called "L'île Clipperton."[7]

In fact, when in 1978 France created "economic zones off the coasts of French overseas departments and territories" in which "foreign fishermen would be permitted to continue their activities . . . temporarily under the same conditions as before," pending specific international agreements, the République specifically included "The Territory of Clipperton (including Clipperton Island)" rather than L'île Passion, which, undoubtedly, no nation besides France (and possibly Mexico) could have identified. "Fishing for tuna by United States vessels off Clipperton Island in the

eastern Pacific Ocean," *Quai d'Orsay* pronounced, "is being conducted in accordance with the conservation and management
program of the Inter-American Tropical Tuna Commission, of
which both the Government of the United States and the Government of France are members."[8]

Aside from an untold number of legal and illegal commercial
fishing ventures around the atoll, the first postwar civilian expedition to the island for which there is considerable information
was led by Robert W. Denniston, an amateur ("ham") radio
operator from Newton, Iowa, who was pursuing what *Time*
magazine has termed "the arcane joys [of] . . . DXing, meaning
long distance communication. The obsessive goal of die-hard
DXers is to make at least one contact with each of the 318
'countries' recognized by hams around the world." Under established criteria, Clipperton qualified as a "country" because it is
more than 225 miles from its governing mainland; however, no
ham could talk to it unless other amateurs went there and put it
"on the air."[9]

Following a similar trip to the Bahamas in 1948 and "suffering
recurring attacks of DXpeditionitis," Denniston organized a visit
to the remote atoll, hardly appreciating as he did the difficulty he
and companion hams would face. He talked up the project over
the airwaves and immediately received support and encouragement, including financial underwriting from The Hallicrafters
Co., a shortwave radio manufacturer. DXers elsewhere interceded
with the French government, securing official permission for the
visit; others obtained "the permits necessary to transport sophisticated radio gear through Mexico."[10]

A ham named "Bob," otherwise identified only by call letters
"K2BBZ," had actually "been on Clipperton in 1945 serving
Uncle Sam, . . . [and] provided volumes of information, photographs, and answered countless questions for the landlubbers from
Iowa. He drew sketches showing the contour of the Pacific bottom
and how to land around the stern of the beached LST, using its
hulk as breakwater." Other DXers who had fished those waters
warned Denniston about "man-eating sharks" that patrolled the
reef, and other dangers: "There's no harbor and a terrific surf
sometimes covers the whole island. . . . Be prepared to swim the

last 50 feet. . . . Beware of the wild pigs with tusks that drive men into the surf."[11]

Originally planning to arrive at Clipperton in November 1953, Denniston's DXpedition was delayed several months while he searched the West coast for a charter boat capable of carrying himself, four companions, duplicate sets of three ham radios (HT-18s, HT-20s, and SX-88s), and two gasoline-powered generators to the remote island and returning them all safely to the mainland. Finally, Hallicrafters located and chartered *Sea Raider* (an 83-foot, twin-engine diesel vessel of American registry), and early in 1954 Denniston, Vern Hedman, Leo Olney, Gene O'Leary, and Tom Partridge set out from Iowa in Olney's station wagon, pulling an equipment-laden trailer. Mechanical problems delayed them in Oklahoma and Texas, and "an expensive bout with Customs"[12] postponed their sailing from Acapulco.

At sea, the ship's captain broke his sextant, forcing them either to return to Acapulco for another, or, since they had been unable to raise anyone via the ship-to-shore phone, to determine their location by locking onto radio transmissions from the United States and, based upon known points of origin, determine the position of their pitching ship in the Pacific.

Triangulating radio waves "fixed" them 250 miles east-northeast of the atoll, which, considering the distances and relatively primitive equipment and techniques involved, "turned out to be quite accurate (within 40 miles)." *Sea Raider* arrived at the island low on fuel, and to conserve what remained, the ship's owner, Al Guiberson of Dallas, who had gone along for the adventure, suggested that the captain "shut down the engines, . . . drift during the night, and [in the morning] try to contact a ship to get fuel. But with the engines stopped the craft pitched and rolled so badly fuel drums lashed on deck threatened to break loose. To prevent damage it was necessary to restart the diesels."[13]

A cautious man, the captain returned to the mainland without attempting a landing. Denniston says "morale was very low; frequent sea sickness did not help. . . . we had run into a streak of bad luck (which was destined to last for some six weeks)." In Acapulco, the Americans decided to try once more before giving up altogether, and Denniston flew to Mexico City, where local hams arranged an audience with a Mexican Navy officer to beg the loan of either a ship or a flying boat. The official explained that because of long-standing and still somewhat strained relations with France over Clipperton island his government could not become involved without *Quai d'Orsay*'s blessings, which might take a month or more to obtain. Then, Denniston later wrote, "A deal with the ham pilot of a privately owned Catalina flying boat fell through when the owner decided to sell it to the Navy."[14]

Disappointed, Denniston returned to Acapulco, where the port's chief pilot suggested that he hire *Barca de Oro II*, an 83-foot schooner with an auxiliary diesel engine. Captain Enrique Braun, the ship's owner and skipper, agreed to the trip, and Hallicrafters and the North American Philips Co., a rival radio manufacturer, paid the charter. Tony Rivas, owner of Hotel La Riviera, where the DXers had resided since their return, and Toby Dorantes, who was "experienced in dugouts and surf landings," also enlisted.

Following "the usual wrangle with customs," the DXers loaded up *Barca* and shoved off with thirteen men aboard. While still in the harbor, the engine's generator broke down, delayng departure for two hours. Then, during the following five days at sea, they "battled oil- and water-line leaks, thunderstorms, torn sails, leaky hull, a dead battery in the ship's 32-volt system, and generator-starting trouble." Late on the sixth day, they spotted Clipperton Rock, but, apparently aware of the dangers, Captain Braun decided to stand by until morning, by which time the atoll "had disappeared from view."[15]

A stout wind had blown them away. Then, when they headed toward the island under power, the engine quit—just as a squall with 35-knot winds smashed into the ship, sending huge waves crashing over the bow. Through it all the DXers kept their portable generator running on deck, maintaining ham contact in case they required rescue, which seemed increasingly likely.

Its diesel fuel diluted with seawater, *Barca*'s engine would not restart, and alerted to the DXers plight by hams around the world, the Mexican Navy dispatched three vessels to assist, the first of which, *G-38,* arrived the following day. Several officers and a mechanic bearing fuel boarded the schooner and rendered assistance, but the balky diesel refused to cooperate. Consequently, the gunboat towed the disabled schooner to Clipperton, and both vessels anchored off the northeast point, within sight of the beached LST. The next morning, three men (Gene O'Leary, Toby Dorantes, and someone identified only as David) set out for shore in a canoe, only to be capsized by a giant breaker 50 feet from shore. O'Leary later reported that while he was swimming for shore he felt something brush his leg, he presumed a shark. With him refusing to reenter the water, Dorantes and David swam back to the schooner just as the second warship, *Tomas Marin,* arrived on the scene.

With Leo Olney remaining on *Barca* to maintain communications with the outside world, Tom Partridge, Vern Hedman, Denniston, and a man identified only as Juan loaded aboard a rubber raft a "complete ham radio station in watertight boxes," along "with water bottle, tent, guns, [and] cameras," lashed it all down securely so that if the raft upset the gear would remain intact, and set out toward the LST. Paddling frantically as they hit the breakers, they "managed to get into the protected area between the LST and the shore . . . [for] a perfect landing on smooth sandy beach without shipping a drop of water." Following a brief rest on shore eating coconuts, they carried their gear to a spot near the lagoon, pitched tents, and set up "a 20-meter quarter-wave vertical [radio antenna] on a fish[ing] pole. . . . Just then," Denniston later recalled, "a pig walked nonchalantly by our tent. We grabbed our guns and edged toward him but he took off on the run. Others we saw later did the same."[16]

Hams soon discovered that their lightweight generator, repeatedly pressed into service aboard *Barca* to power the bilge pump, was showing wear by making considerable noise in the radio receiver. Then, just as they switched to the 15-meter band, "the generator's gasoline engine ran out of oil, [burned out a bearing,] and quit. This is no streak," Denniston mused, "this is a permanent state of bad luck!"[17]

Hedman and O'Leary dismantled the machine but could not repair it. Unable to radio Leo Olney on *Barca* to send the spare generator ashore, they were reduced to wigwag signals with improvised flags. Olney replied in kind that Captain Braun said the surf was running far too heavy for a landing. That evening, the third warship, *G-36,* arrived from Salina Cruz, carrying food, fuel, lubricants, and spare parts for *Barca*'s engine. After dark, when he attempted to "blinker" Olney by flashlight, Denniston says, "whammo!—the whole armada climbed on the frequency with their California k[ilo]W[att] blinkers and pointed their beams at the beach and me. . . . It took many exchanges before I could get across to them that I wanted to talk to Leo. This may have been because I was using English and they Spanish. Eventually I got to work Leo for suggestions, but we still couldn't get the generator engine to run."[18]

The next morning, Captain Braun sent Toby Dorantes ashore to inform the hams that the Mexican warships had been ordered to depart and that *Barca,* disabled, must sail with them. Denniston wigwagged Braun that the DXers had not contacted anyone, that they could not possibly leave yet. Braun relayed this to the Mexican task force commander, who radioed Mexico City, which granted a twenty-four-hour stay on the execution of its orders. Vern Hedman, Tom Partridge, Gene O'Leary, and apparently one of the Mexicans took the rubber raft back through the pounding surf to *Barca* to load the spare generator and to bring to the island Leo Olney, who had not been ashore. This they did without incident.

At 3:00 P.M., Central Standard Time, Sunday, April 25, 1954, "FØ8AJ" was finally "on the air." They broadcast continuously over the next eighteen hours, talking with hams around the world even as the tent came down around the radio and as gear not in use was carried to the beach. At 9:53 A.M. on the twenty-sixth, Denniston reluctantly signed off, and they packed up the radio.

The surf was running high as they prepared to embark, all equipment and five men aboard a single rubber raft. Straddling the outside ring and paddling hard, they emerged from behind the LST just as a huge breaker struck; it tossed several of them off their perches and into the raft, which was nearly swamped with water. Those remaining in position stroked the sea furiously with their paddles, the raft gradually pulling through the surf and into calmer water where travel was easier. As they came along the lee side of *Barca,* swells lifted the raft six feet or more and pounded it against the side of the schooner, nearly crushing them. Finally, "after several close calls,"[19] they unloaded and climbed aboard.

Two of the three Mexican warships having departed the evening before, *Tomas Marin* took *Barca* in tow and, after steaming a circuit around the island for a farewell look, set course for Acapulco.

Three days from Clipperton, the gunboat cut *Barca* loose, and it sailed on under tattered and torn canvas, limping into port twenty-two days after having departed. All told, they had made 1,108 radio contacts and had lost about fifteen pounds each. At that point the DXers "had just one thing in mind," Denniston says, "food!"[20]

Since Denniston's day, the majority of visitors have been scientists, some of whom were merely sailing by. A case in point is the dredging done in May 1952 by USS *Shuttle,* a research vessel of the U.S. Navy's Electronics Laboratory, which hauled up two scoops full of underwater life (mostly mollusks) from 100 to 200 fathoms off Clipperton peak's eastern submarine slope. Given to paleontologists at the University of California at Berkeley to identify, more than half of these invertebrates proved to be unknown in eastern Pacific waters; moreover, one gastropod, a snail named *Clanculus (Panocochlea) clippertonensis,* was altogether new to science. Such discoveries made the place increasingly "intriguing to students of natural history."[21]

That fascination took three members of the Scripps Institution of Oceanography's Acapulco Trench Expedition—Robert L. Fisher, James B. Jordan, and Stanley O'Neil—to the island aboard *Spencer F. Baird* on December 12, 1954, while geophysical investigations were under way in the vicinity. They collected mollusks, crustaceans, and coral from the lagoon beach and from the outer rim of the atoll, all specimens later being given to University of California paleontologists for identification. Although they purposely looked, visiting scientists found no living marine invertebrates in the lagoon.[22] Efforts at underwater collecting in the adjacent sea were equally unsuccessful, because the "effort was disrupted by aggressive sharks."[23]

Two years later, *Spencer F. Baird,* then engaged in "The Acapulco Geological Expedition of 1956," again stopped off at the atoll primarily to "install a tide gauge." On the island from October 20 through 26, Scripps Institution scientists Edwin Allison, Wayne Baldwin, Townsend Cromwell, George Hohnhaus, Conrad Limbaugh, and Alan Smith collected "six vials of invertebrates, [which they] preserved in alcohol,"[24] but their tide gauge was soon "obliterated" by a "storm of great violence that [must have] burst over the island"[25] sometime after May 1958, when USS *Monticello* visited.

Acting on behalf of both the U.S. Navy's Hydrographic Office and its Office of Coast and Geodetic Survey, *Monticello,* a dock landing ship (LSD-35), and USS *Segundo,* a submarine (SS-398), steamed to Clipperton island "in order to accurately fix its position." While *Segundo* was submerged nearby, "in connection with gravity studies," *Monticello* collected "the maximum amount of intelligence on Clipperton Island," which was forwarded to fleet headquarters. Well aware of the inherent dangers in landing through the atoll's turbulent surf, the Pentagon had directed Captain F. D. Kellogg, *Monticello's* skipper, to transport personnel to and fro by helicopter—flying "Lt. Pierre D'Anglejan-Chattilon [liaison officer] of the French Navy, . . . in first group . . . [so that he might] raise the French National Ensign on Clipperton Rock." Although operating under secret orders, the task force obviously had *Quai d'Orsay's* blessings, for, in addition to D'Anglejan-Chattilon, on board was "French Government Geologist, Professor [Alphonse G.] Obermuller," whose "scientific studies"[26] were later published.

All told, *Monticello's* helicopter flew thirty-three sorties through fair weather and foul to ferry men and equipment back and forth to the island. On the afternoon of 30 October, heavy rain reduced visiblity to less than one mile, and the LSD "commenced sounding fog signals,"[27] lest it collide with *Segundo,* which, alternately submerged and surfaced, was taking bottom soundings around the perimeter of the dangerous island. The weather improved somewhat the next day, rains ending and the sky partially clearing. With blue skies and 8-knot winds on the afternoon of Saturday, 2 November, *Monticello* even launched an LCVP with a recreation party that went ashore for about three hours. The following day, its assignment completed, "Task Unit 16.4" disbanded, *Segundo* and *Monticello* going their separate ways—the LSD returning to port at San Diego to debark its passengers.

Difficult and dangerous though its mission had been, the navy unit executed its orders efficiently, precisely fixing the geographical center of the atoll at 10°18′41″ N, 109°12′34″ W. The expedition also accurately measured the elevation of Clipperton Rock at 68 feet 10 inches, which heretofore had been variously reported between 62 and 100 feet tall, including a 1935 report by a French *(Jeanne-d'Arc)* survey team that had it towering 29 meters (90 feet) above sea level. Geodetic soundings by *Segundo* confirmed theories that the atoll actually was constructed upon the remains of an ancient sea mount and that Clipperton island was quite alone in the deep, dark sea. Although those findings were never published, they correlated closely with those of the Scripps Institution, which were. So too were Obermuller's, who judged the atoll's phosphates to be too marginal in quality and quantity to be commercially exploitable.

Whatever its economic potential, Clipperton's ecology continued to fascinate scientists. In 1958, the Scripps Institution undertook the most ambitious investigation ever as part of the Third International Geophysical Year Cruise, "The Doldrums Expedition." The International Geophysical Year, or IGY as it is known among scientists, was an eighteen-month period (July 1957 through December 1958) designated for study of the earth and its cosmic environment by sixty-six cooperating nations—the largest and most far-reaching international scientific venture ever, one of its many ramifications being the designation of Antarctica as a nonmilitary region. The United States' IGY efforts, among other things, led to the discovery of the Van Allen radiation belt and to soundings in the world's seabeds that identified seismically active rifts, which give substance to plate tectonic theory that explains movement in the earth's crust, such as around Clipperton island.

Scripps's "IGY Clipperton Island Expedition" of August–September 1958 lasted eight weeks, thirteen scientists and technicians residing on the atoll for all or part of the period. Blessed with calm seas and fair weather, they landed without incident on August 7 at the northeast point, beside the beached LST, and unloaded what they believed to be sufficient equipment and supplies to see them through the month; however, warm temperatures, ranging from 75° to 90° F, and intermittent rain, as much as four inches coming in a single cloudburst, played havoc with perishable supplies, equipment, and specimens. Leather and cotton cloth quickly molded. Observing the "burned appearance of the vegetation," the scientists quickly concluded "that the rainy season had just started." Taking advantage of the increasing moisture, they transplanted fifty young palm trees from the southwestern shore to the northeast point, "with the hope that they will eventually afford cover there."[28]

All told, the 1958 IGY Clipperton Island Expedition was an extraordinarily productive scientific venture, resulting in a microscopic study of, arguably, the most obscure spot on earth. Episodic investigation heretofore had revealed little in depth of the atoll's ecology, and the IGY's experts purposely set out to fathom it. With most work done by August 25, nine scientists departed "according to plan," going on to Panama to pursue another project, while four persons remained on the atoll until September 25. "In spite of the many difficult logistical problems involved," one of them, Conrad Limbaugh, later concluded that "we were able to collect rather thoroughly on and around the island; in fact, it is [now] probably the best collected island in the entire Eastern Pacific."[29]

Limbaugh's undersea exploration two years earlier had been greatly disrupted by sharks, and in 1958 he employed underwater cages, which, along with scuba gear, "permitted many hours of under water collecting and observing. . . . Although dives were made to a depth of 130 feet, the adequacy of data from below 60 feet is limited by the relatively brief duration of the few deeper dives."[30]

The combined scrutiny eventually produced a dozen articles and monographs, among them the first serious study of the island's history.[31]

Their stay also forever affected the island's ecology. Struck by what they considered to be a comparatively lush flora, especially as contrasted with numerous historical accounts that described the atoll as barren, scientists speculated about the cause of change. Biologist Marie-Hélène Sachet suggested the pigs were to blame. "At the time of our visit in 1958 there were fifty-eight of them on the island and from an examination of their droppings it was obvious that they ate crabs" which no longer infested the place as they had reportedly done at the turn of the century. Wild swine obviously had "eaten enough of them . . . to give the vegetation a chance to take hold. By that time the flora had [also] been increased by various introduced species."[32]

Seemingly likewise affected were the island's birds. Ornithologist Kenneth Stager later wrote:

Early accounts of the bird life of the island had repeatedly mentioned the colonies of thousands of sea birds of several species which used this atoll as their breeding ground. Upon our arrival, however, it soon became apparent that something had happened to the tremendous bird populations as only a few hundred birds of various species of terns and boobies were in evidence. . . . The ground-nesting birds had fallen prey to these feral pigs and no young birds or eggs were safe from the pigs' rooting depredations.

I immediately launched a one-man war against the pigs of Clipperton and by using sound infantry combat tactics and a bit of pig psychology—which consisted of asking the question of, "if I were a pig, where would I hide?"—I managed to completely liquidate the pig population of the island. The final score was 58 pigs of all shapes, sizes and colors. The end of my 20-day sojourn on Clipperton found the island restored as an important breeding site for the oceanic birds of the eastern pacific, completely free from the depredations of pigs.[33]

Apparently unaware that nesting birds rarely resided on the atoll until the hurricane season had passed, or about November 1, Stager's condemnation of the pigs may well have been flawed. Moreover, with the crab population significantly reduced, porkers very likely were merely replacing crustaceans as predators. Even so, most wildlife experts would heartily endorse Stager's eradication program, however much contemporary animal rights' activists may deplore it. Ecology professor Bruce Coblentz of Oregon State University has asserted: "It is a well-recognized fact that feral animals, when left unchecked, can destroy entire ecosystems. . . . if you can shoot feral animals and shoot them to extinction, go ahead and do it."[34]

Interestingly, it seems that neither Stager nor any of his colleagues questioned the propriety of transplanting palm trees, identified by them as an introduced species. They sincerely believed that their modification of the environment was for the better.

High winds and a tempestuous sea throughout September hampered the work of those who remained on the island, and when it came time to leave, they did so only with much difficulty. "Removing the final group with their equipment and specimens was a hazardous and exhausting undertaking," Limbaugh recalled, "and took the entire day"[35] of September 25. Although they lost some equipment, they escaped with their lives.

Thereafter, circumstantial evidence suggests two additional visits by the U.S. Navy, and one rather spectacular miss. As to the visits, no information exists, save for inferences drawn from a description of the island contained in the Navy's *Sailing Directions* (1979):

> *There were (1972) some sheds, a framework building, and an extensive grove of coconut palms [on the island] about midway along the SW coast. Farther SE are several clumps of coconut trees. The N corner of the atoll was covered by thick undergrowth (1976), with a derelict hut and mast near the middle of the NE side.*[36]

The purpose for either the 1972 or 1979 visit is unknown.

The reason for the spectacular miss is entwined with Clipperton's murky history. In 1960, the nuclear-powered submarine USS *Triton* circumnavigated the globe underwater, "following as near as possible the route of the first great circumnavigator, Ferdinand Magellan,"[37] a public-relations idea attributed to Captain E.P. (Pete) Aurand, then naval aide to President Dwight D. Eisenhower. *Triton*'s skipper, Edward L. Beach, an accomplished submariner and the author of the best-selling World War II novel *Run Silent, Run Deep* (1955), had limited time to research Magellan's epochal voyage and hence relied principally upon what he thought was a "most thoroughly researched book," *So Noble a Captain: The Life and Times of Ferdinand Magellan* (1953), penned by lay historian Charles McKew Parr, who, Beach believed, "knows more about Magellan than any man of the present era."[38]

After rounding Cape Horn, *Triton* proceeded diagonally across the South Pacific along the heading that Parr laid down for Magellan: northwestward to the Marianas, skirting by numerous islands that Magellan had somehow failed to spot. In his book *Around the World Submerged* (1962), Captain Beach merely hints at the inherent problem of retracing Magellan's route according to Parr: "From Easter Island to Guam would take about two weeks. Aside from the necessity of threading rather neatly between the outlying reefs of one or two archipelagoes, we foresaw no need to slow down. . . ."[39] *Triton*'s crew was able to identify neither St. Paul nor Shark's island, the lone landfalls sighted by Magellan's men, for, without knowing it, the submarine was thousands of miles off its desired course.

No matter: Even had the submarine followed Magellan's probable route and therefore skimmed close by Clipperton island at periscope depth, those aboard could have seen little; nor is it likely that they would have surfaced and landed a shore party. *Triton*'s objective was elsewhere.

The most recently reported landing was in 1980, when world-renowned oceanographer Jacques-Yves Cousteau visited to assess French development schemes (a manganese nodule processing facility, or a tuna boat station), to investigate the atoll's submerged volcanic vent, and to film the event for American television. He found a desolate island largely devoid of vegetation—a place completely reclaimed by the crabs.

Cousteau's odyssey entailed the most elaborate private expedition ever to the atoll. While the Frenchman was in Manzanillo, Mexico, interviewing octogenarian Altagracia Quiroz about the island's sinister past and gathering together an international (French, Canadian, and American) scientific contingent to study the place, regular members of the Cousteau team headed by Bernard Delemotte sailed *Calypso* to Clipperton and surfed ashore aboard their rubber raft, *Zodiac*. Eventually they ferried tons of supplies (drums of fuel and even fresh water) to the island by helicopter, and later cleared away coral debris to permit Cousteau and his companions from the mainland to land an airplane on the coral rim, as both Admiral Byrd and Captain Taylor had once envisioned.

When the Canadian amphibious aircraft touched down, aboard was seventy-year-old Ramón Arnaud, Jr., who had last seen his birthplace on July 18, 1917. Upon deplaning, he fell to his knees and kissed the ground, saying "My earth." Disoriented, he searched the island for landmarks, for familiar sites with which to get his bearings. Along the southwestern shore, near the coconut grove, he pointed out to sea and said, "My father died over there. . . . He and the other three men died there."[40]

For the television camera, Arnaud verified the story Altagracia

Quiroz had told Cousteau in Manzanillo—of the little colony's ordeal, of being marooned. Then Arnaud led Cousteau to the Rock, the site of Álvarez's hut where, for more than two years, the light keeper had brutalized the women; there, finally, Tirza Randon had crushed his skull with a hammer.

Arnaud described their elation upon being rescued by sailors from USS *Yorktown*. Later, the old man erected a wooden cross on which was inscribed "Capt. Ramón Arnaud, 1915," and sprinkled about it the contents of a flask of holy water that had been blessed in Manzanillo.

Meanwhile, Cousteau's personal inspection of the atoll confirmed much that was already well documented within the scientific community. Feral pigs gone, crabs infested the place in vast numbers. Birds abounded. Television cameras which panned the landscape revealed that, except for the palm groves, much of the low vegetation that botanist Marie-Hélène Sachet had observed twenty-two years before had entirely vanished, apparent victims of resurgent crustaceans.

Cousteau also engaged in original research, thereby adding to the body of knowledge about the atoll. Using Aqua-Lungs, a device he coinvented in 1943, his team explored the lagoon and found that, cut off from the sea and infused with fresh water from frequent rainfall, it supported relatively few life-forms. In shallower stretches the water was clogged with aquatic weeds, and, fertilized by bird droppings, was rich in algae and plankton; however, the lagoon was virtually devoid of larger forms of animal life. Even so, biologist Rene Taxit's analyses of both fresh and salt water showed the lagoon to be far richer in microorganisms than the surrounding ocean.

Far more intriguing to Cousteau was the hole in the Grand Reef, an apparent volcanic vent in the southeastern quadrant of the lagoon. His team placed a diving platform directly over the circular, well-like curiosity and, using a sonar device, found that at 60 feet there was ambiguous indication of bottom. Not knowing exactly what to expect, Cousteau, Delemotte, and Jacques Delcoutere donned watertight unisuits and protective masks for a dive into the strange hole, taking with them special underwater camera equipment designed to film in murky water. Delemotte entered the water first, followed quickly by Delcoutere and Cousteau.

Cousteau narrated the adventure for television:

The journey begins. Above us, for an instant, hangs a rectangle of sunlight—the window from which we have slipped from one element to another. Then, it is dark. I test my camera and the cone shielding the lens against the murkiness of the surrounding water. An apparition looms into view, and I think I recognize Bernard. He signals, and a moment later the lights reveal the inner wall of the crater covered with vegetation. At this level, we still are in a zone of light. Slowly, we continue our descent along the weighted cable, our single reference point as we move into the increasing darkness. Gradually, the character of the water around us seems to be changing, both in temperature and chemical composition—giving it a glycerin-like appearance.

Then, at sixty feet, the light reveals what appears to be the bottom; instead, it proves to be a dense, four-foot layer of accumulated plant debris, a thickly matted net in which material falling from the surface is quickly trapped. Through it, Delcoutere vanishes, and for a moment, all we can see are the air bubbles rising from his breathing apparatus. Then, we too pass through the floating layer. Around us, great globs of matter float by—strange constellations, drifting through a space in which all familiar landmarks have ceased to exist. We seem to have entered a world of dreams, ghostly and insubstantial, in which the cable has become the only thread connecting us to reality. Out of the depths, an outcrop appears. From it, our slightest movement lifts little storms of settled particles, the dead chaff of once living matter.

Deeper. In this submerged desolation the water temperature again seems to rise, burning our hands in spite of our gloves. We take samples, hoping later to learn what chemical changes have occurred at successive levels. Now, at nearly a hundred feet, we pass through a second suspended layer—and enter a silent chaos in which masses of ruptured material move around us, more sensed than seen. Slowly we are enveloped in total darkness. It is only with our flippers that we finally feel the bottom.

Earlier, our hands seemed scalded by the water. Now, despite our watertight suits and masks, our eyes are burning—tears fall down

our faces, blurring our vision. The pain is unbearable. I signal our
return. I know now that it is not heat that is burning us; it is
hydrogen sulfide, the toxic product of vegetation rotting when all
oxygen has been consumed. We have penetrated a zone of death, a
region where no living thing can long survive. Blinded and burned,
we begin an ascent that seems endless. Eager to hurry to escape this
hostile inferno, we still must obey the divers' discipline—return to
the surface at a carefully prescribed pace. Slowly, hand over hand
along the cable, we rise through the successive layers toward the
clearer water at the top. The glow of light at last appears from the
platform's rectangular well. It is no longer simply a window in the
sky. It is deliverance.[41]

Hydrogen sulfide that seeped into his mask temporarily blinded
Delemotte, and both Delcoutere and Cousteau suffered some
distress from the noxious chemical, which was potent enough to
discolor their air tanks.

Later, while on a final tour of the island, Cousteau encountered
"rusted evidence of man's brief, ill-fated intrusion" on the atoll:
"a little [toy] boat, a toy soldier, [the head of] a dismembered
doll—bits and pieces of human existence, even unspent ammunition, salvaged from a [U.S. Navy] wreck [during World War II]
and then abandoned. In this cosmic theatre of the absurd," he
speculated as he prepared to depart, "perhaps it is the crab that
may survive, not we."[42] Fortunately for Clipperton island, the
French government has not decided to pursue developmental
schemes.

Quite likely crabs again dominate life on Clipperton island, but,
with Cousteau's departure, reliable information about the lonely
atoll comes to an end, for no one is known to have been back since
and lived to tell about it—or to have reported it publicly.

Notes

1. "Shipwrecked crew rescued," p. 13.

2. "Five, shipwrecked on isle, rescued," p. 1. There may have been yet another shipwreck since World War II. Biologist Marie-Hélène Sachet, the first academic to research the history of the atoll in depth, says on "31 [sic] Novembre [1950] deux hommes régugiés d'un naufrage," (Sachet, "Histoire," p. 22), but she provides neither details of the two castaways and their apparent rescue nor the source of her information. The atoll may also have been visited in 1950 by "two aviators," Sachet says, "if one believes the messages [graffiti] penciled on the ruined [Navy] barracks." *Ibid.*, p. 19.

3. *Ibid.*, p. 18. Details of visits by *Jeanne-d'Arc* (1952) and *Le Durmont-d'Urville* (1957) have never been made public. Another French naval visit, by *Annamite*, which arrived off the atoll on June 6, 1949, failed because bad weather prevented a landing.

4. Goua, pp. 231–32.

5. *Ibid.*

6. Bourgau, pp. 68–69.

7. For instance, see France, *French Polynesia*, pp. 4, 9.

8. Nash, pp. 1,008–1,010.

9. "In the Caribbean," p. 7.

10. Denniston, p. 10.

11. *Ibid.*, p. 10.

12. *Ibid.*, p. 11.

13. *Ibid.*

14. *Ibid.*

15. *Ibid.*, p. 12.

16. *Ibid.*, p. 14.

17. *Ibid.*, pp. 14–15.

18. *Ibid.*

19. *Ibid.,* p. 15.

20. *Ibid.*

21. Hertlein and Emerson (1953), p. 354. See also Hamilton for details of the 1950 expedition and works by Johnson; Lipps (1968, 1969); Menard; Menard and Fisher; Truchan and Larson; and Wardley relating to underwater research in the vicinity of Clipperton island by the Scripps Institution and others interested in its nearby fracture zone.

22. Hertlein and Emerson (1957), p. 1.

23. Allison, "Distribution of *Conus,"* p. 32.

24. Charles F. Harbison, "Clipperton island: a short history of visits of scientists to this atoll" (MS, 1958), p. 9 (Harbison Papers).

25. Sachet, "Histoire," p. 19.

26. USS *Monticello,* Operation Order, 11 October 1957, in U.S. Navy Records, File No. 003/57 (Operational Archives). See also, Obermuller, *passim.*

27. USS *Monticello,* "Deck log," 3 November 1957, in U.S. Navy Records, Fleet Support Branch (Chief of Naval Operations office).

28. Limbaugh, p. 2. Expedition members were Edwin C. Allison, a paleontologist with the University of California, Berkeley; Wayne J. Baldwin, an ichthyologist also at Berkeley; Robert Bucaro, a radio operator with the Scripps Institution; James Robert Chess, a Scripps deep-sea diver; Alvin S. Hambly, a physician with the University of California Medical School in San Francisco, who doubled as a diver; Charles F. Harbison, an entomologist with the San Diego Society of Natural History; expedition leader Conrad Limbaugh, a biologist interested in shark behavior who had visited the atoll in 1956 with the Scripps Institution; Douglas Magill, a ham radio operator from San Diego; David Peterson, an entomologist with the San Diego Natural History Society; Ernest S. Reese, an invertebrate specialist with the University of California, Los Angeles; Marie-Hélène Sachet, a botanist with the National Academy of Science, Washington; Kenneth E. Stager, an ornithologist with the Los Angeles County Museum; and John Wintersteen, an ichthyologist at UCLA.

29. *Ibid.,* pp. 2–3.

30. Allison (1959), p. 32.

31. See works by Allison (1958, 1959); W. J. Baldwin, *et al.*; Harbison; Limbaugh; Sachet (1959, 1960, 1962); and Stager, as well as related work by Chace. Botanist Marie-Hélène Sachet was by far the most productive of the scientists who journeyed to Clipperton island with the 1958 IGY expedition. All told, she wrote five treatises on the atoll, ranging from history to ecology, all of which were published and are cited in the bibliography.

32. Sachet, "Flora and vegetation," pp. 288–89.

33. Stager, "Expedition to Clipperton island," p. 14.

34. Quoted in Wells, p. 1.

35. Limbaugh, p. 2.

36. U.S. Navy, *Sailing directions,* p. 5.

37. Beach, "Introduction," p. vii.

38. *Ibid.,* p. ix.

39. Beach (1962), p. 181. See also Dibner, *passim.*

40. J. Y. Cousteau (1981), n.p.

41. *Ibid.* Cousteau and his fellow underwater explorers found no igneous rock whatsoever in the walls of the hole, as should have been the case with a volcanic vent; rather, they brought back to the surface only calcium carbonate material, which is characteristic of sedimentary accumulation. Thus, the origin and nature of the hole in Grand Reef remains as much a mystery as before. Richard C. Murphy, Cousteau Society, Los Angeles, March 31, 1989, to JMS.

42. Cousteau, n.p. See also Murphy (1980).

Bibliography

Following is a comprehensive list pertaining to Clipperton island. It includes all works consulted, cited, and directly relevant to the study of the island. Modern library style is used in the unabridged entry format, except for those items that contain *q.v.* (*quod vide*), which refer the reader to a complete citation elsewhere. To facilitate the location of often elusive public documents, SuDocs (U.S. Superintendent of Documents) and/or Serial Set numbers are appended where appropriate.

Unpublished Material

American Geographical Society. Records. New York, N.Y.

Harbison, Charles F. Papers. Archives, Museum of Natural History, San Diego, Calif.

[Morganthau, Henry, Jr.]. The presidential diaries of Henry Morganthau, Jr. (1938–1945). 2 reels. Frederick, Md.: The Presidential Documents Series (Franklin D. Roosevelt), a microfilm project of University Publications of America, Inc., 1981.

Roosevelt, Franklin D. Papers as President. 1933–45. Franklin D. Roosevelt Library, Hyde Park, N.Y.

Truman, Harry S. "War room messages of President Truman (1945–1946)." 5 reels. Frederick, Md.: The Presidential Documents Series (Harry S. Truman), a microfilm project of University Publications of America, Inc., 1980.

U.S. Navy department. Records. National Archives, Washington, D.C.

———. Records. Chief of Naval Operations, Washington, D.C.

———. Records. Operational Archives, Washington Navy Yard, Washington, D.C.

U.S. State department. Records. National Archives, Washington, D.C.

Published Material

"Acapulco total wreck; tidal wave finishes earthquake's work; people without food." New York *Times,* August 2, 1909, p. 1.

Acheson, Dean. *Present at the creation; my years in the State department.* New York: W. W. Norton, Inc., 1969.

"Adee, Alvey Augustus." *Who was who in America, 1897–1942* 1 (1942): 9, q.v.

Agassiz, Alexander. "Reports on the scientific results of the expedition to the eastern tropical Pacific in charge of Alexander Agassiz by the U.S. fish commission steamer *Albatross* from October, 1904, to March, 1905, Lieut. Commander L. M. Garrett, U.S.N., commanding." Museum of Comparative Zoology at Harvard College *Memoirs* 33 (January 1906): 1–75.

"Air transport services; agreement signed at Paris March 27, 1946, with annex, schedules, and protocol of signatures." U.S. State department. *Treaties and other international agreements of the United States of America* 7 (1962): 1109–1121, q.v.

Allison, Edwin C. "Clipperton island; easternmost atoll of the Pacific (abstract)." American Malacological Union *Annual Report for 1958:* 38.

―――. "Distribution of *Conus* on Clipperton island." *The Veliger* (April 1959): 32–34.

―――. "Invertebrates." International Geophysical Year. *Clipperton island expedition field report* (1958): 3–4, q.v.

"American flag displaced; armed Mexican marines haul down the stars and stripes on Clipperton island." New York *Times,* January 1, 1898, p. 9.

"Americans retracted; hauled down their flag when Mexicans claimed Clipperton." Los Angeles *Times,* January 6, 1898, p. 2.

Anderson, Roger N., and Earl E. Davis. "A topographic interpretation of the Clipperton ridge, Mathematicians ridge, East Pacific rise system." American Geophysical Union Transaction *Eos* 53 (April 1972): 414.

"*Argus.*" U.S. Navy. *Dictionary of American naval fighting ships* 1 (1959): 59, q.v. D207.10:1

"Arrangements for concession of Clipperton island to France nearing completion." New York *Times,* March 1, 1933, p. 11.

"*Atlanta.*" U.S. Navy. *Dictionary of American naval fighting ships* 1 (1959): 71, q.v. D207.10:1

Atwater, Tanya. "Implications of plate tectonics for the Cenozoic tectonic evolution of western North America." Geological Society of North America *Bulletin* 81 (1970): 3513–36.

"Awards Pacific isle to France in dispute; king of Italy decides against claims made by Mexico to Clipperton island." New York *Times,* February 4, 1931, p. 10.

Baarslag, Karl. *Islands of adventure.* New York: Farrar & Rinehart, Inc., 1941.

"Babes cast away on lonely isle of Clipperton; skipper of wrecked schooner, wife and kiddies, arrive after a trying time; lived on fish and eggs; crew of lost Nokomis taken off Clipperton island by the cruiser Cleveland." San Francisco *Chronicle,* July 11, 1914, p. 1.

Bailey, Thomas A. *A diplomatic history of the American people.* 6th ed. New York: Appleton-Century-Crofts, Inc., 1958.

Baldwin, Thomas, assisted by several other gentlemen. *A universal pronouncing gazetteer; containing topographical, statistical, and other information of all the more important places in the known world, from the most recent and authoritative sources, with a map.* Philadelphia: Lindsay & Blakiston, 1845.

————. *A universal pronouncing gazetteer; containing topographical, statistical and other information, of all the more important places in the known world, from the most recent and authentic sources to which is added an appendix containing more than ten thousand additional names, chiefly of the small towns and villages of the United States and Mexico; with a supplement, giving the pronunciation of nearly two thousand names, besides those pronounced in the original work, forming in itself a complete vocabulary of geographical pronunciation; a new edition, carefully revised with the population inserted according to the census of 1850, and enriched with many new and extensive articles on California, Oregon, Minnesota, New Mexico, Utah, Australia, France, etc.* Philadelphia: Lippincott, Grambo & Co., 1854.

Baldwin, Wayne J., Ernest S. Reese, and John Wintersteen. "Ichthyology." International Geophysical Year. *Clipperton island expedition field report* (1959): 4, q.v.

Banks, N. "Papers from the Hopkins Stanford Galapagos expedition, 1898–1899; entomological results, Thysanura and Termitidae." Washington Academy of Science *Proceedings* 3 (1901): 541–46.

"Barren reef may be international pawn; Clipperton island in Pacific, claimed by France and Mexico, has curious history." New York *Times,* November 27, 1932, p. 7.

Bartsch, Paul, and Harald Alfred Rehder. "Mollusks collected on the presidential cruise of 1938." *Smithsonian miscellaneous collections* 98 (1939): No. 10. SI1.7:98

Beach, Edward L. *Around the world submerged; the voyage of the Triton.* New York: Holt, Rinehart and Winston, 1962.

————. "Introduction." Charles McKew Parr. *Ferdinand Magellan, circumnavigator,* q.v.

Beck, R. H. "Notes from Clipperton and Cocos islands." *The condor* 9 (1907): 109–110.

Belcher, Edward. *Narrative of a voyage around the world, performed in her majesty's ship Sulphur, during the years 1836–1842, including details of the naval operations in China, from Dec. 1840 to Nov. 1841.* 2 vols. London: Dawsons of Pall Mall, 1843.

Bennett, Frederick Debell. *Narrative of a whaling voyage round the globe, from the year 1833 to 1836; comprising sketches of Polynesia, California, the Indian archipelago, etc., with an account of southern whales, the sperm whale fishery, and the natural history of the climates visited.* 2 vols. London: Richard Bentley, 1840.

Benson, E[dward] F. *Ferdinand Magellan.* London: John Lane the Bodley Head, Ltd., 1929.

Betagh, William. *A voyage around the world with Capt. Shelvocke on the Speedwell; being an account of a remarkable enterprise, begun in the year 1719, chiefly to cruise on the Spanish in the great south ocean; relating the true historical facts of that whole affair, testified by many imployd therein, and confirmed by authorities from the owners.* London: printed for T. Combes, 1728.

"Bid of £575,000; shipping company's huge purchase of shares." *The times,* July 27, 1917, p. 6b.

Blumenthal, Henry. *France and the United States; their diplomatic relations, 1789–1914.* Chapel Hill: The University of North Carolina Press, 1970.

Boorstin, Daniel J. *The discoverers.* New York: Random House, 1983.

"Bottle up a gunboat; federals try the Hobson trick on vessel whose men mutinied." *New York Times,* March 11, 1914, p. 2.

Bourgau, A. "Journal touristique; Clipperton." *La revue maritime* 93 (1954): 66–73.

Briggs, Herbert W., ed. *The law of nations.* 2d ed. New York: Appleton-Century-Crofts, Inc., 1952.

Brinton, Crane. *The Americans and the French.* Cambridge: Harvard University Press, 1968.

Burney, James. *A chronological history of the voyages and discoveries on the south seas or Pacific ocean.* 4 vols. London: G & W Nicol, 1816.

Burns, Josephine Joan. "The Clipperton island case; Mexico v. France." *Cumulative digest of international law and relations* 2 (1932): No. 42.

Byrnes, James F. *Speaking frankly.* New York and London: Harper & Brothers Publishers, 1947.

Cassels, Alan. *Mussolini's early diplomacy.* Princeton: Princeton University Press, 1970.

Castel, J.-G. [ed.] *International law, chiefly as interpreted and applied in Canada.* Toronto: University of Toronto Press, 1965.

"Cession of island to France delayed; Mexican Senate seeks to avoid embarrassing Roosevelt on Monroe doctrine issue; award opposed there; Italian king's decision on Clipperton island assailed as swayed by desire for concessions." New York *Times,* November 15, 1932, p. 14.

"Cession urged on Mexico; acceptance of isle's award to France held a point of honor." New York *Times,* November 16, 1932, p. 5.

Chace, Fenner A., Jr. "The non-brachyuran decapod crustaceans of Clipperton island." United States National Museum Journal *Proceedings* 113 (1962): 605–35.

Chubb, Lawrence John. "Geology of Galapagos, Cocos, and Easter islands." Bishop Museum *Bulletin* 110 (1933): 3–67.

Churchill, Winston S. *Triumph and tragedy.* New York: Houghton Mifflin Company, 1953.

[Churchill, Winston S., and Franklin D. Roosevelt]. *Churchill & Roosevelt; the complete correspondence,* edited by Warren F. Kimball, q.v.

"Claims the islet for Uncle Sam; an Oakland man's title to Clipperton; Captain Permien's story; affidavits filed at State department; phosphate and guano syndicates, British or American, must deal with him." San Francisco *Chronicle,* August 19, 1897, p. 12.

Clark, Austin H. "Echinoderms (other than holothurians) collected on the presidential cruise of 1938." *Smithsonian miscellaneous collections* 98 (1939): No. 11. SI1.7:98

Clark, H. L. "The holothurians of Clipperton island." Washington Academy of Science *Proceedings* 4 (1902): 521–31.

Clark, Martin. *Modern Italy, 1871–1982.* London: Longman, 1984.

"Cleveland." U.S. Navy. *Dictionary of American naval fighting ships* 2 (1968): 129, q.v. D207.10:2

"Clipperton atoll." *The geographical journal* 11 (June 1898): 671–72.

"Clipperton island." Angelo Heilprin and Louis Heilprin, eds. *A complete pronouncing gazetteer* (1905, 1911, 1922): 431, q.v.

———. Leon E. Seltzer, ed. *Columbia Lippincott gazetteer of the world* (1952): 420, q.v.

———. *Lippincott's gazetteer of the world* (1883): 498, q.v.

———. *Lippincott's gazetteer of the world* (1896): 912, q.v.

"Clipperton island affair; Mexico sends a warship to see if the British are in possession." New York *Times,* December 17, 1897, p. 3.

"Clipperton island American." New York *Times,* August 25, 1897, p. 1.

"Clipperton island and the routes of Spanish ships, sixteenth and seventeenth centuries." *The geographical journal* 55 (1920): 154–55.

"Clipperton island arbitration; France-Mexico, 1931." Herbert W. Briggs, ed. *The law of nations,* q.v.

"Clipperton island case; France v. Mexico." D. J. Harris, ed. *Cases and materials on international law*, q.v.

"Clipperton island case; Italy offers to arbitrate disputed ownership between France and Mexico." New York *Times*, August 23, 1909, p. 3.

"Clipperton island flag." New York *Times*, January 3, 1898, p. 1.

"Clipperton island incident; a statement from Mexico." San Francisco *Chronicle*, January 6, 1898, p. 7.

"Clipperton island incident; Mexican official says there was no conflict over flag." New York *Times*, January 6, 1898, p. 2.

"Clipperton island seizure; no news in Washington of the alleged action of Mexico." New York *Times*, January 2, 1898, p. 1.

"Clipperton rock." Joseph Thomas and Thomas Baldwin, eds. *Lippincott's pronouncing gazetteer* (1863, 1864, 1865, 1876): 467, q.v.

"Colonial concessions." *The times*, July 21, 1910, p. 6c.

Con, Stetson, Rose C. Engelman, and Byron Fairchild. *United States army in World War II; the western hemisphere: guarding the United States and its outposts*. Washington: Department of the Army, Office of the Chief of Military History, 1964. D114.7:W52h/v.2

Coquillett, D. W. "Papers from the Hopkins Stanford Galapagos expedition, 1898–1899; entomological results, Diptera." Washington Academy of Science *Proceedings* 3 (1901): 371–79.

[Cortés, Hernán]. *Conquest; dispatches of Cortés from the new world*, edited by Irwin R. Blacker and Harry M. Rosen. New York: Grosset & Dunlap, 1962.

Cousteau, Jacques Yves. *Cousteau odyssey; Clipperton, the island time forgot*. Los Angeles: KCET-TV, 1981.

———. "View from the bridge; so fragile . . . my island." *Calypso log*. 7 (June 1980): 2–3.

Cousteau, Jean-Michel. "Project ocean search, 1980; Clipperton island." *Calypso log* 7 (March 1980): 8–9.

"Covets Clipperton island for England; a syndicate after guano; return of an expedition of inspection; hoisting the British flag high follows control of the deposits." San Francisco *Chronicle*, August 14, 1897, p. 4.

Currie, Rolla P. "Papers from the Hopkins Stanford Galapagos expedition, 1898–1899; entomological results, Odonata." Washington Academy of Science *Proceedings* 3 (1901): 381–89.

Dahlgren, M. E. W. *Voyages Francais; à destination de la mer du sud avant Bougainville (1695–1749)*. Paris: Imprimerie Nationale, 1907.

Darwin, Charles R. *Coral reefs; volcanic islands, South American geology*. [Originally issued in three parts (1842, 1844, and 1846)]. New York: Harper & Brothers, [1925].

Davis, William Morris. *The coral reef problem.* New York: American Geographical Society Special Publication No. 9, 1928; reprinted, AMS, 1969.

Dawson, E. Yale. "Some algae from Clipperton island and the Danger islands." *Pacific naturalist* 1 (1958): 2–8.

DeLaubenfels, M. W. "Sponges collected on the presidential cruise of 1938." *Smithsonian miscellaneous collections* 98 (1939): No. 15. SI1.7:98

Denniston, Robert W. "DXpedition to Clipperton; the story of FØ8AJ." *OST* 38 (1954): 10–15.

"*Detroit.*" U.S. Navy. *Dictionary of American naval fighting ships* 2 (1963): 269–70, q.v. D207.10:2

Dibner, Bern. *The Victoria and the Triton.* New York: Blaisdell Publishing Company, 1962.

Dickinson, Edwin D. "The Clipperton island case." *American journal of international law* 27 (1933): 130–33.

Digest of international law. 56th Cong., 2d Sess. 1900–1901, House Documents, Vol. 128, ser. 4202–4206/2.

"Discovery of Clipperton atoll." *The geographical journal* 51 (1918): 405.

Dod, Karl C. *United States army in World War II; the technical services: the corps of engineers, the war against Japan.* Washington: United States Army, Office of the Chief of Military History, 1966. D114.7:EN3/v.2

"Earthquake wrecks two Mexican towns; Chilpancingo overthrown and Acapulco partly razed by violent shocks early yesterday." New York *Times,* July 31, 1909, p. 1.

Edwords, Clarence E. "Clipperton island and its strange birds." San Francisco *Chronicle* Sunday Magazine, September 9, 1906, pp. 3–4.

"England in the Pacific." *The times,* September 6, 1906, p. 10a.

"England to seize an island? British flag may be hoisted over Clipperton island; supposed to belong to Mexico." New York *Herald,* August 15, 1897, p. 3.

"England's claim to Clipperton; prospect that there may be trouble over the island; the United States is in commercial control and may oppose seizure; Mexico has been regarded as the owner but the island is lightly valued; return of Freeth's expedition; English capitalists who assert that Britain's flag will fly if they buy the phosphate beds." San Francisco *Examiner,* August 18, 1897, p. 12.

"Fear islands are gone; Acapulco thinks 'quake sunk Clipperton island group [sic] in the sea." New York *Times,* August 24, 1909, p. 1.

Fenwick, Charles G. *International law.* 3d ed. New York: Appleton-Century-Crofts, Inc., 1948.

Finger, Charles J. *Magellan and the Pacific.* Girard, Kans.; Haldeman-Julius Company, 1924.

"Five, shipwrecked on isle, rescued; San Pedro fishermen found on bleak atoll off Mexico, 1,700 miles from home." *Los Angeles Times,* June 30, 1947, p. 1.

[Forrestal, James]. *The Forrestal diaries,* edited by Walter Mills with the collaboration of E. S. Duffield. New York: The Viking Press, 1951.

"Found them safe; Clipperton's two Crusoes home again." *San Francisco Morning Call,* October 31, 1893, p. 8.

France. *French Polynesia.* New York: Ambassade de France, Service de Presse et d'Information, 1961.

————. *Mémoire défensif présenté par le gouvernement de la République Française dans le litige relatif à la souveraineté de l'île Clipperton; soumis à la décision arbitrale de sa majesté Victor-Emmanuel III, roi d'Italie en exécution de la convention dentre de France et le Mexico, du 2 Mars 1909.* Paris: Imprimerie Nationale, 1912.

Fraser, C. McLean. "General Account of the scientific work of the *Valero III* in the eastern Pacific, 1931–41; Part I: historical introduction, *Valero III,* personnel." *Allan Hancock Pacific expeditions.* Los Angeles: University of Southern California Press, 1943.

————. "General account of the scientific work of the *Velero III* in the eastern Pacific, 1931–41; Part II: geographical and biological associations." *Allan Hancock Pacific expeditions.* Los Angeles: University of Southern California Press, 1943.

————. "General account of the scientific work of the *Valero III* in the eastern Pacific, 1931–41; Part III: a ten-year list of the *Valero III* collecting stations." *Allan Hancock Pacific expeditions.* Los Angeles: University of Southern California Press, 1943.

Funnell, William. *A voyage round the world; containing an account of captain Dampier's expedition into the south-seas in the ship St. George, in the years 1703 and 1704; with various adventures, engagements, &c., and a particular and exact description of several islands in the Atlantick ocean, the Brazilian coast, the passage round Cape Horn, and the coasts of Chili, Peru, and Mexico, together with the author's voyage from Amapalla on the west-coast of Mexico, to east-India, his passing by three unknown islands, and thro' a new-discover'd streight near the coast of New Guinea, his arrival at Amboyna, with a large description of that and other Spice islands, as also of Batavia, the Cape of Good Hope, &c.* London: James Knapton, 1707.

Garman, Samuel. "Concerning a species of lizard from Clipperton island." *New England Zoological Club Proceedings* 1 (1899): 59–62.

————. "A species of goby from the shores of Clipperton island." *New England Zoological Club Proceedings* 1 (1899): 63–64.

Gauroy, Pierre. "Une terre Francise presque inconnue Clipperton." *Historania* 17 (1953): 44–45.

Gauthier, M. L. "Levé hydrographique de l'île Clipperton (2 Décembre 1934 et 26–27 Janvier 1935)." *Annales hydrographique* 3 (1949): 5–12.

Gautier, Émile. "Océanie." *L'anne scientifique et industrielle* 49 (1906): 308–309.

Gerhard, Peter. *Pirates on the west coast of New Spain, 1575–1742.* Glendale, Calif.: The Arthur H. Clark Company, 1960.

Gifford, Edward Winslow. "The birds of the Galapagos islands, with observations on the birds of Cocos and Clipperton islands (Columbi-formes to Pelecaniformes)." California Academy of Sciences *Proceedings* 2 (1913): 1–7.

"Gordon, Arthur Charles Hamilton." *Dictionary of national biography, 1912–1921.* London: Oxford University Press, 1927.

Goua, A. "Clipperton terre française." *Revue maritime* 70 (1952): 226–34.

"*Grand Island.*" U.S. Navy. *Dictionary of American naval fighting ships* 3 (1968): 134, q.v. D207.10:3

Greenfield, Kent Roberts, ed. *Command decisions.* Washington: Department of the Army, Office of the Chief of Military History, 1960. D114.2:D35

Grew, Joseph C. *Turbulent era; a diplomatic record of forty years, 1904–1945,* edited by Walter Johnson. 2 vols. Boston: Houghton Mifflin Company, 1952.

Gross, Leo, ed. *International law in the twentieth century.* New York: Appleton-Century-Crofts, Inc., 1969.

"Guano Islands Act." U.S. *Code.,* q.v.

Guillemard, F. H. H. *The life of Ferdinand Magellan and the first circumnavigation of the globe.* London: George Philip & Son, 1890.

"Gunboat to be dismantled; rebels will use the Tampico's guns in land battle." New York *Times,* March 27, 1914, p. 2.

Guppy, Henry Brougham. *Observations of a naturalist in the Pacific between 1896 and 1899.* 2 vols. London: Macmillan and Co., Ltd., 1903, 1906.

Hackett, C[harles] W. "Clipperton island award." *Current history* 37 (January 1933): 466–67.

Hackworth, Green Haywood. "Hemispheric security; the Monroe doctrine interpretations, pronouncements, etc." U.S. State department *Digest of international law* 5 (1943): 435–57ff, q.v. S7.12:943/5

———. "Territory and sovereignty of states; acquisition and loss, general observations." U.S. State department, *Digest of international law,* 1 (1940): 393–443, q.v. S7.12:940/1

Hamilton, E. L. *Sunken islands of the mid-Pacific mountains.* Baltimore: Geological Society of America Memoir [No.] 64, 1956.

Harbison, Charles F. "Entomology." International Geophysical Year. *Clipperton island expedition field report* (1959): 4–6, q.v.

Harris, D. J., ed. *Cases and materials on international law.* London: Sweet & Maxwell, 1973.

Hartman, Olga. "The polychaetous annelids collected on the presidential cruise of 1938." *Smithsonian miscellaneous collections* 98 (1939): No. 13. SI1.7:98

Harvey, T. "Notes of a voyage to the Pacific in *H.M.S. Havana.*" *Nautical magazine* 29 (1860): 302–307, 358–61, 420–25, 521–25, 587–91.

"Has an option on Clipperton island; John T. Arundel of London about to buy the guano island." San Francisco *Chronicle,* November 7, 1897, p. 7.

"Hauled down; Mexican gunboat strikes old glory; buzzard and snake run up in its place; high-handed proceedings in the Pacific; Clipperton island, where an American guano company was at work, seized by the Mexican government." Los Angeles *Times,* January 1, 1898, p. 1.

"Hauled down the stars and stripes; Mexico lowers our flag; takes formal possession of Clipperton island." San Francisco *Chronicle,* January 1, 1898, p. 3.

Heidemann, Otto. "Papers from the Hopkins Stanford Galapagos expedition, 1898–1899; entomological results, Hemiptera." Washington Academy of Science *Proceedings* 3 (1901): 364–70.

Heilprin, Angelo, and Louis Heilprin, eds. *A complete pronouncing gazetteer; or geographical dictionary of the world, containing the most recent and authentic information respecting the countries, cities, towns, resorts, islands, rivers, mountains, seas, lakes, etc., in every portion of the globe.* Philadelphia: J. B. Lippincott Company, 1905, 1911, 1922.

Heller, Edmund. "Papers from the Hopkins Stanford Galapagos expedition, 1898–1899; reptiles." Washington Academy of Science *Proceedings* 5 (1903): 39–98.

Heller, Edmund, and Robert E. Snodgrass. "Descriptions of two new species and three new subspecies of birds from the eastern Pacific; collected by the Hopkins Stanford expedition to the Galapagos islands." *The Condor* 3 (May 1901): 74–77.

———. "Papers from the Hopkins Stanford Galapagos expedition, 1898–1899; new fishes." Washington Academy of Science *Proceedings* 5 (1903): 189–229.

Hertlein, Leo George, and William K. Emerson. "Additional notes on the invertebrate fauna of Clipperton island." *American Museum novitates* 1859 (1957): 1–9.

———. "Mollusks from Clipperton island (eastern Pacific) with the description of a new species of gastropod." San Diego Society of Natural History *Transactions* 11 (1953): 347–63.

Hetherington, John. *Uncommon men*. Melbourne: F. W. Cheshire, 1965.

Hildebrand, Arthur Sturges. *Magellan; a general account of the life and times and remarkable adventures, by land and sea, of the most eminent and renowned navigator Ferdinand Magellan (Fernão de Magalhães), Commander of the order of Santiago, his majesty's Captain General of the armada which first went around the world*. New York: Harcourt, Brace and Company, 1924.

Holstein, Otto. "Geographical record." *Geographical review* 24 (1931): 488–89.

"*Houston*." U.S. Navy. *Dictionary of American naval fighting ships* 3 (1968): 274–275, q.v. D207.10:3

"How island earth works." *Calypso log* 8 (September 1981):8–11.

Hoyt, Edwin P. *The last explorer; the adventures of Admiral Byrd*. New York: The John Day Company, 1968.

Hurd, Willis Edwin. "Tropical cyclones of the eastern Pacific ocean." *Monthly weather review* 57 (1929): 43–49. C55.11:929

Hutchinson, George Evelyn. "The biochemistry of vertebrate excretion." American Museum of Natural History *Bulletin* 96 (1950): 1–476.

Hyman, Libbie H. "Polyclad worms collected on the presidential cruise of 1938." *Smithsonian miscellaneous collections* 98 (1939): No. 17. SI1.7:98

"In the Caribbean; hams and goats." *Time*, May 3, 1982, pp. 7–8.

"In the *Clipperton island* case, Mexico-France: arbitration (1931)." J.-G. Castel, [ed.]. *International law, chiefly as interpreted and applied in Canada*, q.v.

International Geophysical Year. *Clipperton island expedition field report, August-September, 1958*. Mimeographed; La Jolla, Calif.: Scripps Institute of Oceanography, 1959.

"Islands may have sunk into ocean; fears that Clipperton group [sic] disappeared during recent earthquake." San Francisco *Chronicle*, August 24, 1909, p. 2.

"Italy would be arbitrator; is willing to decide ownership of Clipperton islands [sic]." San Francisco *Chronicle*, August 23, 1909, p. 5.

Ives, Ronald L. "Hurricanes on the west coast of Mexico." Seventh Pacific Science Conference *Proceedings* 3, (1949): 21–31.

Jacobs, Madeleine. "Sea snake research sheds light on diving biology of marine reptiles." Smithsonian Institution *Research reports* 45 (Spring 1985): 5.

Jennings, Gary. *Aztec*. New York: Avon Books, 1980.

Johnson, David A. "Eastward-flowing bottom currents along the Clipperton fracture zone." *Deep sea research* 19 (1972): 253–57.

Jones, Stephen P., and Klas Mehnert. "Hawaii and the Pacific; a survey of political geography." *Geographical review* 30 (1940): 358–75.

Jones v. *United States*. 173 U.S. 202, 217, 222 (1890).

"Kept old glory up; Americans hold the fort at Clipperton island." Los Angeles *Daily times*, August 25, 1897, p. 2.

Killip, Ellsworth P. "Flowering plants collected on the presidential cruise of 1938." *Smithsonian miscellaneous collections* 98, (1939): No. 8. SI1.7:98

Kimball, J. H. "A Pacific hurricane of September 1915." *Monthly weather review* 43 (September 1915): 486. C55.11:915

Kimball, Warren F., ed. *Churchill & Roosevelt; the complete correspondence.* 3 vols. Princeton, N.J.: Princeton University Press, 1984.

King, Ernest J. *U.S. navy at war, 1941–1945; official reports to the secretary of the navy.* Washington: United States Navy Department, 1946. N27.1:941–45

King, Ernest J., and Walter Muir Whitehill. *Fleet admiral King; a naval record.* New York: W. W. Norton & Company, Inc., 1952.

"Kinkora crew on the Clippertons [sic]." San Francisco *Chronicle,* June 5, 1897, p. 12.

La Barbinais, Le Gentil. *Nouveau voyage au tour du monde; enrichi de plufieurs plans, vûës & perspectives de principales viles & ports du Pérou, Chilly, Bresil, & de la Chine—avec une description de l'empire de la Chine beoucoup plus ample & plus circonstanciée que celles qui ont paru jusqu'à present, où il est traité des moeurs, religion, politique, éducation & commerce des peuples de cet empire.* 3 vols. Amsterdam: Chez Pierre Mortier, [1728].

La Veyrie, Jean. "Le passage di croiseur *Jeanne-d'Arc* a l'île Clipperton." *L'Illustration* 190 (January 1935): 39.

Lacroix, Alfred. "Clipperton, îles de Pâques et Pitcairn." L'institut Océanographique *Annales* (nouvelle série) 18 (1939): 289–304.

Lamer, Mirko. *The world fertilizer economy.* Stanford, Calif.: Stanford University Press, 1957.

Leahy, William D. *I was there; the personal story of the chief of staff to presidents Roosevelt and Truman based on his notes and diaries made at the time.* New York: McGraw-Hill Book Company, Inc., 1950.

Limbaugh, Conrad. "Introduction." International Geophysical Year. *Clipperton island expedition field report* (1959): 1–3, q.v.

Lippincott's gazetteer of the world; a complete pronouncing gazetteer, or geographical dictionary of the world, containing notices of over one hundred and twenty-five thousand places with recent and authentic information respecting the countries, islands, rivers, mountains, cities, towns, etc., in every portion of the globe. New edition; thoroughly revised and greatly enlarged, [etc.]. Philadelphia: J. B. Lippincott & Co., 1883.

————. . . . *originally edited by Joseph Thomas, M.D., Ll.D., [etc.].* New revised edition: amplified by a series of statistical tables, [etc.]; Philadelphia: J. B. Lippincott Company, 1896.

Lipps, Jere H. "Fossil calcareous plankton from the Clipperton fracture zone, equatorial east Pacific; interregional correlation and zoogeography." Geological Society of America *Special paper* 101 (1968): 122–23.

———. "Tertiary plankton from the Clipperton fracture zone." Geological Society of America *Bulletin* 80 (1969): 1,801–1,808.

Lloyd, Christopher. *William Dampier*. Hamden, Conn.: Archon Books, 1966.

Lowe, C. J., and F. Marzari. *Italian foreign policy, 1870–1940*. London & Boston: Routledge & Kegan Paul, 1975.

Lowe, Herbert N. "The cruise of the *Petrel*." *Nautilus* 46 (1933): 73–77, 109–115.

"*LST-563*." U.S. Navy. *Dictionary of American naval fighting ships* 7 (1981): 642, q.v. D207.10:7

"Macabre isle of Passion given up to war as landing site for French navy planes." New York *Times*, January 20, 1935, II, p. 1.

"*McDougal*." U.S. Navy. *Dictionary of American naval fighting ships* 4 (1969): 298–99, q.v. D207.10:4

McDowell, Eleanor C. "Uninhabited territories." U.S. State department, *Digest of United States practice in international law* (1975): 92–94ff, q.v. S7.12/3:978

McIntire, Ross T., in collaboration with George Creel. *White House physician*. New York: G. P. Putnam's Sons, 1946.

McKay, Donald C. *The United States and France*. Cambridge: Harvard University Press, 1951.

McNeill, Jerome. "Papers from the Hopkins Stanford Galapagos expedition, 1898–1899; entomological results, Orthoptera." Washington Academy of Science *Proceedings* 3 (1901): 487–506.

"Mariscal, Ignacio (1829–1910)." *Diccionario porrúa; de historia, biografía y geografía de Mexico; cuarta edución corregida y augmentada, con suplemento*. 2 tomos. Mexico City: Editorial Porrúa, S.A., 1964.

Markham, Jesse W. *The fertilizer industry; study of an imperfect market*. Nashville: Vanderbilt University Press, 1958.

"Marooned 2 years on isle; naval commander reports on rescue of Mexican women and children." New York *Times*, August 13, 1917, p. 18.

Maximilian of Transylvania. "Voyage made by the Spaniards round the world," Charles E. Nowell, ed. *Magellan's voyage around the world*, q.v.

Memoirs of the Bernice Pauahi Bishop Museum of Polynesian ethnology and natural history. Honolulu: Bishop Museum Press, 1899–1903.

Menard, H. W. "Extension of northeastern-Pacific fracture zones." *Science* 155 (1967): 72–74.

Menard, H. W., and Robert L. Fisher. "Clipperton fracture zone in the northeastern equatorial Pacific." *Journal of geology* 66 (May 1958): 239–53.

"Mexicans accede to loss of island; lengthy dispute is ended; verdict by ruler in 1931 on lonely Pacific isle was outcome of arbitration begun in 1909." New York *Times,* November 10, 1932, p. 10.

"Mexicans ask indemnity; attempt to enforce their claims on Clipperton island." New York *Times,* March 11, 1898, p. 5.

"Mexicans demand an indemnity; guano taken from Clipperton must be paid for; the isle in the Pacific they claim belongs to them; the phosphate company is compelled to suspend shipments; $1,500,000 the sum asked." San Francisco *Call,* March 10, 1898, p. 11.

"Mexicans vote to buy isle; Senate asks to recover Clipperton." New York *Times,* December 17, 1932, p. 12.

Mexico. *Constitución politica de los Estados Unidos Mexicanos, expedida el 31 Enero de 1917 y promulgada el 5 de Febrero del mismo año, reforma la de 5 de Febrero de 1857.* Mexico, [D. F.]: Imprenta de la Secretaria de Gobernación, 1917.

———. *Constitution of Mexico, 1917 (as amended).* Washington, D.C.: Organization of American States, 1972.

———. *Diario de los congreso constituyente 1916–1917; ediciones de la comision nacional para la celebracion del sesquicentenario de la proclamacion de la independencia nacional y del cincuenenario de la revolucion Mexicana.* 2 tomas. Mexico City: Estados Unidos Mexicanos, 1960.

[———]. *Leyes fundamentales de Mexico, 1808–1957,* [compiled and edited by] Felipe Tena Ramirez. Mexico, D. F.: Editorial Porrúa, S.A., 1957.

———. Secretaria de Relaciones Exteriores. *Isla de la Pasión, llamada de Clipperton.* México: Publicación Oficial, 1909.

"Mexico finally accepts King Victor Emmanuel's decision and returns Clipperton island to France." New York *Times,* July 9, 1933, IX, p. 2.

"Mexico; France to get almost forgotten island." *Newsweek,* March 11, 1933, p. 16.

"Mexico owns the island; had a right to take down the stars and stripes." Los Angeles *Times,* January 2, 1898, p. 1.

Michelson, Charles. *The ghost talks.* New York: G. P. Putnam's Sons, 1944.

Monroe, James. "Seventh annual message (December 2, 1823)." U.S. Presidents. *A compilation of the messages and papers of the presidents* II, 776–89, q.v.

Moore, John Bassett. "Clipperton island." U.S. State department, *Digest of international law* 1 (1906): 573–74, q.v. S7.12:906/1

"More shocks at Acapulco; sea recedes thirty feet; people still living in the open." New York *Times,* August 18, 1909, p. 4.

Morga, Antonio de. *History of the Philippines from their discovery by Magellan in 1521 to the beginning of the XVII century,* translated and edited by E. H. Blair and J. A. Robertson. 2 vols. Cleveland: Arthur H. Clark Company, 1907.

Morrell, Benjamin. *A narrative of four voyages, to the south seas, north and south Pacific ocean, Chinese sea, Ethiopic and southern Atlantic ocean, Indian and Antarctic ocean, from the year 1822 to 1831; comprising critical surveys of coasts and islands, with sailing directions and account of some new and valuable discoveries, including the Massacre islands, where thirteen of the author's crew were massacred and eaten by cannibals, to which is prefaced a brief sketch of the author's early life.* New York: J. & J. Harper, 1832.

Morris, C. Edward. "The island the world forgot." *New outlook* 164 (July 1934): 31–35.

Morton, Louis. "Germany first; the basic concept of allied strategy in World War II." Kent Roberts Greenfield, *Command decisions,* q.v.

"Mother, babies, sea castaways, on way to city; City of Sydney bringing captain's wife and children after shipwreck; survive deadly perils; three weeks' battle against sea in open boat to reach distant point." San Francisco *Examiner,* July 5, 1914, p. 63.

Murphy, Richard C. "Clipperton island." *Calypso log* 7 (September 1980):4–5.

Murphy, R. C., and J. N. Kremer. "Community metabolism in Clipperton lagoon." *American zoologist* 20 (1980):951.

———. "Community metabolism of Clipperton lagoon." Marine Science *Bulletin.* 33 (1983):152–64.

"Mutineers took gunboat; imprisoned Tampico's captain; to attack federals at Mazatlan." New York *Times,* February 26, 1914, p. 63.

Nash, Marian Lloyd. "Fisheries; Pacific tuna." U.S. State department, *Digest of United States practice of international law* (1978): 964–1,010ff, q.v. S7.12/3:978

"National and private contests for Clipperton island." San Francisco *Call,* February 13, 1898, p. 21.

National geographic atlas of the world. 5th ed. Washington, D.C.: National Geographic Society, 1981.

"Nautical notices." *Nautical magazine* 20 (1851): 612.

Nelson, C., L. D. Bibee, N. T. Edgar, E. L. Winterer, and J. L. Matthews. "Seismic structure along a 'flow line' of the Pacific plate." American Geographical Union Transactions *Eos* 57 (1976): 333.

"*Nevada.*" U.S. Navy. *Dictionary of American naval fighting ships* 5 (1970): 52, q.v. D207.10:5

"New issue; the Pacific Phosphate Company (Limited)." *The times,* May 7, 1906, p. 13e.

"*New Orleans.*" U.S. navy. *Dictionary of American fighting ships* 5 (1980): 67–68, q.v. D207.10:5

"New territory acquired for Uncle Sam; the stars and stripes now fly over Clipperton island, in the Pacific." San Francisco *Chronicle,* August 25, 1897, p. 7.

"*New York.*" U.S. Navy. *Dictionary of American naval fighting ships* 5 (1970): 71, q.v. D207.10:5

New York *Times,* January 3, 1898, p. 6; January 6, 1898, p. 8.

Niemeyer, E. V., Jr. *Revolution at Querétaro; the Mexican constitutional convention of 1916–1917.* Austin: University of Texas Press, 1974.

"No valid claim to Clipperton island, State department opinion; Oceanic Phosphate Company loses; the island declared to be French property; Uncle Sam has no title." San Francisco *Chronicle,* January 29, 1898, p. 2.

"Notes; in the *Clipperton island* case, Mexico-France: arbitration (1931)." J.-G. Castel, [ed.], *International law, chiefly as interpreted and applied in Canada,* q.v.

Nowell, Charles E., ed. *Magellan's voyage around the world; three contemporary accounts.* Evanston: Northwestern University Press, 1962.

Nunn, George E. "Magellan's route across the Pacific." *Geographical review* 24 (1934): 615–33.

Obermuller, A. G. "Contribution à l'étude géologique et minérale de l'île Clipperton (Polynésie francaise)." *Recherche géologique et minérale en Polynésie française.* Paris: L'inspection Générale des Mines at de la Géologie, 1959.

" 'Old glory' waves on Clipperton island; stars and stripes flying above coral island; hoisted by Americans and guarded with shovels and guns; San Francisco seamen, by order of their employers, assert the national claim; flag kept in the breeze despite objections by a British shipmaster; warship *Comus* on the scene; Captain Dyke has not regarded the island as United States territory, but he may not protest." San Francisco *Examiner,* August 24, 1897, p. 1.

Olinger, John Peter. "The guano age in Peru." *History today* 30 (June 1980): 13–18.

Osing, Olga. "Jan Mayen; a little known but important island." *Sea frontiers* 31 (1985): 10–14.

Owen, Launcelot. "Notes on the phosphate deposit of Ocean island, with remarks on the phosphates of the equatorial belt of the Pacific ocean." Geological Society of London *Quarterly journal* 79 (1923): 1–15.

"Ownership of Clipperton island." *The times,* October 24, 1908, p. 10b.

"Pacific Phosphate." *The times,* October 31, 1912, p. 19f.

"Pacific Phosphate, a romantic enterprise." *The times,* May 22, 1913, p. 17d.

"Pacific Phosphate Company." *The times,* December 19, 1912, p. 11b.

"Papers from the Hopkins Stanford Galapagos expedition, 1898–1899; introduction." Washington Academy of Science *Proceedings* 3 (1901): 363–64.

Parr, Charles McKew. *Ferdinand Magellan, circumnavigator.* New York: Thomas Y. Crowell Company, 1964.

———. *So noble a captain; the life and times of Ferdinand Magellan.* New York: Thomas Y. Crowell Company, 1953.

Pease, W. H. "On the existence of an atoll near the west coast of America, and proof of its elevation." California Academy of Natural Sciences *Proceedings* 3 (1868): 199–201.

Peckham, Howard H. "Introduction." Antonio Pigafetta, *The voyage of Magellan,* q.v.

"Permien's title is sadly clouded; Clipperton island guano; Oceanic Phosphate Company in possession; J. T. Arundel treating for the purchase; claims of France and England." San Francisco *Chronicle,* August 20, 1897, p. 4.

Perrill, Charlotte K., [ed.]. "Forgotten island, in which a navigator's ruler played a most important part in the destinies of several people." United States Naval Institute *Proceedings* 63 (1937): 796–805.

Perrill, H. P. "Island the world forgot." *New outlook* 164 (October 1934): 4–5.

"Personal." New York *Times,* January 27, 1898, p. 6.

[Pigafetta, Antonio]. *The voyage of Magellan; the journal of Antonio Pigafetta,* translated by Paula Spurlin Paige. Englewood Cliffs, N.J.: Prentice-Hall, Inc., 1969.

[———, Maximilian of Transylvania, and Gaspar Corrêa]. *Magellan's voyage around the world; three contemporary accounts,* edited by Charles E. Nowell, q.v.

Pratt, Julius W. *Expansionists of 1898; the acquisition of Hawaii and the Spanish islands.* Baltimore: The Johns Hopkins University Press, 1936.

"Presidency; brief annals." *Time,* July 30, 1934, p. 14.

"Presidency; Frank III." *Time,* August 1, 1938, p. 7.

"Presidency; wahoos for McAdoo." *Time,* July 25, 1938, p. 7.

Priestley, Herbert Ingram. *France overseas; a study of modern imperialism.* New York: Octagon Books, Inc., 1966.

"Quakes in Mexico continue violent; thirteen shocks recorded in Mexico City in 30 hours before 1 o'clock yesterday; Friday's disturbance razed largest and strongest buildings in Acapulco." New York *Times,* August 1, 1909, p. 2.

Rathbun, Mary J. "The grapsoid crabs of America." United States National Museum *Bulletin* 97 (1918): 1–461.

————. "Papers from the Hopkins Stanford Galapagos expedition, 1898–1899; Brachyura and Macrura." Washington Academy of Science *Proceedings* 4 (1902): 275–92.

"Rebel gunboat sunk; captain and engineer commit suicide; U.S. ships save many." *New York Times,* June 18, 1984, p. 2.

Reilly, Michael, as told to William J. Slocum. *Reilly of the White House.* New York: Simon and Schuster, 1947.

"Reopens Clipperton case; Mexico names board to study award of island to France." New York *Times,* December 30, 1931, p. 8.

Richardson, H. "Papers from the Hopkins Stanford Galapagos expedition, 1898–1899: the Isopods." Washington Academy of Science *Proceedings* 3 (1901): 565–68.

Roberts, Stephen H. *The History of French colonial policy, 1870–1925.* London: P. S. King & Co., 1929.

Robertson, Dougal. *Survive the savage sea.* New York: Praeger Publishers, 1973.

Roditi, Edouard. *Magellan of the Pacific.* London: Faber and Faber, 1972.

Roncagli, C. "Circa la scoperta dell'isola di Clipperton (ocean Pacifico, zona equatoriale nord-orientale)." Societa Geografica Italiana *Bolletino* (1917): 821–26.

[Roosevelt, Franklin Delano]. *F.D.R.; his personal letters, 1928–1945,* edited by Elliott Roosevelt. 4 vols. New York: Duell, Sloan and Pearce, 1959.

[Roosevelt, Franklin D., and Winston S. Churchill]. *Churchill & Roosevelt; the complete correspondence,* edited by Warren F. Kimball, q.v.

"Roosevelt heads for Clipperton island, where the fishing is reportedly excellent." New York *Times,* July 16, 1934, p. 34.

Roosevelt, James, and Sidney Shalett. *Affectionately, F.D.R.; a son's story of a lonely man.* New York: Avon Book Corporation, 1959.

"Roosevelt lucky off Clipperton; his launch gets big haul of fish; cruiser later sails for Galapagos islands." New York *Times,* July 22, 1938, p. 19.

"Roosevelt on tour; visits Mexican president; they pledge fight for 'good neighbor world.' " New York *Times,* April 21, 1943, p. 1.

"Roosevelt on way to fishing grounds; cruiser Houston speeding to Clipperton island, a Pacific coral atoll." New York *Times,* July 17, 1934, p. 17.

"Roosevelt stops at Clipperton; off Mexican island he gets strike reports by radio but makes no comment." New York *Times,* July 18, 1934, p. 1.

"Roosevelt watches naval 'hide and seek'; President sees cruisers Houston and New Orleans in tactical manoeuvres in Pacific." New York *Times,* July 19, 1934, p. 3.

Saavedra Cerón, Alvaro de. "Log." Mexico. *Isla de la Pasión,* q.v.

Sachet, Marie-Hélène. "Botany." International Geophysical Year. *Clipperton island expedition field report* (1959): 6–7, q.v.

———. "Flora and vegetation of Clipperton island." California Academy of Science *Proceedings* 31 (1962): 249–307.

———. *Geography and land ecology of Clipperton island.* Washington, D.C.: National Academy of Science Atoll Research Bulletin No. 86, 1962.

———. "Histoire de l'île Clipperton." *Cashiers du Pacifique* 2 (1960): 1–32.

———. "Vegetation of Clipperton island." Ninth International Botanical Congress *Proceedings* 2 (1959): 337–38.

"Sail 670 miles for help; two volunteers get warship to rescue castaways on an island." New York *Times,* July 5, 1914, p. 6.

San Francisco *Chronicle,* August 4, 1897, p. 4; August 19, 1897, p. 12; August 20, 1897, p. 4; November 7, 1897, p. 15; January 29, 1898, p. 2.

Sauchelli, Vincent. *Phosphates in agriculture.* New York: Reinhold Publishing Corporation, 1965.

Schmitt, Waldo L. "Decapod and other crustacea collected on the presidential cruise of 1938 (with introduction and station data)." *Smithsonian miscellaneous collections* 98 (1939): No. 6 SI1.7:98

———. "The presidential cruise of 1938." *Explorations and field work of the Smithsonian Institution in 1938.* Washington: Smithsonian Institution publication [No.] 3525, 1939. SI1.13:938

———, and Leonard P. Schultz. "List of fishes taken on the presidential cruise of 1938." *Smithsonian miscellaneous collections* 98 (1940): No. 25. SI1.7:98

Schurz, William Lytle. "The voyage of the Manila galleon from Acapulco to Manila." *Hispanic American historical review* 2 (November 1919): 632–38.

Schwarzenberger, Georg. "Title to territory; response to a challenge" Leo Gross, ed. *International law in the twentieth century,* q.v.

"Seeks delay on island; Mexican soldiers' group would hold up cession of Clipperton." New York *Times,* November 22, 1932, p. 6.

304 □ B I B L I O G R A P H Y

*"Seize"*U.S. Navy. *Dictionary of American naval fighting ships* 6 (1976): 431, q.v. D207.10:6

Seltzer, Leon E., ed. *The Columbia Lippincott gazetteer of the world.* Morningside, New York: Columbia University Press, by arrangement with J. B. Lippincott Company, 1952.

"Senators of Mexico accept loss of isle; cession of Clipperton to France is urged to maintain honor in arbitral award." New York *Times,* December 15, 1932, p. 6.

"Shannon." U.S. Navy. *Dictionary of American naval fighting ships* 6 (1976): 465, q.v. D207.10:6

Shelvocke, George. *A privateer's voyage around the world.* London: Jonathan Cape, 1726.

Sherwood, Robert E. *Roosevelt and Hopkins; an intimate history.* New York: Harper & Brothers, 1948.

"Shipwrecked crew coming." San Francisco *Chronicle,* July 5, 1914, p. 63.

"Shipwrecked crew rescued; five men survive 6 weeks on tiny island." San Francisco *Examiner,* June 30, 1947, p. 13.

"Shipwrecked sailors here." San Francisco *Chronicle,* July 21, 1897, p. 12.

Shoemaker, C. R. "Amphipod crustaceans collected on the presidential cruise of 1938." *Smithsonian miscellaneous collections* 101 (1942): No. 11. SIl.7:101

Slevin, Joseph R. *Log of the schooner Academy on a voyage of scientific research to the Galapagos islands, 1905–1906.* San Francisco: California Academy of Sciences, 1931.

Smithsonian Institution. *Explorations and field work of the Smithsonian Institution in 1938.* Washington: The Smithsonian Institution, 1939.

Snodgrass, Robert Evans, and Edmund Heller. "Birds of Clipperton and Cocos islands." Washington Academy of Science *Proceedings* 4 (September 30, 1902): 501–520.

———. "Papers from the Hopkins Stanford Galapagos expedition, 1898–1899; birds." Washington Academy of Science *Proceedings* 5 (1904): 231–372.

Stager, Kenneth E. "Expedition to Clipperton island." Los Angeles County Museum *Quarterly* 15 (1959): 13–14.

———. "Ornithology." International Geophysical Year. *Clipperton island expedition field report* (1959): 7, q.v.

"Statement on France." New York *Times,* May 17, 1945, p. 7.

Stephens, H. Morse, and Herbert E. Bolton, eds. *The Pacific ocean in history; papers and addresses presented at the Panama-Pacific Historical*

Congress held at San Francisco, Berkeley, and Palo Alto, California, July 10–23, 1915. New York: The Macmillan Company, 1917.

[Stettinius, E. R., Jr.] *The diaries of Edward R. Stettinius, Jr., 1943–1946,* edited by Thomas M. Campbell and George C. Herring. New York: New Viewpoints, 1975.

Stiller, Jesse H. *George S. Messersmith; diplomat of democracy.* Chapel Hill: The University of North Carolina Press, 1987.

"Story of the Kinkora men; long voyage in leaking ship; stranded on Clipperton; days of severe labor at the pumps; the men rescued by the warship Comus and now on way here from Monterey." San Francisco *Chronicle,* July 20, 1897, p. 2.

"Strange experiences of the lone man who is defending Clipperton island." San Francisco *Call,* February 13, 1898, p. 21.

Strauss, David. *Menace in the west; the rise of French anti-Americanism in modern times.* Westport, Conn.: Greenwood Press, 1978.

"Survivors due today." San Francisco *Chronicle,* July 10, 1914, p. 16.

Taylor, P[atrick] G[ordon]. *Forgotten island.* London: The Shakespeare Head, 1948.

———. *The sky beyond.* Boston: Houghton Mifflin Company, 1963.

Taylor, Paul S. "Spanish seamen in the new world during the colonial period." *Hispanic American historical review* 5 (November 1922): 631–61.

Taylor, W[illia]m. Randolph. "Algae collected on the presidential cruise of 1938." *Smithsonian miscellaneous collections* 98 (1939): No. 9. SI1.7:98

Teall, J. J. H. "A phosphatized trachyte from Clipperton atoll (northern Pacific)." Geological Society of London *Quarterly journal* 54 (1898): 230–33.

"*Tenino.*" U.S. Navy. *Dictionary of American naval fighting ships* 7 (1981): 86, q.v. D207.10:7

Thomas, J[oseph], and T[homas] Baldwin, *et al.,* eds. *Lippincott's pronouncing gazetteer; a complete pronouncing gazetteer or dictionary of the world, containing a notice of the pronunciation of the names of nearly one hundred thousand places, with recent and authentic information respecting the countries, islands, rivers, mountains, cities, towns, &c., in every portion of the globe, including the latest and most reliable statistics of population, commerce, etc.; also, a complete etymological vocabulary of geographical names, and many other valuable features to be found in no other gazetteer in the English language.* Philadelphia: J. B. Lippincott & Co., 1863, 1864.

———. *Lippincott's pronouncing gazetteer; a complete pronouncing gazetteer or dictionary of the world, containing a notice of the pronunciation of the names of nearly one hundred thousand places, with recent and authentic information respecting the countries, islands, rivers, mountains, cities, towns,*

&c., in every portion of the globe; revised edition, with an appendix containing nearly ten thousand new notices and the most recent statistical information, according to the latest census returns, of the United States, and foreign countries. Philadelphia: J. B. Lippincott & Co., 1866.

―――. *Lippincott's pronouncing gazetteer; a complete pronouncing gazetteer or geographical dictionary of the world, containing a notice and the pronunciation of the names of nearly one hundred thousand places with recent and authentic information respecting the countries, islands, rivers, mountains, cities, towns, &c., in every portion of the globe; revised edition of 1866, with an appendix containing nearly ten thousand new notices and new tables of population according to the latest census returns of the United States and foreign countries.* Philadelphia: J. B. Lippincott & Co., 1876.

Thompson, J. M. *Louis Napoleon and the second empire.* New York: The Noonday Press, 1955.

The times. April 20, 1899, p. 11e; April 29, 1911, p. 26d; May 23, 1912, p. 21a; June 24, 1914, p. 13a; June 7, 1917, p. 13d; July 7, 1917, p. 13e; July 19, 1917, p. 12d; July 30, 1917, p. 11b.

Toniolo, A. R. "A proposito della situazione e della prima conoscenza dell'isola di Clipperton." *Rivista geografica Italiana* 26 (1919): 86–105.

Truchan, Marek, and Roger L. Larson. "Eastern extension of the Siqueiros and Clipperton fracture zones and the Cocos (Farallon)-Pacific plate motions." American Geophysical Union Transaction *Eos* 53 (1972): 413–14.

Truman, Harry S. *Memoirs.* 2 vols. New York: New American Library, 1955.

"Truman proposes De Gaulle meeting in hailing French; President Bidault he recognizes the importance of France to Europe; chief executive also states aid in far eastern war will be welcomed." New York *Times,* May 19, 1945, p. 1.

U.S. *Code* (1978). Title 43, Ch. 8: "Guano islands."

U.S. Agriculture department. *Report of the commissioner of agriculture for the year 1869.* Washington: Government Printing Office, 1870. A1.1:869

U.S. Foreign Commerce bureau. *Commercial relations of the United States with foreign countries during the year 1898.* 2 vols. Washington: Government Printing Office, 1899. S4.1:898

U.S. Navy department. *Dictionary of American naval fighting ships.* 8 vols. Washington: Government Printing Office, 1959–81. D207.10: [volume number]

―――. *Kite balloons to airships . . . ; the Navy's lighter-than-air experience,* edited by Roy A. Grossnick. [Washington: Government Printing Office, 1987]. D202.2:Av5/4/v.4

————. *Register of commissioned and warrant officers of the United States navy and marine corps.* Washington: Government Printing Office, periodical. N1.10:[date]

————. *United States submarine losses, World War II; reissued with an appendix of Axis submarine losses, fully indexed.* Washington: Office of the Chief of Naval Operations, Naval History Division, 1963. D207.10/2: Su 1/2

————. Defense Mapping Agency, Hydrographic/Topographic Center. *Sailing directions (en route) for the west coasts of Mexico and central America.* 2d ed. N.p.: n.p., 1979. DMA Stock No. SDPUB153

U.S. Presidents. *A compilation of the messages and papers of the presidents, prepared under the direction of the Joint Committee on Printing, of the House and Senate, pursuant to an act of the 52nd Congress of the United States (with additions and encyclopedia by private enterprise),* [compiled and edited by James David Richardson]. 20 vols. New York: Bureau of National Literature, Inc., 1897–1917.

[U.S. State department]. *Digest of international law* [compiled and edited by Green Haywood Hackworth]. 8 vols. Washington: Government Printing Office, 1940–43. S7.12:date/vol.

[————]. *A digest of international law as embodied in diplomatic discussions, treaties and other international agreements, international awards, the decisions of municipal courts, and the writings of jurists, and especially in documents, published and unpublished, issued by presidents and secretaries of state of the United States, the opinions of attorneys-general, and the decisions of courts, federal and state* [compiled and edited by John Bassett Moore]. 8 vols. Washington: Government Printing Office, 1906. S7.12:date/vol.

[————]. *Digest of United States practice of international law.* Serial; various compilations. Washington: [Government Printing Office, annual]. S7.12/3:date

————. *Foreign relations of the United States; diplomatic papers.* Serial. Washington: United States Government Printing Office, annual. S1.1:date/vol.

————. *Friendship and territorial sovereignty; treaty between the United States of America and Tuvala, signed at Funafuti February 7, 1979.* Washington: Treaties and Other International Acts series no. 10776, [1985]. S9.10:10776

————. *Proceedings of the International Civil Aviation Conference, Chicago, Illinois, November 1–December 7, 1944.* 2 vols. Washington: United States Government Printing Office, 1949. S1.70/4:In85/3/v.1–2

————. *Treaties and other international agreements of the United States of America, 1776–1949.* Serial. Washington: United States Government Printing Office, annual. S9.12/date:vol.

————. *Treaties in force; a list of treaties and other international agreements of the United States in force on January 1, 1981.* [Washington: Government Printing Office, 1981]. S9.14:981

————. "United States national security policy; the extension of military assistance to foreign nations; estimates of threats to the national security; coordination of political and military policy with respect to the acquisition of military bases, and air transit rights," U.S. State department. *Foreign relations of the United States* 1 (1946): 1,108–1,191, q.v. S1.1:946/1

U.S. Treasury department. *Circular no. 1, relative to the guano islands appertaining to the United States.* Washington: Government Printing Office, 1869. T1.4:869

Van Denburg, J., and J. R. Slevin. "Reptiles and amphibians of the islands of the west coast of America." *California Academy of Science Proceedings* 4 (1914): 129–52.

Victor Emmanuel III. "Arbitral award on the subject of the difference relative to the sovereignty over Clipperton island." *American journal of international law* 26 (1932): 390–94.

————. "Decision of the controversy between France and Mexico regarding sovereignty over Clipperton island." *Cumulative digest of international law and relations* 2 (1932): 95–98.

"Victor Emmanuel III, king of Italy." *Current biography; who's news and why, 1943.* New York: H. W. Wilson Company, 1944.

"*Viking.*" U.S. Navy. *Dictionary of American fighting ships* 7 (1981): 519–21, q.v. D207.10:7

Villari, Luigi. *Italian foreign policy under Mussolini.* New York: The Devin-Adair Company, 1956.

Viorst, Milton. *Hostile allies; FDR and Charles de Gaulle.* New York: The Macmillan Company, 1965.

Visher, Stephen S. "Tropical cyclones in the northeast Pacific, between Hawaii and Mexico." *Monthly weather review* 50 (June 2, 1922): 295–97. C55.11:922

————. "Tropical cyclones of the Pacific." Bishop Museum *Bulletin* 20 (1925): 1–163.

Wardley, A. "The great fault zones of the N. E. Pacific." University of Sheffield Geological Society *Journal* 5 (1969): 164–68.

"Washington records shocks; seismograph experts thought it was about 2,800 miles away." New York *Times,* July 31, 1909, p. 1.

Watson, Mark Skinner. *United States army in World War II; the war department: chief of staff, prewar plans and preparations.* Washington, D.C.: Historical Division, Department of the Army, 1950. D114.7:W19/v.1

Welles, Sumner. *The time for decision.* New York: Harper & Brothers Publishers, 1944.

Wells, Ken. "Ecologists fret over outlaw hogs, goats gone wrong; once-tamed 'feral' animals vandalize environment; remedy is controversial." *Wall street journal,* October 17, 1985, pp. 1, 16.

Welty, Joel Carl. *The life of birds.* 2d ed. Philadelphia: W. B. Saunders Company, 1975.

"Were stranded on Clipperton island; shipwrecked crew of the Kinkora rescued by the cruiser Comus; the steamer Navarro goes after." San Francisco *Call,* July 21, 1897, p. 8.

Wetmore, Alexander. "Birds from Clipperton island collected on the presidential cruise of 1938." *Smithsonian miscellaneous collections* 98 (1939): No. 22. SI1.7:98

Wharton, G. W. "Acarina collected on the presidential cruise of 1938." *Smithsonian miscellaneous collection* 99 (1941): No. 12. SI1.7:99

Wharton, W. J. "Note on Clipperton island." Geological Society of London *Reports and proceedings* (May 1898): 233–34.

————. "Notes on Clipperton atoll (northern Pacific)." Geological Society of London *Quarterly journal* 54 (1898): 228–29.

Who was who in America, 1897–1942; a companion volume to who's who in America; biographies of the non-living with dates of death appended. Serial. Chicago: The A. N. Marquis Company, 1942.

Wilkinson, Clennell. *William Dampier.* London: John Lane the Bodley Head, Ltd., 1929.

"William Dampier." *Dictionary of national biography* 5 (1900): 452–57.

"The wreck of the Kinkora." San Francisco *Chronicle,* June 15, 1897, p. 10.

Wroth, Lawrence C. "The early cartography of the Pacific." Bibliographical Society of America *Papers* 38 (1944): 87–267ff.

Wycherley, George. *Buccaneers of the Pacific.* Indianapolis: Bobbs-Merrill Publishers, 1928.

Yaldwyn, J. C., and Kasimierz Wodzicki. "Systematics and ecology of the land crabs (*Decapoda: Coenobitidae, Grapsidae and Gecarcinidae*) of the Tokelau islands, central Pacific." Smithsonian Institution *Atoll research bulletin* 235 (1979): 37–44. SI1.25:233–239.

"*Yorktown.*" U.S. Navy. *Dictionary of American naval fighting ships* 8 (1981): 531–32, q.v. D207.10:8

Zahniser, Marvin R. *Uncertain friendship; American-French diplomatic relations through the cold war.* New York: John Wiley & Sons, Inc., 1975.

Zweig, Stefan. *Conqueror of the seas; the story of Magellan,* translated by Eden and Cedar Paul. New York: The Literary Guild of America, Inc., 1938.

Index